Mining Software Specifications

Methodologies and Applications

Chapman & Hall/CRC
Data Mining and Knowledge Discovery Series

SERIES EDITOR
Vipin Kumar
University of Minnesota
Department of Computer Science and Engineering
Minneapolis, Minnesota, U.S.A

AIMS AND SCOPE

This series aims to capture new developments and applications in data mining and knowledge discovery, while summarizing the computational tools and techniques useful in data analysis. This series encourages the integration of mathematical, statistical, and computational methods and techniques through the publication of a broad range of textbooks, reference works, and handbooks. The inclusion of concrete examples and applications is highly encouraged. The scope of the series includes, but is not limited to, titles in the areas of data mining and knowledge discovery methods and applications, modeling, algorithms, theory and foundations, data and knowledge visualization, data mining systems and tools, and privacy and security issues.

PUBLISHED TITLES

UNDERSTANDING COMPLEX DATASETS:
DATA MINING WITH MATRIX DECOMPOSITIONS
David Skillicorn

COMPUTATIONAL METHODS OF FEATURE
SELECTION
Huan Liu and Hiroshi Motoda

CONSTRAINED CLUSTERING: ADVANCES IN
ALGORITHMS, THEORY, AND APPLICATIONS
Sugato Basu, Ian Davidson, and Kiri L. Wagstaff

KNOWLEDGE DISCOVERY FOR
COUNTERTERRORISM AND LAW ENFORCEMENT
David Skillicorn

MULTIMEDIA DATA MINING: A SYSTEMATIC
INTRODUCTION TO CONCEPTS AND THEORY
Zhongfei Zhang and Ruofei Zhang

NEXT GENERATION OF DATA MINING
**Hillol Kargupta, Jiawei Han, Philip S. Yu,
Rajeev Motwani, and Vipin Kumar**

DATA MINING FOR DESIGN AND MARKETING
Yukio Ohsawa and Katsutoshi Yada

THE TOP TEN ALGORITHMS IN DATA MINING
Xindong Wu and Vipin Kumar

GEOGRAPHIC DATA MINING AND
KNOWLEDGE DISCOVERY, SECOND EDITION
Harvey J. Miller and Jiawei Han

TEXT MINING: CLASSIFICATION, CLUSTERING,
AND APPLICATIONS
Ashok N. Srivastava and Mehran Sahami

BIOLOGICAL DATA MINING
Jake Y. Chen and Stefano Lonardi

INFORMATION DISCOVERY ON ELECTRONIC
HEALTH RECORDS
Vagelis Hristidis

TEMPORAL DATA MINING
Theophano Mitsa

RELATIONAL DATA CLUSTERING: MODELS,
ALGORITHMS, AND APPLICATIONS
Bo Long, Zhongfei Zhang, and Philip S. Yu

KNOWLEDGE DISCOVERY FROM DATA STREAMS
João Gama

STATISTICAL DATA MINING USING SAS
APPLICATIONS, SECOND EDITION
George Fernandez

INTRODUCTION TO PRIVACY-PRESERVING DATA
PUBLISHING: CONCEPTS AND TECHNIQUES
**Benjamin C. M. Fung, Ke Wang, Ada Wai-Chee Fu,
and Philip S. Yu**

HANDBOOK OF EDUCATIONAL DATA MINING
**Cristóbal Romero, Sebastian Ventura,
Mykola Pechenizkiy, and Ryan S.J.d. Baker**

DATA MINING WITH R: LEARNING WITH
CASE STUDIES
Luís Torgo

MINING SOFTWARE SPECIFICATIONS:
METHODOLOGIES AND APPLICATIONS
David Lo, Siau-Cheng Khoo, Jiawei Han, and Chao Liu

DATA CLUSTERING IN C++: AN OBJECT-ORIENTED
APPROACH
Guojun Gan

Chapman & Hall/CRC
Data Mining and Knowledge Discovery Series

Mining Software Specifications

Methodologies and Applications

David Lo
Siau-Cheng Khoo
Jiawei Han
Chao Liu

CRC Press
Taylor & Francis Group
Boca Raton London New York

CRC Press is an imprint of the
Taylor & Francis Group, an **informa** business

A CHAPMAN & HALL BOOK

CRC Press
Taylor & Francis Group
6000 Broken Sound Parkway NW, Suite 300
Boca Raton, FL 33487-2742

© 2011 by Taylor and Francis Group, LLC
CRC Press is an imprint of Taylor & Francis Group, an Informa business

No claim to original U.S. Government works

Printed in the United States of America on acid-free paper
10 9 8 7 6 5 4 3 2 1

International Standard Book Number: 978-1-4398-0626-5 (Hardback)

Visit the Taylor & Francis Web site at
http://www.taylorandfrancis.com

and the CRC Press Web site at
http://www.crcpress.com

Contents

List of Figures

Preface

Data mining and machine learning techniques have been used to learn models of software behavior. These models appear in various forms following different formalisms of software specifications, each capturing different aspects of a software system. The mined models can later be tuned, adapted, and used for various purposes.

Mined models help in understanding existing systems and hence reduce the cost incurred during software maintenance (i.e., when features are added, bugs are fixed, etc.). This is particularly advantageous in the cases of maintaining legacy systems and keeping pace with changes in evolving systems, where significant maintenance cost can be saved through better understanding of such systems with the help of mined models.

The mined models/specifications can also be used to aid program testing efforts and help program verification tools to find bugs and ensure correctness of systems. As reported by US National Institute of Standards and Technology (NIST) in 2002, bugs have been causing US economy to lose 59.5 billion dollars annually. Also, the first test flight of Ariane 5 ended up in an explosion due to a software bug. Automated methods to find bugs and ensure correctness of systems are certainly valuable.

There has been a proliferation of research in the area of specification mining in both academia and industry. Research and development in specification mining have been performed in various institutions across the globe with results presented in various venues such as conferences on software engineering, programming languages, data mining, and databases. Due to its appearance in a wide range of research domains, it is often hard to find and relate different works on mining specification in the literature. There has not been a single reference to describe and categorize these studies in a unified setting. This book aims to serve as the first reference to the wealth of knowledge in this new emerging field of mining software specifications.

There are diverse forms of target formalism considered in various research work. Two of the most common ones are finite state machines and rules/patterns of behavior. A finite state machine is typically larger and captures more complex behavior. Many works on mining finite state machine extract models that capture the overall behavior of a system. A set of rules or patterns tends to be smaller and decompose complex behavior into simpler parts. Much work on mining rules/patterns extracts strongly observed sub-behaviors either in terms of their frequency of appearance or some other statistical measures. In this book, we present in detail a number of past studies on mining finite state machines (Chapters 2-6) and also those on mining rules/patterns (Chapters 7-12).

There are also differences in terms of how the raw data used as input for the mining and learning tasks are obtained. Some works analyze program code (i.e., static analysis) while others analyze execution traces (i.e., dynamic analysis). There are also works that analyze both code and execution traces. Either static or dynamic analysis has its own advantages and disadvantages. Static analysis could potentially consider all possible behaviors as all the behaviors of the system are in the code. Dynamic analysis on the other hand only analyzes a sample of the behaviors of a system exhibited on a set of runs of a system. However, dynamic analysis can be more precise as exact events that happen during runtime are collected rather than inferred. Its performance is not affected by the difficulties arising from dealing with infeasible paths in a software system or pointer analysis. This book presents both approaches and even some synergies of the two: Some chapters present works that employ dynamic analysis, some others present works that employ static analysis, and yet a few present works that employ a combination of both static and dynamic analyses.

We would like to thank the chapter authors (in alphabetical order): Mithun Acharya, Anindya Banerjee, Kirill Bogdanov, David Evans, Stephen Fink, Ananth Grama, Thomas R. Gross, Suresh Jagannathan, Benjamin Livshits, Leonardo Mariani, Madhuri R. Marri, Aditya V. Nori, Fabrizio Pastore, Mauro Pezzé, Marco Pistoia, Michael Pradel, Sriram K. Rajamani, Muralikrishna Ramanathan, Mauro Santoro, Sharon Shoham, Suresh Thummalapenta, Neil Walkinshaw, Andrzej Wasylkowski, Tao Xie, Eran Yahav, Jinlin Yang, Thomas Zimmermann, and Andreas Zeller, for their valuable contributions without which this book would not be possible. We would also like to thank the various reviewers (in alphabetical order): Mithun Acharya, Suresh Jagannathan, Lingxiao Jiang, and Venkatesh Prasad Ranganath, who help to review submitted chapters. Last but not least, we also thank various members of the SpecMine group, National University of Singapore, and Software Mining and Analysis Group, Singapore Management University, for performing some final checks during the compilation of the book.

We sincerely hope that this book can help in raising interest, growth, and collaboration in the area of specification mining. We also hope to see more industry adoption of specification mining techniques and more incorporation of these techniques to standard IDEs in the near future.

David Lo, Siau-Cheng Khoo, Jiawei Han, and Chao Liu

Contributors

Mithun Acharya
ABB Corporate Research
North Carolina, US

Anindya Banerjee
IMDEA Software
Madrid, Spain

Kirill Bogdanov
The University of Sheffield
Yorkshire, UK

David Evans
University of Virginia
Virginia, US

Stephen Fink
IBM T.J. Watson Research Center
New York, US

Ananth Grama
Purdue University
Indiana, US

Thomas R. Gross
ETH Zurich
Zurich, Switzerland

Jiawei Han
University of Illinois at
    Urbana-Champaign
Illinois, US

Suresh Jagannathan
Purdue University
Indiana, US

Siau-Cheng Khoo
National University of Singapore
Singapore

Chao Liu
Microsoft Research–Redmond
Washington, US

Benjamin Livshits
Microsoft Research–Redmond
Washington, US

David Lo
Singapore Management University
Singapore

Leonardo Mariani
University of Milano Bicocca
Milan, Italy

Madhuri R. Marri
North Carolina State University
North Carolina,US

Aditya V. Nori
Microsoft Research–Redmond
Washington, US

Fabrizio Pastore
University of Milano Bicocca
Milan, Italy

Mauro Pezzè
University of Lugano and University
   of Milano Bicocca
Lugano, Switzerland and Milan, Italy

Marco Pistoia
IBM T.J. Watson Research Center
New York, US

Michael Pradel
ETH Zurich
Zurich, Switzerland

Sriram K. Rajamani
Microsoft Research–Bangalore
Bangalore, India

Muralikrishna Ramanathan
Coverity, Inc.
California, US

Mauro Santoro
University of Milano Bicocca
Milan, Italy

Sharon Shoham
Technion–Israel Institute of
   Technology
Haifa, Israel

Suresh Thummalapenta
North Carolina State University
North Carolina, US

Neil Walkinshaw
The University of Leicester
Yorkshire, UK

Andrzej Wasylkowski
Saarland University
Saarbrücken, Germany

Tao Xie
North Carolina State University
North Carolina, US

Eran Yahav
IBM T.J. Watson Research Center
   and Technion–Israel Institute
   of Technology
New York, US and Haifa, Israel

Jinlin Yang
Microsoft–Redmond
Washington, US

Andreas Zeller
Saarland University
Saarbrücken, Germany

Thomas Zimmermann
Microsoft Research–Redmond
Washington, US

Chapter 1

Specification Mining: A Concise Introduction

David Lo

School of Information Systems, Singapore Management University

Siau-Cheng Khoo

School of Computing, National University of Singapore

Chao Liu

Microsoft Research–Redmond

Jiawei Han

Department of Computer Science, University of Illinois at Urbana-Champaign

1.1   Introduction

Many software systems are poorly documented. Developers tend to spend most of their time in developing functionalities rather than documenting them. This causes an issue as after some time it is hard to understand the existing system. A software maintenance task could be harder to perform as there is no documentations of existing functionalities. Indeed, past studies have shown that the cost of software maintenance could be up to 90% of the total software cost [22]. Another study reported that up to 50% of the maintenance cost could be attributed to the difficulty in understanding legacy/existing systems [12, 27, 67].

1

From another perspective, software bugs are prevalent. Bugs not only make it more expensive in developing software systems due to the high cost involved in debugging, but also may cause various security vulnerabilities. For many mission and safety critical system faults and bugs could mean the loss of lives or billions of dollars. The absence of specifications has made it harder to locate bugs. Many existing bug finding tools, e.g., model checking [13], require the availability of specifications in order to locate bugs which are defined as anomalies or violations of these specifications.

To address the above challenges (i.e., to improve program understanding and to find bugs), *specification mining* has been proposed. The term specification mining is first coined by Ammons et al. in [6]. Specification mining is a process of inferring models or properties that hold for a system. Many techniques have been proposed to mine or extract these specifications. Techniques used range from data mining, grammar inference, static analysis, etc.

Specification mining starts with a program under analysis and/or a set of test cases. Techniques employing dynamic analysis require the running of the test cases to produce a set of traces which is later analyzed. Often traces could also be generated statically by "walking through" the code. Some techniques employ symbolic execution to mitigate the effect of infeasible paths. Various learning or mining techniques can be employed on these sets of dynamically or generated traces to infer models.

Various formalisms have been proposed to specify a software system. Similarly, the models mined by these specification mining engines are also varied. They range from temporal properties, finite state machines, etc. In Section 1.2, we discuss in more detail the type of specifications that many past studies have considered.

Models mined in turn could be used to aid various activities. They could be used to guide novice developers in using an existing/legacy software system or a library. Many systems and libraries are hard to understand. Poor understanding of a system in turn could lead to the introduction of bugs. Mined specification describes the constraints that a system would need to obey and thus could help in either reducing the time needed to develop and maintain a system or reduce the number of bugs introduced.

One could also use the mined model as input to a model checking or other lightweight verification process to detect violations. The central tenet of many specification mining-based anomaly detection techniques is stated in [21], namely: If a model is observed "999 out of 1000 times, then it is probably a valid belief and the sole deviation a probable error." Many specification mining studies have been successful in locating bugs from software systems. Employing model-based testing, mined models could also be used to generate regression tests or reduce the number of test cases and thus improves the quality of software systems while still ensure that the testing process could be performed in a limited amount of time.

In this chapter, we start the book by presenting a concise summary of many existing works on specification mining. This family of studies on specification mining has been ongoing for over a decade and more than 50 papers have been published on this topic. We provide a brief summary starting from one of the first papers on this topic published in 1995 by Cook and Wolf [14], to many recent papers. The remaining chapters of this book describe 11 different techniques appearing in recent literature in detail.

Section 1.2 describes a general scheme to categorize existing works into several groups. Section 1.3 describes studies on the extraction of finite state machines. Section 1.4 describes works that mine for value-based invariants. Section 1.5 describes approaches to mine rules and patterns. Section 1.6 presents yet another family of studies extracting sequence diagram-like specifications. We conclude our discussion in Section 1.7.

1.2 Categorization

There are various ways to organize the many studies on specification mining. We choose to categorize them in terms of the specifications forms produced by the miners. These include finite state machine or automata, value-based invariants, patterns/rules, and sequence diagram-like representations. Some examples of studies mining the various specification formalisms are shown in Table 1.1.[1]

A finite state machine consists of states and transitions. The states or the transitions could be labeled – depending on whether a Mealy or Moore machine is mined. These labels could correspond to various pieces of information depending on the level of granularity considered. Typically, the labels correspond to method calls of interest. Most studies on the extraction of finite state machines listed in Table 1.1 propose the extraction of models governing the order in which methods of a particular library could be invoked. An example of a model specifying how a file access library should be used is shown in Figure 1.1. The finite state machine specifies that a call to *open* needs to be made before any call to *read* or *write*. At the end of an interaction, with the library a call to *close* is made.

A value-based invariant captures a constraint among various global or local variables at a particular point in a program. Various constraints could be considered ranging from a simple equality constraint involving two variables/-values to more complex inequalities or even conditional constraints involving multiple variables. Value-based invariants thus capture the constraints among the various variables characterizing a system's state. An example of a value-based invariant is shown in Figure 1.2. It illustrates that at the end of a simple program that computes a square, the computation result is greater than or equal to zero.

---

[1] Our list might not be complete.

TABLE 1.1: Categorization Based on Target Formalisms

Formalisms	Past Studies
Automata	Cook & Wolf [14], Ammons et al. [6], Ammons et al. [7], Alur et al. [5], Henzinger et al. [31], Mariani & Pezzè [53], Acharya et al. [3], Dallmeier et al. [15], Lo & Khoo [38], Acharya et al. [1], Mariani et al. [52], Shevertalov & Mancoridis [65], Quante & Koschke [60], Walkinshaw et al. [72], Gabel & Su [30], Gabel & Su [29], Lorenzoli et al. [49], Mariani & Pastore [54], Walkinshaw & Bogdanov [71], Lo et al. [46], Pradel & Gross [58], Zhong et al. [77], and Gabel & Su [28]
Value-Based Invariants	Ernst et al. [23–26], Perkins & Ernst [57], Nimmer & Ernst [56], Pytlik et al. [59], Brun & Ernst [11], and Boshernitsan et al. [9]
Patterns/Rules	Engler et al. [21], El-Ramly et al. [20], Li & Zhou [37], Livshits & Zimmermann [37], Mandelin et al. [50], Weimer & Necula [75], Kremenek et al. [34], Safyallah & Sartipi [64], Yang et al. [76], Lo et al. [39], Ramanathan et al. [61], Ramanathan et al. [62], Thummalapenta & Xie [68], Lo et al. [40], Ramanathan et al. [63], Zhong et al. [79] , Zhong et al. [78], Acharya & Xie [2], Heydarnoori et al. [32], Lo et al. [47], Nguyen et al. [55], Thummalapenta & Xie [70], Thummalapenta & Xie [69], Wasylkowski & Zeller [73], Zhong et al. [77], and Lo et al. [41]
Sequence Diagrams	Briand et al. [10], Lo et al. [48], de Sousa et al. [17], Lo & Maoz [43], Lo & Maoz [42], Lo & Maoz [44], and Doan et al. [19]

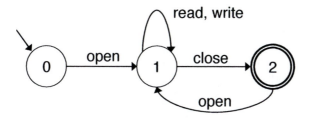

FIGURE 1.1: Finite state machine. File access library.

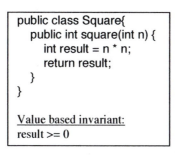

FIGURE 1.2: Value-based invariants. A program that computes the square of an integer.

There are many different approaches that mine for frequent patterns. A pattern corresponds to a template that matches many concrete instances obeying the pattern in a trace or in a program. Data mining concepts such as itemset, sequential pattern, and graph pattern are often used. An itemset is a set of items. A sequential pattern is a series of items/events. A graph pattern captures relationships between labeled nodes and labeled edges. Each item/event/label could denote various pieces of information although typically they represent method calls. A pattern is frequent if it appears frequently in a dataset of interest. Various types of patterns have been mined including sequential patterns that appear often in execution traces to graph patterns that appear often in code bases. For example, a sequential pattern specifying a partial method call sequence to implement a context menu using JFace is shown in Figure 1.3 – c.f. [32].

There are other studies that mine for significant rules. Different from a pattern that captures things which appear frequently, a rule captures a *constraint* between two things; namely, the premise/pre-condition and the consequent/post-condition of the rule. A rule can capture a constraint between itemsets, sequential patterns, or graph patterns. There are many rules that programmers obey, for example, a "lock" must eventually be followed by an "unlock", an "allocation" must eventually be followed by a "free", a "use"

```
Viewer.getControl()
AppAction.<init>()
AppAction.setText(String)
AppAction.setToolTipText(String)
MenuManager.<init>(String)
MenuManager.setRemoveAllWhenShown(Boolean)
AppMenuListener.<init>()
MenuManager.addMenuListener(AppMenuListener)
MenuManager.createContextMenu(Control)
```

FIGURE 1.3: Frequent pattern of usage. Context menu using JFace.

must be preceded by an "allocation", etc. Some examples of these rules are shown in Figure 1.4.

```
KeAcquireSpinLock -> KeReleaseSpinLock
ExAcquireFastMutex -> ExReleaseFastMutex
ExAllocatePoolWithTag -> ExFreePool

zfcp_reqlist_alloc -> zfcp_reqlist_free
zfcp_fsf_alloc -> zfcp_fsf_req_free
xfrm_policy_alloc -> xfrm_policy_destroy
```

FIGURE 1.4: Temporal rules: Windows (top) and Linux (bottom).

Another form of specifications is sequence diagram which is composed of lifelines and messages. They are intuitive to capture the communication among the various objects through various method calls. There are also some extensions to standard UML sequence diagrams including Message Sequence Charts (MSC), which is the standard of International Telecommunication Union (ITU) [33] and Live Sequence Chart (LSC) [16] that extends MSC with modalities. LSC is able to express a rule-like property in the form of a modal sequence diagram. An example of a Live Sequence Chart is shown in Figure 1.5. It captures the constraint "whenever `PictureChat` calls the `Backend` method `getMyJID()`, and sometime in the future the `PictureHistory` calls the `Backend` method `send()`, eventually the latter must call the `send()` method of `Connect` and `Connect` must call the `send()` method of `Output`."

From Table 1.1, we notice that there are many studies extracting finite state machines and rules/patterns. There are also a good number of studies mining other forms of specifications including value-based invariants and sequence diagrams.

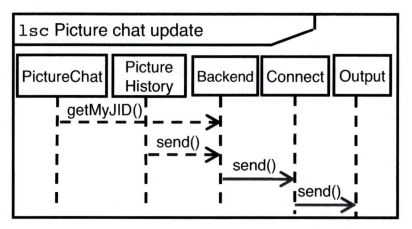

FIGURE 1.5: Sequence diagram. Jeti instant messaging application.

1.3   Mining Finite State Machines

In this section, we describe past studies on mining finite state machines. In this and the following sections, we present the studies in a semi-chronological order.

One of the pioneer works on the inference of finite state machines from software systems is done by Cook and Wolf [14]. They investigate various approaches to infer a finite state model of a process from a set of event sequences. Various approaches ranging from neural network to grammar inference (i.e., k-tails [8]) are investigated.

The work by Cook and Wolf is later extended by Ammons et al., who coin the term "mining specification" [6]. Ammons et al. directly address software specifications rather than generic process models. They employ a program analysis technique to extract related trace segments from dynamic executions of a program. These trace segments are later fed into a probabilistic grammar inference engine. They also develop a process to prune potentially wrong edges from the resultant finite state machine. In their later work [7], they propose an approach to reduce the amount of user manual feedback needed in their system to debug and correct errors in mined specifications.

Whaley et al. propose a static and a dynamic analysis approach to extract specifications in the form of a finite state machine [74]. Rather than producing a single finite state machine, they produce multiple finite state machines. Each finite state machine models a sub-behavior corresponding to a group of method calls implementing the same Java interface or accessing a particular field. They distinguish method calls into two types: state-preserving (side effect free) and state-modifying (with side effect). For the static analysis approach, for each method m they find fields and predicates that guard exceptions. Next, they detect other methods m' that set the values of the fields and the predicates that would trigger some exceptions in m. Calls to m' which are directly followed by m are thus illegal. A model that excludes the illegal behaviors is finally produced. For the dynamic analysis approach, their approach keeps track of the history of the last state-modifying method that was called. Each method corresponds to a unique state. Their algorithm then builds a graph connecting two methods that are called one after another.

Alur et al. propose an approach to infer a finite state machine from Application Programming Interface (API) code [5]. Given a library code and certain assertions that must hold, the task is to describe the most general way to invoke the methods in the API such that the assertions are not violated. A sequence of method calls that does not lead to a violation of the assertions is considered safe. Alur et al. provide a sound algorithm to solve this problem. The work is extended by Henzinger et al. [31]. In the latter work, they could assure that all safe sequences of method calls are represented in the mined finite state machine. The resulting model learned is termed as "permissive interface" as it does not wrongly forbid any client from using the API.

Mariani and Pezzé propose a new grammar inference engine specially suited for program executions named k-behavior [53]. They employ k-behavior along with a value-based invariant generation engine (see Section 1.4) to concisely capture the various behaviors of a software system. These behaviors could later be replayed to test the correctness of the software system.

Acharya et al. [3] propose a static analysis approach to mine finite state machines from systems. Their tool leverages a model checker to statically generate traces of a system. Based on certain trigger automata, the model checker could generate concrete labels corresponding to various condition checks and method calls as transition labels of the automata. These concrete labels are then further analyzed to generate a mapping between high level concepts, e.g., check, free, etc., to concrete statements. Users could then specify a generic automata to be automatically converted to a concrete automata that could in turn be used to find violations using a model checker.

Dallmeier et al. propose a hybrid static and dynamic analysis approach to infer a finite state machine [15]. First, a set of methods termed as mutators (i.e., those that change a system state) and another set termed as inspectors (i.e., those that read/inspect a system state) are determined statically. A dynamic analysis approach is then employed to get possible states of a system based on abstracted values of variables, e.g., size>0, size=0, etc. These states form the nodes in finite state machine. Invocations of the mutator methods that transform one state to another act as transitions in the resultant finite state machine.

Lo and Khoo extend the work by Ammons et al. by proposing a metric of precision and recall in evaluating the quality of a specification mining engine producing finite state machines [38]. They also introduce trace clustering and trace filtering to reduce the effect of bad traces and inaccuracies during the inference of mined specifications.

Acharya et al. extend their previous work [3] in [1]. Static traces are first extracted from program code similar to their previous work [3]. Relevant segments of traces are then recovered. These segments of traces fed to a frequent partial order miner. The resultant partial orders are then composed to generate a specification in the form of a finite state machine.

Mariani et al. extend their previous work [53] in [52]. They propose a technique to generate prioritized regression test cases for the integration of Commercial-off-the-Shelf (COTS) components. A model in the form of a finite state machine and a set of boolean expressions on a set of variables, operators, and values is learned based on an older version of a system. This model is used to generate test cases to verify whether there are problems in a future version of the system when a component is replaced.

Shevertalov and Mancoridis propose an approach to extract a finite state machine capturing a network protocol [65]. Their system first captures packets from a network traffic. These packets are then clustered using a hierarchical clustering approach with a distance metric defined based on the longest common subsequence of two packets when compared byte per byte. Each cluster is given a unique identifier. A set of traces of captured packets can then be converted to a set of sequences of identifiers. A set of states and transitions between states are then inferred. Various refinement operations to split and merge states are also proposed.

While many specification mining approaches extract a finite state machine from sequences or stream of events, Quante and Koschke develop an approach that extracts a finite state machine from graphs [60]. An object process graph, which is a projection of a control flow graph on a single object, is used. The approach takes in a set of object process graphs corresponding to the various usage scenarios of a particular application and generalizes them to form a finite state machine via some transformation operations.

Walkinshaw et al. employ a state-of-the-art grammar inference technique that incorporates active learning [72]. The inference engine asks a series of membership questions while performing the inference. A membership question asks whether a series of events is valid or not. Inputs from a user or new test cases could be used to answer these membership questions. With answers to membership questions serving as feedbacks, the quality of the mined specification could be improved.

Gabel and Su use a Binary Decision Diagram (BDD) based approach to mine small size automata efficiently [30]. They show that the problem of specification mining under a particular setting, i.e., given an automaton template A and a trace T, enumerate all possible concrete automata following A that are satisfied by T, is inherently NP-Complete. A BDD-based approach could be used to speed up the process. In the process they show that they are able to mine small size automata from traces of sizes up to millions of events. They extend their approach by proposing a technique to merge multiple small size finite state machines to a larger one [29].

Lorenzoli et al. mine extended finite state machines (EFSMs) in [49]. An extended finite state machine enriches a standard finite state machine with value-based invariants. Value-based invariants make the finite state machine more expressive: It could specify that if a certain constraint is met a set of behaviors becomes possible, otherwise another set of behaviors becomes possible. Their approach consists of merging of equivalent traces, generating value-based invariants, creating an initial model, and merging the initial model's states to result in a final model.

Mariani and Pastore mine finite state machines to identify failure causes from system logs [54]. System logs are first collected. Several pre-processing modules to detect for events in logs and to transform data to an appropriate format that abstracts away concrete values are first employed. Based on the transformed log a model is learned using the approach proposed in [53]. When a failure occurs, the corresponding log and the mined model are analyzed to produce suspicious statements as potential root causes.

Shoham et al. propose an approach to infer specifications via an inter-procedural static analysis using abstract interpretation [66]. Their approach works in two steps. The first step is abstract-trace collection. In this step, abstract histories in automata form are learned. Next, a summarization step is performed. A statistical approach is employed in this step to consolidate information collected in the first step and remove noise.

In [71], Walkinshaw and Bogdanov further automate their active learning finite state machine inference approach [72]. The approach in [72] potentially asks a large number of questions to users. The work in [71] reduces the amount of questions by asking users to provide a set of constraints. This set of constraints is used to automatically answer many of the generated questions.

In [46], Lo et al. propose mining of short temporal rules (in future and past-time temporal logics) that are incorporated to finite state machine inference. Different from the approach in [71], these rules are mined rather than specified. This approach addresses a technical concern about undesired merges of states during an inference leading to an imprecision in the constructed finite state machine. Specifically, the mined rules are used to prevent these bad merges, resulting in the learning of a more accurate finite state machine. A sound but incomplete approach to efficiently check the mined rules on the intermediate finite state machines is also proposed.

In [58], Pradel and Gross develop an efficient solution to mine for specifications involving multiple objects from a large amount of traces. Their approach first splits the traces into multiple smaller traces consisting of calls to related objects and methods. Each set of splitted traces is analyzed separately. This divide and conquer approach scales their approach to process a large amount of events in traces collected from various applications; each can contain up to tens of millions of events.

In [80], different from previous approaches, Zhong et al. extract specifications from natural language documentations (specifically Javadocs). These Javadocs are analyzed to form action-resource pairs. These pairs are later combined into a finite state machine. They have shown that the generated finite state machines are accurate and are able to detect bugs.

Gabel and Su propose an online specification mining approach [28]. Rather than performing an offline mining on a set of traces, they devise a technique to perform mining at the same time as traces are generated. A trace is processed window by window. Specification is mined/updated based on information collected in each window. Mining and checking of mined specifications are performed along the way as new traces are collected.

1.4   Mining Value-Based Invariants

In this section, we describe past studies mining value-based invariants.

The pioneer work in extracting value-based invariants is Daikon by Ernst et al. [23–26]. Daikon contains many value-based invariant templates. It monitors a program in execution and matches one or more invariant templates to particular program points of interest. It then reports the invariants that holds at the program point. Various filtering and template selection strategies are provided by Daikon. Daikon is also integrated with constraint solvers to reduce the redundancy in the mined invariants. Optimization strategies have also been proposed to speed up the extraction of value-based invariants, e.g., by incremental detection of invariants [57].

Many other studies leverage Daikon to perform other software engineering tasks. For example, Nimmer and Ernst integrate Daikon with ESC/Java to evaluate the effectiveness of the mined invariants in, detecting bugs via static analysis [56]. Pytlik et al. leverage Daikon invariants for fault localization [59]. Given a set of execution traces that fail and those that are successful Pytlik et al. find invariants that discriminate failing and correct traces in an effort to localize or pinpoint the wrong statement which is the root cause of the failure. They encounter a negative result in their experiment as many of the invariants are not related to bugs. Their study is later extended by Brun and Ernst in [11]. The latter study is able to show that with machine learning, Daikon invariants could be used to localize bugs. Demsky et al. use Daikon to learn data structure consistency invariants for automatic data structure repair [18].

In several studies the work on mining value-based invariants is combined with mining other invariant types. For example, Ramanathan et al. mine both value-based invariants and precedence rules as pre-conditions of various methods using an inter-procedural path-sensitive static analysis [62]. Lorenzoli et al. integrate Daikon invariants into a finite state machine inference algorithm to mine specifications that capture both the temporal ordering constraints and invariants among values/variables [49]. Lo and Maoz also extend their algorithm with Daikon to enable the extraction of sequence diagrams in the form of Live Sequence Charts with value-based invariants from program executions [45].

1.5   Mining Patterns and Rules

In this section, we describe past studies mining rules and patterns.

Engler et al. are among the first pioneers in proposing statistical approaches to find bugs [21]. Their tool is built upon the tenet: "If two beliefs contradict, we know that one is an error without knowing what the correct belief is." Their system works on a set of templates that associates a few variables together, e.g., "Does lock ⟨L⟩ protect a resource ⟨R⟩?" "Must IS_ERR be used to check the return value of function F?" etc. Instances of these templates with sufficient statistical values are then identified. Violations of these instances are reported as potential bugs in a ranked list based on statistical likelihood of them being errors.

El-Ramly et al. extract frequent patterns of usage termed as interaction patterns from a set of sequences of events extracted from runtime program executions [20]. They formulate a new frequent pattern mining semantics and an efficient algorithm to mine the patterns. They applied their solution in a software maintenance task. In particular, they show the viability of the mined patterns in helping the migration of a legacy system to a new web-based solution.

Li and Zhou propose an approach that mines for rules from program code [37]. In their approach, every function is mapped into a transaction. The database of transactions corresponding to functions in a program under analysis is later mined. Association rule mining is employed to find rules that satisfy minimum support and confidence thresholds. The mined rules are used for the detection of anomalies.

Livshits and Zimmermann propose an approach that combines repository mining with the analysis of program execution traces to infer specifications [35]. First, transactions are formed from sets of method calls that are added together in a revision in a software repository. These transactions are later subject to association rule mining to mine for rules satisfying minimum support and confidence thresholds. Mined rules are later filtered and ranked. For the remaining set of rules, a user can choose some of them. These selected rules would be verified using a dynamic analysis approach. If there are many violations of a rule in execution traces, the rule is less likely to be valid. On the other hand, if the traces conform to the rule, the rule is more likely to be valid. Mined rules are used for the detection of anomalies.

Mandelin et al. propose a concept referred to as *jungloid mining* [50]. The process accepts a pair of input and output types of a desired code fragment. The system then produces a piece of code fragment that would transform the input type to the output type (i.e., jungloid). The resultant code fragment refer to the variables in the program under investigation and thus can be inserted with ease. The system behaves like a programmer's search engine and produces a list of possible jungloids based on a user query.

Weimer and Necula extract temporal rules statically by analyzing program code [75]. A temporal rule specifies an ordering constraint among events. In particular, their work focuses on an approach to mine two event rules, e.g., a lock is eventually followed by an unlock, etc. First, a set of static traces is extracted from program code. These traces are categorized into error and normal traces. An error trace passes through an error handling code. Next, based on the intuition that programmers tend to make more bugs in handling exceptional conditions, they devise a set of heuristics to automatically extract temporal rules that can result in finding a set of violations, particularly those that go through error handling code.

Kremenek et al. mine for annotations of methods in a code base [34]. As the first step, a set of annotations is defined, e.g., allocation and deallocation. Next, a model is built based on the annotations. Using the assumption that a program is generally correct they make use of a factor graph. A factor is a relationship that maps the deduction that a variable (i.e., the methods to be annotated) has a particular value (i.e., the annotation, e.g., allocation, etc.) to a positive real number. A factor graph is used to represent the relationship between various factors and variables. It is powerful enough to represent the fusion of various pieces of information and to propagate information learned on one method to other related methods.

Safyallah and Sartipi develop an approach to find frequent behavioral patterns from program traces [64]. They propose a frequent sub-string mining algorithm to realize the task. A sub-string mining algorithm is more efficient than a regular sub-sequence mining algorithm first proposed in [4] as it does not need to consider gaps between the events in a pattern. They also propose a two-step process in which the result of a mining operation is used as an input of another mining operation to detect higher level patterns.

Yang et al. develop a linear time solution to extract two-event rules from execution traces [76]. They particularly focus on expressing alternating behavior in which two events must occur in a strict alternating ordering. A concept of satisfaction rate is used to detect interesting rules. The linear time algorithm is realized by maintaining a matrix-like data structure of quadratic size to the number of unique events in the trace. As each event in the trace is processed a corresponding row and a corresponding column in the matrix are updated. They also propose a chaining process to link multiple two event rules that are mined.

Lo et al. mine iterative patterns to capture frequent software behaviors [39]. An iterative pattern captures pattern instances that appear within a sequence and across multiple sequences. It merges frequent subsequence mining [4] with frequent episode mining [51]. Since a program contains loops, recursions, etc., patterns of interest could appear many times in an execution of a program. A depth-first pattern mining solution is employed. A notion of *closed patterns* (i.e., the longest pattern without a super-sequence pattern having the same support) for iterative patterns is also proposed. Several pruning strategies to remove search space containing infrequent and redundant patterns (i.e., non-closed patterns) are detected early and those patterns are removed en masse.

Ramanathan et al. propose a static analysis technique to generate inter-procedural path-sensitive constraint repository from program code [61]. The constraint repository captures precedence relationships in the form of a sequence/chain of elements. From these trace-like chains of elements, a sequence mining operation is performed to find frequent patterns in the repository. These frequent patterns are then used to detect anomalies.

Ramanathan et al. next propose another inter-procedural path-sensitive static analysis technique to infer pre-conditions that must be observed before a method call is made [62]. The pre-conditions are in two forms: dataflow and control flow properties. The data flow property is in the form of value-based invariants, e.g., when a procedure X is called the integer parameter n must be less than or equal to zero. The control flow property captures ordering constraints among method calls, e.g., when "unlock" is called, "lock" must be called before.

Thummalapenta and Xie mine for frequent event sequences from the source code repositories on the web [68]. The approach first downloads code from source code repositories, e.g., Google code. The code is then analyzed to extract Method-Invocation Sequences (MIS) that could transform an object of a particular type to another. The extracted MISs are later clustered and ranked before being presented to the user. Two ranking heuristics based on frequency and length are used.

Lo et al. extends the algorithm in [76] to mine rules of longer length [40]. Recall that the approach in [76] mines for rules of length two and later composes them to rules of longer lengths. However some rules might be omitted and some other generated rules might not be valid (i.e., when the satisfaction rate is not perfect). Mined temporal rules are in the format: "Whenever a series of events occurs, another series of events must eventually occur." Their algorithm follow a depth first approach to traverse the rule search space. Search spaces containing non-significant rules are identified and those rules are removed en masse. The resulting algorithm guarantees that 1) all mined rules satisfy the user defined threshold of support and confidence, 2) all interesting rules satisfying support and confidence thresholds are mined. A redundancy criterion is also defined and a process to identify and remove search space containing redundant rules is proposed. The early detection of redundant rules could greatly reduce the runtime needed and the number of rules mined.

Ramanathan et al. provide a summarization mechanism to statically generate paths in programs [63]. The proposed technique summarizes static paths that reach a particular point in a program. The static paths are collected by propagating and merging predicate information in an inter-procedural path-sensitive analysis. For each node in a control flow graph (CFG) information on the number of paths that reach it, and the number of paths satisfying various predicates that go through it, is collected. The summary is termed as static path profile. The static path profile is used to mine pre-conditions of various methods.

Zhong et al. extract specifications from code in the form of a rule graph [79]. Nodes in the rule graph correspond to method calls and edges correspond to relationships between these methods. Their approach starts with a set of basic known rule graphs. These rule graphs are extended to form new rule graphs. Basic facts are extracted from program source code. These facts are used to infer other graphs based on the existing pool of known rule graphs in an iterative manner. The rule graphs could later be visualized to show the relationships among various methods.

Zhong et al. study the effect of trace quality on the quality of mined specifications [78]. They focus on mining specifications in the form of frequent sub-sequence patterns in a trace set. They introduce the notion of "polluting" events. They show that some events in the trace might lower the quality of the mined specifications. Several automated filtering strategies are proposed to remove these polluting events. They show that the quality of mined specifications is improved after the polluting events are filtered and mining is performed on the resultant traces.

Acharya and Xie mine for error-handling specifications from program code [2]. Their approach first extracts traces corresponding to error-handling and correct behaviors. Two types of specifications are mined, namely, error checking specification (i.e., a particular check is performed before a returned result is used) and multiple-API specification (i.e., right clean-up API methods are called). To mine for multiple-API specification, a frequent sub-sequence mining algorithm is employed. The sub-sequence mining algorithm is used to extract frequent sequences of method calls from correct executions.

Heydarnoori et al. propose an automated approach to extract *concept implementation templates* [32]. A concept implementation template is a sequence of method calls together with related information (e.g., a set of import statements in Java, etc.) to implement a particular generic functionality in a particular framework, e.g., implementing a context menu in JFace, etc. The approach starts with a collection of execution traces that is relevant to the context of interest. The extracted traces are later marked and sliced to get the relevant method calls. Events in the extracted sliced traces are then generalized. Several sets of facts, e.g., the dependency among events, etc., are extracted from the generalized traces. An intersection of these sets is taken.

Based on the generalized traces and common facts, a code corresponding to the template is finally generated.

Livshits et al. mine explicit information flow specifications [36]. They first extract a propagation graph which is a directed graph whose nodes are methods and transitions are explicit information flow between these methods. The task of explicit flow information is to label the nodes in the propagation graph by one of the following labels: sources, sinks, sanitizers, and regular. Given the labels and the graph, one could find information flow issues by running a reachability analysis. A probabilistic inference approach is used based on the intuition that most paths in the propagation graph are valid or secure.

Lo et al. propose an algorithm to mine for quantified temporal rules [47]. They propose a linear time algorithm to mine such quantified rules of length two. The approach could mine regular temporal rules, temporal rules with equality constraints, and quantified temporal rules with equality constraints. An example of quantified temporal rules is "for all object z, all calls to method m1(z), must eventually be followed by a call to method m2(z)." Only significant rules that satisfy minimum support and confidence thresholds are reported. A redundancy criterion is also proposed and redundant rules are filtered before being reported to the user.

Nguyen et al. capture common usage patterns of one or multiple objects from program code [55]. Their approach first constructs a graph-based object usage model (groum). The nodes in a groum correspond to various method calls or control structures. The edges in a groum correspond to temporal usage orders or data dependencies among various nodes. The groums are extracted from all the methods in a code base. The set of groums are input to a frequent graph mining algorithm. The resultant patterns are reported and are used to detect for anomalies in the code base.

Thummalapenta and Xie mine a set of exception handling rules to capture the behaviors that should occur when an exception is encountered [70]. Exception handling rules are expressed in a rule format: "A function F should be followed by a series of function $G_1,\ldots,G_m$ if it is preceded by a series of function $E_1,\ldots,E_n$." They also propose an extension to control flow graph termed exception flow graph that captures the flow of a program when exception happens. Static traces are extracted from the EFG, post-processed, and input to the mining algorithm. Rules are then produced and used to detect for anomalies.

Thummalapenta and Xie also mine for alternative patterns to detect for neglected conditions [69]. An alternative pattern captures a disjunction among patterns. To capture alternative patterns a frequent itemset mining algorithm is run multiple times. The first run would obtain the set of frequent patterns. For each frequent pattern, two sub-databases are formed: One corresponds to itemsets that do not contain all items in the frequent pattern, another corresponds to itemsets that support the frequent pattern. Alternating patterns are mined on the first sub-database by re-running the frequent itemset mining algorithm. The support of an alternating pattern is the support of the pattern in the first sub-database minus that of the second sub-database. The mined patterns are then used to detect for anomalies corresponding to neglected condition checks.

Wasylkowski and Zeller mine temporal rules in the form of Computational Tree Logics (CTL) from program code [73]. Their approach, named Tikanga, takes as input a program code to be analyzed and a set of CTL templates (of one or two placeholder events). An object usage model capturing how an object is being used in a program is first created via an intra-procedural static analysis. Each of these models is later converted into a Kripke structure (i.e., a finite state machine representation normally used in model checking). Next, a model checking procedure is used to check the satisfiability of CTL formulas from the templates on the Kripke structures. For each formal parameter of a method, a set of common CTL formulas that holds for objects passed as the actual arguments is mined via concept analysis. The resultant CTL formulas are used to detect for a list of violations ranked from the most probable to the least probable.

Zhong et al. mine frequent usage patterns from code bases in the web, e.g., Google code [77]. API call sequences are first extracted from a code base. The call sequences are then clustered. Each of the clusters is then input to a frequent subsequence mining algorithm. The resultant patterns are indexed to code snippets that exhibit such patterns. The patterns are presented to the user and once the user selects a particular pattern, all corresponding code snippets are also displayed. The approach is shown to be better than using Google code alone as it could automatically extract and utilize the context of an API method call.

In [19], Doan et al. package the algorithm described in [48] into a tool. The tool supports the creation of mining projects, management of traces, and running of the mining algorithm. The resultant mined scenarios could also be saved and re-visited later. It also supports identification of segments of the traces that satisfy/violate the mined scenarios. A set of pre-processing and post-processing options is also available to help users in refining the result of the mining process.

In [41], Lo et al. extend the mining of closed iterative patterns [39]. They propose an approach to mine for *generators* of iterative patterns. A generator is a frequent pattern without any sub-sequence pattern of the same support. Whereas closed patterns are the maximal patterns, generators are the minimal patterns. Aside from closed patterns, generators are another alternative set of patterns to compactly represent a set of frequent patterns. The concept of *representative rules* that merge closed patterns and generators is also proposed. The resultant rules can capture interesting temporal constraints including specifying a set of events that must happen before, after, and in-between sequences of precursor events.

1.6   Mining Sequence Diagrams

In this section, we describe past studies mining sequence diagrams.

Briand et al. extract a UML sequence diagram from execution traces [10]. A UML sequence diagram contains lifelines corresponding to objects, and messages corresponding to method calls between these objects. They propose a framework to instrument a distributed system via an aspect-oriented language (i.e., AspectJ). Running an instrumented program would produce a trace. The collected traces are then analyzed to form a sequence diagram that could capture the caller, callee, and method signature information. In addition, branching points and loops in the trace would also be represented in the extracted sequence diagram.

Lo et al. extract modal sequence diagrams [48]. Such modal sequence diagram is represented as Live Sequence Charts (LSCs) [16]. An LSC is composed of a prechart and a mainchart. It could express a constraint: "Whenever the pre-chart is satisfied, the post-chart would eventually be satisfied." Both the pre- and post-charts are sequence diagrams capturing caller, callee, and method signature information. Mined LSCs could be used as input to a runtime verification tool to find for anomalies.

Sousa et al. extract implied scenarios from execution traces [17]. Their approach starts with trace collection with each trace corresponding to an execution of a scenario. The collected traces are later filtered to distill the method calls that are relevant to the scenario and remove irrelevant ones. Based on this set of scenarios, their approach infers implied scenarios that are not present in the original set. The final set of scenarios is output and presented to the user.

In [42], Lo and Maoz extend the initial work on mining Live Sequence Charts published in [48]. The work introduces the concept of *triggers and effects*. The task is: Given a trigger, mine all significant effects. Similarly, given an effect, find all significant triggers. Thus users could help in directing the specification miner by providing a trigger or an effect. The resultant specification mining process could reduce both the runtime cost and the number of mined specifications. Only specifications related to the trigger or effect of interest would be mined.

In [43], Lo and Maoz further extend the work in [48]. They focus on the semantics of *symbolic* Live Sequence Charts. Symbolic LSCs have symbolic lifelines. A symbolic lifeline specifies a set of objects of a particular type or class. The work in [48] only approximates the symbolic LSCs by aggregating all frequent object-level/concrete LSCs in which all lifelines correspond to concrete objects. However it could be the case that a symbolic LSC is frequent while the corresponding object level LSCs are not. In this case, the work in [48] would miss the symbolic LSCs. This issue is addressed in [43].

In [44], Lo and Maoz introduce the concept of hierarchical specification mining. Given a hierarchical structure, they mine a set of specifications at a certain abstraction level of interest. The resultant mined patterns could be zoomed-in or zoomed-out by expanding or collapsing lifelines of interest. It helps users by mining specifications at the right abstraction level. If more information is needed, the mined specification could be zoomed in. If there is too much information, the mined specification could be zoomed out. Thus, it provides an interactive mining experience to the user.

In [45], Lo and Maoz incorporate mining value-based invariants to mining Live Sequence Charts. They introduce the concept of *scenario-based slicing*. A set of scenarios is first mined. For a desired scenario of interest, slices of program traces that satisfy the scenario are extracted. These slices are fed to a value-based invariant miner, namely, Daikon [24], to produce a set of invariants. These invariants are then incorporated to the mined LSC of interest. Thus the work could capture both temporal ordering constraints and value-based invariants from execution traces.

1.7   Conclusion

Specification mining corresponds to the inference of models in various formats from programs either from code or execution traces or even natural language documents. Mined specifications are useful for various software engineering activities. These include program comprehension, software maintenance, bug finding, and test cases generation.

Categorizing based on the type of specification formalisms that were mined, the work on specification mining could be grouped into these mining: finite state machines, value-based invariants, patterns/rules, and sequence diagrams. More than 50 papers have been published on specification mining and we have surveyed many of them in this chapter.

In the following chapters, various works are discussed in more detail. We focus particularly on specification mining works that extract finite state machines and patterns/rules. The book covers approaches employing static analysis, dynamic analysis, and even the combination of the two.

Bibliography

[1] M. Acharya, T. Xie, J. Pei, and J. Xu. Mining API patterns as partial orders from source code: from usage scenarios to specifications. In *Proceedings of Joint Meeting of the European Software Engineering Conference and the ACM International Symposium on Foundations of Software Engineering*, pages 25–34, 2007.

[2] M. Acharya and T. Xie. Mining API error-handling specifications from source code. In *Proceedings of International Conference on Fundamental Approaches to Software Engineering*, pages 370–384, 2009.

[3] M. Acharya, T. Xie, and J. Xu. Mining interface specifications for generating checkable robustness properties. In *Proceedings of International Symposium on Software Reliability Engineering*, pages 311–320, 2006.

[4] R. Agrawal and R. Srikant. Mining sequential patterns. In *Proceedings of IEEE International Conference on Data Engineering*, pages 3–14, 1995.

[5] R. Alur, P. Cerny, G. Gupta, and P. Madhusudan. Synthesis of interface specifications for java classes. In *Proceedings of ACM Symposium on Principles of Programming Languages*, pages 98–109, 2005.

[6] G. Ammons, R. Bodik, and J.R. Larus. Mining specification. In *Proceedings of ACM Symposium on Principles of Programming Languages*, pages 4–16, 2002.

[7] G. Ammons, D. Mandelin, R. Bodik, and J.R. Larus. Debugging temporal specifications with concept analysis. In *Proceedings of ACM Conference on Programming Language Design and Implementation*, pages 182–195, 2003.

[8] A.W. Biermann and J.A. Feldman. On the synthesis of finite-state machines from samples of their behaviour. *IEEE Transactions on Computers*, 21:591–597, 1972.

[9] M. Boshernitsan, R-K. Doong, and A. Savoia. From Daikon to agitator: lessons and challenges in building a commercial tool for developer testing. In *Proceedings of International Symposium on Software Testing and Analysis*, pages 169–180, 2006.

[10] L.C. Briand, Y. Labiche, and J. Leduc. Toward the reverse engineering of UML sequence diagrams for distributed Java software. *IEEE Transactions on Software Engineering*, 32:642–663, 2006.

[11] Y. Brun and M.D. Ernst. Finding latent code errors via machine learning over program executions. In *Proceedings of ACM/IEEE International Conference on Software Engineering*, pages 480–490, 2004.

[12] G. Canfora and A. Cimitile. Software maintenance. In S.K. Chang, editor, *Handbook of Software Engineering and Knowledge Engineering*, pages 91–120. World Scientific, 2002.

[13] E.M. Clarke, O. Grumberg, and D.A. Peled. *Model Checking*. MIT Press, 1999.

[14] J.E. Cook and A.L. Wolf. Automating process discovery through event-data analysis. In *Proceedings of ACM/IEEE International Conference on Software Engineering*, pages 73–82, 1995.

[15] V. Dallmeier, C. Lindig, A. Wasylkowski, and A. Zeller. Mining object behavior with ADABU. In *Proceedings of International Workshop on Dynamic Analysis*, pages 17–24, 2006.

[16] W. Damm and D. Harel. LSCs: breathing life into message sequence charts. *Journal on Formal Methods in System Design*, 19(1):45–80, 2001.

[17] F.C. de Sousa, N.C. Mendonça, S. Uchitel, and J. Kramer. Detecting implied scenarios from execution traces. In *Proceedings of Working Conference on Reverse Engineering*, pages 50–59, 2007.

[18] B. Demsky, M.D. Ernst, P.J. Guo, S. McCamant, J.H. Perkins, and M.C. Rinard. Inference and enforcement of data structure consistency specifications. In *Proceedings of International Symposium on Software Testing and Analysis*, pages 233–244, 2006.

[19] T.A. Doan, D. Lo, S. Maoz, and S-C. Khoo. LM: a tool for scenario-based specification mining. In *Proceedings of ACM/IEEE International Conference on Software Engineering*, pages 319–320, 2010.

[20] M. El-Ramly, E. Stroulia, and P. Sorenson. From run-time behavior to usage scenarios: an interaction-pattern mining approach. In *Proceedings of ACM International Conference on Knowledge Discovery and Data Mining*, pages 315–324, 2002.

[21] D. Engler, D.Y. Chen, S. Hallem, A. Chou, and B. Chelf. Bugs as deviant behavior: a general approach to inferring errors in systems code. In *Proceedings of Symposium on Operating Systems Principles*, pages 57–72, 2001.

[22] L. Erlikh. Leveraging legacy system dollars for e-business. *IEEE IT Pro*, pages 17–23, 2000.

[23] M.D. Ernst, J. Cockrell, W.G. Griswold, and D. Notkin. Dynamically discovering likely program invariants to support program evolution. In *Proceedings of ACM/IEEE International Conference on Software Engineering*, pages 213–224, 1999.

[24] M.D. Ernst, J. Cockrell, W.G. Griswold, and D. Notkin. Dynamically discovering likely program invariants to support program evolution. *IEEE Transactions on Software Enginering*, 27(2):99–123, 2001.

[25] M.D. Ernst, A. Czeisler, W.G. Griswold, and D. Notkin. Quickly detecting relevant program invariants. In *Proceedings of ACM/IEEE International Conference on Software Engineering*, pages 449–458, 2000.

[26] M.D. Ernst, J.H. Perkins, P.J. Guo, S. McCamant, C. Pacheco, M.S. Tschantz, and C. Xiao. The Daikon system for dynamic detection of likely invariants. *Science of Computer Programming*, 1-3:35–45, 2007.

[27] R. Fjeldstad and W. Hamlen. Application program maintenance-report to our respondents. In G. Parikh and N. Zvegintzov, editors, *Tutorial on Software Maintenance*, pages 13–27. IEEE Computer Society Press, 1983.

[28] M. Gabel and Z. Su. Online inference and enforcement of temporal properties. In *Proceeding of IEEE/ACM International Conference on Software Engineering*, pages 15–24, 2010.

[29] M. Gabel and Z. Su. Javert: fully automatic mining of general temporal properties from dynamic traces. In *Proceedings of ACM International Symposium on Foundations of Software Engineering*, pages 339–349, 2008.

[30] M. Gabel and Z. Su. Symbolic mining of temporal specifications. In *Proceedings of ACM/IEEE International Conference on Software Engineering*, pages 51–60, 2008.

[31] T.A. Henzinger, R. Jhala, and R. Majumdar. Permissive interfaces. In *Proceedings of Joint Meeting of the European Software Engineering Conference and the ACM International Symposium on the Foundations of Software Engineering*, pages 31–40, 2005.

[32] A. Heydarnoori, K. Czarnecki, and T.T. Bartolomei. Supporting framework use via automatically extracted concept-implementation templates. In *Proceedings of European Conference on Object-Oriented Programming*, pages 344–368, 2009.

[33] ITU-T. ITU-T Recommendation Z.120: Message Sequence Chart (MSC). 1999.

[34] T. Kremenek, P. Twohey, G. Back, A. Ng, and D. Engler. From uncertainty to belief: inferring the specification within. In *Proceedings of Symposium on Operating Systems Design and Implementation*, pages 161–176, 2006.

[35] Z. Li and Y. Zhou. PR–miner: automatically extracting implicit programming rules and detecting violations in large software code. In *Proceedings of SIGSOFT Symposium on the Foundations of Software Engineering*, pages 306–315, 2005.

[36] B. Livshits, A.V. Nori, S.K. Rajamani, and A. Banerjee. Merlin: specification inference for explicit information flow problems. In *Proceedings of SIGPLAN Conference on Programming Language Design and Implementation*, pages 75–86, 2009.

[37] B. Livshits and T. Zimmermann. DynaMine: finding common error patterns by mining software revision histories. In *Proceedings of ACM Symposium on the Foundations of Software Engineering*, pages 296–305, 2005.

[38] D. Lo and S.-C. Khoo. SMArTIC: towards building an accurate, robust and scalable specification miner. In *Proceedings of ACM International Symposium on Foundations of Software Engineering*, pages 265–275, 2006.

[39] D. Lo, S.-C. Khoo, and C. Liu. Efficient mining of iterative patterns for software specification discovery. In *Proceedings of ACM International Conference on Knowledge Discovery and Data Mining*, pages 460–469, 2007.

[40] D. Lo, S.-C. Khoo, and C. Liu. Mining temporal rules for software maintenance. *Journal of Software Maintenance and Evolution*, 20(4):227–247, 2008.

[41] D. Lo, J. Li, L. Wong, and S.-C. Khoo. Mining iterative generators and representative rules for software specification discovery. *IEEE Transaction on Knowledge and Data Engineering*, 25(2), 2011.

[42] D. Lo and S. Maoz. Mining scenario-based triggers and effects. In *Proceedings of IEEE/ACM International Conference on Automated Software Engineering*, pages 109–118, 2008.

[43] D. Lo and S. Maoz. Mining symbolic scenario-based specifications. In *Proceedings of ACM Workshop on Program Analysis for Software Tools and Engineering*, pages 29–35, 2008.

[44] D. Lo and S. Maoz. Mining hierarchical scenario-based specifications. In *Proceedings of IEEE/ACM International Conference on Automated Software Engineering*, pages 359–370, 2009.

[45] D. Lo and S. Maoz. Scenario-based and value-based specification mining: better together. In *Proceedings of ACM/IEEE International Conference on Automated Software Engineering*, pages 387–396, 2010.

[46] D. Lo, L. Mariani, and M. Pezzè. Automatic steering of behavioral model inference. In *Proceedings of Joint Meeting of the European Software Engineering Conference and the ACM International Sympopsium on Foundations of Software Engineering*, pages 345–354, 2009.

[47] D. Lo, G. Ramalingam, V.P. Ranganath, and K. Vaswani. Mining quantified temporal rules: formalisms, algorithms, and evaluation. In *Proceedings of Working Conference on Reverse Engineering*, pages 62–71, 2009.

[48] D. Lo, S. Maoz, and S.-C. Khoo. Mining modal scenario-based specifications from execution traces of reactive systems. In *Proceedings of IEEE/ACM International Conference on Automated Software Engineering*, pages 465–468, 2007.

[49] D. Lorenzoli, L. Mariani, and M. Pezzè. Automatic Generation of Software Behavioral Models. In *Proceedings of ACM/IEEE International Conference on Software Engineering*, pages 501–510, 2008.

[50] D. Mandelin, L. Xu, R. Bodik, and D. Kimelman. Jungloid mining: helping to navigate the API jungle. In *Proceedings of ACM Conference on Programming Language Design and Implementation*, pages 48–61, 2005.

[51] H. Mannila, H. Toironen, and A. Verleamo. Discovery of frequent episodes in event sequence. *Data Mining and Knowledge Discovery*, 1:259–289, 1997.

[52] L. Mariani, S. Papagiannakis, and M. Pezzè. Compatibility and regression testing of COTS-component-based software. In *Proceedings of ACM/IEEE International Conference on Software Engineering*, pages 85–95, 2007.

[53] L. Mariani and M. Pezzè. Behavior capture and test: automated analysis for component integration. In *Proceedings of IEEE International Conference on Engineering of Complex Computer Systems*, pages 292–301, 2005.

[54] L. Mariani and F. Pastore. Automated identification of failure causes in system logs. In *Proceedings of International Symposium on Software Reliability Engineering*, pages 117–126, 2008.

[55] T.T. Nguyen, H.A. Nguyen, N.H. Pham, J.M. Al-Kofahi, and T.N. Nguyen. Graph-based mining of multiple object usage patterns. In *Proceedings of Joint Meeting of the European Software Engineering Conference and the ACM International Symposium on Foundations of Software Engineering*, pages 383–392, 2009.

[56] J.W. Nimmer and M.D. Ernst. Automatic generation of program specifications. In *Proceedings of International Symposium on Software Testing and Analysis*, pages 229–239, 2002.

[57] J.H. Perkins and M.D. Ernst. Efficient incremental algorithms for dynamic detection of likely invariants. In *Proceedings of ACM International Symposium on Foundations of Software Engineering*, pages 423–432, 2004.

[58] M. Pradel and T.R. Gross. Automatic generation of object usage specifications from large method traces. In *Proceedings of IEEE/ACM International Conference on Automated Software Engineering*, pages 371–382, 2009.

[59] B. Pytlik, M. Renieris, S. Krishnamurthi, and S.P. Reiss. Automated fault localization using potential invariants. *The Computing Research Repository*, cs.SE/0310040, 2003.

[60] J. Quante and R. Koschke. Dynamic protocol recovery. In *Proceedings of Working Conference on Reverse Engineering*, pages 219–228, 2007.

[61] M.K. Ramanathan, A. Grama, and S. Jagannathan. Path-sensitive inference of function precedence protocols. In *Proceedings of ACM/IEEE International Conference on Software Engineering*, pages 240–250, 2007.

[62] M.K. Ramanathan, A. Grama, and S. Jagannathan. Static specification inference using predicate mining. In *Proceedings of ACM Conference on Programming Language Design and Implementation*, pages 123–134, 2007.

[63] M.K. Ramanathan, K. Sen, A. Grama, and S. Jagannathan. Protocol inference using static path profiles. In *Proceedings of International Symposium on Static Analysis*, pages 78–92, 2008.

[64] H. Safyallah and K. Sartipi. Dynamic analysis of software systems using execution pattern mining. In *Proceedings of IEEE International Conference on Program Comprehension*, pages 84–88, 2006.

[65] M. Shevertalov and S. Mancoridis. A reverse engineering tool for extracting protocols of networked applications. In *Proceedings of Working Conference on Reverse Engineering*, pages 229–238, 2007.

[66] S. Shoham, E. Yahav, S. Fink, and M. Pistoia. Static specification mining using automata-based abstractions. In *Proceedings of International Symposium on Software Testing and Analysis*, pages 174–184, 2008.

[67] T. Standish. An essay on software reuse. *IEEE Transactions on Software Engineering*, 5(10):494–497, 1984.

[68] S. Thummalapenta and T. Xie. Parseweb: a programmer assistant for reusing open source code on the web. In *Proceedings of IEEE/ACM International Conference on Automated Software Engineering*, pages 204–213, 2007.

[69] S. Thummalapenta and T. Xie. Alattin: mining alternative patterns for detecting neglected conditions. In *Proceedings of IEEE/ACM International Conference on Automated Software Engineering*, pages 283–294, 2009.

[70] S. Thummalapenta and T. Xie. Mining exception-handling rules as sequence association rules. In *Proceedings of ACM/IEEE International Conference on Software Engineering*, pages 496–506, 2009.

[71] N. Walkinshaw and K. Bogdanov. Inferring finite-state models with temporal constraints. In *Proceedings of IEEE/ACM International Conference on Automated Software Engineering*, pages 248–257, 2008.

[72] N. Walkinshaw, K. Bogdanov, M. Holcombe, and S. Salahuddin. Reverse engineering state machines by interactive grammar inference. In *Proceedings of Working Conference on Reverse Engineering*, pages 209–218, 2007.

[73] A. Wasylkowski and A. Zeller. Mining temporal specifications from object usage. In *Proceedings of IEEE/ACM International Conference on Automated Software Engineering*, pages 295–306, 2009.

[74] J. Whaley, M.C. Martin, and M.S. Lam. Automatic extraction of object oriented component interfaces. In *Proceedings of International Symposium on Software Testing and Analysis*, 2002.

[75] W. Weimer and G. Necula. Mining temporal specifications for error detection. In *Proceedings of International Conference on Tools and Algorithms for the Construction and Analysis of Systems*, pages 461–476, 2005.

[76] J. Yang, D. Evans, D. Bhardwaj, T. Bhat, and M. Das. Perracotta: mining temporal API rules from imperfect traces. In *Proceedings of ACM/IEEE International Conference on Software Engineering*, pages 282–291, 2006.

[77] H. Zhong, T. Xie, L. Zhang, J. Pei, and H. Mei. MAPO: mining and recommending API usage patterns. In *Proceedings of European Conference on Object-Oriented Programming*, pages 318–343, 2009.

[78] H. Zhong, L. Zhang, and H. Mei. Early filtering of polluting method calls for mining temporal specifications. In *Proceedings of Asia-Pacific Software Engineering Conference*, pages 9–16, 2008.

[79] H. Zhong, L. Zhang, and H. Mei. Inferring specifications of object oriented APIs from API source code. In *Proceedings of Asia-Pacific Software Engineering Conference*, pages 221–228, 2008.

[80] H. Zhong, L. Zhang, T. Xie, and H. Mei. Inferring resource specifications from natural language API documentation. In *Proceedings of IEEE/ACM International Conference on Automated Software Engineering*, pages 307–318, 2009.

Chapter 2

Mining Finite-State Automata with Annotations

Leonardo Mariani, Fabrizio Pastore, Mauro Pezzè, and Mauro Santoro

Department of Informatics, Systems and Communication
University of Milano Bicocca

2.1   Introduction

Many software design and verification techniques assume the availability of some kind of behavioral models of the systems under analysis [2, 4, 10, 11, 28]. Unfortunately, manually specifying and maintaining behavioral models is expensive and error prone, and requires specific skills that are not always available in development teams. This reduces the applicability of model-based approaches in industrial projects. The problem of generating behavioral models can be solved with techniques that automatically generate behavioral models by mining program executions and thus reducing the effort required to generate models [3, 5, 18, 20, 24].

Many of these techniques generate finite state automata (FSA) that model the relations between sequences of events, but do not capture information about the attributes that are associated with the events, like parameters of method calls, thus missing details that may be important to support test and verification activities. For example, FSA can represent the causal relation between `open` and `close` actions on files, but cannot distinguish between actions on the same or different files, and cannot model the access mode of a specific file (being it `read-only`, `write-only`, or `read-write`) without modeling the parameters associated with the operations.

Recently, researchers explored mining techniques that extract FSA annotated with information about attribute values to capture both the relations among events and between events and attributes. In this chapter, we discuss and compare two mining techniques, *gkTail* and *KLFA*, that represent two different strategies to extend FSA with attribute values. gkTail mines Extended Finite State Automata (EFSA) that represent both the relations between sequences of events and the constraints on the values associated with the events [19]. KLFA mines FSAs that represent both the relations between sequences of events and data-flow patterns that model the occurrence of attribute values among events [21]. We introduce and compare the two techniques with the help of a running example, a simple flight booking system.

This chapter is organized as follows. Section 2.2 discusses the main techniques to generate annotated FSAs. Section 2.3 presents the running example that is used to illustrate the techniques discussed in this chapter. Sections 2.4 and 2.5 present gkTail and KLFA, respectively. Section 2.6 summarizes the main results obtained with gkTail and KLFA. Section 2.7 surveys techniques that mine different kinds of behavioral models from program executions. Section 2.8 summarizes the content of the chapter and describes challenges for the future.

2.2 Modeling Software Systems with Annotated FSA

The problem of inferring an FSA that accepts a language that contains a given set of samples is well known and has been extensively studied. There exist several algorithms whose applicability depends both on the nature of the samples and the knowledge about the FSA to be inferred. Some algorithms require only positive samples, that is, samples that belong to the language to be inferred [3, 6, 18, 20], while other algorithms require both positive and negative samples, that is, both samples that belong and samples that do not belong to the language to be inferred [23]. Other algorithms take advantage of additional information like *teachers* that answer to membership queries, that is, they assume to know if any specific sample does or does not belong to the language to be inferred [5].

FSAs can model sequences of events, but they do not capture other important behavioral elements, like conditions and relations between values. To build accurate behavioral models that integrate different aspects, for example, event order and data flow information, classic inference algorithms have been extended to generate annotated FSA. Here we distinguish three main ways of annotating FSA: adding information to the states, adding information to the transitions, and adding probabilities to the transitions.

Adding information to the states consists of annotating the states of the FSA with constraints that specify the set of concrete states of the program represented by the state of the FSA. These constraints usually include the variables relevant for the program under analysis. For example, the ADABU technique infers FSA annotated with constraints that specify the changes in the object states caused by method executions [7]. The ADABU constraints are predicates on the inspector methods implemented by the object under analysis. Figure 2.1 shows an example FSA inferred with ADABU for a Java object of type `Vector`. The example is taken from [7].

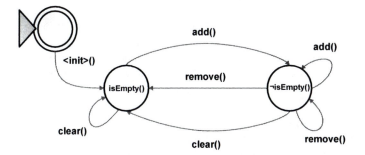

FIGURE 2.1: The ADABU model of a `Vector` object.

Adding information to the transitions consists of annotating the transitions with constraints on the values that are assigned to the attributes associated with the events modeled by the transitions. The techniques to infer such constraints differ for the aspects of the attributes specified by the inferred constraints. In this chapter, we discuss two techniques that can derive complementary annotations. *gkTail* derives constraints that specify the concrete values that can be assigned to attributes. Figure 2.10 shows an example of an annotated FSA inferred by gkTail. KLFA labels transitions to represent the repeated occurrence of the attribute values across events, regardless of their concrete values. Figure 2.12 shows an example of an annotated FSA inferred by KLFA. We discuss in detail gkTail and KLFA in Sections 2.4 and 2.5, respectively.

Adding probabilities to transitions consists of annotating transitions with probabilities that specify the likelihood that the event modeled by the transition occurs in a state modeled by the source state of the transition [1, 24]. Probabilities associated to transitions can distinguish the frequency of different behaviors, and can identify infrequent behaviors that correspond to failures. Since this chapter focuses on the inference of FSA annotated with information about attribute values, we do not analyze further this class of techniques.

2.3   Introducing a Running Example

This section presents the example that we use to illustrate the gkTail and KLFA approaches. The example consists of an application that interacts with several Web Services to reserve flights for a number of people. In this section, we illustrate the approaches referring to the `reserveFlight` component that implements the logic to reserve the cheapest flight that allows the party of people to fly together from the start to the final destination. If there are no flights that allow the party of people to flight together from the start to the final destination, the `reserveFlight` component reserves different flights for different subsets of people. The `reserveFlight` component interacts with other components responsible for communicating with the Web Services required to finalize the job. In this chapter we show how gkTail and KLFA infer behavioral models that represent the interactions between the `reserveFlight` component and the other components involved in the computation. Interactions consist of method calls. We refer to the method calls that cross the boundaries between the `reserveFlight` and the other components as the *inter-component method invocations*. Listing 2.1 shows part of the implementation of the `reserveFlight` component.

Both gkTail and KLFA build behavioral models from a set of execution traces. In the example, we assume to extensively execute the client component

```
1    public class Booking    {
2
3            List<Flight> allInOneFlight = new ArrayList<>();
4            List<Flight> splittedInMultipleFlights = new ArrayList<>();
5
6            /**
7             * Books a flight from an airport to another given a departure
                   and returning date
8             */
9            public void bookFlight( int persons, String from, String to,
                   Date departure, Date back){
10                   Iterator<Airline> it = CompaniesRegistry.INSTANCE.
                          getCompanbiesIterator();
11
12                   if ( !it.hasNext() ){
13                           ErrorLogger.configurationError();
14                   }
15
16                   while ( it.hasNext() ) {
17                           Airline airline = it.next();
18                           processAirline(airLine);
19                   }
20
21                   if ( allInOneFlight.size() > 0 ) {
22                           SingleSolution solution = findBestSolution(
                                  allInOneFlight);
23                           reservationMaker.book(solution);
24                   } else {
25                           CompositeSolution solution =
                                  findCompositeSolution(
                                  splittedInMultipleFlights);
26                           reservationMaker.book(solution);
27                   }
28
29           }
30
31            /**
32             * Identifies the available flights for a given airline
33             */
34            private void processAirline ( AirLine airLine,int persons,
                   String from, String to, Date departure, Date back ){
35                   List<Flight> flights = airLine.getAvailableFlights(
                          persons,from,to,departure,back);
36                   Iterator<Flight> it = flights.iterator();
37                   while ( it.hasNext() ) {
38                           Flight flight = it.next();
39
40                           if ( flight.getAvailableSeats() >= persons ){
41                                   allInOneFlight.add(flight);
42                           } else {
43                                   splittedInMultipleFlights.add(flight);
44                           }
45                   }
46
47           }
48
49   }
```

Listing 2.1: An excerpt of the reserveFlight component.

and record the inter-component method invocations. A trace is a sequence of inter-component method invocations that are represented with the name of the invoked method, the values of the parameters, and the return values, if any.

If a parameter (or the return value) of a method invocation is of primitive type, the trace records its value as a simple pair $\langle parameter\_name, value \rangle$. For example, $'\langle firstname, "John" \rangle$ indicates that the parameter *firstname* of type `String` has been passed with value "John". If the parameter (or the return value) is of a non-primitive type, the trace records the values of all its attributes. If any of the attributes is of a non-primitive type, the trace recursively records the values until all the recorded values are of primitive types. Thus, a non-primitive parameter results in a set of pairs $\langle parameter\_name.path\_to\_attribute, value \rangle$, where *parameter_name* is the name of the parameter, *path_to_attribute* is a path from the parameter to an attribute and is represented with the dot notation, and *value* is the value of the attribute. For example $\{ \langle address.street, "Examplestreet" \rangle, \langle address.city, "London" \rangle, \langle address.number, 1 \rangle \}$ represents values that can be extracted from a parameter of name *address*.

In the example there are several methods that exchange objects as parameters and return values. For instance, the method `findBestSolution` returns an object of type `SingleSolution`, which includes a field `totalSeatsAvailable`. When executing `findBestSolution`, the monitor can produce a trace that contains $\langle$`returnValue.totalSeatsAvailable`$, 6 \rangle$, which indicates that the field `totalSeatsAvailable` of the object returned by the method `findBestSolution` has value 6. This strategy for extracting values from objects has been already applied in other contexts [20].

Figure 2.2 shows four traces recorded during the execution of method `bookFlight`: The sequence of inter-component method invocations are reported from left to right, and on multiple lines when necessary. Since all traces refer to the execution of a same method, they all start with an invocation to `bookFlight`. Values of the attributes associated with the invoked methods are reported below the name of the method. For brevity, we show only the name of the invoked method omitting the full signature and the name of the class that implements the invoked method. The complete information can be easily obtained by pairing the traces in Figure 2.2 with the code in Listing 2.1. Solid lines separate the different traces.

We can include the information about the attribute values into FSAs by directly annotating the transitions with the set of attribute values that have been recorded in the traces, but in this way we would overfit the observed data and do not generalize the component behavior. For example, the FSA that can be derived from the traces in Figure 2.2 by simply annotating transitions with attribute values would accept an invocation to `bookFlight` with a value of 7, 4, 10, or 6 for the attribute `person`, but would not accept an invocation to `bookflight` with a number of persons equals to 5. The automaton

Trace 1

bookFlight	**→getCompaniesIterator**	**→hasNext**	**→hasNext**	**→next**
persons=7	return=Iterator		return=true	return=true	return.name
from=MXP				="KLM"
to=NYC				
depDate= 03/18/10				
retDate= 04/02/10				

→getAvailableFlights	**→iterator**		**→hasNext**	**→next**
persons=7	return=Iterator		return=true	return.availSeats=8
				return.flightNo=KL1017

→getAvailableSeats	**→add**	**→hasNext**	**→hasNext**	**→size**
return=8	object.availSeats=8	return=false	return=false	return=1
	object.flightNo=KL1017			

→findBestSolution	**→book**
allInOne=List	solution.seats=7
return.seats=7	

Trace 2

bookFlight	**→getCompaniesIterator**	**→hasNext**	**→hasNext**	**→next**
persons=4	return=Iterator		return=true	return=true	return.name
from=BGY				="Ryanair"
to=JFK				
depDate= 03/22/10				
retDate= 03/31/10				

→getAvailableFlights	**→iterator**		**→hasNext**	**→next**
persons=4	return=Iterator		return=true	return.availSeats=9
				return.flightNo=KL1027

→getAvailableSeats	**→add**	**→hasNext**	**→hasNext**	**→size**
return=9	object.availSeats=9	return=false	return=false	return=1
	object.flightNo=KL1027			

→findBestSolution	**→book**
allInOne=List	solution.seats=4
return.seats=4	

Trace 3

bookFlight	**→getCompaniesIterator**	**→hasNext**	**→hasNext**	**→next**
persons=10	return=Iterator		return=true	return=true	return.name
from=BGY				="KLM"
to=JFK				
depDate= 03/22/10				
retDate= 03/31/10				

→getAvailableFlights	**→iterator**		**→hasNext**	**→next**
persons=10	return=Iterator		return=true	return.availSeats=4
				return.flightNo=KL1022

→getAvailableSeats	**→add**	**→hasNext**	**→next**
return=4	object.availSeats=4	return=true	return.availSeats=7
	object.flightNo=KL1022		return.flightNo=KL1028

→getAvailableSeats	**→add**	**→hasNext**	**→next**
return=7	object.availSeats=7	return=true	return.availSeats=5
	object.flightNo=KL1028		return.flightNo=KL1058

→getAvailableSeats	**→add**	**→hasNext**	**→hasNext**
return=5	object.availSeats=5	return=false	return=false
	object.flightNo=KL1058		

→size	**→findCompositeSolution**	**→book**
return=0	allInOne=List	solution.seats=10
	return.seats=10	

Trace 4

bookFlight	**→getCompaniesIterator**	**→hasNext**	**→configurationError**
persons=6	return=Iterator	return=true	
from=BDS			
to=CIA			
depDate= 03/16/10			
retDate= 03/20/10			

FIGURE 2.2: Traces of the execution of method `bookFlight`.

clearly overfits the observed behavior. gkTail and KLFA extract information from attribute values and synthesize automata that generalize the observed behaviors.

2.4   Inferring FSA Annotated with Constraints

In this section we present gkTail [19], a technique to automatically generate Extended Finite State Automata (EFSA), that is, automata augmented with constraints on transitions. gkTail derives EFSA from a set of interaction traces (positive samples) that include information about both the ordering of the events and the values of the attributes associated with the events, such as the ones shown in Figure 2.2. gkTail processes traces in four steps:

1. merge similar traces

2. generate constraints associated with the events in the traces

3. produce an initial EFSA

4. merge equivalent states in the EFSA

In the first step, gkTail identifies similar traces, namely, traces with the same sequences of method invocations and possibly different values of the parameters, and merges sets of similar traces into traces where method invocations are annotated with sets of attribute values. In the second step, gkTail derives constraints that represent the set of attribute values associated with the same method invocation. In the third step, gkTail creates an initial EFSA from interaction traces annotated with constraints. In the fourth step, gkTail iteratively merges states that can accept similar sequences of method calls.

Hereafter, we describe in detail the four steps referring to the running example introduced in Section 2.3.

2.4.1   Merging Similar Traces

In the first step, gkTail processes a sequence of interaction traces $\{it^1 \ldots it^m\}$. Each interaction trace is a sequence of inter-component method invocations. An inter-component method invocation in the jth trace is a tuple $(x_i^j, p_{1_{x_i}}^j \ldots p_{n_{x_i}}^j)$, where x_i^j is the signature of the ith invoked method, and $p_{1_{x_i}}^j \ldots p_{n_{x_i}}^j$ are its parameter and return values, if any. Figure 2.2 shows four examples of interaction traces collected from the execution of the running example.

When the monitored component executes similar tasks, we obtain similar traces, namely, traces that share the same sequence of method invocation, and differ only for the values of the parameters and return values. For example, the first and second trace in Figure 2.2 are similar. To produce models that capture the general nature of the interactions, gkTail identifies and merges sets of similar traces, and produces traces where each method is associated with a set of parameter values. The set of values associated with a method in the merged traces corresponds to the parameter values associated to the same method in the original traces. For example, merging the first and second trace in Figure 2.2 produces a trace whose first element is a call to the method `bookFlight` associated to a set that includes the following two items: {*persons=7 from=MXP to=NYC depDate=03/18/10 retDate=04/02/10, persons=4 from=BGY to=JFK depDate=03/22/10 retDate=03/31/10*}.

Figure 2.3 shows the merged traces obtained from the interaction traces shown in Figure 2.2.

More formally, let us consider a set of interaction traces $IT = \{it^1 \ldots it^m\}$ all including the same sequence of invoked methods, and let the ith trace be $it^i = (x_1^i, p_{1_{x_1}}^i, \ldots, p_{n_{x_1}}^i) \ldots (x_n^i, p_{1_{x_n}}^i, \ldots, p_{n_{x_n}}^i)$ where $x_j^i = x_j^1 \; \forall i = 1 \ldots m$, the trace obtained by merging the interaction traces in IT is $it = (x_1, p_{1_{x_1}}^1 \ldots p_{n_{x_1}}^1 \cup \ldots \cup p_{1_{x_1}}^m \ldots p_{n_{x_1}}^m) \ldots (x_n, p_{1_{x_n}}^1 \ldots p_{n_{x_n}}^1 \cup \ldots \cup p_{1_{x_n}}^m \ldots p_{n_{x_n}}^m)$.

The next section describes how gkTail generates constraints from the set of attribute values associated with each event in the merged traces.

2.4.2 Generating Constraints

Transition constraints are predicates that specify the values that can be assigned to the attributes associated with the events. In the case of the running example, constraints represent the values that can be assigned to parameters and return variables. gkTail generates predicates from interaction traces using Daikon, an invariant inference engine originally proposed to derive likely invariants from execution traces [9]. Daikon transforms the values assumed by sets of variables across multiple executions into likely invariants that hold for all the executions. We run Daikon on the sets of values associated with the method calls in the merged execution traces, to produce constraints associated to the method calls in the traces. For example, Daikon can infer the predicate $x \geq 0$ from the values associated with the event `book` as shown in Figure 2.4.

gkTail uses Daikon to transform the set of merged traces into a set of traces annotated with constraints. A trace annotated with constraints is a sequence $(x_1, P_{x_1}) \ldots (x_n, P_{x_n})$ where P_{x_i} is a boolean predicate on the attribute of x_i, for all $i = 1 \ldots n$.

2.4.3 Initializing EFSA

In the third step, gkTail builds an initial EFSA by simply creating tree where each branch of the tree accepts a different merged trace. The initial EFSA is refined in the fourth and last step. Figure 2.5 shows the initial EFSA built from the traces in Figure 2.3.

Traces 1-2

bookFlight	→getCompaniesIterator	→hasNext	→hasNext	→next
{persons=7 from=MXP to=NYC depDate=03/18/10 retDate=04/02/10, persons=4 from=BGY to=JFK depDate=03/22/10 toDate=03/31/10}	{return=Iterator, return=Iterator}	{return =true, return =true}	{return =true, return =true}	{return.name ="KLM", return.name ="Ryanair"}
→getAvailableFlights	→iterator	→hasNext	→next	
{persons=7, persons=4}	{return=Iterator, return=Iterator}	{return =true, return =true}	{return.availSeats=8 return.flightNo=KL1017, return.availSeats=9 return.flightNo=KL1027}	
→getAvailableSeats	→add	→hasNext	→hasNext	→size
{return=8, return=9}	{object.availSeats=8 object.flightNo=KL1017, object.availSeats=9 object.flightNo=KL1027}	{return =false, return =false}	{return =false, return =false}	{return=1, return=1}
→findBestSolution	→book			
{allInOne=List return.seats=7, allInOne=List return.seats=4}	{solution.seats=7, solution.seats=4}			

Trace 3

bookFlight	→getCompaniesIterator	→hasNext	→hasNext	→next
{persons=10 from=BGY to=JFK depDate= 03/22/10 retDate= 03/31/10}	{return=Iterator}	{return =true}	{return =true}	{return.name ="KLM"}
→getAvailableFlights	→iterator	→hasNext	→next	
{persons=10}	{return=Iterator}	{return =true}	{return.availSeats=4 return.flightNo=KL1022}	
→getAvailableSeats	→add	→hasNext	→next	
{return=4}	{object.availSeats=4 object.flightNo=KL1022}	{return =true}	{return.availSeats=7 return.flightNo=KL1028}	
→getAvailableSeats	→add	→hasNext	→next	
{return=7}	{object.availSeats=7 object.flightNo=KL1028}	{return =true}	{return.availSeats=5 return.flightNo=KL1058}	
→getAvailableSeats	→add	→hasNext	→hasNext	
{return=5}	{object.availSeats=5 object.flightNo=KL1058}	{return =false}	{return =false}	
→size	→findCompositeSolution		→book	
{return=0}	{allInOne=List return.seats=10}		{solution.seats=10}	

Trace 4

bookFlight	→getCompaniesIterator	→hasNext	→configurationError
{persons=6 from=BDS to=CIA depDate= 03/16/10 retDate=03/20/10}	{return=Iterator}	{return =true}	

FIGURE 2.3: The set of merged traces obtained from the traces in Figure 2.2.

FIGURE 2.4: An example predicate generated by Daikon.

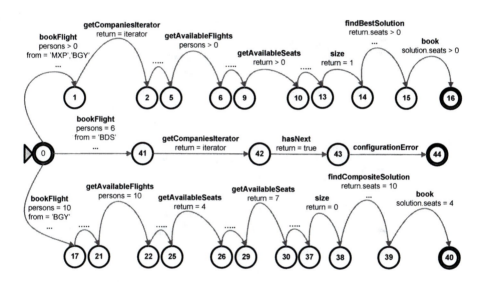

FIGURE 2.5: The initial EFSA obtained from the traces in Figure 2.3.

2.4.4   Merging Equivalent States in EFSA

In the previous steps, gkTail generalizes the values of the attributes and produces transition constraints. In the last step, gkTail generalizes the ordering of the events and produces compact EFSA. The initial EFSA produced in the third step accepts only sequences of method calls that correspond to the input traces. However in general, the finite set of input traces is a sample of the infinitely many behaviors of a component. By generalizing the ordering of the events in the initial EFSA, gkTail extends the model of the program behavior including a possibly infinite set of sequences of method calls. gkTail generalizes the ordering of the events with a heuristic inspired from the heuristics proposed in the kTail algorithm that iteratively merges likely equivalent states [3].

The heuristics adopted by gkTail suggests to merge states that accept equivalent sets of behaviors up to a maximum length k. The heuristic is based on the observation that the initial version of the model may include multiple representations of a same logical state, and merging states with the same future can expand and generalize the set of behaviors accepted by the model, likely increasing the model accuracy as well.

More formally, given an EFSA *efsa* with a set of states S and a state $s \in S$, we define the *k-future(s)* as the set of sequences $\{seq^1, \ldots seq^m\}$ where $seq^i = \{(x_1^i, P_{x_1}^i) \ldots (x_l^i, P_{x_l}^i)\}$ such that $\exists$ a transition sequence $(s, x_1^i, P_{x_1}^i, s_1)(s_1, x_2^i, P_{x_2}^i, s_2) \ldots (s_{l-1}, x_l^i, P_{x_l}^i, s_l)$ with $l \leq k$. Figure 2.6 shows the *2-future* of the initial state of the EFSA shown in Figure 2.5.

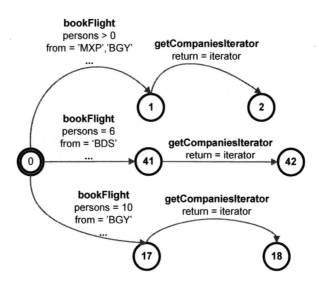

FIGURE 2.6: The 2-future of the initial state of the EFSA in Figure 2.5.

gkTail modifies the initial EFSA by iteratively merging the states with an equivalent k-future. gkTail merges states according to three equivalence criteria: *equivalence, weak subsumption*, and *strong subsumption*. Two states are *equivalent* if the sequences of events in their k-futures are the same, and the predicates associated with each pair of corresponding events are equivalent. Figure 2.7 shows two states that are 2-equivalent in the running example.

Since behavioral models are generated from incomplete traces, merging only equivalent state may lead to poor generalization, especially in presence of partial samples, for example, when traces derive from shallow testing. gkTail proposes also strong and weak subsumption to increase the effectiveness of generalization even in presence of incomplete samples.

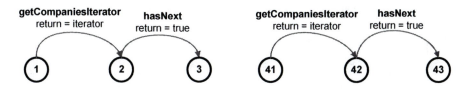

FIGURE 2.7: Two 2-equivalent states.

A state s_1 weakly subsumes a state s_2 if the sequences of events in the k-future of s_1 and s_2 are the same, and the constraints in the k-future of s_1 are more general than the corresponding constraints in the k-future of s_2. Given a pair of corresponding events and their associated constraints P_1 and P_2, P_1 is more general than P_2 if whenever P_1 holds, P_2 holds as well. Figure 2.8 shows an example of a state (4) that weakly subsumes another state (20) for $k = 2$.

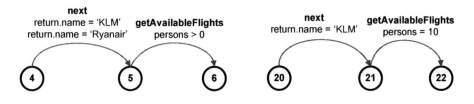

FIGURE 2.8: State 4 weakly subsumes state 20.

A state s_1 strongly subsumes a state s_2 if the sequences of event in the k-future of s_1 includes the sequences of events in the k-future of s_2, and the predicates in the k-future of s_1 are more general than the corresponding predicates in the k-future of s_2. Figure 2.9 shows an example of a state (4) that strongly subsumes another state (20) for $k = 2$.

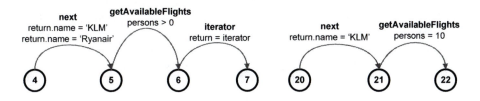

FIGURE 2.9: State 4 strongly subsumes state 20.

Given a merging criterion and a value for k, gkTail iteratively merges pairs of equivalent states until there are no equivalent states according to the given equivalence criterion. gkTail merges two states s and s' by removing the state s, adding to s' all incoming and outgoing transitions of s, and replacing the specific predicates with the more general predicates on the transitions (if strong or weak subsumption is applied). If a merging step produces an EFSA with two or more transitions that share input and output state, gkTail merges these transitions into a unique transition annotated with the OR disjunction of the predicates of the original transitions. Finally, if any of the merged states is a final state, the merged state is final. Figure 2.10 shows the EFSA obtained from the initial EFSA shown in Figure 2.5 with $k = 2$ and weak subsumption.

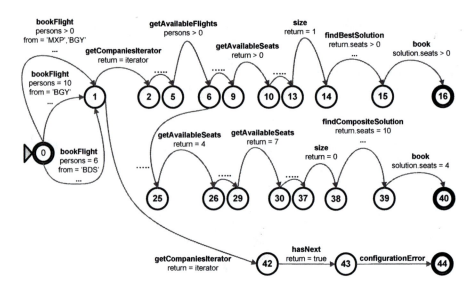

FIGURE 2.10: The EFSA produced by gkTail from the interaction traces in Figure 2.2 by using weak subsumption and $k = 2$ as merging criteria.

gkTail correctly generalized some of the observed behaviors. For instance, the transition between states 37 and 38 shows that the component under analysis looks for composite solutions only if no normal solutions exist. On the other hand, the constraints associated to some transitions have limited validity with respect to the system. For instance, the model indicates that an invocation to `bookflight` method is accepted only for some specific values of the departure and destination airports, while the system behavior is more general. This is a typical effect of monitoring a limited set of executions of the component under analysis. This effect can be reduced by generating the model from a more thorough set of executions.

2.5 Inferring FSA Annotated with Data-Flow Information

This section describes KLFA, a technique that derives FSAs annotated with data-flow information [21]. While gkTail focuses on the values that are assigned to attributes, KLFA focuses on the patterns of occurrence of values across events within the same trace (we call this recurrences data-flow patterns). KLFA represents data-flow patterns by replacing the monitored events (both the event names and their attribute values) with new events that do not include attributes but incorporate information about the occurrence of the attribute values within the labels, as illustrated by the example in Figure 2.12. KLFA implements three rewriting strategies that can identify different data flow patterns: *global ordering*, *relative to instantiation*, and *relative to access* rewriting strategy.

The KLFA inference process consists of two phases: *data preprocessing* and *model generation*. In the data preprocessing phase, KLFA rewrites traces. In the model generation phase, KLFA infers a FSA that incorporates data-flow information from the preprocessed traces.

2.5.1 Preprocessing Data

KLFA rewrites the events in the traces in three steps. In the first step, KLFA identifies clusters of related attributes, that is, attributes that refer to homogeneous types. This step avoids identifying data-flow patterns that incorrectly relate heterogeneous quantities. For instance, it may make sense to relate occurrences of values that represent distances, but it does not make sense to relate occurrences of values that represent distances with values that represent names of persons. In the second step, each cluster with homogeneous attributes is rewritten according to three rewriting strategies implemented by KLFA, thus producing three versions of each data cluster (global ordering, relative to instantiation and relative to access rewriting strategies). In the third step, KLFA heuristically identifies the best rewritten version of each cluster among the three available alternatives. KLFA may select different rewriting strategies for different data clusters in the same system.

2.5.1.1 Identifying Data Clusters

In the first step, KLFA automatically identifies sets of attributes that are assigned with homogeneous values, namely, the *data clusters*.

KLFA automatically identifies data clusters by comparing the values assigned to attributes in the traces. Given the sets of distinct values assigned to two attributes in the traces, KLFA heuristically assumes that these two attributes refer to a same or comparable quantity if they share a relevant number of concrete values. In particular, if two attributes share at least the 70% of their values, KLFA assigns them to the same *two-elements data cluster*. KLFA identifies *data clusters* as the transitive closure of the *two-elements data cluster* relation: If we consider a graph where nodes are attributes and edges represent the *two-elements data cluster* relation, the *data clusters* are the connected components of the graph.

For example, one of the data clusters that KLFA automatically identifies from the execution traces in Figure 2.2 is composed of the following attributes: attribute `persons` of event `bookFlight`, attribute `persons` of event `getAvailableFlights`, attribute `return.seats` of event `findBestSolution`, attribute `return.seats` of event `findCompositeSolution`, and attribute `solution.seats` of event `book`.

2.5.1.2   Global Ordering Rewriting Strategy

The simplest way to annotate traces with data-flow information is to consistently replace all occurrences of the same concrete value with the same symbol, for example, a number. KLFA incrementally introduces numbers according to the order of appearance of new values. Thus, the first concrete value that occurs in a data cluster is rewritten with a 1, the second concrete value is rewritten with a 2 if never observed before, otherwise the same number is consistently used, and so on for all attribute values within a data cluster. The numbers represent the re-occurrence by abstracting from concrete values. This rewriting strategy is named *global ordering rewriting strategy*. The new event labels are obtained by concatenating the event names with the numbers produced by the global rewriting strategy.

Since the attribute `persons` of event `bookFlight` is always assigned with a same value within a trace (see the traces in Figure 2.2), the global rewriting strategy would replace all occurrences of this value with the same symbol 1. This replacement identifies the re-occurrence of the value assigned to `persons`, i.e., all the rewritten traces contain the symbolic value 1 for the attribute `persons`.

Since the attributes of the events `bookFlight`, `getAvailableFlights`, `findBestSolution`, `findCompositeSolution`, and `book` belong to the same data cluster, the global rewriting strategy will replace all attributes with the same symbolic value. Table 2.1 shows the symbolic values used to replace the concrete values associated with these attributes: column # indicates the position of the event in the original trace in Figure 2.2, column *Events* reports the name of the event, column *Attributes* indicates the name of the rewritten attribute, while columns *Actual Values* and *GO* show the value associated to the attribute in the trace and the symbolic value derived by applying the *global rewriting strategy*. Table 2.1 shows that in all the four considered executions the *global ordering rewriting strategy* generates the same symbolic values for all the values in the data cluster thus suitably identifying their re-occurrence. We can observe that the execution traces 1 and 2 are rewritten in the same way.

TABLE 2.1: Common Patterns That Span over Different Executions

#	Events	Attributes	Actual Values	GO
Execution 1				
1	bookFlight	persons	7	1
6	getAvailableFlights	persons	7	1
15	findBestSolution	return.seats	7	1
16	book	solution.seats	7	1
Execution 2				
1	bookFlight	persons	4	1
6	getAvailableFlights	persons	4	1
24	findBestSolution	return.seats	4	1
16	book	solution.seats	4	1
Execution 3				
1	bookFlight	persons	10	1
6	getAvailableFlights	persons	10	1
23	findCompositeSolution	return.seats	10	1
16	book	solution.seats	10	1
Execution 4				
1	bookFlight	persons	6	1

The perfect match between the two rewritten sequences indicates that they share the same sequence of events and the same data-flow pattern. Trace 3 is a variant of the behavior represented by traces 1 and 2, since trace 3 differs from traces 1 and 2 only for the third event that is findCompositeSolution. These behaviors correspond to the cases in which the application finds a single flight (traces 1 and 2) or a set of flights (trace 3) for the passengers. Trace 4 corresponds to an early termination of the execution due to the lack of flights available for satisfying the traveling request.

2.5.1.3 Instantiation Rewriting Strategy

A common behavioral pattern consists of producing and consuming values. Such behaviors produce traces where new values are iteratively generated and then used. The global ordering rewriting strategy does not represent these behavioral patterns in a compact way, because it produces a new symbol every time a new value is introduced. The *relative to instantiation rewriting strategy* aims to explicitly represent the re-occurrence of the generation and

TABLE 2.2: A Pattern of Data Reuse

#	Events	Attributes	Actual Values	GO	RI
8	hasNext				
9	next	return.availSeats	4	1	0
10	getAvailableSeats	return	4	1	1
11	add	flight.availSeats	4	1	1
12	hasNext				
13	next	return.availSeats	7	2	0
14	getAvailableSeats	return	7	2	1
15	add	flight.availSeats	7	2	1
16	hasNext				
17	next	return.availSeats	5	3	0
18	getAvailableSeats	return	5	3	1
19	add	flight.availSeats	5	3	1
20	hasNext				

use of values rather than the re-occurrence of the same concrete values, to obtain a compact representation of produce-consume behavioral patterns.

Let us consider the sequence of events `next`, `getSeatsAvailable`, and `add` that occurs three times in the third trace in Figure 2.2. The three occurrences of the sequence share a common data-flow pattern that indicates that the number of seats available remains constant within a cycle but changes among different cycles. Table 2.2 shows the attribute values within these sequences (we omit the attribute values that do not belong to the same data-flow cluster to keep the table small). The column # shows the position of the event in the trace 3 in Figure 2.2. The column *Events* reports the event names. The column *Attributes* indicates the names of attributes. The columns *Actual Values* and *GO* specify the attribute values and the corresponding symbols generated by the global ordering rewriting strategy. The last column *RI* reports the symbols generated by the relative to instantiation rewriting strategy.

The relative to instantiation rewriting strategy rewrites values following the generation and use of the new values. Each time a new value occurs in a trace, it is rewritten with 0. If an existing value occurs in the traces, the value is replaced with a number that indicates the number of new values that have been introduced from its first occurrence plus 1. Columns *RI* in Tables 2.2 and 2.3 show how values are rewritten according to the relative to instantiation rewriting strategy.

Table 2.2 shows that the global ordering rewriting strategy does not represent the generation and usage of values compactly, since it generates a different symbol every time a new concrete value is rewritten. Consequently, similar sequences cannot be merged into a unique abstract sequence to obtain a compact

TABLE 2.3: A Pattern of Data Reuse

#	Events	Attributes	Actual Values	GO	RI
1	hasNext				
2	next	return.availSeats	5	1	0
3	getAvailableSeats	return	5	1	1
4	add	flight.availSeats	5	1	1
5	hasNext				
6	next	return.availSeats	7	2	0
7	getAvailableSeats	return	7	2	1
8	add	flight.availSeats	7	2	1
9	hasNext				
10	next	return.availSeats	8	3	0
11	getAvailableSeats	return	8	3	1
12	add	flight.availSeats	8	3	1
13	hasNext				
14	next	return.availSeats	9	4	0
15	getAvailableSeats	return	9	4	1
16	add	flight.availSeats	9	4	1
17	hasNext				

representation. For example, Table 2.3 shows the events generated in an execution that differs from the one reported in Table 2.2 for the number of times the same sequence of operations is executed. The extra iteration is classified as a new sequence by the global ordering rewriting strategy due to the new abstract symbol that is generated to rewrite it. On the contrary, the relative on instantiation rewriting strategy rewrites values according to the same schema. Thus, the relative to instantiation rewriting strategy successfully captured the common behavioral patterns represented in the traces.

2.5.1.4   Access Rewriting Strategy

The relative to instantiation rewriting strategy can deal with the generation and subsequent use of new concrete values, but does not handle well the case of multiple production of concrete values. This case is exemplified in Table 2.4, which presents three sequences of events that reuse the same attribute values multiple times across iterations. We can observe that symbols in column *RI* in Table 2.4 do not fully capture the repeated pattern of values that are generated and used multiple times. The *relative to access rewriting strategy* is designed to capture this case.

The *relative to access rewriting strategy* replaces the first occurrence of a concrete value with 0, and the subsequent occurrences with a number that

TABLE 2.4: Capturing Patterns with Repeated Values

#	Events	Attributes	Actual Values	RI	RA
1	hasNext				
2	next	return.availSeats	4	0	0
3	getSeatsAvailable	return	4	1	1
4	add	flight.availSeats	4	1	1
5	hasNext				
6	next	return.availSeats	7	0	0
7	getSeatsAvailable	return	7	1	1
8	add	flight.availSeats	7	1	1
9	hasNext				
10	next	return.availSeats	4	2	4
11	getSeatsAvailable	return	4	2	1
12	add	flight.availSeats	4	2	1
13	hasNext				

indicates the number of events observed from its last occurrence. Column *RA* in Table 2.4 shows the values produced by the relative to access rewriting strategy. We can observe that these values capture well the patterns occurring in these traces.

2.5.1.5   Choosing a Rewriting Strategy

The three rewriting strategies discussed above address complementary aspects, and it is hard to identify a priori strategy that best adapts to a data cluster. The choice of a strategy mainly depends on the nature of the observed behaviors and on the collected data. Since the amount of data can be extremely large, testers can seldom manually inspect data clusters to choose a proper rewriting strategy. KLFA automatically identifies the best rewriting strategy for each data cluster, based on the observation that the effectiveness of a rewriting strategy depends on the ability of capturing the regularity of the data flows. We measure such regularity as the number of symbols used by a rewriting strategy to rewrite a data cluster: The smaller the number of symbols used to rewrite the concrete values, the better the rewriting strategy captures the regularity of the data flow.

KLFA selects the best rewritten version of each data cluster by choosing the one with the smallest number of distinct symbols. To reduce the noise of spurious values that cause the generation of additional symbols, KLFA selects the technique that rewrites 50% of the attribute values with the fewer number of symbols. In this way, it selects the rewritten version of a data cluster that better captures the regularity of the core behavior of a data cluster.

TABLE 2.5: Automatically Identify Data Clusters and Rewriting Strategies

#	Events	Attributes	Cl.	Actual Values	Symb. val.	Rewritten trace
1	hasNext					hasNext
2	next	return.availSeats	A	4	0	next_A0_B0
		return.flightNo	B	KL1022	0	
3	getAvailableSeats	return	A	4	1	getAvailableSeats_A1
4	add	flight.availSeats	A	4	1	add_A1_B1
		flight.flightNo	B	KL1022	1	
5	hasNext					hasNext
6	next	return.availSeats	A	7	0	next_A0_B0
		return.flightNo	B	KL1028	0	
7	getAvailableSeats	return	A	7	1	getAvailableSeats_A1
8	add	flight.availSeats	A	7	1	add_A1_B1
		flight.flightNo	B	KL1028	1	
9	hasNext					hasNext
10	next	return.availSeats	A	4	4	next_A4_B0
		return.flightNo	B	KL1058	0	
11	getAvailableSeats	return	A	4	1	getAvailableSeats_A1
12	add	flight.availSeats	A	4	1	add_A1_B1
		flight.flightNo	B	KL1058	1	
13	hasNext					hasNext

Legend
Cl.   data cluster
Symb. val.   symbolic value

Table 2.5 shows some of the events recorded during an execution of the running example. KLFA automatically identifies two data clusters: one that groups attributes that represent the number of available seats (indicated as A in column *Cl.*) and one that groups the flight numbers (indicated as B in column *Cl.*). After the application of the three rewriting strategies to these two data clusters, KLFA is able to identify the rewriting strategy that better rewrites the concrete values. The value of the flight number changes at every iteration, thus the *relative to instantiation rewriting strategy* works better than the other strategies. The number of available seats tends to be the same for different flights, thus the *relative to access rewriting strategy* better adapts to this cluster.

Column *Rewritten trace* shows how KLFA rewrites event names and attributes. Each rewritten event consists of the event name followed by the symbolic values of the parameters separated by underscores. To ease the understanding of the data-flow relations among attributes, KLFA specifies the name of the data cluster before the symbolic value of each attribute.

In some cases, data clusters can include attribute values whose distribution does not match the requirements of any of our strategies, producing in poor results. To avoid poor results due to inadequate strategies, KLFA applies a rewriting strategy for a data-flow cluster only if at least 50% of the attribute values can be rewritten by using at most 10 symbols (we empirically derived these thresholds). If more than 10 symbols are used to rewrite a data cluster, KLFA simply ignores the attributes and work by considering the events without their attributes.

2.5.2   Generating Models

The rewritten traces are traces of event names where the attributes are implicitly represented as part of the event labels. Thus, we can generate models with classic engines to infer automata from traces.

The current KLFA prototype uses the KBehavior incremental inference engine to infer automata [20]. At each step, KBehavior reads a trace and updates the current FSA according to the content of the trace. The updated FSA generates all the traces that have been analyzed.

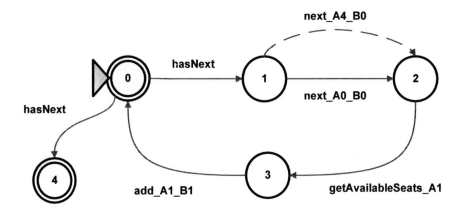

FIGURE 2.11: An example FSA extended with a new trace.

Given a new trace, KBehavior extends the current FSA by identifying sub-machines in the current FSA that generate sub-sequences in the input trace, and suitably connecting them to accept the new trace. For example, Figure 2.11 shows how kBehavior extends a FSA according to the new trace shown in Table 2.5. State 0 is the initial state of the automaton, while State 4 is the final state. Events from 1 to 9 in the table are accepted by the given automaton up to state 1, while event 10, next_A4_B0, is not accepted by any submachine. Since events 11 to 13 are accepted from state 2, kBehavior extends the automaton with a new branch from state 1 to state 2.

Figure 2.12 shows the automaton that KLFA derives from the traces recorded during the execution of the running example. For brevity the model includes only the attributes reported in the traces of Figure 2.2.

The automaton in Figure 2.12 suitably represents data-flow information. For example, KLFA used the *relative to instantiation strategy* to rewrite the

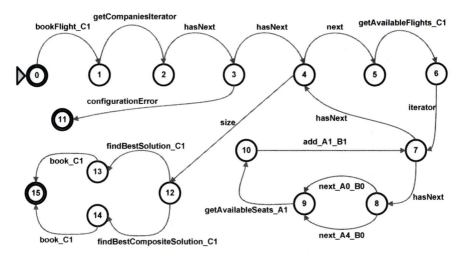

Legend
We added a letter that identifies the cluster before the number that rewrites a concrete value to increase the readability of the model. The strategies used to rewrite each cluster are:
A *Relative to Access* rewriting strategy
B *Relative to Instantiation* rewriting strategy
C *Global Ordering* rewriting strategy

FIGURE 2.12: A KLFA model of the behavior of method `bookFlight`.

second attribute (`return.fligtNo`) of the two transitions from state 8 to state 9. The resulting automaton indicates that new values are always introduced at that point of the execution (due to the presence of label B0), thus a new flight number is produced every time the loop through states 7, 8, 9, and 10 is covered.

Similarly, KLFA used the *relative to access strategy* to rewrite the first attribute (`return.availSeats`) associated with the transitions from state 8 to state 9. The symbolic values show that `return.availSeats` can be associated with either a new value (symbolic value equals to A0) or a value observed two iterations before (symbolic value equals to A4).

The transition from state 10 to state 7 shows that the two attributes of event `add`, `object.flightNo` and `object.availSeats`, are always equal to attributes `return.fligthNo` and `return.availSeats` associated with the event `next` (A1 and B1 denote the reuse of concrete values).

Finally, transitions from state 0 to state 1, from state 12 to state 13, and from state 13 to state 15 show an example of attributes rewritten with *Global Ordering*. Symbols associated with these values show that `persons`, `return.seats`, and `solution.seats` have the same values across all executions.

2.6   Comparing the Generated Models

The models generated with gkTail and KLFA represent the interplay between the ordering of the events and the values of the attributes (corresponding to the interplay between method invocations and parameters in the cases discussed in this paper). The models generated with gkTail and KLFA represent the ordering of events in the same way, as sequences of events accepted by the automaton, but differ in the way they represent the attribute values: gkTail represents the concrete values that can be assigned to attributes with constraints, while KLFA represents how concrete values reoccur across different events of a trace with symbols. For instance, the EFSA in Figure 2.10 correctly indicates that the attribute **persons** is a non-negative attribute; while the FSA in Figure 2.12 correctly indicates that the attribute **persons** has the same value every time it occurs, and such value is also the same as the value of attribute **seats**. This information is different and complemental. Ideally, this information could be integrated into a unique model that specifies both the legal attribute values and how values are reused among events.

The choice of analyzing traces with either gkTail or KLFA mainly depends on the aspect targeted by the analysis. For instance, if testers monitor independent attributes, gkTail is probably the best choice because identifying the legal concrete values is more important than identifying the recurrence of values. On the contrary, if testers monitor dependent variables, their recurrence would be extremely relevant and thus KLFA is preferable.

We empirically validate both gkTail and KLFA with several case studies. gkTail has been used to build models of the interactions between components for 5 Java applications [19]. In such study, gkTail derived a total of 62 EFSAs, out of which 33 (53%) include interactions that can be represented only by exploiting constraints on attribute values. A manual comparison between the models and the applications code highlighted that at least 21 (34%) of these EFSAs represent non coincidental relations between attributes and event sequences. These results show that interactions frequently include behaviors that need EFSAs rather than FSAs to be accurately represented.

KLFA has been used to identify failure causes from log files produced by several applications, including well-known application servers such as Glassfish and Tomcat [21]. The FSAs produced by KLFA have been extremely useful to relate the events produced by application servers from the values of the many attributes commonly recorded in log files. Incorporating the recurrence of attribute values into FSAs, in addition to producing more accurate models, has been necessary to identify 18 failure causes out of the 46 (39%) identified failure causes. This result confirms the importance of considering attribute values when building behavioral models.

In summary, these early empirical results show that both the models produced with gkTail and KLFA can be useful and the choice between the two depends on the nature of traces, the characteristics of the applications, and the kind of analysis that these models should support.

2.7 Related Work

We already discussed techniques that generate FSAs and annotated FSAs from execution traces in Section 2.2. Here we discuss other techniques that generate models that represent either the ordering of the events or the values that can be assigned to the program variables.

2.7.1 Mining Models That Represent Ordering of Events

Some mining techniques derive models different from FSA to represent information about the ordering of events. Some techniques simply derive a visual representation of the execution traces without mining any extra information that is not already in the traces. These techniques are useful to simplify the manual inspection of execution traces, but do not derive compact representations of the (general) program behaviors. For instance, techniques presented in [14, 22] can represent execution traces as sequence diagrams.

Other techniques analyze execution traces to derive frequent patterns of events [8, 16, 26]. Frequent patterns can be useful to discover anomalous behaviors, but their usage is restricted to anomalies that impact the frequent events. On the contrary, FSAs represent the entire behavior of a software program and can include all the events recorded in execution traces. Thus, FSAs can discover anomalies impacting any behavior of a software program, regardless the frequency of these behaviors. The cost of this wider scope of the model is a stronger dependency of the quality of the model on the completeness of the samples used to infer the model.

Other techniques mine temporal rules that capture a set of dependencies between events [17, 29]. These models focus on the relations between key events, rather then the exact ordering of the single events. Temporal rules have an interesting complementarity with respect to FSA: Temporal rules can suitably represent relations between events occurring at arbitrary points of an execution, while FSAs can well represent relations between non-consecutive events only by suitably representing the relations between the intermediate events, which is typically harder to achieve. This complementarity has been exploited in [18, 27] to derive FSAs that satisfy inferred relations between events that occur at arbitrary points within traces.

Yet other techniques mine algebraic specifications and graph transformations from program traces. They rely on a ground mathematical background and can compactly represent a large number of behaviors [12, 15], but so far, they have been applied only to rather simple software components (single classes and containers), while FSAs have been shown to be useful with a broader set of applications.

2.7.2   Mining Models That Represent Program Variables

Several techniques can infer models on the values assigned to program variables during program executions. Such data-oriented models well complement FSAs that focus on the ordering of the events rather than on the data values that occurred in a given execution.

A well-known technique for inferring models that represent the values that can be assigned to program variables is Daikon [9]. Daikon accepts a set of variables and their values across several executions as input, and generates a set of Boolean properties on these variables. Daikon is integrated in gkTail to derive transition constraints.

Hangal and Lam present a technique for generating models about program variables expressed as bit masks [13]. The technique traces the values of these variables across multiple executions and builds a model out of these observations. The technique is very efficient, but the derived models are of little use for tester designers because they do not explicitly represent meaningful relations. These models can be hardly integrated with FSAs because they represent code level information useful for fault-localization, but less useful for understanding executions.

A complementary approach about models that capture program properties that may involve multiple program variables is the case of models on single variables. For instance Raz et al. generate statistical indexes that represent the range of values assigned to single variables in order to automatically detect anomalous values in new executions [25].

2.8   Concluding Remarks

In this chapter we illustrated two algorithms, gkTail and KLFA, that can infer finite state models from traces. Differently from classic FSAs that represent only the ordering of events, gkTail and KLFA models have the unique capability of representing the interplay between the ordering of events and the values of attributes. The two algorithms differ in the way attributes are handled. gkTail produces EFSAs where transitions are annotated with constraints that indicate the legal values of attributes. KLFA produces FSAs that represent the recurrence of attribute values with symbols added to transition labels. These two aspects are complemental and useful, as also confirmed by the early empirical results.

gkTail and KLFA can represent constraints and recurrences on the values that can be assigned to attributes, but cannot identify more complicated relations that may occur in program behaviors. Adding such capabilities, for instance by integrating static and dynamic analysis, is still an open research direction.

Bibliography

[1] G. Ammons, R. Bodík, and J.R. Larus. Mining specifications. In *Proceedings of the 29th Symposium on Principles of Programming Languages*. ACM Press, 2002.

[2] J.H. Andrews and Y. Zhang. Broad-spectrum studies of log file analysis. In *Proceedings of the 22nd International Conference on Software Engineering*, 2000.

[3] A. Biermann and J. Feldman. On the synthesis of finite state machines from samples of their behavior. *IEEE Transactions on Computer*, 21:592–597, June 1972.

[4] M. Broy, B. Jonsson, J.-P. Katoen, M. Leuckerand, and A. Pretschner, editors. *Model-Based Testing of Reactive Systems*, volume 3472 of *Lecture Notes in Computer Science*. Springer, 2005.

[5] Orlando Cicchello and Stefan C. Kremer. Inducing grammars from sparse data sets: a survey of algorithms and results. *Journal of Machine Learning Research*, 4:603–632, 2003.

[6] J.E. Cook and A.L. Wolf. Discovering models of software processes from event-based data. *ACM Transactions on Software Engineering and Methodology*, 7(3):215–249, 1998.

[7] V. Dallmeier, C. Lindig, A. Wasylkowski, and A. Zeller. Mining object behavior with ADABU. In *Proceedings of the International Workshop on Dynamic Systems Analysis (WODA)*. ACM Press, 2006.

[8] M. El-Ramly, E. Stroulia, and P. Sorenson. Interaction-pattern mining: extracting usage scenarios from run-time behavior traces. In *ACM SIGKDD International Conference on Knowledge Discovery and Data Mining*, 2002.

[9] M.D. Ernst, J. Cockrell, W.G. Griswold, and D. Notkin. Dynamically discovering likely program invariants to support program evolution. *IEEE Transaction on Software Engineering*, 27(2):99–123, February 2001.

[10] H. Foster, S. Uchitel, J. Magee, and J. Kramer. Ltsa-ws: a tool for model-based verification of web service compositions and choreography. In *Proceedings of the 28th International Conference on Software Engineering*. ACM Press, 2006.

[11] G. Friedman, A. Hartman, K. Nagin, and T. Shiran. Projected state machine coverage for software testing. In *Proceedings of the 2002 ACM SIGSOFT International Symposium on Software Testing and Analysis*. ACM Press, 2002.

[12] C. Ghezzi, A. Mocci, and M. Monga. Synthesizing intensional behavior models by graph transformation. In *Proceedings of the International Conference on Software Engineering*, 2009.

[13] Sudheendra Hangal and Monica S. Lam. Tracking down software bugs using automatic anomaly detection. In *Proceedings of the International Conference on Software Engineering (ICSE)*. ACM Press, 2002.

[14] J.G. Hosking. Visualisation of object oriented program execution. In *Proceedings of the IEEE Symposium on Visual Languages*, 1996.

[15] J. Henkel and A. Diwan. Discovering algebraic specifications from java classes. In *Proceedings of the European Conference on Object Oriented Programming*, 2003.

[16] D. Lo, S.-C. Khoo, and C. Liu. Efficient mining of iterative patterns for software specification discovery. In *ACM SIGKDD International Conference on Knowledge Discovery and Data Mining*, 2007.

[17] D. Lo, S.-C. Khoo, and C. Liu. Mining temporal rules for software maintenance. In *Journal of Software Maintenance and Evolution: Research and Practice*, volume 20, pages 227–247, 2008.

[18] D. Lo, L. Mariani, and M. Pezzé. Automatic steering of behavioral model inference. In *Proceedings of the 7th Joint Meeting of the European Software Engineering Conference (ESEC) and the ACM SIGSOFT Symposium on the Foundations of Software Engineering (FSE)*, 2009.

[19] Davide Lorenzoli, Leonardo Mariani, and Mauro Pezzè. Automatic generation of software behavioral models. In *30th International Conference on Software Engineering (ICSE)*. IEEE Computer Society, May 2008.

[20] L. Mariani and M. Pezzè. Dynamic detection of COTS components incompatibility. *IEEE Software*, 24(5):76–85, September/October 2007.

[21] Leonardo Mariani and Fabrizio Pastore. Automated identification of failure causes in system logs (issre). In *Proceedings of the International Symposium on Software Reliability Engineering*. IEEE Computer Society, 2008.

[22] M. McGavin, T. Wright, and S. Marshall. Visualisations of execution traces (VET): an interactive plugin-based visualisation tool. In *Proceedings of the 7th Australasian User Interface Conference*, 2006.

[23] J. Oncina and P. Garcia. Inferring regular languages in polynomial update time. In N. Pérez de la Blanca, A. Sanfeliu, and E.Vidal, editors, *Pattern Recognition and Image Analysis*, pages 49–61. World Scientific, 1992.

[24] A.V. Raman and J.D. Patrick. The sk-strings method for inferring PFSA. In *Proceedings of the Workshop on Automata Induction, Grammatical Inference and Language Acquisition*, 1997.

[25] Orna Raz, Philip Koopman, and Mary Shaw. Semantic anomaly detection in online data sources. In *Proceedings of the International Conference on Software Engineering (ICSE)*. ACM Press, 2002.

[26] H. Safyallah and K. Sartipi. Dynamic analysis of software systems using execution pattern mining. In *Proceedings of the International Conference on Program Comprehension*, 2006.

[27] N. Walkinshaw and K. Bogdanov. Inferring finite-state models with temporal constraints. In *Proceedings of the 23rd IEEE/ACM International Conference on Automated Software Engineering*, 2008.

[28] J. Whittle and P.K. Jayaraman. Synthesizing hierarchical state machines from expressive scenario descriptions. *ACM Transactions on Software Engineering and Methodologies*, 19(3):1–45, 2010.

[29] J. Yang, D. Evans, D. Bhardwaj, T. Bhat, and M. Das. Perracotta: mining temporal api rules from imperfect traces. In *Proceedings of the International Conference on Software Engineering*, 2006.

Chapter 3

Adapting Grammar Inference Techniques to Mine State Machines

Neil Walkinshaw

Department of Computer Science, The University of Leicester

Kirill Bogdanov

Department of Computer Science, The University of Sheffield

3.1 Introduction

State-based models are valuable for a range of software development tasks. They help the developer to understand how the system works. They formally document the system behaviour. Most importantly, a range of powerful, automated model-based testing techniques can be used to rigorously test implementations against their state-based specifications. Numerous automated model-based testing frameworks have been developed that are tailored to suit a range of development paradigms and domain-specific software systems such as telecoms systems [10] or network protocols [3].

Despite their apparent value, the use of state-based models is not widespread. The main reason is their expense; generating the specifications in the first place requires a substantial amount of manual effort, which developers are usually reluctant or unable to invest. In practice, the system is often developed without a comprehensive specification. If state-based models are used at all, they are only used to model selected aspects of the system. Even if a specification is produced, its maintenance is usually hampered by time and cost constraints. As a consequence, developers are forced to resort to ad-hoc testing approaches, and end up having to read the source code to understand how the system behaves.

This reluctance to manually generate specifications has spurred research into reverse-engineering approaches. These can broadly be divided into two camps (as reflected in the chapter structure of this book): *static* approaches, which are largely based on the analysis of source code, and *dynamic* approaches, which are based on the analysis of program traces. Both have their respective merits, and a detailed discussion of those is beyond the scope of this chapter. In this chapter we focus on dynamic state machine mining techniques.

The dynamic state machine mining challenge is to, given a set of program traces, accurately infer the underlying state machine. The final machine should be accurate [6,37]; it should represent every sequence of events that is possible in the subject program, but should also omit every impossible sequence of events. The majority of current state machine mining approaches are based on an inference technique known as the *k-tails* algorithm [4,5]. This algorithm is however subject to four important problems:

1. Traces only show valid behaviors this makes it difficult for the inference algorithm to omit impossible/invalid sequences of events.

2. The *k*-tails heuristic (described later) is prone to making mistakes that lead to inaccurate state machines.

3. It is up to the developer to supply a suitable set of traces, even though they are rarely sufficiently familiar with the system.

4. Reliance upon traces alone tends to render the inference process too expensive for practical use.

A selection of advances, most of which are inspired by developments in the field of Grammar Inference [27], can be employed to attenuate or even eliminate the above problems. Most current grammar inference techniques employ the notion of "negative traces" to facilitate the inference process. Improved heuristics have been developed to vastly improve the accuracy of the final

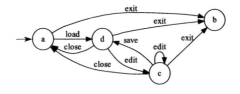

FIGURE 3.1: Model of a simple text editor.

state machines. Active techniques have been developed to guide the collection of traces. Constraints can be added to summarize large numbers of traces, further enhancing the accuracy and efficiency of inference techniques.

This chapter will describe the conventional reverse-engineering approach and its problems in more detail in Section 3.2. Section 3.3 will describe the advances that are key to addressing these individual problems. Where appropriate it will contain algorithms that show how these advances can be (and have been) combined to produce more powerful state machine mining techniques. Section 3.4 shows how temporal constraints that are supplied by the user can be integrated into the inference process as well. Finally, Section 3.5 offers some conclusions, and outlines some areas for future work.

3.2 The Conventional Reverse-Engineering Approach and Its Problems

We begin this section by providing a short introduction to state machines, (partial) labeled transition systems, and their languages. This is followed by an introduction to the conventional reverse-engineering techniques such as the *k*-tails algorithm. The section is concluded by a more detailed treatment of the problems mentioned in the introduction that tend to hamper the practical application of such reverse-engineering techniques.

3.2.1 State Machines and Their Languages

The basic structure of a state machine can be visualized diagrammatically, as a Labelled Transition System (LTS). An LTS is a quadruple $A = (Q, \Sigma, \delta, q_0)$, where Q is a finite set of states, Σ is a finite alphabet, $\delta : Q \times \Sigma \rightarrow Q$ is a partial functions and $q_0 \in Q$. An example of an LTS is shown in Figure 3.1, which shows the state-based behavior of a simple, fictional text editor. We shall use this example later on to illustrate some of the basic state machine inference concepts.

State-based models are usually presumed to be complete; if a particular transition does not exist in the model, it is assumed to be impossible in practice. Such models are represented as straightforward LTSs. Although this can be valid when reasoning about a finished design, in our setting we will be dealing with unfinished models – hypothesized models of system behavior. As stated by Uchitel et al. [33]: "In this setting the distinction between proscribed behaviour and behaviour that has not yet been defined is an important one." To accommodate this, the technique presented here is defined with respect to an extension of conventional LTSs: partial LTSs (PLTSs) [33]. If they are known to be incomplete, it is possible to explicitly distinguish between model transitions that are known to be invalid, and transitions that are simply not known to exist at all.

Definition 1 (Partial LTS (PLTS)). *A PLTS is a tuple $A = (Q, \Sigma, \delta, q_0, \Psi)$. This is defined as an LTS, but it is assumed to be only partial. To make the explicit distinction between unknown and invalid behavior, Ψ makes the set of invalid labels from a given state explicit – $\Psi \subseteq Q \times \Sigma$ where $(q, \sigma) \in \Psi$ implies that σ will be rejected in q.*

To define the language of a PLTS, we draw on the inductive definition for an extended transition function $\hat{\delta}$ used by Hopcroft et al. [18] to define two notions of language: prescribed and proscribed which are used below.

Definition 2 (Prescribed and Proscribed Languages). *For a state p and a string w, the extended transition function $\hat{\delta}$ returns the state p that is reached when starting in state p and processing sequence w. For the base case $\hat{\delta}(q, \epsilon) = q$. For the inductive case, let w be of the form xa, where a is the last element, and x is the prefix. Then $\hat{\delta}(q, w) = \delta(\hat{\delta}(q, x), a)$.*
Given the extended transition function, the prescribed *language of a PLTS A can be defined as follows:*
$PreL(A) = \{w | \hat{\delta} \text{ is defined for } (q_0, w)\}$.
The proscribed *language of a PLTS can be defined as:*
$ProL(A) = \{xas | \hat{\delta} \text{ is defined for } (q_0, x) \text{ and } (\hat{\delta}(q_0, x), a) \in \Psi \text{ and } s \in \Sigma^*\}$.
By construction $PreL(A) \cap ProL(A) = \emptyset$.

It is important to note that the prescribed language of a *PLTS* is prefix-closed. This means that, for every sequence in $PreL(A)$, any prefix of it is also in $PreL(A)$.

3.2.2   State Merging

Numerous techniques have emerged that attempt to reverse-engineer state machines from program traces [1, 5, 11, 21–23, 31]. The high-level process they follow is shown in Figure 3.2. The developer records a set of traces that are deemed to comprehensively exercise the target program; these are fed to a machine-learning technique, which produces a hypothesis state machine. Such

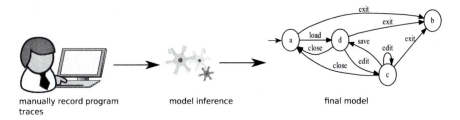

manually record program   model inference   final model
traces

FIGURE 3.2: Conventional reverse-engineering process.

inference approaches are referred to as *passive* techniques; they take the given set of traces and generate a corresponding model without requiring any further input. A range of passive techniques exists to infer state machines from traces (e.g., using Markov models or Neural Nets [11]), but the most popular technique is called *state merging*.[1]

State-merging techniques arrange the traces into a tree-shaped deterministic state machine called the Prefix Tree Acceptor (PTA), which exactly represents the sequences in the trace. In the PTA, traces that share a prefix also share a common path in the tree, but different trace suffixes lead to different states. Figure 3.3(a) shows an example of how a set of traces from a fictional text editor is arranged into a PTA.

Once the traces are arranged as a PTA, the challenge is to merge those states together that are deemed to be equivalent. Every time a pair of states is merged, the resulting machine is more general; it represents a broader range of behaviors (has a larger prescribed language). For the inference of software models, suitable pairs of states are usually selected by adopting the *k-tails* heuristic [4]. A value k is selected by the developer, the PTA is traversed, and every pair of states that share an identical set of outgoing paths of length k is merged. The process is illustrated in Figure 3.3(b). If we assume that $k = 2$, the first pair of nodes to be merged would be b and f; both have identical k-tails.

Input: $(Traces)$
1 $PLTS \leftarrow generatePTA(Traces)$;
2 **while** $(q, q') \leftarrow findKPair(PLTS)$ **do**
3 $\quad | \quad PLTS \leftarrow merge(PLTS, (q, q'))$;
4 **end**
5 **return** $PLTS$

Algorithm 1: k-tails

The k-tails algorithm [4] is presented in algorithm 1. It starts by generat-

---

[1]Although this section describes the state-merging process, the problems to be discussed in Section 3.2.3 apply to other passive inference techniques as well.

Initial traces
< *load, edit, edit, save, close* >
< *load, edit, save, edit, edit* >
< *load, close, exit* >
< *load, edit, save, edit, save* >
< *load, edit, save, close, exit* >

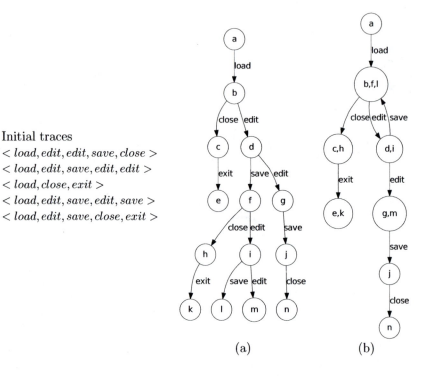

(a)   (b)

FIGURE 3.3: Prefix Tree Acceptor for traces from the text editor example, and the merging of states b and f when $k = 2$.

ing the PTA from the set of positive traces *Traces*, using the *generatePTA* function. In line 2 the PTA is given to the *findKPair* function, which uses a breadth-first search to identify the first pair of states that have identical k-tails. If such a pair exists, the states are merged with the *merge* function. It takes two states q and q', along with the current state machine A. In effect, the state q' is removed, all of its incoming transitions are routed to q instead, and all of its outgoing transitions are routed from q. Every time a pair of states is merged, the resulting state machine may be non-deterministic. Nondeterminism is eliminated by recursively merging the targets of non-deterministic transitions. This merging process continues until *findKPair* cannot find any further pairs, and the current state machine A is returned as the inferred hypothesis.

3.2.3   Problems with This Approach

The solution described above is at best partial. It will reverse-engineer a state transition system, but is prone to inaccuracies. The inference of the transition system has several intrinsic, interrelated weaknesses, which means that it is in practice rarely possible to obtain an accurate result. These problems are elaborated below.

(1) Traces only show what sequences of actions are possible, and not what is *im*possible. For the inferred state machine to be accurate, it must not only incorporate every valid sequence of traces, but also omit every *in*-valid sequence. In other words, correctly inferring its prescribed and proscribed languages is equally important. The conventional k-tails algorithm assumes that all traces represent valid system executions (belong to the prescribed language of the underlying system). There is no guidance for the inference algorithm to describe which sequences are invalid. As a result, whenever the inference algorithm attempts to produce a machine that generalizes from the supplied set of traces, it runs a big risk of falsely inferring that invalid sequences are valid, because there is no evidence to the contrary.

(2) The k-Tails merging rule is prone to erroneous merges. The k-tails technique described above forms the basis for the majority of current software state machine inference techniques. Its weakness is due to the fact that just because two states share a tail of length k does not necessarily mean that they are equivalent. Furthermore, a pair of states that do not share a k-tail are also not necessarily distinct. This is particularly notable when the set of traces is underpopulated (as is usually the case in a practical reverse-engineering scenario). Finally its use depends on the selection of some value k, which is critical to the outcome, but for which there is no way of determining which value is correct. Higher values may lead to the avoidance of erroneous merges but also rule out merges that should happen. Conversely, lower values may lead to erroneous merges, but will end up incorporating valid merges as well.

(3) The selection of traces is critical to the accuracy of the inferred machine. If the set of traces is incomplete, it is impossible for an algorithm to ensure that those states that are merged are in fact equivalent (and that unmerged states are actually distinct). The problem is that, in the context of the conventional state machine inference scenario, there is no notion of what constitutes a *complete* set of traces. In his influential work on grammar inference, Gold proved [16] that the inference of a grammar from positive samples alone was undecidable – a principle that also applies to our state machine inference scenario (his proof is succinctly summarized by Pullum [29]). Thus, a complete set of traces must somehow include traces that are impossible or invalid, which belong to the *pro*scribed language of the software system. For certain state-merging algorithms such as the RPNI algorithm [26] (which accounts for negative samples as well as positive ones), it has been shown that a set of traces is complete if they are *characteristic* of the target system. Informally, this means that the set of traces must contain traces that cover every transition in the target system, as well as a sufficiently large set of positive and negative samples to distinguish between every pair of distinct states to avoid erroneous merges. A characteristic sample is usually vast and, even if we do find a way to collect negative traces, identifying and collecting a characteristic set of traces is practically infeasible for any non-trivial software system.

(4) Reliance on traces alone often renders the inference process more expensive than it needs to be. As stated in the previous point, the size of the trace-set that is necessary to infer an accurate state machine tends to be too large to collect in practice. However, it is often the case that the user of the technique is aware of certain constraints or rules that would obviate the need for a potentially vast number of traces. The problem is that the conventional reverse-engineering process does not provide a means for supplying such facts.

The rest of this chapter will introduce selection approaches that can be used to address these problems. For problems 1 through 3, we resort to techniques that are either directly lifted from or inspired by the closely related field of (regular) grammar inference (presented in the following section). For problem 4 we describe a technique of our own [34], which enables the integration of temporal constraints into the inference process.

3.3   Applying Advances from the Field of Grammar Inference

The field of grammar inference is concerned with the development of algorithms or procedures that can be used to infer grammars from samples of their languages. Its roots can be traced back to the 1950s, in Moore's work on "gedanken experiments" on state machines [24] and Nerode's work on the synthesis of machines from equivalence relations [25]. However it was Gold's work in 1967 that was arguably most influential, establishing the theoretical limits of grammar learnability [16, 29], and forming a theoretical framework for the current techniques.

The field is very broad; a host of different approaches have been developed to suit different grammar classes and learning settings. Regular grammars are the simplest class of formal grammars, and have consequently been the subject of most inference research. The reason that regular grammar inference is of particular import to this chapter is that regular grammars can be represented as deterministic labeled transition systems [18]. Consequently, techniques that apply to the inference of regular grammars automatically apply to the problem of inferring state machines.

The k-tails technique was initially published as in the context of generic state machine inference [4], without any specific applications to the domain of software engineering. It was four years later [5] that the authors applied it to infer state machines from program traces. Since then the k-tails technique has formed the basis for most state machine inference techniques in the domain of software engineering [1, 11, 21–23, 31].

However, since then a host of advances have been made in the field of grammar inference that have not been exploited in the software engineering community [36]. The rest of this section will show how these can be applied to solve three of the key problems with the k-tails technique that were outlined in the previous section.

3.3.1   Negative Samples

As stated in Section 3.2.3 problem 1, the k-tails technique assumes that all traces are valid. This means that it is never possible to obtain a *characteristic sample* of traces (which requires negative samples – see the discussion of problem 3), making it impossible to ensure an accurate state machine. It is only by providing a large and diverse set of positive as well as negative examples, that the inference of accurate (or at least reasonably accurate) state machines becomes a possibility. So what is meant by a "negative" program trace? If the state machine inference process is akin to that shown in Figure 3.2, where should these negative traces come from? Some answers to these questions are provided below.

The usual assumption is that a trace must be by definition positive – it represents an observed, valid program execution. This assumption is however not necessarily correct. There are two circumstances that can give rise to "negative" program traces:

1. **Program executions that fail:** Depending on the nature of the software (and the choice of semantics attributed to program traces), executions that end by throwing an exception, or terminate with an outright failure can be deemed to produce negative traces.

2. **Infeasible executions:** For most software systems, the vast majority of theoretically conceivable program executions are in fact infeasible. For example, with respect to the text editor in Figure 3.1, to begin an execution with a "close" action is not even an option, because no file has been opened in the first place.

These two notions enable us to distinguish between valid and invalid traces; those that belong to the prescribed and proscribed language of the underlying software system. This in turn enables us to employ more sophisticated inference algorithms than the k-tails algorithm, as will be discussed in following subsections.

3.3.2   Improved State-Merging Heuristics

As detailed previously, the k-tails strategy is prone to merging states that are not equivalent, and not merging states when they should be merged. The latter mistake tends to be amplified when the set of traces is sparse. Even if the given sample of traces incorporated negative samples, the heuristic is still error-prone. Since the k-tails was developed in the early 1970s, there have however been notable advances in the grammar inference community, leading to much more sophisticated merging heuristics. Two key advances came about as a result of the "Abbadingo-One" competition [19]; (1) Rodney Price's Evidence Driven State Merging heuristic takes advantage of the characteristics of the given set of traces to make improved state-merging decisions. (2) The associated "Blue-Fringe" search strategy substantially reduces the number of pairs of candidate states that have to be compared with each other to assess whether or not they should be merged. These two strategies are presented in more detail below.

3.3.2.1   Evidence-Driven State Merging

The central idea behind Price's Evidence Driven State Merging (EDSM) algorithm [19] is that states are merged based on the likelihood that they are equivalent, based on the similarity of their outgoing paths.[2] This is in contrast to the k-tails strategy that will simply merge the first pair of states to share a tail of length k. The EDSM algorithm computes what is called a *similarity score* for all pairs of states, and uses this scoring to select those state-pairs that are deemed to be most similar to each other. The rationale is that this reduces the number of merging errors, thus increasing the likelihood that the final model is accurate.

Input: (Pos, Neg)
1   $PLTS \leftarrow generateAPTA(Pos, Neg)$;
2   **while** $(q, q') \leftarrow selectStatePair(PLTS)$ **do**
3      $PLTS' \leftarrow merge(PLTS, (q, q'))$;
4   **if** $compatible(PLTS', Neg)$ **then**
5         $PLTS \leftarrow PLTS'$;
6   **end**
7   **end**
8   **return** $PLTS$

Algorithm 2: EDSM algorithm

The EDSM algorithm is presented in algorithm 2. There are several important differences between the EDSM and k-tails algorithms. The involvement of negative traces means that the prefix-tree acceptor has to be augmented, to distinguish between valid and invalid traces. This is referred to as the "Augmented Prefix-Tree Acceptor" [9], and is generated by the *generateAPTA* function. Figure 3.4 shows the APTA for the set of traces in Figure 3.3 that has been augmented with a negative trace (indicating that it is impossible to

---

[2]This notion of equivalence is referred to as their *Nerode equivalence* based on Nerode's early work [25].

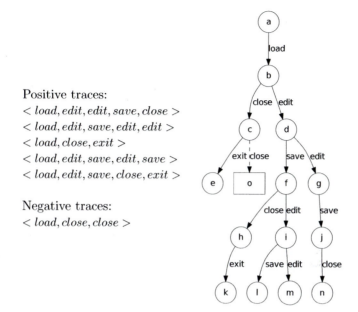

Positive traces:
< *load, edit, edit, save, close* >
< *load, edit, save, edit, edit* >
< *load, close, exit* >
< *load, edit, save, edit, save* >
< *load, edit, save, close, exit* >

Negative traces:
< *load, close, close* >

FIGURE 3.4: Prefix Tree Acceptor with added negative trace.

close a file twice in a row). The rectangular state with the dashed transition leading to it implies that it corresponds to an impossible execution.

Unlike *findKPair* in algorithm 1, the *selectStatePair* function does not simply select the first pair of states that are deemed to be compatible. It computes a "similarity score" for each pair, and then merges pairs in the order of their scores (highest to lowest). Given that the initial set of traces contains traces that are invalid, as well as valid traces, the merge is only accepted if the resulting machine is compatible with both valid and invalid traces – this is established by the *compatible* function.

The similarity score for a pair of states is computed by counting the extent to which their outgoing paths overlap with each other. The greater the overlap, the greater the score. Thanks to the availability of negative traces, it is also possible to rule out state merges if they have a conflicting set of outgoing paths (i.e., a sequence is deemed to be possible from one state but not from another). If this is the case, the pair is assigned a score of -1 to prevent a merge from occurring.

We select some examples to provide an idea of how they are scored. Pair (b, f) produces the highest score, because their outgoing paths contain the largest number of overlapping transitions. The scoring process is illustrated in Figure 3.5; the outgoing paths from both states b and f that overlap are displayed beside each other. A count of the number of overlapping transitions gives us a score of 5. On the other hand, pair (b, c) produces a score of -1,

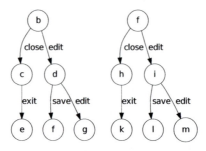

FIGURE 3.5: Example of score computation for pair (b, f) in the APTA in Figure 3.4.

because "close" is possible from b, but not from c. Any pair that involves node a produces a score of 0, because "load" only appears once in the machine.

3.3.2.2 Blue-Fringe Search Strategy

It becomes apparent that computing the score for every pair of states at every iteration of the algorithm can become very expensive. The problem is amplified when we are dealing with non-trivial state machines, or PTAs that are generated from large trace sets. The Blue-Fringe strategy [19] is a windowing method for limiting the number of pairs of nodes that have to be compared to each other. The algorithm keeps a list of nodes that are mutually unmergable, which reduces the number of state comparisons by orders of magnitude.

In terms of the EDSM algorithm shown in algorithm 2, the Blue-Fringe strategy is implemented as part of the *selectStatePairs* function. It operates by coloring the states of the state machine such that unmergable pairs are red, and candidates to be compared to the red states are colored blue. To begin with, the initial state is colored red, and its neighbouring states are colored blue (the rest remain uncolored). Every red-blue pair of nodes is compared according to the EDSM algorithm shown above, and the pairs are ranked. If a blue state cannot be merged to any red state, it is colored red and the process iterates. Otherwise, if none of the red-blue pairs are incompatible, they are ranked according to their similarity scores and merged, starting with the highest-scoring and finishing with the lowest scoring pair. Every time a pair is merged the blue state disappears since it is merged into a red node. As an example, we refer to Figure 3.4. Let us imagine that nodes a and b are red, and that nodes c and d form the blue fringe. If d is merged to b, the merged state bd becomes red. Once there are no further merges to be carried out, the blue-fringe is recomputed, nodes c, f, and g are colored blue, and the whole process iterates until all nodes in the state machine are red. For a more in-depth discussion the reader is referred to the original paper by Lang et al. [19] or the overview by Cicchello and Kremer [9].

3.3.3   Active Approaches

Any analysis approach that attempts to derive information about a software system from traces alone is vulnerable to problem 3 in Section 3.2.3. The selection of traces is critical to be able to draw valid conclusions about the underlying software system [14]. This presents us with an important problem. In a setting where the developer is wanting to mine the specification for the software system, it is unreasonable to expect very much (if any) prior knowledge about how the system behaves. Consequently, it is unrealistic to expect the ability to derive a collection of traces that is sufficiently diverse to adequately exercise every aspect of software behavior.

There is an analogous problem in the field of grammar inference: How does one obtain the set of sentences that are necessary to accurately infer a grammar? One solution was proposed by Angluin in 1987 [2] in the form of the L^* learning algorithm. This algorithm does not require any initial samples at all; instead it proposes its own traces (called "membership queries"), and assumes that there is an oracle (called a "minimally adequate teacher") that can provide feedback to the algorithm. This feedback is provided in two forms: (1) being able to state whether individual traces do or do not belong to the target machine, and (2) being able to state whether a hypothesis machine is equivalent to the target, and if not why not. Given that these answers can be provided, Angluin established that it is possible to infer the exact state machine in polynomial time.

The L^* algorithm works by constructing an "observation table," which records whether certain sequences over Σ^* are accepted or not. These sequences are asked in the form of membership queries, and the querying process stops once the table has been fully populated (or in more formal terms – it is *closed* and *consistent*). Once this is the case, it is possible to conjecture a hypothesis LTS. This solution is suitable for situations where the target machine is relatively simple, and we have an oracle that can be asked as many questions as are necessary. However, if the state machines are large and complex, or there is a limit on the number of queries that can be answered by the oracle, the algorithm becomes impractical.

Nonetheless, the L^* approach is appealing from the point of view that it is *active*. The provision of an initial set of traces is no longer critical to its ability to produce an accurate result. This idea of active inference has subsequently motivated work by Dupont et al., who developed an active variant of the EDSM-Blue Fringe algorithm called the Question State Merging (QSM) algorithm [12, 13]. The inference process is the same as with EDSM, but this time the algorithm is equipped with the ability to ask questions after every state-merge, to ensure that the merge is correct. In comparison to the L^* algorithm, no guarantees can be made about the absolute correctness of the final

Input: (Pos, Neg)

1 $PLTS \leftarrow generateAPTA(Pos, Neg)$;
2 **while** $(q, q') \leftarrow selectStatePair(PLTS)$ **do**
3 | $PLTS' \leftarrow merge(PLTS, (q, q'))$;
4 | **if** $compatible(PLTS', Neg)$ **then**
5 | | **while** $query \leftarrow generateQueries(PLTS, PLTS')$ **do**
6 | | | $counter \leftarrow askOracle(query)$;
7 | | | **if** $counter \neq \epsilon$ **then**
8 | | | | **if** $counter \in PreL(PLTS')$ **then**
9 | | | | | $Neg \leftarrow Neg \cup counter$;
10 | | | | **else**
11 | | | | | $Pos \leftarrow Pos \cup counter$;
12 | | | | **return** *QSM(Pos, Neg)*;
13 | | | **else if** $query \in PreL(PLTS')$ **then**
14 | | | | $Pos \leftarrow Pos \cup query$;
15 | | | **else**
16 | | | | $Neg \leftarrow Neg \cup query$;
17 | | | **end**
18 | | **end**
19 | | $PLTS \leftarrow PLTS'$;
20 | **end**
21 **end**
22 **return** $PLTS$

Algorithm 3: QSM algorithm

state machine (unless the initial set of traces fulfills a particular constraint, which is discussed below). Nonetheless, it does not rely on exhaustively querying an oracle, and can handle incomplete sets of traces. Consequently, it will at least provide an approximate model, given an incomplete set of traces and an oracle that is capable of answering some queries about it.

The QSM algorithm is shown in algorithm 3. When compared to the EDSM algorithm in algorithm 2, the difference is the while-loop in lines 5 – 19. Once a merge has been found to be compatible with *Pos* and *Neg* (i.e., all positive traces are accepted and negative traces are not), a set of membership queries are generated with the *generateQuery* function, and are posed to the oracle by the *askOracle* function.

The purpose of the queries is to verify that the decision to merge a pair of states is indeed correct. The *generateQuery* function achieves this by generating sequences from the merged machine that do not already belong either to *Pos* or *Neg*. Depending on the answers to the queries, these are added to one of the two sets. If the answer conflicts with the language of the current hypothesis $PLTS'$, the inference process is restarted so that it can take into account the augmented sets *Pos* and *Neg*.

The accuracy of the final model depends on the strategy that is employed by the *generateQuery* function. Dupont et al. [12, 13] base their strategy on the goal of obtaining a characteristic sample. Their question generation strategy takes advantage of the fact that blue states are always at the root of an acyclic part of the *PLTS*. For a particular merge of a red and a blue state, a set of queries is built by taking the cross-product of the shortest path from the initial state to the red state, and set of paths in the outgoing tree from the blue state. Any paths generated in this way that do not already belong to the set *Pos* or *Neg* are posed as questions.

There is a lot of flexibility in the choice of question generation strategy. The above strategy is guaranteed to produce an accurate state machine on the condition that the sample of traces used to infer the initial PLTS is *structurally complete*; i.e., it covers every transition in the target machine at least once. In practice, especially in the reverse-engineering domain, it is unrealistic to rely on the initial PLTS being structurally complete. When this is the case, it is however possible to employ more rigorous question-generation strategies. Customizing and augmenting the *generateQuery* function is straightforward. As an example, previous work by the authors [35] has enabled the use of a slightly more elaborate question-generation strategy, which makes sure that any loops that arise from a merge are explicitly accounted for in the questions.

3.3.4   Applying These Advances in Practice

The integration of negative traces, coupled with more powerful heuristics and the ability to acquire missing information through queries, forms the basis for specification mining algorithms that are much more powerful than the *k*-tails algorithm. Work on applying these algorithms in the domain of software engineering has been pioneered by Dupont et al. [12, 13], who applied the QSM algorithm in the context of forward-engineering models from developer-supplied scenarios. In this setting, the developer maps out a selection of scenarios that best characterize the software system in question, and the QSM algorithm generates further queries (presented to the user as scenarios) to infer the final machine.

Initial work by the authors [35] employed the QSM algorithm to directly guide the tracing process. The QSM algorithm would ask a question in the form of a hypothetical trace, and the user would attempt to execute it manually, supplying the algorithm with a suitable response which would lead to a further question. This however turned out to be a tedious process; the number of traces required tended to be too large to collect by hand.

3.3.4.1   The Software System as Oracle

One important benefit to reverse-engineering techniques versus the forward-engineering work described by Dupont et al. is the fact that the oracle responsible for answering questions or providing scenarios does not necessarily

Input: $Prog$, Σ
1 $Pos \leftarrow \emptyset$; $Neg \leftarrow \emptyset$;
2 $PLTS \leftarrow generateInitPLTS(\Sigma)$;
3 $Test \leftarrow generateTests(PLTS)$;
4 **foreach** $test \in Test$ **do**
5 | $(trace, pass) \leftarrow runTest(test, Prog)$;
6 | **if** $pass$ **then**
7 | | $Pos \leftarrow Pos \cup \{trace\}$;
8 | | **if** $trace \in ProL(PLTS)$ **then**
9 | | | $PLTS \leftarrow EDSM(Pos, Neg)$;
10 | | | $Test \leftarrow generateTests(PLTS)$;
11 | |
12 | **else**
13 | | $Neg \leftarrow Neg \cup \{trace\}$;
14 | | **if** $trace \in PreL(PLTS)$ **then**
15 | | | $PLTS \leftarrow EDSM(Pos, Neg)$;
16 | | | $Test \leftarrow generateTests(PLTS)$;
17 | |
18 | **end**
19 **end**
20 **return** $PLTS$

Algorithm 4: InferWithTests

need to be human. If the software system exists already, there is no need for any manual intervention to decide whether a trace is feasible or not; it can simply be attempted automatically. This fact is crucially important; it substantially reduces the necessary involvement from the developer's perspective. Traces can be gathered automatically (or at least semi-automatically).

Several techniques that are based on Angluin's L^* have emerged that exploit this. Techniques by Raffelt and Steffen [30] and Shahbaz and Groz [32] have adapted Angluin's L^* technique [2] to convert its queries directly into tests that can be executed on the system. However, even without relying on a human to answer queries, the key challenge with such techniques is their scalability. The number of questions required tends to rise exponentially with the number of states and the alphabet size of the target machine.

Recent work by the authors has combined the use of heuristics such as EDSM/Blue-Fringe with the ablity to automatically collect traces as tests. Instead of tying the inference process to a rigid question-generation strategy as is the case with L^*-based techniques, their work allows the user to choose their own model-based testing strategy as a basis for selecting traces. In their work on reverse engineering models of Erlang processes [38], they show how a simple random test-set generator can be used to automatically generate a large number of traces, without relying on any initial sets of traces from the developer.

The InferWithTests algorithm is shown in algorithm 4. It takes as input the subject program *Prog*, along with an alphabet Σ. It begins by producing a special initial PLTS with the *generateInitPLTS* function. This produces the most general transition system, consisting of a single state with one looping transition that is labeled by all of the elements in Σ. Formally, the resulting PLTS is defined as $A = (Q, \Sigma, \Delta, q_0, \Psi)$ where: $Q = \{q_0\}$, $\forall \sigma \in \Sigma$, $\delta(q_0, \sigma) = q_0$, and $\Psi = \emptyset$. For this machine the proscribed language $ProL(PLTS) = \emptyset$ and $PreL(PLTS) = \Sigma^*$.

Given this initial state machine, it uses the model-based tester generator to generate a test set *Test*, and proceeds to execute the tests. Every time a test execution conflicts with the expected outcome (i.e., every time a test fails when it is valid in the PLTS or vice versa), it is added to the appropriate *Pos* or *Neg* sets. Subsequently a new PLTS is inferred with the *EDSM* algorithm and the process iterates until no conflicting tests are found. For this approach the accuracy of the final machine depends on the test sets produced by the *generateTests* function, which can be customized to suit the circumstances.

One of the biggest advantages of this approach is its modularity. Like the *generateQueries* function in the *QSM* algorithm, it is possible to customize the *generateTests* function. Given a *PLTS*, it is possible to select from a broad range of established state-machine testing algorithms [20]. If accuracy is crucial, it is possible to employ a more expensive but rigorous algorithm such as the W-Method [8]. However, if efficiency is more important, a cheaper algorithm can be used instead – for example, in their work on Erlang processes [38], the authors used an off-the-shelf random state machine testing framework [10].

3.4 Integrating Constraints

So far the chapter has shown how traces can be collected and analyzed more efficiently, with the result of inferring state machines that are more accurate. However, even if the traces are collected automatically by using the test-based techniques described in Section 3.3.4, there still remains the essential problem that the necessary set of traces simply becomes too large when the target system increases in size.

One way to address this problem is to integrate additional non-trace-based knowledge about the underlying system into the inference process. This idea has been adopted by various authors in different guises. A brief overview of these approaches, which annotate states with data constraints, is provided in Section 3.4.1 (some of these are already described more comprehensively in other chapters in this book). We will subsequently focus on the description of a technique for integrating temporal rules [34] that extend the QSM algorithm presented in Section 3.3.3.

3.4.1   Integrating Data Constraints

Both Dupont et al. [12, 13] and Lorenzoli et al. [23] describe techniques for integrating data-constraints into the inference process. They deal with different settings; Dupont et al. assume a forward-engineering scenario, where the developer can manually provide the relevant rules for particular sets of states, whereas Lorenzoli et al. describe a reverse-engineering scenario, where data constraints are mined from the variable values in a given set of traces.

In the approach proposed by Dupont et al., additional domain knowledge about the system is added in the form of *fluents*. A fluent is in effect a two-state state machine that is given an initial state, and this state can be altered by a selection of events in Σ. Given that the relevant fluents are specified for the initial state, the rest of the states in the state machine can be annotated in terms of the fluents by symbolic execution. Consequently, these state annotations can be fed into the inference process; the QSM algorithm may determine that, based purely on trace information, a pair of states can be merged. However, if they are annotated with conflicting data states, then this domain information can prevent false merges from occurring.

Lorenzoli et al. approach the problem from a reverse-engineering angle. In their setting, there is no well-informed developer who can supply suitable fluent-like constraints. Instead, they extract data constraints from variable values in execution traces, and use these to augment the k-tails state-merging algorithm. Data constraints are obtained with the Daikon tool [15], and state comparisons take account of these constraints. The final state machine can be formally defined as an extended finite state machine [7] – a state machine that is augmented with data constraints. It is worth noting that their process of using Daikon to annotate states is not necessarily restricted to the k-tails algorithm, which falls prey to several weaknesses as mentioned in Section 3.2.3. Their annotation approach could be used to extend most inference techniques.

3.4.2   Integrating Temporal Constraints

An alternative approach to the integration of data constraints is to integrate constraints directly in terms of the alphabet of the state machine [34]. Whereas the approaches described above use data variables or domain knowledge to annotate states, the following approach shows how constraints can be expressed directly in terms of the elements in Σ. In this scenario, we envisage that the user is not only able to obtain a selection of traces, but can also provide selected, simple facts or rules that govern the behavior of the underlying software system.

Returning to the editor example in Figure 3.1, one example of a tempo-

Input: (Pos, Neg, LTL)

1   $PLTS \leftarrow generateAPTA(Pos, Neg)$;
2   **while** $(q, q') \leftarrow selectStatePair(PLTS)$ **do**
3      $PLTS' \leftarrow merge(PLTS, (q, q'))$;
4   **if** $Compatible(PLTS', Neg)$ **then**
5          $CounterEx \leftarrow modelCheck(PLTS', LTL)$;
6   **if** $(CounterEx = \emptyset)$ **then**   /* If consistent with LTL */
7   **while** $query \leftarrow generateQueries(PLTS, PLTS', LTL)$ **do**
8                  $constraint \leftarrow newConstraintsFromUser(query)$;
9   **if** $constraint \neq \epsilon$ **then**
10   **return** $ltlInfer(Pos, Neg, \emptyset, LTL \cup \{constraint\})$;
11   **end**
12                  $counter \leftarrow askOracle(query)$;
13   **if** $counter \neq \epsilon$ **then**
14   **if** $counter \in PreL(PLTS')$ **then**
15                          $Neg \leftarrow Neg \cup counter$;
16   **else**
17                          $Pos \leftarrow Pos \cup counter$;
18   **return** $ltlInfer(Pos, Neg, \emptyset, LTL)$;
19   **else if** $query \in PreL(PLTS')$ **then**
20                      $Pos \leftarrow Pos \cup query$;
21   **else**
22                      $Neg \leftarrow Neg \cup query$;
23   **end**
24   **end**
25   **else**   /* Not consistent with LTL */
26              $PLTS' \leftarrow rebuild(Pos, Neg \cup CounterEx, LTL)$;
27              $StatePairs \leftarrow selectStatePairs(PLTS')$;
28   **end**
29   **end**
30 **end**
31 **return** $PLTS'$

Algorithm 5: $ltlInfer$

ral constraint could be: *"You cannot save a file unless it has been edited."* Although this rule is relatively straightforward, it is virtually impossible to ensure that the hypothesis model will conform to the rule without supplying an impractically large number of traces. However, such rules can be succinctly expressed in well-established formalisms such as linear temporal logic (LTL) [28].

LTL expressions enable the behavior of a system to be characterised in terms of propositions that describe the state of a system. A set of temporal modal operators can be used to describe the temporal relationships between these propositions. Important operators are listed below:

- The *next* operator $\bigcirc$, where $\bigcirc\phi$ means that the property ϕ has to hold in the next state.

- The *global* operator $\square$, where $\square\phi$ means that the property ϕ has to hold for every future state.

- The *eventually* operator $\diamond$, where $\diamond\phi$ means that the property ϕ has to hold eventually.

- The *until* operator U, where $\varphi U\phi$ means that the property φ has to hold until property ϕ holds.

- The *release* operator R, where $\varphi R\phi$ means that the property ϕ is true until φ becomes true, or forever if φ is never true.

So, for example, the property that you cannot save a file unless it has been edited can be expressed as follows:

$$(edit\,R\,\neg\,save) \wedge \square(save \rightarrow \bigcirc(edit\,R\,\neg\,save))$$

There exist several powerful model-checking techniques to ensure that a labeled transition system conforms to such properties [17]. Model checkers not only state whether or not a model conforms to a particular constraint, but also provide *counter examples* of paths in the model that violate a given constraint. The approach described by the authors [34] shows how the QSM algorithm can be extended to integrate constraints. Depending on the choice of initial traces and the constraints provided, the number of questions and traces can be substantially reduced, whilst increasing the accuracy of the final machine.

The algorithm is shown in algorithm 5 and assumes the existence of some model-checker (invoked by the *modelCheck* function), and the availability of a set of constraints (provided as a set LTL). Lines 1–4 are the same as the QSM algorithm; an APTA is constructed, pairs of states are selected to be merged, and for each merge the hypothesis machine $PLTS'$ is checked to ensure that it is compatible with Neg. Once this has happened, the model checker is used to check that $PLTS'$ is compatible with LTL (line 5). If this is not the case, the counter-examples are used to build a new $PLTS'$, and new candidate state merges are computed (lines 26–27). Otherwise, if there are no counter-examples, a set of queries is generated.[3] For each query, the user is given the opportunity to answer it with a new LTL constraint, in which case the process is restarted with the new LTL query (lines 8–10). If no new LTL queries are supplied, the algorithm carries on as with QSM, allowing the developer to state whether a query is valid or not.

As with traces, it is unrealistic to expect the developer to supply a suitable set of LTL constraints without guidance. The QSM process of asking questions enables this; the developer can either choose to answer queries as they would with the conventional QSM algorithm, or queries can be answered more comprehensively with an LTL constraint that will also prevent other similar questions from being asked. Preliminary results on small case studies have produced promising results [34]; depending on the initial set of traces and the supplied set of LTL constraints the number of questions can be substantially reduced, whilst maintaining or even slightly improving the accuracy of the inferred machine.

3.5   Conclusions and Future Work

This chapter has presented a selection of advances on the traditional reverse-engineering process, many of which have been inspired by advances in the field of grammar inference. The rigid process described in Figure 3.2 has been gradually augmented. The process can be iterative. It can accept inputs from a developer in the form of answers to queries, from model-based testers in the form of passed/failed test cases, and from model-checkers in the form of counter-examples to constraints.

The result is that state machines can be reverse-engineered with less input required from the user. The collection of traces can be automated with model-based testers and counter-examples from model checkers. The use of negative traces reduces the reliance upon primitive heuristics, and enables the inference of state machines that are much more accurate.

Nonetheless, there still remains a host of important challenges to be addressed by future work. Current techniques do not account for the task of abstracting traces into sequences of symbols. A typical trace will record sequences of low-level events (i.e., method calls in an object-oriented system). A relatively trivial program trace can incorporate hundreds of different events and be extremely large. Current approaches assume that there is some "abstraction function" that automatically lifts a low-level trace to a sequence

---

[3]The *generateQueries* function here is slightly different from QSM; it ensures that none of the queries contradict the given set of LTL constraints.

of symbols in Σ. Constructing such a function is often non-trivial and error prone. Therefore one area of future work is concerned with the development of (semi-)automated abstraction techniques.

Although the presented EDSM Blue-Fringe algorithm is currently accepted to be the most accurate inference algorithm, the evidence so far has concentrated on state machines from the domain of grammar-inference. These tend to be restricted to alphabets of size 2, whereas a typical software-engineering state machine contains much larger alphabets. Although the EDSM algorithm is undoubtedly more accurate than the k-tails algorithm (thanks to its ability to incorporate negative traces), there is still the potential that other algorithms are more accurate for state machines that are characteristic of software systems.

Bibliography

[1] G. Ammons, R. Bodík, and J. Larus. Mining specifications. In *29th SIGPLAN-SIGACT Symposium on Principles of Programming Languages (POPL)*, pages 4–16, Portland, Oregon, 2002.

[2] D. Angluin. Learning regular sets from queries and counterexamples. *Information and Computation*, 75:87–106, 1987.

[3] G. Banks, M. Cova, V. Felmetsger, K. Almeroth, R. Kemmerer, and G. Vigna. SNOOZE: toward a stateful network protocol fuzzer. In *Information Security, 9th International Conference, ISC 2006*, volume 4176 of *Lecture Notes in Computer Science*, pages 343–358. Springer, 2006.

[4] A. Biermann and J. Feldman. On the synthesis of finite-state machines from samples of their behavior. *IEEE Transactions on Computers*, 21:592–597, 1972.

[5] A.W. Biermann and R. Krishnaswamy. Constructing programs from example computations. *IEEE Trans. on Software Engineering*, SE-2:141–153, 1976.

[6] K. Bogdanov and N. Walkinshaw. Computing the structural difference between state-based models. In *16th IEEE Working Conference on Reverse Engineering (WCRE)*, 2009.

[7] K. Cheng and A. Krishnakumar. Automatic functional test generation using the extended finite state machine model. In *30th ACM/IEEE Design Automation Conference*, pages 86–91, 1993.

[8] T. Chow. Testing software design modelled by finite state machines. *IEEE Transactions on Software Engineering*, 4(3):178–187, 1978.

[9] O. Cicchello and S. Kremer. Inducing grammars from sparse data sets: a survey of algorithms and results. *Journal of Machine Learning Research*, 4:603–632, 2003.

[10] K. Claessen and J. Hughes. Quickcheck: a lightweight tool for random testing of Haskell programs. In *Proceedings of the International Conference on Functional Programming (ICFP)*, pages 268–279, 2000.

[11] J. Cook and A. Wolf. Discovering models of software processes from event-based data. *ACM Transactions on Software Engineering and Methodology*, 7(3):215–249, 1998.

[12] C. Damas, B. Lambeau, P. Dupont, and A. van Lamsweerde. Generating annotated behavior models from end-user scenarios. *IEEE Transactions on Software Engineering*, 31(12):1056–1073, 2005.

[13] P. Dupont, B. Lambeau, C. Damas, and A. van Lamsweerde. The QSM algorithm and its application to software behavior model induction. *Applied Artificial Intelligence*, 22:77–115, 2008.

[14] M. Ernst. Static and dynamic analysis: synergy and duality. In *Proceedings of the International Workshop on Dynamic Analysis (WODA)*, 2003.

[15] M. Ernst, J. Cockrell, W. Griswold, and D. Notkin. Dynamically discovering likely program invariants to support program evolution. *Transactions on Software Engineering*, 27(2):1–25, February 2001.

[16] M. Gold. Language identification in the limit. *Information and Control*, 10:447–474, 1967.

[17] G. Holzmann. *The SPIN Model Checker: Primer and Reference Manual*. Addison-Wesley, 2004.

[18] J. Hopcroft, R. Motwani, and J. Ullman. *Introduction to Automata Theory, Languages, and Computation, Third Edition*. Addison-Wesley, 2007.

[19] K. Lang, B. Pearlmutter, and R. Price. Results of the Abbadingo One DFA Learning Competition and a new evidence-driven state merging algorithm. In *Proceedings of the International Colloquium on Grammar Inference (ICGI)*, volume 1433, pages 1–12, 1998.

[20] D. Lee and M. Yannakakis. Principles and methods of testing finite state machines — a survey. In *Proceedings of the IEEE*, volume 84, pages 1090–1126, 1996.

[21] D. Lo and S. Khoo. SMArTIC: towards building an accurate, robust and scalable specification miner. In *SIGSOFT FSE*, pages 265–275, 2006.

[22] D. Lo, L. Mariani, and M. Pezzè. Automatic steering of behavioral model inference. In *ESEC/SIGSOFT FSE*, pages 345–354. ACM Press, 2009.

[23] D. Lorenzoli, L. Mariani, and M. Pezzè. Automatic generation of software behavioral models. In *ICSE '08: Proceedings of the 30th International Conference on Software Engineering*, pages 501–510, New York, ACM Press, 2008.

[24] E.F. Moore. Gedanken–experiments on sequential machines. In C.E. Shannon and J. McCarthy, editors, *Annals of Mathematics Studies (34)*, *Automata Studies*, pages 129–153. Princeton University Press, Princeton, NJ, 1956.

[25] A. Nerode. Linear automata transformations. *Proceedings of the American Mathematical Society*, 9:541–544, 1958.

[26] J. Oncina and P. Garcia. Inferring regular languages in polynomial update time. In *Pattern Recognition and Image Analysis*, volume 1, pages 49–61. 1992.

[27] R. Parekh and V. Honavar. *The Handbook of Natural Language Processing*, chapter Grammar Inference, Automata Induction and Language Acquisition, pages 727–764. Marcel-Dekker, New York, 2000.

[28] A. Pnueli. The temporal logics of programs. In *18th IEEE Symposium on the Foundations of Computer Science*, 1977.

[29] G. Pullum. *The Oxford International Encyclopedia of Linguistics*, 2nd edition, chapter Learnability: Mathematical Aspects, pages 431–434. Oxford University Press, 2003.

[30] H. Raffelt and B. Steffen. Learnlib: a library for automata learning and experimentation. In *FASE*, volume 3922 of *Lecture Notes in Computer Science*, pages 377–380. Springer, 2006.

[31] S. Reiss and M. Renieris. Encoding program executions. In *ICSE*, pages 221–230. IEEE Computer Society, 2001.

[32] M. Shahbaz and R. Groz. Inferring mealy machines. In *Proceedings of Formal Methods (FM'09)*, volume 5850 of *LNCS*, pages 207–222, 2009.

[33] S. Uchitel, J. Kramer, and J. Magee. Behaviour model elaboration using partial labelled transition systems. In *4th Joint Meeting of the European Software Engineering Conference and ACM SIGSOFT Symposium on the Foundations of Software Engineering (ESEC/FSE)*, pages 19–27, 2003.

[34] N. Walkinshaw and K. Bogdanov. Inferring finite-state models with temporal constraints. In *Proceedings of the 23rd International Conference on Automated Software Engineering (ASE)*, 2008.

[35] N. Walkinshaw, K. Bogdanov, M. Holcombe, and S. Salahuddin. Reverse engineering state machines by interactive grammar inference. In *14th IEEE International Working Conference on Reverse Engineering (WCRE)*, 2007.

[36] N. Walkinshaw, K. Bogdanov, M. Holcombe, and S. Salahuddin. Improving dynamic software analysis by applying grammar inference principles. *Journal of Software Maintenance and Evolution: Research and Practice*, 2008.

[37] N. Walkinshaw, K. Bogdanov, and K. Johnson. Evaluation and comparison of inferred regular grammars. In *Proceedings of the International Colloquium on Grammar Inference (ICGI)*, St. Malo, France, 2008.

[38] N. Walkinshaw, J. Derrick, and Q. Guo. Iterative refinement of reverse-engineered models by model-based testing. In *Proceedings of Formal Methods (FM'09)*, volume 5850 of *LNCS*, pages 305–320. Springer, 2009.

Chapter 4

Mining API Usage Protocols from Large Method Traces

Michael Pradel

ETH Zurich

Thomas R. Gross

ETH Zurich

4.1   Introduction

Large software is typically built from several components that are reused among different projects. Programmers access functionality from such components via an application programming interface (API). While reusing existing components can increase programmer productivity, API usage also implies certain difficulties. One such difficulty is that many APIs implicitly constrain the order of API method calls. For instance, using an output stream typically follows the protocol: open the stream, write to it an arbitrary number of times, and close the stream. Violating this protocol can lead to severe programming errors, such as resource leakage due to unreleased resources. Although such constraints exist for most APIs, few of them are documented appropriately. Moreover, ordering constraints of method calls are rarely formalized, making it impossible to check them automatically.

We address the problem of missing specifications of typical and correct API usage by automatically inferring API usage protocols. This chapter presents a dynamic analysis that mines common usage patterns from existing programs using an API. The analysis produces finite state machines (FSMs) that describe the order in which API methods are typically called. Our approach is to learn from the runtime behavior of programs, which provides several benefits. First of all, dynamic analysis has precise and unambiguous information about the program's control flow, aliasing between objects, and the type of each object. Furthermore, execution frequencies help to focus on recurring patterns while ignoring incidental call sequences.

A major challenge of dynamic specification inference is the large volume of runtime events occurring in real-world programs. The presented analysis focuses on small sets of related objects and method calls, *object collaborations*, that appear together during program execution. Each object collaboration can be analyzed separately. As a result, the analysis scales linearly with the number of runtime events to analyze.

Experiments with an implementation of the analysis show that it infers typical API usage protocols while being scalable to large volumes of runtime events. Overall, we applied the analysis to 10 Java programs and analyzed 280 million method calls and returns. The largest set of runtime events contains

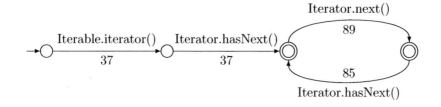

FIGURE 4.1: An inferred API usage protocol that shows correct iterator usage in Java. The weights describe how often each transition was observed.

84 million runtime events and can be analyzed in 26 minutes. Analyzing the inferred protocols for an API used by almost all Java programs, *java.util*, shows that 28% of the protocols found in one program are independently found in another program as well, and hence, can be considered typical. For example, Figure 4.1 shows an inferred protocol that describes typical iterator usage in Java.

The API usage protocols that our analysis infers can be used for different applications. At first, they help in program understanding and provide documentation on common ways to use an API. Usage protocols can enrich existing documentation by showing temporal constraints between methods in the context of a particular usage scenario. Furthermore, static program analysis can use specifications to formally prove the absence of certain errors [12] or to identify uncommon programming patterns that may be due to bugs [13, 39, 40]. Moreover, the inferred specifications can serve as input to runtime monitoring tools that check whether a program violates certain usage rules [9, 26].

Our analysis infers typical API usage protocols from large method traces of real-world applications. In particular, we make the following contributions:

- *Reduced complexity.* The analysis focuses on small sets of related objects and method calls, which can be analyzed separately. As a result, the analysis scales to large traces of runtime events.

- *Mining techniques.* We extract relevant parts of a program execution and identify recurring patterns using a set of novel mining techniques, such as comparing the roles that objects play within a certain context.

- *Specifications of interacting objects.* The analysis produces API usage protocols that describe common method call sequences on *multiple* objects.

- *Experimental validation.* We apply an implementation of the analysis to 10 Java programs. The results show that the analysis infers typical API usage patterns.

This chapter is based on a previously presented paper [29]. Besides providing additional material and experimental results, we here describe several enhancements of our approach: A dataflow analysis helps to focus on related method calls. Moreover, the analysis now produces FSMs with transitions labeled with method calls, instead of labeling states and having anonymous transitions. Therefore, the language accepted by the FSMs directly reflects the call sequences that a protocol permits. Finally, all inferred protocols are written to a specification database that accumulates results from analyzing different programs over time.

The remainder of this text is organized as follows. Section 4.2 describes the components of our analysis and shows how they work together. Sections 4.3 and 4.4 report on an implementation of the analysis and our experimental results. A discussion of our approach and possible applications of it follows in Section 4.5. Finally, we discuss related work and conclude.

4.2   Mining API Usage Protocols

This section describes a dynamic analysis to infer API usage protocols. The analysis requires a program using an API and some input to run the program. The output of the analysis are FSMs that describe typical API method call sequences. The general idea is to learn common usage patterns from existing programs by analyzing in which order these programs call methods. The underlying assumption is that frequently observed behavior is likely to be correct [6].

Figure 4.2 provides an overview of the analysis. At first, we instrument a program that uses a particular API so that it emits information about method calls during execution. Running the instrumented program yields method traces, that is, a sequences of method call and method return events. An analysis of the traces identifies small sets of related API objects and the methods that are called on them, which we call object collaborations. To focus on call sequences that are relevant for inferring API usage protocols, different *collaboration transformers* refine collaborations and filter irrelevant parts of them. Afterward, the analysis summarizes collaborations into recurring patterns, which finally are translated into FSMs that describe API usage protocols.

The remainder of this section details the components of our analysis and explains how they work together to mine API usage protocols.

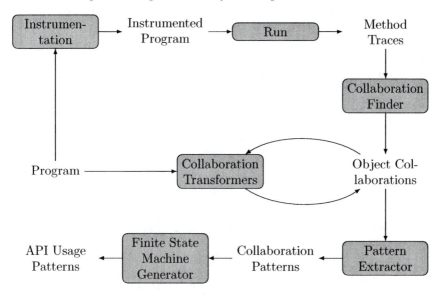

FIGURE 4.2: Overview of the protocol mining approach.

4.2.1   Collecting Method Traces

The first step of our analysis is to modify programs so that they emit runtime information during their execution. Since we are interested in specifications of method call sequences, each method call and method return is relevant. More precisely, we log the following for each call and return:

- Unique object identity and type of caller and callee.

- Name of the called method.

- Unique object identity and type of parameters and return value.

- Source code location of the event.

The source code location is necessary to disambiguate several calls to a particular method within one method. Each call and return is called an *event*. A sequence of events is referred to as *method trace*. The instrumented program writes all events into text files. For each thread of execution, a separate text file is written.

As a running example consider the Java source code in Figure 4.3(a). Instrumenting the program and executing method *callM()* can produce the method trace shown in Figure 4.4, which assumes that the list *li* contains two elements. Method traces of larger programs can contain millions of events. The largest program run we analyzed during our experiments consists of over 83 million runtime events.

```
class A {                                    class B {
  public void callM(LinkedList<B> li) {        SomeClass f;
    Iterator<B> iter = li.iterator();
    while (iter.hasNext()) {                    public void m() {
      B b = iter.next();                          f.g();
      b.m();                                    }
    }                                         }
  }
}
```

(a) Method *callM()* uses an iterator to traverse a *LinkedList*.

```
class C {
  public int addElements(HashSet<Integer> s) {
    int sum = 0;
    for (Iterator<Integer> i = s.iterator(); i.hasNext(); ) {
      sum += i.next();
    }
    return sum;
  }
}
```

(b) Method *addElements()* iterates over a *HashSet*.

FIGURE 4.3: Two examples of iterator usage.

```
...
    --> a.callM()
                    --> li.iterator()
                    --> iter.hasNext()
                    --> iter.next()
                    --> b1.m()
                              --> f1.g()
                    --> iter.hasNext()
                    --> iter.next()
                    --> b2.m()
                              --> f2.g()
                    --> iter.hasNext()
```

FIGURE 4.4: Method trace from executing *callM()* in Figure 4.3(a) (return events and other details omitted).

4.2.2 Finding Object Collaborations

Our analysis scans the method traces from one or more program executions and extracts semantically related subsequences of manageable size to be analyzed separately. Doing so involves two challenges: First, the analysis must be able to deal with large volumes of method traces as they result from real-world programs. Ensuring scalability allows us to analyze a variety of traces from different programs, and hence, helps to increase the coverage of the API by the inferred protocols. Second, the analysis should focus on typical API usage scenarios and discard incidental call sequences that are not representative.

We address these two challenges using an abstraction given by the programmer, namely, the grouping of related method calls into methods. A method typically implements a small piece of functionality. Therefore, the API methods called within a method often constitute a small and coherent piece of API usage. We exploit this observation by considering the objects used within a method execution and the methods called on them to form a collaboration.

For example, the execution of method *callM()* depicted in Figure 4.4 involves four callee objects: the list *li*, the iterator *iter*, and two instances of *B*, *b1* and *b2*. On each of them, one or more methods are called within the context of *callM()*. We say that these objects collaborate and that the sequence of calls on them is an object collaboration.

Definition 1. *Object collaboration. The sequence of method calls within the execution of a method and their receiver objects form an object collaboration. Let a method call be a pair (o, s) of the receiver object o and the called method's signature s. A collaboration is an ordered sequence*

$$S = (o_1, s_1), \ldots, (o_n, s_n)$$

of calls issued within the execution of a method (o_{outer}, s_{outer}). The following objects are said to collaborate:

$$O = \{o \mid \exists (o, s) \in S\}$$

Splitting method traces into object collaborations yields small and semantically coherent sequences of method calls. Each collaboration can be analyzed independently from other collaborations, which is crucial for keeping the analysis scalable.

While many typical API call sequences can be observed within the execution of one method, some usage scenarios may span across multiple methods. Often, related calls happen in several methods that are called from one "root method." To address such situations, our analysis has a parameter called *nesting level*. With nesting level one only calls issued directly within a method are considered to belong to a collaboration. By increasing the nesting level, the analysis also considers indirect calls. For example, the calls to method $g()$ in Figure 4.4 are included in *callM()*'s collaboration with nesting level two. The larger the nesting level, the more method calls belong to a collaboration. If not mentioned otherwise, we use nesting level one.

Of course, not all method calls within the execution of a method are relevant for inferring API usage protocols. We therefore refine and filter the extracted object collaborations using a set of techniques explained in the following.

4.2.3   Collaboration Transformers

Our analysis modifies object collaborations to make them more suitable for inferring API usage protocols. Different ways to do so are unified as *collaboration transformers*. Each transformer takes one collaboration and returns zero, one, or more collaborations. The following transformers are part of our analysis:

- *Generalizing types.* Generalize observed behavior to more general types than those that were observed.

- *Merging objects.* Merge objects if they only repeat information in the resulting protocol.

- *Package-based filtering.* Focus on method calls that relate to a particular API package.

- *Dataflow relations.* Focus on method calls that are dataflow-related.

The following explains each transformer in detail.

4.2.3.1   Generalizing Types

Many API usage patterns that can be observed during program execution are more specific than the general API protocol followed by the programmer. In particular, the types visible at runtime can often be generalized. Reconsider the example in Figure 4.3(a) and its trace in Figure 4.4. The observed sequence of API calls is not specific to *LinkedList*. Instead, changing the type of *li* to *Iterable* captures a more general API protocol.

We address such situations by generalizing the type of each object in a collaboration as far as the methods that are required within the collaboration permit. Specifically, we determine which *role* each object plays within a collaboration.

Definition 2. *Role. The role of an object in a collaboration is the subset of its methods that are called in the scope of the collaboration:*

$$\forall o \in O : role(o) = \{s \mid \exists(o, s) \in S\}$$

Note that the order of calls is not considered to computing the role of an object. The roles of the objects involved in the collaboration built from Figure 4.4

are as follows: li has role $\{iterator()\}$, $iter$ has role $\{hasNext(), next()\}$, and $b1$ and $b2$ each have role $\{m()\}$.

Based on the role r of an object o, we compute its best-fitting type by considering all supertypes of o's dynamic type that fulfills r (that is, that provides all methods of r). For each such supertype t, we compute the ratio of the number of methods in r and the number of methods in t:

$$fit(r, t) = \frac{|methods(r)|}{|methods(t)|}$$

For each object, we choose the type that maximizes fit, or in other words, that minimizes the number of methods provided by the type that is not required in the collaboration.

For the above example, li's best-fitting type is *Iterable*, where $fit = 1$ since *Iterable* provides exactly the methods required by li's role. Generalizing types transforms one collaboration into another one.

4.2.3.2   Merging Objects

Another way to make collaborations more suitable for inferring API usage protocols is to remove objects and method calls that do not add additional information. For instance, the number of elements in the list li in Figure 4.3(a) is not relevant for the way the API is used and may vary from one execution of *callM()* to another. Considering all elements of li individually would give a different usage protocol for each list with a different length.

Such a situation occurs whenever a program iterates over a collection and calls the same methods on each element. To avoid polluting protocols with incidental method calls, we merge all objects that have exactly the same role into one artificial object. In the example, the analysis merges all instances of B into one artificial instance that receives all calls to instances of B. Merging objects transforms one collaboration into another one.

4.2.3.3   Package-Based Filtering

Most recurring API usage patterns are specific to a particular package. By focusing on one package in each collaboration, our analysis can automatically remove irrelevant method calls from the inferred protocols. For example, Figure 4.3(a) contains several calls related to *java.util* and a call to $m()$, which seems irrelevant for a specification describing iterator usage.

To filter a collaboration for a package p, we remove all calls that do not relate to p. A method call is said to relate to a package p if its callee, its return value, or one of its parameters is an instance of a class in p. This approach generalizes ideas from Weimer et al. [40], where two method calls can only be part of the same specification if they are declared in the same package. In contrast, we also consider calls that are in a direct dataflow relation to a particular package. Filtering the collaboration created by *callM()* in

```
public class DataflowExample {
  PrintWriter debugLog;

  public void readFile(File f) throws Exception {
    FileInputStream is = new FileInputStream(f);
    byte[] b = new byte[1000];
    while (is.read(b) != -1) {
      // use b
    }
    is.close();
    debugLog.write("Reading file: Done.");
  }
}
```

FIGURE 4.5: Several calls to objects from *java.io*. Dataflow analysis extracts the highlighted calls, which are relevant for showing a typical use of *FileInputStream*.

Figure 4.3(a) for package *java.util* removes the calls to *m()*, and hence, leaves only calls relevant for using an iterator.

The package to focus on can be given as a parameter to our analysis. Alternatively, we provide an automatic mode, where relevant packages are determined for each collaboration. For that purpose, each package with at least two calls related to it is considered. Package-based filtering transforms one collaboration into zero, one, or more collaborations. For example, a method may use an iterator (related to *java.util*) and write to an output stream (related to *java.io*). Such a collaboration is transformed into two collaborations: one with calls related to *java.util* and one with calls related to *java.io*.

4.2.3.4   Dataflow Filtering

Larger methods that call many other methods can result in large collaborations. Sometimes, two or more API usages are interleaved within a method. For instance, Figure 4.5 shows a method that uses a *FileInputStream* and a *PrintWriter*. To obtain a protocol of using *FileInputStream*, the call to the *PrintWriter* is unnecessary, but since both belong to *java.io* package-based filtering cannot split the collaboration accordingly.

Our analysis tries to separate interleaved method call sequences based on dataflow relations between method calls. Since our approach is dynamic, precise and unambiguous information about object identities and the dataflow between objects is available. Based on this knowledge, the analysis computes dataflow-related subsequences of calls:

- First, the analysis computes the set of objects that are related to each call, that is, its callee, parameters, and return value. Based on these sets of related objects, two calls are considered to be related if they share at least one related object.

- Second, the analysis extracts subsets of calls so that within each subset, all calls are directly or indirectly related to each other. The relations between calls can be thought of as a graph, where calls are nodes and edges denote a dataflow relation between them. To extract dataflow-related subsequences of calls, our analysis computes connected subgraphs of this graph.

For the example in Figure 4.5, the highlighted calls are dataflow-related as they all share the same callee. As a result, the analysis will put them into a separate collaboration. Dataflow filtering transforms one collaboration into one or more collaborations.

This concludes the description of four collaboration transformers that our analysis employs to focus on method call sequences that expose typical API usage. The order in which transformers are applied to collaborations can influence the result. For instance, generalizing types may change the callee package of certain calls, which again influences the package-based filtering. Our analysis repeatedly applies transformers in the order of their description in this chapter until the set of transformed collaborations stabilizes.

4.2.4 Extracting Collaboration Patterns

The preceding parts of our analysis yield a set of object collaborations, of which each contains several API method calls. In the following, we explain how to identify recurring API usage patterns, called *collaboration patterns*, within this set of collaborations. Extracting collaboration patterns proceeds in two steps. At first, the analysis summarizes collaborations into patterns by comparing the roles that objects play. Afterward, the analysis removes infrequent patterns to ignore incidental call sequences and uncommon API usage patterns.

4.2.4.1 Summarizing Frequent Collaborations

To learn common API usage protocols, we need to identify call sequences that are similar but may expose different orders of calls. Comparing conceptually similar collaborations, we observe that the involved objects often require the same methods. Exploiting this observation, we map collaborations into patterns as follows:

Definition 3. *Collaboration pattern. Two collaborations belong to the same collaboration pattern if their objects play the same roles and have the same types. That is, given two collaborations with object sets O_1 and O_2, they belong* *to the same pattern if and only if there exists a bijective map* $: O_1 \rightarrow O_2$ *with*

$$o_1 \mapsto o_2 \in map \quad \Leftrightarrow \quad role(o_1) = role(o_2)$$

For example, executing method *addElements()* in Figure 4.3(b) leads to a collaboration that is similar to that from Figure 4.3(a). After applying all of the collaboration transformers, both contain two objects with exactly the same roles and types: an instance of *Iterable* with role $\{iterator\}$ and an instance of *Iterator* with role $\{hasNext(), next()\}$. Hence, both collaborations belong to the same collaboration pattern.

4.2.4.2   Removing Infrequent Collaborations

In performing a dynamic analysis, there are two notions of frequency we can use. On the one hand, each pattern occurs in a certain number of collaborations, that is, it appears a certain number of times at runtime. We refer to that number as *dynamic frequency*. On the other hand, our analysis considers the number of different static call sites in which a pattern is found. This number is referred to as *static frequency*.

When extracting frequent collaboration patterns, our analysis removes all patterns with static and dynamic frequencies below certain thresholds. Requiring a large dynamic frequency favours patterns that appear often at runtime, while a minimal static frequency enforces a certain spread of a API usage pattern in the source code.

4.2.5   Generating Finite State Machines

The final part of our analysis generates FSMs that encode commonly observed API usage patterns. Each FSM contains a protocol of using one or more API objects and specifies in which order the objects' methods are typically called. The analysis maps each collaboration pattern to a weighted FSM as follows:

- *States*. For each object, create a state for each of the methods called on it.

- *Methods*. Whenever two methods are observed consecutively in one of the collaborations that belong to the pattern, connect the two corresponding states with a transition and assign weight one to it. If there is already such a transition, increment its weight. Label the transitions with the method of the destination state.

As a result, the FSM describes which method sequences occur in the collaborations of a pattern. Furthermore, the weights indicate how often each transition was observed, and hence, provide an estimate of how likely one method call is to follow another.

Figure 4.1 shows a protocol inferred from the collaborations produced by the methods in Figure 4.3. The protocol describes a typical usage of iterators in Java.

This concludes the description of an analysis that infers API usage protocols from running programs. Starting from method traces, the analysis extracts small sets of related methods calls (object collaborations), transforms and filters them, identifies frequently occurring API usage patterns, and finally outputs them as FSMs. The analysis is modular in the sense that each of its components is exchangeable. For example, one can use another approach to identify recurring patterns in the set of collaborations, while retaining the rest of the analysis.

4.3   Implementation

This section describes an implementation of the analysis presented in Section 4.2. At first, we give details on instrumenting programs and running instrumented programs, followed by a brief description of the specification mining tool itself. We implemented the analysis for Java programs. The only input that is required are JAR files containing the programs to analyze, as well as JAR files of all third-party libraries they depend on.

4.3.1   Instrumentation and Program Run

We instrument programs with AspectJ [1] so that all method calls and returns are reported when the program is executed. Additional instructions at each method call and return pass information about each event to a logging component. Figure 4.6 shows a simplified version of the aspect we use for instrumentation. The pointcut *tracedCall* applies to all non-static method invocations, including constructor calls. A before (after) advice reports call (return) events to the *CallLogger*. Besides regular method returns, we also log exceptional returns. Both are handled as normal return events.

The logging component retrieves runtime information from the instrumented program and writes it into text files. For each thread of execution, a separate file is created. We only instrument classes and methods of the program that is analyzed, excluding libraries and other third-party components it may use.

Instead of writing runtime events into files and analyzing them offline, one could infer API usage protocols while a program is using an API. We opted for an offline analysis because it facilitates the experiments as each program must

```
public aspect CallTracing {
  pointcut tracedCall(): call(!static * * (..)) || call(new(..));

  before(): tracedCall() {
    CallLogger.addCall(...);
  }

  after() returning(Object retVal): tracedCall() {
    CallLogger.addReturn(...);
  }

  after() throwing : tracedCall() {
    CallLogger.addReturn(...);
  }
}
```

FIGURE 4.6: Skeleton of the aspect used to instrument programs so that they log method calls and returns.

be executed only once, making the slowdown caused by the instrumentation negligible.

4.3.2 Specification Inference

The specification inference tool is implemented in Scala. It consists of different modules that roughly reflect the structure depicted in Figure 4.2. For analyzing the static structure of classes, for instance in the collaboration transformer that generalizes types (Section 4.2.3.1), we use the Java reflection facilities. The internal representation of FSMs is based on the *dk.brics.automaton* library [27].

All inferred API usage protocols are written into a specification database. This allows us to easily accumulate protocols from different programs over time. Moreover, we merge protocols from different programs when they contain exactly the same states and transitions by adding the weights of each pair of matching transitions. The specification database supports different output formats, such as DOT files [2], a textual representation of protocols, and different summaries of the inferred protocols.

4.4 Experiments

We evaluate our analysis by applying it to several real-world Java programs that overall produced around 280 million runtime events. This section presents our results, which where driven by the following research questions:

TABLE 4.1: Programs Used for Our Experiments with Number of Produced Runtime Events, Extracted Collaborations (Measured after Applying Collaboration Transformers), and Inferred FSMs

Program	Classes loaded	Runtime events	Collaborations	FSMs
antlr	126	9,359,100	1,172	38
chart	219	28,875,810	490	10
eclipse	795	499,296	7,388	133
fop	231	6,813,674	9,945	54
hsqldb	131	18,618,350	4,164	8
jython	251	54,222,673	59,371	75
luindex	128	19,358,160	69	10
lusearch	118	83,888,242	32	3
pmd	325	295,748	144	20
xalan	244	57,340,996	9,645	56
Sum		279,272,049	92,420	407

- *Number and size of inferred protocols.* How many protocols does the analysis infer and how large are they? Producing a reasonable number of protocols of manageable size is desirable, for instance, to use them as API usage documentation.

- *Influence of coverage.* How much does the coverage of the API by the method traces influence the results? Answering this question helps to decide when it is worth to gather and analyze more traces.

- *Quality of inferred protocols.* Do the inferred protocols show typical API usage scenarios? This question is important since specification miners risk to produce incidental call sequences that are not representative.

- *Performance and scalability.* How does the analysis perform for large method traces? Real-world programs produce millions of runtime events and only a scalable analysis can analyze them in reasonable time.

4.4.1   Experimental Setup

For our experiments, we use the DaCapo benchmark suite [8]. It contains real-world Java programs from different application domains and provides input to each program to run them in a controlled and reproducible manner. The first three columns of Table 4.1 show the analyzed programs, how many classes were loaded during their execution, and how many runtime events we analyzed.

All experiments are done on a 3.16 GHz Intel Core 2 Duo machine with

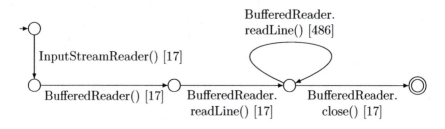

FIGURE 4.7: Inferred protocol that shows a typical usage of a reader.

4 GB memory. We use the Java Hotspot Server virtual machine version 1.6.0 running on Debian/GNU Linux.

4.4.2   Examples

Before addressing the above research questions, we illustrate the outcome of our analysis with two representative examples. Figure 4.7 shows a usage protocol of *BufferedReader*. At first, an *InputStreamReader* is created and given as a parameter to the constructor of *BufferedReader*. Then, the *readLine()* method is called multiple times; eventually, the reader is closed. As indicated by the weights of transitions, this protocol was observed 17 times.

Figure 4.8 shows a more complex protocol that involves three objects. It

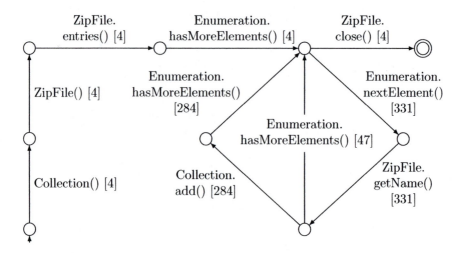

FIGURE 4.8: Complex protocol showing how to read entries of a ZIP file to store them in a collection.

describes how to read the entries of a *ZipFile* using an *Enumeration*. Information about each entry is added to a collection, which is initialized at the beginning of the protocol. After reading all entries, the *ZipFile* is closed.

4.4.3   Number and Size of Inferred Protocols

To assess whether the inferred API usage protocols are of a manageable number and size, we measure how many protocols the analysis infers and how many states and transitions each protocol contains. Table 4.1 shows the number of collaborations and protocols inferred for the Java standard library. The number of collaborations is measured after applying transformers and after removing trivial collaborations with less than two calls. The results show that extracting and filtering object collaborations significantly reduce the amount of data to analyze compared with the number of analyzed runtime events. Furthermore, the analysis mines a reasonably small number of FSMs from each program (between 3 and 133).

Figure 4.9 illustrates the number of states and transitions of the inferred protocols. Most protocols have less than 10 states and less than 10 transitions. The largest protocol contains 25 states and 53 transitions. We conclude from the results that most protocols are small enough to be understandable for humans.

4.4.4   Influence of Coverage

An obvious question is how the coverage of the API by the method traces influences the number of usage protocols that our analysis infers. To answer it, we measure the overall number of calls to API classes c_{all} within the analyzed traces and the number of distinct API methods called $c_{distinct}$. Then, we compute the correlation of c_{all} and $c_{distinct}$ with the number of inferred

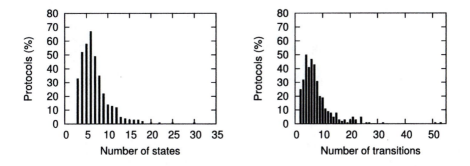

FIGURE 4.9: Distribution of number of states and number of transitions of the inferred protocols.

FSMs n. Using the Pearson correlation coefficient r, which is a measure for the linear dependence of two data sets, we find that $r(c_{all}, n) = -0.1$. Hence, there is no correlation between the overall number of API calls and the number of inferred FSMs. In contrast, $r(c_{distinct}, n) = 0.95$, indicating a strong correlation between the two data sets. The results confirm the intuition that simply adding more traces does not necessarily lead to more inferred protocols. Instead, the number of distinct API methods called in the set of method traces matters.

4.4.5   Quality of Inferred Protocols

Measuring the quality of inferred API usage protocols in an objective way is difficult. Instead of presenting a manual classification of protocols into "useful" and "not useful," we assess which protocols represent typical API usage scenarios by comparing the results from different programs using the same API. We consider a protocol to be typical if it is confirmed by at least one other program, that is, if it independently appears in the results of at least two programs. There are two ways of confirming a protocol:

- *Confirmed by identity.* If a protocol $P1$ inferred from one program is identical to a protocol $P2$ inferred from another program, then both $P1$ and $P2$ are confirmed by identity.

- *Confirmed by inclusion.* If a protocol $P1$ inferred from one program is included in a protocol $P2$ inferred from another program, then $P1$ is confirmed by inclusion. We consider $P1$ to be included in $P2$ if each state of $P1$ can be mapped to a state of $P2$ so that all outgoing transitions of $P1$'s states are included in the outgoing transitions of $P2$'s states.

Table 4.2 shows the number of confirmed protocols that our analysis infers for the *java.util* package. On average over all programs, 28% of the protocols inferred from one program also appear in the results of another. Hence, at least 28% of the inferred protocols can be considered typical. A manual inspection of the remaining protocols shows that many of them describe common usage patterns, even though they are not confirmed according to the above definition. The results show that a significant part of the protocols that our analysis infers are described as typical API usage patterns.

4.4.6   Performance and Scalability

To show that our analysis scales to large method traces, we measure the execution time required to infer protocols for the Java standard library. Figure 4.10 shows the execution time for analyzing traces depending on the number of runtime events in the traces. The execution time of all but one program behaves linearly with respect to the number of events to analyze. The max-

TABLE **4.2**: Number and Percentage of Confirmed Protocols Inferred for *java.util*

Program	FSMs	Confirmed		
		By identity	By inclusion	Overall
antlr	2	0	0	0%
chart	2	0	0	0%
eclipse	54	3	3	11%
fop	15	2	2	27%
hsqldb	0	0	0	0%
jython	22	2	5	32%
luindex	5	2	0	40%
lusearch	2	2	0	100%
pmd	6	0	1	17%
xalan	10	1	4	50%
Average				28%

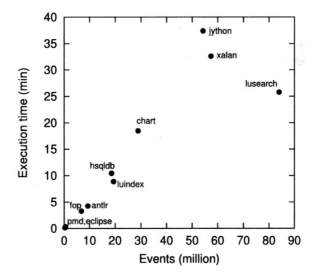

FIGURE 4.10: Runtime of the analysis by number of events in the analyzed trace files.

imum execution time is around 37 minutes (*jython* with 54 million runtime events); the analysis of most method traces requires less than 20 minutes.

The reason for the linearity of the execution times in Figure 4.10 is that our analysis analyzes each collaboration independently from the others. Hence, a larger method trace with more collaborations only influences the analysis execution time linearly.

4.5   Discussion and Applications

This section discusses various issues related to our work and possible applications of it.

4.5.1   Dynamic versus Static Analysis

Our analysis derives protocols of typical API usage by observing the runtime behavior of existing applications. Such a dynamic analysis is limited to the execution paths taken in the analyzed programs, and hence, cannot infer every possible API usage. Static analysis of API source code can infer specifications that cover the entire API, for instance, by considering all non-exceptional paths to be legal [5, 19] or based on known facts about array accesses [44]. In contrast to these static approaches, our analysis focuses on common API usage that actually happens at runtime, ignoring dead code and infrequent program paths. Moreover, dynamic analysis provides precise information about types and aliasing properties of objects, whereas static approaches can only approximate actual behavior.

Achieving a satisfying coverage of typical ways to use an API is a particular challenge for dynamic specification miners. We address it by providing an analysis that scales linearly with the number of runtime events to analyze. As a result, API usage patterns from different programs can be gathered, which together provide a broad view of the API's usage.

Another potential problem is erroneous behavior in the analyzed programs. Given an execution trace containing mostly incorrect sequences of API calls, our analysis obviously infers incorrect protocols. However, our experiments and those reported by others [6] show that executed program paths are mostly correct. By removing infrequent collaborations and weighting each transition in an FSM, the protocols our analysis infers can be considered correct in most cases.

4.5.2   Limitations

The mining techniques presented in Section 4.2 assume certain properties of API usage protocols. By considering object collaborations, our analysis is limited to call sequences that happen within the execution of a method (and then therein called methods if the nesting level is larger than one). Global patterns, such as an API object accessed from several, otherwise unrelated methods, cannot be detected with our tool. However, our results show that many relevant protocols can be found within the scope of methods.

Our definition of collaboration patterns maps all collaborations whose objects play exactly the same roles into a pattern. That is, a single additional method prevents two similar call sequences from ending up in the same protocol. As a result, our results contain numerous protocols with overlapping methods. Finding alternative ways to group collaborations into recurring patterns, or techniques to merge similar protocols remains as future work. Modifications such as an enhanced pattern extraction can be performed with relatively little effort, as our analysis and its implementation are built in a modular way.

4.5.3   Applications

Developers perceive API usage to be difficult, among other reasons, for lack of appropriate documentation that describes how to use an API for a particular task [33]. The protocols produced by our analysis can help developers to understand in which order to call API methods, and hence, are valuable documentation artifacts. Preliminary results on recovering existing API usage documentation show that the inferred specifications can produce such documentation automatically.

Another application of inferred specifications is to use them for error discovery. Several runtime monitoring frameworks [4, 9, 26] check programs for event patterns, such as violations of API usage protocols. Similarly, static analysis can detect incorrectly ordered calls to API methods [7] or erroneous framework interactions [20].

Although our implementation targets Java programs, we consider our analysis to be applicable to other statically typed, object-oriented languages. The analysis does not depend on Java-specific language features. Language-dependent parts of our implementation (for instance, inspecting the type hierarchy to generalize types) could be adapted to other languages with little effort.

4.6   Related Work

4.6.1   Mining of Finite State Machines

There are several approaches to infer finite state machines that describe sequences of method calls. We first present static analyses for that purpose, followed by a description of dynamic approaches.

One static approach is to build several FSMs by assuming two consecutive calls to be legal if they do not cause an exception [41]. In [41], several FSMs are built for one class so that each FSM covers methods that access a particular field, which is assumed to encode the state of the class. A generalization of these ideas is to detect the most general temporal interface of a class that does not lead to an unsafe valuation of the class' fields [5]. Henzinger et al. [19] present a model checking-based approach to derive a "permissive" interface of a class. A temporal interface is permissive if it permits all legal call sequences without leading to a marked error condition, such as an exception. The above approaches differ from ours by statically analyzing API source code, while our analysis mines execution traces of API clients. Furthermore, we obtain protocols of typical usage, instead of FSMs permitting all call sequences that do not violate some error condition. Finally, our protocols can cover several related objects.

Instead of analyzing API source code, Shoham et al. [36] statically mine API clients. At first, traces are collected through abstract interpretation and stored as automata. Afterward, automata are summarized and merged based on their static frequencies. The authors of [36] acknowledge their approach to be limited to smaller programs. Moreover, only one API class is described in each inferred FSM.

There are several dynamic approaches to infer finite state machines. Ammons et al. [6] propose to learn probabilistic FSMs from method traces of C programs. Gabel and Su [15] describe Javert, which extracts FSMs that may involve multiple objects. Javert addresses the scalability problem by scanning method traces for predefined templates and assembling them afterward. In contrast, our analysis reduces complexity by considering small sets of related objects and method calls separately. Protocols inferred with our analysis can describe arbitrary sequence constraints and are not dependent on predefined templates.

Ghezzi et al. [16] synthesize FSMs describing the use of classes by distinguishing modifier methods from observer methods. States correspond to canonical sequences of calls that lead to a particular observable behavior. In contrast to [16], we infer protocols that can involve multiple objects and report on experiments with APIs used by real-world software. Lo and Khoo [24] present a specification mining framework that divides the mining process into trace filtering, event clustering, automata learning, and automata merging. Their work focuses on inferring precise specifications instead of scalability.

Dallmeier et al. [11] extract finite state models for individual objects and merge all models for one class. States are built based on the return values of pure methods of the class. Quante and Koschke [30] infer protocols from dynamic object process graphs, a representation of an object's usage based on an interprocedural control flow graph, which are combined into one protocol per class. In contrast to [11] and [30], our approach considers collaborations of an arbitrary number of objects, instead of building a model around one core object.

4.6.2   Mining of Temporal Rules and Other Specifications

Besides specification miners that produce FSMs, numerous approaches to infer other kinds of rules and recurring patterns from programs have been proposed. Zhong et al. [44] produce graphs that describe dependencies between API method calls based on known facts, such as that arrays must be initialized before writing to them. Acharya et al. [3] mine frequent partial orders of method calls from static traces extracted with a model checker. Henkel et al. [18] infer algebraic specifications for Java container classes, which describe equalities resulting from different sequences of method calls.

Several static rule miners are presented together with bug finding techniques that exploit rarely occurring violations of the inferred rules. Engler et al. [13] statically detect frequently occurring instances of predefined rule templates and check violations of the rules. Li and Zhou [21] mine association rules that relate functions or variables that are often used together and present call paths where those rules may be violated to the user. Weimer and Necula [40] extract pairs of methods that occur together in exception handling paths and use them to identify potential bugs. Thummalapenta and Xie [38] mine sequence association rules in exception handling code and use anomalies to identify bugs. Wasylkowski and Zeller [39] learn conditions that should be fulfilled before passing a particular parameter to a method and search bugs through anomalies. Nguyen et al. [28] present a graph-based miner of usage protocols that can be used to identify bugs and to provide code skeletons showing a usage scenario. The specifications inferred by our analysis could be combined with existing bug-finding techniques. Having a scalable analysis for mining usage patterns that can analyze many different API clients leads to more complete specifications, and hence, reduces the problem of false warnings reported by a checker.

Among the dynamic approaches to infer usage rules, Yang et al. [43] also focus on scalability. Their approach is, similar to [15], based on predefined templates. Salah et al. [34] infer usage scenarios for a class by grouping similar method invocation sequences on instances of this class into canonical sets. Lo and Maoz [25] infer scenario-based specifications and present them hierarchically, which allows users to inspect them at different levels of abstraction.

An alternative source to infer typical programming patterns is the history of version control systems. Livshits and Zimmermann [23] mine association rules from sets of methods that are checked-in together. Similarly, Williams and Hollingsworth [42] infer relations between pairs of methods from version control histories. Liu et al. [22] propose a method for checking the likelihood of API usage patterns using a model checker that counts the number of validations and violations for each pattern. Such an approach could be used to further filter the protocols found by our analysis.

4.6.3   Invariant Inference

Another stream of research that relates to our work is invariant inference. Ernst [14] pioneered dynamic invariant inference. An example of using inferred invariants for error detection is [17]. Inferred invariants hold at a specific point during the execution of a program. In contrast, API usage rules are recurring patterns that can be found in different parts of a program and even different programs.

4.6.4   Other Related Work

The terminology used for some of our mining techniques, collaborations and roles that objects play within them is inspired by work in conceptual modeling [37] and program understanding [32]. The problem of learning temporal patterns from observed events is also relevant for other applications than inferring usage specifications. For example, one can derive FSMs that describe software development processes [10], use FSMs to reduce space when encoding method call sequences [31], or detect attacks to systems by learning system call sequences and checking for anomalies [35].

4.7   Conclusions

Our work addresses the question of how to infer API usage protocols from executing programs in a practical manner. We present a dynamic analysis that extracts short sequences of related method calls from large method traces and summarizes them as FSMs. The inferred FSMs encode typical API method call sequences that can, for example, be used as documentation for programmers learning how to use an API, or to check whether a program violates typical usage rules.

The presented approach contributes by using scalable mining techniques to find specifications of multiple interacting objects. We abstract program executions based on the idea that objects participate in collaborations, where each object plays a certain role. Since each collaboration contains a small number of runtime events that can be analyzed separately, the runtime of our analysis scales linearly with the number of runtime events to analyze.

Bibliography

[1] The AspectJ project. http://www.eclipse.org/aspectj.

[2] Graphviz – graph visualization software. http://www.graphviz.org.

[3] Mithun Acharya, Tao Xie, Jian Pei, and Jun Xu. Mining API patterns as partial orders from source code: from usage scenarios to specifications. In *European Software Engineering Conference and Symposium on Foundations of Software Engineering (ESEC/FSE)*, pages 25–34. ACM Press, 2007.

[4] Chris Allan, Pavel Avgustinov, Aske Simon Christensen, Laurie Hendren, Sascha Kuzins, Ondřej Lhoták, Oege de Moor, Damien Sereni, Ganesh Sittampalam, and Julian Tibble. Adding trace matching with free variables to AspectJ. In *Conference on Object-Oriented Programming, Systems, Languages, and Applications (OOPSLA)*, pages 345–364. ACM Press, 2005.

[5] Rajeev Alur, Pavol Cerný, P. Madhusudan, and Wonhong Nam. Synthesis of interface specifications for Java classes. In *Symposium on Principles of Programming Languages (POPL)*, pages 98–109. ACM Press, 2005.

[6] Glenn Ammons, Rastislav Bodík, and James R. Larus. Mining specifications. In *Symposium on Principles of Programming Languages (POPL)*, pages 4–16. ACM Press, 2002.

[7] Kevin Bierhoff. API Protocol Compliance in Object-Oriented Software. Ph.D. thesis, School of Computer Science, Carnegie Mellon, 2009.

[8] Stephen M. Blackburn, Robin Garner, Chris Hoffmann, Asjad M. Khan, Kathryn S. McKinley, Rotem Bentzur, Amer Diwan, Daniel Feinberg, Daniel Frampton, Samuel Z. Guyer, Martin Hirzel, Antony L. Hosking, Maria Jump, Han Bok Lee, J. Eliot B. Moss, Aashish Phansalkar, Darko Stefanovic, Thomas VanDrunen, Daniel von Dincklage, and Ben Wiedermann. The DaCapo benchmarks: Java benchmarking development and analysis. In *Conference on Object-Oriented Programming, Systems, Languages, and Applications (OOPSLA)*, pages 169–190. ACM Press, 2006.

[9] Feng Chen and Grigore Rosu. MOP: an efficient and generic runtime verification framework. In *Conference on Object-Oriented Programming, Systems, Languages, and Applications (OOPSLA)*, pages 569–588. ACM Press, 2007.

[10] Jonathan E. Cook and Alexander L. Wolf. Discovering models of software processes from event-based data. *ACM Transactions on Software Engineering and Methodology*, 7(3):215–249, 1998.

[11] Valentin Dallmeier, Christian Lindig, Andrzej Wasylkowski, and Andreas Zeller. Mining object behavior with ADABU. In *Workshop on Dynamic Systems Analysis (WODA)*, 2006.

[12] Dawson Engler, Benjamin Chelf, Andy Chou, and Seth Hallem. Checking system rules using system-specific, programmer-written compiler extensions. In *Symposium on Operating Systems Design and Implementation (OSDI)*, pages 1–16. ACM Press, 2000.

[13] Dawson Engler, David Yu Chen, Seth Hallem, Andy Chou, and Benjamin Chelf. Bugs as deviant behavior: a general approach to inferring errors in systems code. In *Symposium on Operating Systems Principles*, pages 57–72. ACM Press, 2001.

[14] Michael Dean Ernst. Dynamically Discovering Likely Program Invariants. Ph.D. thesis, University of Washington, 2000.

[15] Mark Gabel and Zhendong Su. Javert: fully automatic mining of general temporal properties from dynamic traces. In *Symposium on Foundations of Software Engineering (FSE)*, pages 339–349. ACM Press, 2008.

[16] Carlo Ghezzi, Andrea Mocci, and Mattia Monga. Synthesizing intensional behavior models by graph transformation. In *International Conference on Software Engineering (ICSE)*, pages 430–440, 2009.

[17] Sudheendra Hangal and Monica S. Lam. Tracking down software bugs using automatic anomaly detection. In *International Conference on Software Engineering (ICSE)*, pages 291–301. ACM Press, 2002.

[18] Johannes Henkel, Christoph Reichenbach, and Amer Diwan. Discovering documentation for Java container classes. *IEEE Transactions on Software Engineering*, 33(8):526–543, 2007.

[19] Thomas A. Henzinger, Ranjit Jhala, and Rupak Majumdar. Permissive interfaces. In *European Software Engineering Conference and Symposium on Foundations of Software Engineering (ESEC/FSE)*, pages 31–40. ACM Press, 2005.

[20] Ciera Jaspan and Jonathan Aldrich. Checking framework interactions with relationships. In *European Conference on Object Oriented Programming*, 2009.

[21] Zhenmin Li and Yuanyuan Zhou. PR-Miner: automatically extracting implicit programming rules and detecting violations in large software code. In *European Software Engineering Conference and Symposium on Foundations of Software Engineering (ESEC/FSE)*, pages 306–315. ACM Press, 2005.

[22] Chang Liu, En Ye, and Debra J. Richardson. Software library usage pattern extraction using a software model checker. In *International Conference on Automated Software Engineering (ASE)*, pages 301–304. IEEE, 2006.

[23] V. Benjamin Livshits and Thomas Zimmermann. DynaMine: finding common error patterns by mining software revision histories. In *European Software Engineering Conference and Symposium on Foundations of Software Engineering (ESEC/FSE)*, pages 296–305. ACM Press, 2005.

[24] David Lo and Siau-Cheng Khoo. SMArTIC: towards building an accurate, robust and scalable specification miner. In *Symposium on Foundations of Software Engineering (FSE)*, pages 265–275, 2006.

[25] David Lo and Shahar Maoz. Mining hierarchical scenario-based specifications. In *International Conference on Automated Software Engineering (ASE)*, 2009.

[26] Michael C. Martin, V. Benjamin Livshits, and Monica S. Lam. Finding application errors and security flaws using PQL: a program query language. In *Conference on Object-Oriented Programming, Systems, Languages, and Applications (OOPSLA)*, pages 365–383. ACM Press, 2005.

[27] Anders Møller. http://www.brics.dk/automaton.

[28] Tung Thanh Nguyen, Hoan Anh Nguyen, Nam H. Pham, Jafar M. Al-Kofahi, and Tien N. Nguyen. Graph-based mining of multiple object usage patterns. In *European Software Engineering Conference and Symposium on the Foundations of Software Engineering (ESEC/FSE)*, pages 383–392. ACM, 2009.

[29] Michael Pradel and Thomas R. Gross. Automatic generation of object usage specifications from large method traces. In *International Conference on Automated Software Engineering (ASE)*, pages 371–382, 2009.

[30] Jochen Quante and Rainer Koschke. Dynamic protocol recovery. In *Working Conference on Reverse Engineering (WCRE)*, pages 219–228. IEEE, 2007.

[31] Steven P. Reiss and Manos Renieris. Encoding program executions. In *International Conference on Software Engineering (ICSE)*, pages 221–230. IEEE, 2001.

[32] Tamar Richner and Stphane Ducasse. Using dynamic information for the iterative recovery of collaborations and roles. In *International Conference on Software Maintenance (ICSM)*, pages 34–43. IEEE, 2002.

[33] Martin P. Robillard. What makes APIs hard to learn? Answers from developers. *IEEE Software*, 26(6):27–34, 2009.

[34] Maher Salah, Trip Denton, Spiros Mancoridis, Ali Shokoufandeh, and Filippos I. Vokolos. Scenariographer: a tool for reverse engineering class usage scenarios from method invocation sequences. In *Conference on Software Maintenance (ICSM)*, pages 155–164. IEEE, 2005.

[35] R. Sekar, M. Bendre, D. Dhurjati, and P. Bollineni. A fast automaton-based method for detecting anomalous program behaviors. In *Symposium on Security and Privacy (SSP)*, pages 144–155. IEEE, 2001.

[36] Sharon Shoham, Eran Yahav, Stephen Fink, and Marco Pistoia. Static specification mining using automata-based abstractions. In *International Symposium on Software Testing and Analysis (ISSTA)*, pages 174–184. ACM Press, 2007.

[37] Friedrich Steimann. On the representation of roles in object-oriented and conceptual modelling. *Data & Knowledge Engineering*, 35(1):83–106, 2000.

[38] Suresh Thummalapenta and Tao Xie. Mining exception-handling rules as sequence association rules. In *International Conference on Software Engineering (ICSE)*, pages 496–506, 2009.

[39] Andrzej Wasylkowski and Andreas Zeller. Mining temporal specifications from object usage. In *International Conference on Automated Software Engineering (ASE)*, 2009.

[40] Westley Weimer and George C. Necula. Mining temporal specifications for error detection. In *Conference on Tools and Algorithms for the Construction and Analysis of Systems (TACAS)*, pages 461–476. Springer, 2005.

[41] John Whaley, Michael C. Martin, and Monica S. Lam. Automatic extraction of object-oriented component interfaces. In *Symposium on Software Testing and Analysis (ISSTA)*, pages 218–228. ACM Press, 2002.

[42] Chadd C. Williams and Jeffrey K. Hollingsworth. Recovering system specific rules from software repositories. In *Workshop on Mining Software Repositories (MSR)*. ACM Press, 2005.

[43] Jinlin Yang, David Evans, Deepali Bhardwaj, Thirumalesh Bhat, and Manuvir Das. Perracotta: mining temporal API rules from imperfect traces. In *International Conference on Software Engineering (ICSE)*, pages 282–291. ACM Press, 2006.

[44] Hao Zhong, Lu Zhang, and Hong Mei. Inferring specifications of object oriented APIs from API source code. In *Asia-Pacific Software Engineering Conference (APSEC)*, pages 221–228. IEEE, 2008.

Chapter 5

Static API Specification Mining: Exploiting Source Code Model Checking

Mithun Acharya

Industrial Software Systems, ABB Corporate Research

Tao Xie

Department of Computer Science, North Carolina State University

5.1 Introduction

As computers penetrate every aspect of our daily life, reliability of software systems is becoming increasingly important. Software reliability is the probability of failure-free software operation for a specified period of time in a specified environment [46]. A software system interacts with its environment (memory, graphics card, network, operating system, other software, etc.) through Application Program Interfaces (APIs[1]). Using these APIs correctly often needs to follow certain programming rules, i.e., API specifications. API specifications specify the required checks (on API input parameters and return values) and other APIs to be invoked before (preconditions) and after (postconditions) an API call.

We identify two types of API specifications – preconditions and postconditions.[2] Preconditions for a given API specify the conditions required before the API is invoked. Preconditions specify the required conditional checks on API input parameters and other APIs to be invoked before invoking the API. For example, the POSIX standard [7] states that the first parameter of the `bind` API, the *socket* identifier, should come from the `socket` API and should be non-negative. Postconditions for a given API specify the conditions required after the API is invoked. Postconditions specify the required conditional checks on API return values and other APIs to be invoked after invoking the API. For example, the return value of the `bind` API should be non-negative and the socket identifier should be `closed` along all paths. Postconditions also specify the correct handling of errors incurred after API invocations. Incorrect usage of APIs (in short, API violations) can lead to security and robustness problems [53], two primary hindrances for the reliable operation of a software system. Hence, for a software system, adherence to the specifications, which govern the correct usage of APIs used by the system to interact with its environment, is paramount for software reliability.

Software testing [4, 5] and more recently, static verification [1–3, 6, 13] have been adopted by the industry to assure software reliability. However, there are several limitations with these approaches. Software testing approaches [28,32,36,38,44,45,52,54,57] typically focus on issues such as correctness of functionality and performance and are often insufficient for assuring the absence of API violations. Most of these approaches consider a target software system as a black box and conduct testing with random or extreme

---

[1]We overload the term API to mean both a set of related library procedures or a single library procedure in the set – the actual meaning should be evident from the context.

[2]Pre/postconditions have enforcement points in a program. Enforcement points are program statements where a pre/postcondition is coded or programmed. For example, the enforcement point for the precondition "return value of `malloc` should be checked for `NULL` value" is the point in the program where the memory pointer returned by `malloc` is explicitly compared against `NULL`. We do not explicitly distinguish between pre/postconditions and their enforcement points – the distinction should be evident from the context.

input values. However, black-box testing approaches cannot easily generate values for testing such as incorrect input values and error return values for APIs. Specifications, when known, can be formally written for third-party APIs and statically verified against a software system. The last decade has witnessed great advances in assuring high software reliability through static verification [13, 15, 20, 21, 23, 26, 27, 29, 33]. Unfortunately, *API specifications are not well documented by the API developers and are often not known to programmers who reuse third-party APIs in the first place. API specifications cut across procedural boundaries and an attempt to infer these specifications by manual inspection of source code (API client code that uses the APIs) is often inefficient and inaccurate.*

In this chapter, we describe a static specification mining framework to address the aforementioned problems faced by programmers in reusing third-party APIs. When API specifications are not known, to automatically mine them from source code (API client code), we present a framework to generate static traces from source code. There are five main challenges in generating static traces and mining specifications from them. First, as API specifications cut across procedural boundaries, the trace generation should be inter-procedural. Second, API specifications may reflect control-flow properties (such as "API b should always precede API a"), data-flow properties (such as "first parameter of API a should always come from API b"), or both. Third, because of the ordering constraints present in API specifications, the trace generation should be flow-sensitive (ordering among program statements should be respected) and the mining should consider the ordering among APIs. Fourth, because of the need for value tracking between API call sites and their corresponding pre/postcondition enforcement points, the trace generation should be path-sensitive (at conditional branches, the trace generation should depend on the branch predicate). Finally, for mining API *error-handling* (proper handling of errors incurred after API invocation) specifications, the static trace generation and mining should be adapted to take into account the fact that programmers often make mistakes in error-handling code [14,31,56,60]. Hence, we need techniques to generate and distinguish error traces (i.e., static traces with API errors along API error paths) and normal traces (i.e., static traces, without API errors), even when the API error behaviors are not known *a priori*. To generate static traces related to APIs of interest, our framework adapts *push-down* model checking [26], meeting the preceding requirements. We then present novel applications of data mining techniques on the generated static traces for specification mining.

The remainder of this chapter is organized as follows. Section 5.2 describes our framework for automatically generating static traces from program source code for mining specifications. Section 5.3 describes how we adapt our trace generation and mining framework for mining API error-handling specifications. In these sections, we also share our experiences of applying our framework on several popular open-source packages to mine API specifications and detect violations, without requiring any user input. Finally, Section 5.4 concludes this chapter.

5.2   Static Trace Generation for Mining Specifications

In this section, we describe our framework [8] for mining specifications automatically by analyzing the API client code. To mine specifications, the framework presented in this section generates static traces related to APIs of interest, directly from source code (API client code). Frequent API patterns are then mined from the generated static traces. We identify two types of API patterns – patterns that are specifications and patterns that are usage *scenarios* (see Section 5.2.1 for the definition of a scenario). Unlike specifications (such as "the `bind` API should be preceded by the `socket` API"), which have to be satisfied by a program to be free from violations, usage scenarios are API patterns specific to a given programming task (such as "*refreshing* a user-interface window" or "displaying a drop-down menu"); usage scenarios are not programming rules.

API patterns are often not documented by the API developers. Hence, it is difficult for the system developers to effectively or correctly reuse these APIs during system development or verify the correct usage of these APIs after the system has been built, necessitating automated specification mining. Our framework mines API patterns from static traces as *partial orders* (see Section 5.2.2). We adapt a model checker to generate inter-procedural control-flow-sensitive static traces related to the APIs of interest. In Section 5.3, we show how our framework is adapted for mining API error-handling specifications. Next, we describe the motivation for mining API patterns as partial orders.

Previous approaches have mined likely API patterns from software systems that reuse APIs. Some approaches [39–41, 43, 60, 62] exploit the static program information extracted from system source code, whereas other approaches [11, 12, 64] exploit the dynamic program information extracted from system executions, which require setup of runtime environments and availability of sufficient system tests. API patterns mined by most of these previous approaches are in the form of frequent association rules, itemsets, or subsequences. Association rules [9, 41, 43] characterize pairs of API calls that are often used together without considering their orders. Frequent itemsets [30, 39] characterize sets of API calls that are often used together without considering their orders. Frequent subsequences [58, 63] characterize sequences of API calls that are often used together while considering their orders. Although these mined API patterns have been shown to be useful to some extent, they cannot completely capture some useful orderings shared by APIs, especially when multiple APIs are involved across different procedures.

To address the issues faced by previous approaches in mining API patterns, we develop a framework to automatically mine frequent partial orders among user-specified APIs, directly from the source code (API client code). Frequent partial orders summarize important ordering information from sequential patterns. Frequent partial orders provide more general and more concise API ordering information than the sequential patterns. The mined partial orders among APIs can assist the correct and effective API reuse by the programmers. This section describes the following main steps required for generating static traces from source code and mining API specifications and usage scenarios from the generated static traces.

Static API Trace Generation: We adapt a model checker to generate inter-procedural control-flow-sensitive static traces related to the APIs of interest. Our framework allows mining of open-source systems that reuse the APIs of interest without requiring environment setup for system executions or availability of sufficient system tests.

Scenario Extraction: A single static trace from the model checker might involve several API scenarios, being often interspersed. We present an algorithm, which considers the data flow between program statements in terms of shared variables, to separate different scenarios from a given trace, so that each scenario can be fed separately to the miner.

API Partial-Order Mining: We present novel applications of a miner in mining partial orders among APIs from static traces. The mined partial orders provide important, useful API ordering information that is not provided by patterns mined by previous approaches.

We describe an implementation of our framework by adapting a publicly available model checker called MOPS [20] and adopting a miner called FRECPO [47]. We apply our framework on 72 clients of X11 with 208 KLOC in total and compare our framework with an existing dynamic specification miner. Our results highlight the unique benefits of our framework and show that the extracted API partial orders are useful in assisting effective API reuse and checking.

The remainder of this section is structured as follows. Section 5.2.1 starts with an example that motivates our framework. Section 5.2.2 introduces the formal framework for mining API partial orders and describes the various components in our framework in detail. Section 5.2.3 presents the implementation details. Section 5.2.4 reports our experience of comparing our framework with an existing dynamic specification miner.

5.2.1 Example

This section illustrates a partial order that our framework extracts for a given set of related APIs, directly from the source code. Figure 5.1(a) shows a simple code snippet in C that uses APIs from a header file <abcdef.h>, namely,

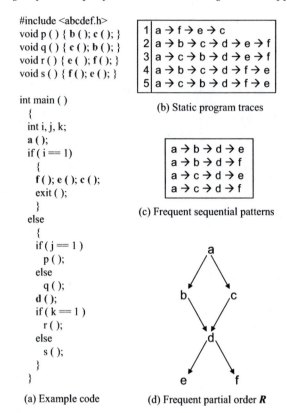

```
#include <abcdef.h>
void p ( ) { b ( ); c ( ); }
void q ( ) { c ( ); b ( ); }
void r ( ) { e ( ); f ( ); }
void s ( ) { f ( ); e ( ); }

int main ( )
 {
 int i, j, k;
 a ( );
 if ( i == 1 )
  {
  f ( ); e ( ); c ( );
  exit ( );
  }
 else
  {
  if ( j == 1 )
   p ( );
  else
   q ( );
  d ( );
  if ( k == 1 )
   r ( );
  else
   s ( );
  }
 }
```

(a) Example code

1 a → f → e → c
2 a → b → c → d → e → f
3 a → c → b → d → e → f
4 a → b → c → d → f → e
5 a → c → b → d → f → e

(b) Static program traces

a → b → d → e
a → b → d → f
a → c → d → e
a → c → d → f

(c) Frequent sequential patterns

(d) Frequent partial order **R**

FIGURE 5.1: A simple example illustrating our framework for mining partial orders from static traces.

a, b, c, d, e, and f. Before proceeding further, we define the terms path, trace, and scenario. A control-flow path exists between two program points if the latter is reachable from the former through some set of control-flow edges, i.e., Control Flow Graph (CFG) edges. For a given path, a trace is the print of all statements that exist along that path. Two APIs are said to be *related* if they manipulate at least one (or more) common variable(s). A *scenario* is a set of related APIs in a given trace. A given trace can have multiple scenarios. Suppose that a programmer wants to investigate whether there are some ordering patterns among the APIs from <abcdef.h>.

Figure 5.1(b) shows five program traces involving these APIs along different possible control-flow paths in the program. Given a support threshold *min_sup*, a sequential pattern is a sequence *s* that appears as the subsequence of at least *min_sup* sequences. For example, let *min_sup* be 4. The four sequences shown in Figure 5.1(c) are sequential patterns since they are subsequences of Sequences 2, 3, 4, and 5 (all except a → f → e → c). Sequential patterns capture the frequent call patterns shared by program traces. However, the four sequential patterns cannot completely capture the ordering shared by APIs a, b, c, d, e, and f. It is easy to see that the partial order R shown in Figure 5.1(d) is shared by the four program traces. We can make the following interesting observations from the partial order R:

- The partial order R summarizes the four sequential patterns: the four sequential patterns are paths in the partial order R. Note that the only sequences with a support greater than 4 are a $\rightarrow$ f, a $\rightarrow$ e, and a $\rightarrow$ c, each with a support of 5.

- The partial order R provides more information about the ordering than the sequential patterns. For example, R indicates that b and c are called in any order, but often before d. Hence the mined partial order R effectively summarizes the sequential patterns among APIs and provides more general and more concise API ordering information to the programmers.

- If the min_sup is sufficiently high, the partial order provides strong hints on likely specifications that should be true for the correct operation of the program. For example, if the partial order R were mined from traces with a very high support, then with high confidence, "d should always follow a along any path" is a specification that should be satisfied by all programs using the APIs a and d.

This example motivates the idea of using frequent partial orders to effectively summarize sequential patterns among APIs and provide more general and more concise ordering information to the programmers. However, there are many issues not obvious in the motivating example, and these issues shall be addressed throughout the section. (1) In general, if T is the set of all traces along all execution paths in the program, then T is an uncomputable set. Furthermore, the length of a trace can be infinite. (2) Along some program paths, APIs might not be used correctly. (3) A given trace might have more than one scenario involving APIs from <abcdef.h>, being all jumbled up (for example, a $\rightarrow$ a $\rightarrow$ b $\rightarrow$ c could be two separate scenarios, a $\rightarrow$ b and a $\rightarrow$ c, instead of one). Each scenario has to be extracted separately before being fed to the miner. We address these issues in the next section, where we present our framework for mining partial orders from static program traces.

5.2.2 Framework

In this section, we formalize the notions introduced in the previous section. We define partial order, total order, and frequent closed partial order (FCPO) [47], and formalize the problem of mining frequent closed partial orders from program traces. After the necessary foundations have been laid, we present the various components of our framework. We conclude this section by providing a complexity analysis of the different components in our framework.

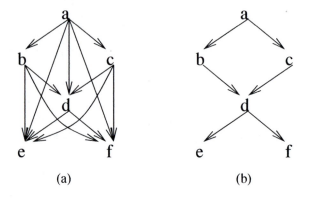

(a)   (b)

FIGURE 5.2: (a) A partial order and (b) its transitive reduction.

5.2.2.1   Partial and Total Order

A *partial order* is a binary relation that is reflexive, antisymmetric, and transitive. A *total order* (or called linear order) is a partial order R such that for any two items x and y, if $x \neq y$ then either $R(x, y)$ or $R(y, x)$ holds.

A partial order R can be expressed in a Directed Acyclic Graph (DAG): the items are the vertices in the graph and $x \to y$ is an edge if and only if $(x, y) \in R$ and $x \neq y$. We also write an edge $x \to y$ as (x, y) or xy. For example, Figure 5.2(a) shows a partial order R, which has 13 edges.

Since a partial order is transitive, some edges can be derived from the others and thus are redundant. For example, in Figure 5.2(a), edge $a \to d$ is redundant given edges $a \to b$ and $b \to d$. Generally, an edge $x \to y$ is *redundant* if there is a path from x to y and this path does not contain the edge. For a partial order R, the *transitive reduction* of R can be drawn in a *Hasse diagram*: for $(x, y) \in R$ and $x \neq y$, x is positioned higher than y; edge $x \to y$ is drawn if and only if the edge is not redundant. Figure 5.2(b) shows the transitive reduction of the same partial order R in Figure 5.2(a). The transitive reduction has only six edges. For an order R, the transitive reduction may have much fewer edges.

We draw a partial order in a Hasse diagram, i.e., its transitive reduction, and omit the isolated vertices. For example, Figure 5.3 shows four partial orders R_1, R_2, R_3, and R_4; R_1 is further a total order.

Let V be a set of items, which serves as the domain of our string database. A *string* defines a global order on a subset of V. A string can be written as $s = x_1 \cdots x_l$, where $x_1, \ldots, x_l \in V$. l denotes the *length* of string s, i.e., $len(s) = l$. For strings $s = x_1 \cdots x_l$ and $s' = y_1 \cdots y_m$, s denotes a *super-string* of s' and s' denotes a *sub-string* of s if (1) $m \leq l$ and (2) there exist integers $1 \leq i_1 < \cdots < i_m \leq l$ such that $x_{i_j} = y_j$ ($1 \leq j \leq m$). We also say s contains s'. For a string database SDB (set of strings), the *support* of a string

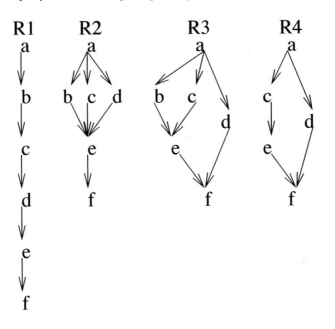

FIGURE 5.3: Four orders $R_1 \supset R_2 \supset R_3 \supset R_4$.

s, denoted by $sup(s)$, is the number of strings in SDB that are super-strings of s.

The *transitive closure* of a binary relation R is the minimal transitive relation R' that contains R. Thus, $(x, y) \in R$ provided that there exist $z_1, \ldots, z_n$ such that $(x, z_1) \in R$, $(z_n, y) \in R$, and $(z_i, z_{i+1}) \in R$ for all $1 \leq i < n$.

The total order defined by string $s = x_1 \cdots x_l$ can be written in the *transitive closure* of s, denoted by $C(s) = \{(x_i, x_j) | 1 \leq i < j \leq l\}$. Note that, in the transitive closure, we omit the trivial pairs (x_i, x_i). For example, for string $s = abcd$, $len(s) = 4$. The transitive closure is $C(s) = \{(a, b), (a, c), (a, d), (b, c), (b, d), (c, d)\}$. Here, we omit the trivial pairs (a, a), (b, b), (c, c), and (d, d).

The *order containment relation* is defined as, for two partial orders R_1 and R_2, if $R_1 \subset R_2$, then R_1 is said to be *weaker* than R_2, and R_2 is *stronger* than R_1. Intuitively, a partially ordered set (or poset for short) satisfying R_2 will also satisfy R_1. For example, in Figure 5.3, $R_4 \subset R_3 \subset R_2 \subset R_1$. Note that R_4 covers fewer items than the other three partial orders. Trivially, we can add the missing items into the DAG as isolated vertices so that every DAG covers the same set of items. To keep the DAG simple and easy to read, we omit such isolated items.

5.2.2.2 Frequent Closed Partial Orders (FCPO)

A *string database SDB* is a multiset of strings. For a partial order R, a string s is said to *support* R if $R \subseteq C(s)$. The *support of R in SDB*, denoted by $sup(R)$, is the number of strings in SDB that support R. Given a minimum support threshold min_sup, a partial order R is *frequent* if $sup(R) \geq min\_sup$. Following the related definitions and the order containment relation, we have the following result: for a string database SDB and partial orders R and R' such that $R' \subset R$, we have $sup(R') \geq sup(R)$. Therefore, if R is frequent, then R' is also frequent. To avoid the triviality, instead of reporting all frequent partial orders, we can mine the representative ones only.

Let us consider the program traces in Figure 5.1 again. The four sequential patterns can be regarded as frequent partial orders, which are supported by Traces 2, 3, 4, and 5. As discussed before, given that the partial order R is also supported by Strings 2, 3, 4, and 5, the four sequential patterns as frequent partial orders are redundant. There does not exist another partial order R' such that R' is stronger than R in Figure 5.1 and is also supported by Strings 2, 3, 4, and 5. In other words, R is the strongest one among all frequent partial orders supported by Strings 2, 3, 4, and 5. Thus, the partial order R is not redundant and can be used as the representative of the frequent partial orders supported by Strings 2, 3, 4, and 5. Technically, R is a frequent closed partial order.

A partial order R is *closed* in a string database SDB if there exists no partial order $R' \supset R$ such that $sup(R) = sup(R')$. A partial order R is a *frequent closed partial order* if it is both frequent and closed. We next formalize the process of mining FCPOs from program traces.

5.2.2.3   Formalizing FCPO Mining from Program Traces

Informally, our framework mines FCPOs for the APIs specified by the user from the program source code. Our framework addresses the following problems:

- Generating sequences of API invocations along different program paths. These sequences are stored as a string multiset database. However, generating all traces along all execution paths is an uncomputable problem and a trace can be of infinite size.

- Finding the complete set of frequent closed partial orders from the API sequence database with respect to a minimum support threshold min_sup.

Formally, let Σ be the set of valid program statements in the given program source code. Let $\mathcal{A}$ be the set of APIs specified by the user. A *trace* $t \in \Sigma^*$, a sequence of statements executed by a path p, is *feasible* if path p is feasible in the program. Let $T \subset \Sigma^*$ be the set of all feasible traces in the program. To simplify the definitions, let us assume that all APIs in $\mathcal{A}$ are empty methods, do not take any arguments, and return void.[3] For a given $t \in T$, let $A(t) \in \mathcal{A}^*$

---

[3] By assuming that APIs are empty methods that do not take any arguments and return void, we restrict the program statements related to APIs from $\mathcal{A}$ in the program to only

be the API invocations along the trace t expressed as a string. $A(t)$ can be an empty string if t does not have any invocation of APIs from the set $\mathcal{A}$. Let $T' \subseteq T$ be the set of all feasible traces such that if $t \in T'$, $A(t)$ is not empty. However, the set T' is uncomputable and $t \in T'$ can be of infinite size. Our framework initially does the following steps:

- Generate the computable approximation of T' from the program and extract $A(t)$ for all t in the approximate set. The extracted $A(t)$'s are stored in a string database, say, V.

- Extract the set of FCPOs among APIs in $\mathcal{A}$ from V, with respect to a minimum threshold *min_sup*.

The high-level overview of our framework is shown in Figure 5.4. Our framework has three main components: trace generator, scenario extractor, and specification miner. The user specifies a set of APIs from which *Triggers* (explained in Section 5.2.2.4) are generated. The Triggers are then used with push-down model checking for trace generation. This process also recommends more APIs related to the user-specified set of APIs. The scenario extractor extracts various API scenarios (explained in Section 5.2.2.5) from the traces. The specification miner feeds the extracted scenarios to a FCPO miner [47] to output specifications and usage scenarios as partial orders. Each process is described in detail in the subsections below. We first explain the process of trace generation.

5.2.2.4 Trace Generation

We first briefly summarize the Push-Down Model Checking (PDMC) process [18, 26], which we adapt for trace generation. To generate API invocation sequences along different program paths, we introduce the concept of *Triggers*. Finally, we discuss the soundness of our framework.

Push-Down Model Checking (PDMC): Informally, given a property represented using a Finite State Machine (FSM), PDMC [26] checks to see if there is any path in the program that puts the FSM in its final state. For example, if the property FSM is specified as shown in Figure 5.5, PDMC reports all program paths in which a is followed by either b or c. PDMC models the program as a Push Down Automata (PDA) and the property as an FSM. PDMC then combines the program PDA and the property FSM to generate a new PDA; the new PDA is then model checked to see if any *final configuration* in the PDA is reachable. A *configuration* of a PDA **P** is a pair $c = \langle q, \omega \rangle$, where q is the state in which the PDA is in and ω is a string of stack symbols in the PDA stack at that state. A configuration is

---

direct API invocations. If this is not the case, for a given API, say a, we have to consider all the program statements that affect and are affected by a through some data-flow dependencies. For example, if we have `i = a(j); if (i != NULL ) b(i);`, then the program statements `if (i != NULL)` and `b(i)` are related to a. We relax this assumption to a certain extent later in the section by incorporating simple data-flow analysis.

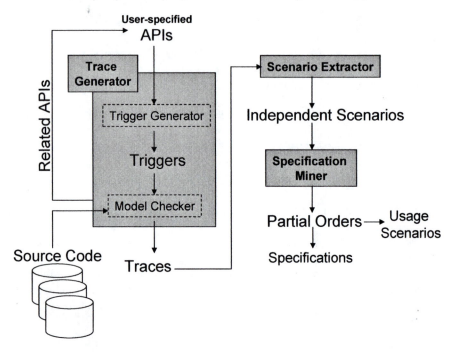

FIGURE 5.4: Our framework for mining usage scenarios and specifications.

said to be a final configuration if q belongs to the set of final states in the FSM. If a final configuration is reachable, PDMC outputs the paths (in the program) that cause the resultant PDA to reach this final configuration. We next describe our *Triggers* technique that adapts PDMC to generate API invocation sequences in a program.

Triggers: Our goal is to generate the set $T' \subseteq T$ from the program and extract $A(t)$ for all $t \in T'$, $A(t) \in \mathcal{A}^*$, $\mathcal{A} = \{a_1, a_2, a_3, ..., a_k\}$, where $a_i, 1 \leq i \leq k$, are the APIs specified by the user. Let us assume that we give the FSM shown in Figure 5.6 to PDMC to be verified against a program $\mathcal{P}$. The FSM in Figure 5.6 accepts any string of the form $e(\sum_{i=1,2,...,k} a_i)^* x$, where e and x are any two points in the program. Given this Trigger FSM, PDMC outputs all program paths that begin with e and end with x in the program. By setting e as the entry point of the main routine and x as any exit point in the program, we can collect sequences of API along paths that begin at the main routine and end at exit points.

Let $B \subseteq \Sigma^*$ be all sequences of program statements in $\mathcal{P}$ that put the FSM in Figure 5.6, say $\mathbb{F}$, in its final state. As defined earlier, $T \subset \Sigma^*$ is the set of all feasible traces in the program, in this case, $\mathcal{P}$. If $T \cap B = \phi$, then the final state of $\mathbb{F}$ is never reached. Since B and T are arbitrary languages and T is uncomputable, deciding if $T \cap B = \phi$ is an undecidable problem.

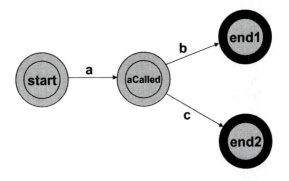

FIGURE 5.5: A property FSM where end1 and end2 are final states.

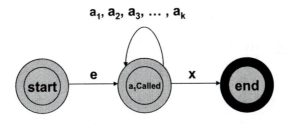

FIGURE 5.6: Trigger FSM that accepts the regular language $e(a_1 + a_2 + ... + a_k)^* x$.

Hence PDMC restricts the form of B and T by modeling B to be a regular language accepted by $\mathbb{F}$ ($B = L(\mathbb{F})$), and T as a context-free language accepted by a PDA $\mathbb{P}$ (of program $\mathcal{P}$). In general, we have $T \subseteq L(\mathbb{P})$, which then implies $T \cap B \subseteq L(\mathbb{F}) \cap L(\mathbb{P})$. Consequently, if $L(\mathbb{F}) \cap L(\mathbb{P})$ is empty, $T \cap B$ is definitely empty. However, if $L(\mathbb{F}) \cap L(\mathbb{P})$ is not empty, $T \cap B$ could either be empty or not. Since $L(\mathbb{F})$ is a regular language and $L(\mathbb{P})$ is a context-free language, $L(\mathbb{F}) \cap L(\mathbb{P})$ can be captured by a PDA, say **P**, and hence the final state of $\mathbb{F}$ is reached if and only if the PDA **P** accepts the empty language. There are efficient algorithms to determine if the language accepted by the PDA is empty [35]. Once **P** is constructed, PDMC checks to see if any final configuration is reachable in **P**. Chen and Wagner [20] use the preceding analysis to adapt PDMC for lightweight property checking. We use the preceding analysis for static trace generation. We call the FSMs such as the one used in Figure 5.6 as Triggers. By using Triggers, we have achieved two purposes:

- We have produced T_{ex}, the set of traces (in the program) that begin with e and end with x instead of $T' \subseteq T$.

- The knowledge of $\mathcal{A} = \{a_1, a_2, a_3, ..., a_k\}$ allows us to extract $A(t)$ from any $t \in T_{ex}$.

Soundness: The consequence of using a context-free language for T introduces imprecision but retains the soundness of analysis. Infeasible traces might occur (being incomplete) because of data-flow insensitivity of the PDMC process, but all the program traces that put the FSM in its final state are reported (being sound). Since determining if $T \cap B = \phi$ is undecidable, no tool can be sound and complete at the same time. Consequently, there could be some infeasible API sequences in the database being fed to the FCPO miner. For example, in Figure 5.1, the variable i might never assume value 1; therefore, the trace $a \to f \to e \to c$ is infeasible in the program. Also, along some feasible paths, the implicit API ordering rules might be violated and APIs could be used incorrectly (producing buggy traces with actual errors). Hence the API sequence database might contain certain wrong API sequences. However, we assume that most programs that we analyze are well written. Hence, we expect only few feasible paths to be buggy, if at all. We expect to handle infeasible and buggy traces by selecting an appropriate *min_sup* value. The traces generated by PDMC with Triggers can still be of infinite size in the presence of loops. We address this problem in Section 5.2.3.

5.2.2.5   Scenario Extraction

A single static trace from the model checker might involve several API usage scenarios, being often interspersed. We have to separate different usage scenarios from a given trace, so that each scenario can be fed separately to the miner. A naive algorithm for scenario extraction would be to remove all duplicate APIs in a given trace and feed the resulting API sequence as a single scenario to the miner. But most traces have multiple scenarios around the same set of APIs. Furthermore, these different scenarios represent different usage patterns among the API set. The naive algorithm of deleting duplicates leads to loss of API ordering information and a drastic decrease in the number of scenarios fed to the miner.

We develop a refined scenario-extraction algorithm based on identifying *producer-consumer* chains (PC-chain; return value *produced* by one API is *consumed* as an input parameter by another API to form a chain) among APIs in the trace. The algorithm (henceforth called the *PC-Chain* algorithm) is based on the assumption that related APIs have some form of data dependencies between them in the form of shared variables. In short, the PC-Chain algorithm first identifies PC-chains among APIs in traces and outputs them as scenarios. Isolated partial orders are then constructed among APIs in related PC-chains. Finally, partial orders are computed between heads of PC-chains, and these partial orders form partial order clusters. As an example, consider three sets of APIs (a, b, c, d), (e, f, g), and (h, i, j). The first API in each set produces a value that is consumed by the remaining APIs in the set. Figure 5.7(a) shows two traces produced by the model checker. The APIs are all interspersed and there are three scenarios in each trace. The arrows in Figure 5.7(a) show the PC-chains among related APIs. Figure 5.7(b) shows six different scenarios extracted from two traces. Figure 5.7(c) summarizes the

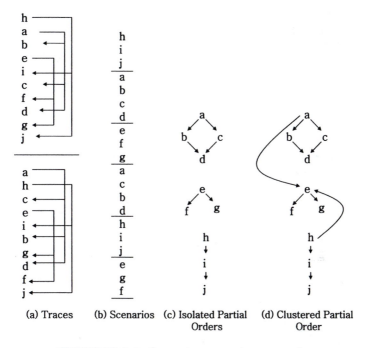

(a) Traces   (b) Scenarios   (c) Isolated Partial Orders   (d) Clustered Partial Order

FIGURE 5.7: Scenario extraction example.

six different API scenarios compactly as three isolated partial orders. Finally, Figure 5.7(d) merges the isolated partial orders into one big partial order. The algorithm outlined in Figure 5.8 summarizes the PC-Chain scenario extraction algorithm.

5.2.2.6   Specification Mining

The independent scenarios from the scenario extractor form the input to the specification miner. The specification miner uses a partial-order miner called FRECPO [47] to mine partial orders among independent scenarios. The partial orders are produced as either usage scenarios (lower support) or specifications (higher support). To mine the complete set of FCPOs, FRECPO [47] searches a set enumeration tree of transitive reductions of partial orders in a depth-first manner. In principle, a partial order can be uniquely represented as the set of edges in its transitive reduction. Moreover, all edges in a set can be sorted in the dictionary order and they can be written as a list. Therefore, we can enumerate all partial orders in the dictionary order. A set enumeration tree of partial orders can be formed: for orders R_1 and R_2, R_1 is an ancestor of R_2, and R_2 is a descendant of R_1 in the tree if and only if the list of edges in R_1 is a prefix of the list of edges in R_2. By a depth-first search of the set enumeration tree of transitive reductions of partial orders, FRECPO does not miss any frequent partial order.

Input: static traces
Output: partial order clusters
Identify all producers;
foreach producer **do**
        Identify consumers;
        Construct PC-chain;
        Output PC-chain as a scenario;
end
Construct isolated partial orders from scenarios;
Collect the head APIs from isolated partial orders;
Construct partial order among head APIs to form partial order clusters;
return partial order clusters

FIGURE 5.8: The **PC-Chain** algorithm for scenario extraction.

To be efficient and scalable, FRECPO prunes the futile branches and narrows the search space as much as possible. Basically, three types of techniques are used. First, FRECPO prunes infrequent items, edges, and partial orders. If a partial order R in the set enumeration tree is infrequent, then the partial orders in the subtree rooted at R, which are stronger than R, cannot be frequent. The subtree can be pruned. Second, FRECPO prunes forbidden edges. Not every edge can appear in the transitive reduction of a partial order. For example, if every string containing ac also contains ab and bc, then edge ac should not appear in the transitive reduction of any frequent closed partial order. Edge ac is called a forbidden edge. Removing the forbidden edges can also reduce the search space. Finally, FRECPO extracts transitive reductions of frequent partial orders directly and does not need to compute the transitive reductions.

5.2.2.7   Complexity

PDMC constructs PDA $\mathbb{P}$ from the program Control Flow Graph (a directed graph $G = (N, E)$) where each node represents a program point and each edge represents a valid program statement. PDMC takes $O(E)$ time to construct the PDA $\mathbb{P}$ from the CFG G, takes $O(E \times |Q|)$ (Q is the number of states in the FSA) for computing $\mathbf{P}$, the product of FSA $\mathbb{F}$ and PDA $\mathbb{P}$, takes $O(|Q|^2 \times E)$ for deciding if the PDA $\mathbf{P}$ is empty and $O(|Q|^2) \times lg|Q| \times E \times lgN$ for backtracking. The derivations are shown by Chen [18].

It has been shown that the problem of counting the complete set of frequent closed partial order is #P-complete. In other words, FRECPO is of exponential complexity with respect to $|A|$. However, FRECPO is pseudo-linear. That is, the runtime is linear with respect to the number of frequent closed partial orders in the data set. In practice, the number of significant frequent closed partial orders of APIs for a program is often small. Thus, it is highly feasible and effective to use FRECPO in our application context.

5.2.3 Implementation

To generate static traces, we adapted a publicly available model checker called MOPS [20]. To mine FCPOs, we adopted a FCPO miner called FRECPO [47]. The FCPO miner employed in our framework does not handle duplicate strings. We handled this implementation limitation by appropriately modifying the scenario extraction algorithm. The process of generating error traces from a final configuration $\langle q, \omega \rangle$ (ω is the stack content containing a list of return addresses) of PDA **P** is called *backtracking* [18]. With the knowledge of a user-specified set of APIs, $\mathcal{A} = \{a_1, a_2, a_3, ..., a_k\}$, our framework extracts $A(t)$ from any trace t produced by MOPS. The PDMC process produces a graph in which certain paths map to violation paths in the program [18]. Multiple program paths (and hence graph paths) can violate a given property specified by a FSM (such as the one shown in Figure 5.5), and many such violations could be similar because they indicate the same programming bug. So instead of reporting all program traces that violate a given property, the MOPS model checker clusters similar traces and reports the shortest trace as a candidate trace for each violation. This mechanism would save the user's time considerably because the user need not review each trace manually.

However, for our purposes, given a Trigger, we need all the traces in the program that contain the APIs specified in the Trigger. We modified the backtracking algorithm of MOPS, wherein, instead of clustering traces, we consider all program paths that satisfy the Trigger, and produce a random number of traces by random walking the graph generated by the PDMC process. In our experiments, we specified a threshold (20 in our experiments) for the number of traces to be generated from each program. MOPS assumes that a loop may

appres	beforelight	bitmap	dpsexec	xload	xlogo
dpsinfo	editres	glxgears	glxinfo	xlsatoms	xlsclients
iceauth	ico	listres	luit	xlsfonts	xmag
makepsres	oclock	proxymngr	rstart	xman	xmessage
setxkbmap	showfont	smproxy	texteroids	xmh	xmodmap
twm	viewres	x11perf	xauth	xpr	xrandr
xbiff	xcalc	xclipboard	xclock	xrdb	xrefresh
xcmsdb	xconsole	xditview	xdpyinfo	xset	xsetmode
xev	xeyes	xf86dga	xfd	xsetpointer	xsetroot
xfindproxy	xfontsel	xfsinfo	xfwp	xstdcmap	xterm
xgamma	xgc	xhost	xinit	xtrap	xvidtune
xkbevd	xkbvleds	xkbutils	xkill	xvinfo	xwud

FIGURE 5.9: X11 client programs used in our evaluation.

XCreateGC	56
XOpenDisplay	32
XCreateWindow	26
XOpenIM	4
XQueryBestSize	2
XFreeModifiermap	1

FIGURE 5.10: Call frequencies for the selected X11 APIs.

execute either one or zero times to avoid generating traces of infinite size. Furthermore, MOPS monitors backtracking and aborts if it detects a loop.

To simplify the definitions, we had assumed in Section 5.2.2.3 that the APIs are empty methods, do not take any arguments, and return void. If we relax this assumption, then we should also consider those statements in the program that affect and are affected by a given API, say a. For example, if we have i = a(j); if (i != NULL) b(i);, then the program statements if (i != NULL) and b(i) are related to a. We should include such statements in the API sequence database before being fed to the FCPO miner. A possible API specification (a path in the partial order) could look like "the return value of a should always be compared to NULL before being passed to b." We implemented simple data-flow extensions to the PDMC process to correlate two program statements related by program variables (for example, FILE* fp = fopen(...) and fread(fp) are related through the file pointer variable, fp), without considering aliasing.

5.2.4   Comparison with a Dynamic Miner

We applied our framework on 72 client programs from the X11R6.9.0 distribution. The analyzed client programs use APIs for the X11 windowing system, with roughly 208 KLOC in total. Figure 5.9 lists the X11 client programs used in our evaluation. We selected X11 client programs because the Inter-Client Communication Conventions Manual (ICCCM) [50] from the X Consortium standard describes several rules for how well-behaved programs should use the X11 APIs, serving as an oracle.

Roughly, 700 distinct X11 APIs were used across 72 client programs. For each X11 API, we calculated the number of call sites across all client programs. Figure 5.10 shows the call site frequencies for selected X11 APIs. APIs such as XCreateGC, XOpenDisplay, and XCreateWindow were called quite often (more than 25 times) among 72 clients. But the usage of APIs such as XCreateGC, XQueryBestSize, and XFreeModifiermap were relatively sparse (less than 5 times) across all the clients. We considered only APIs with more than 10 call sites for specification mining.

We next present an illustrative example of how specifications are mined by

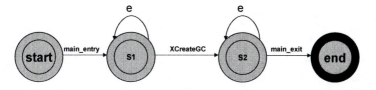

FIGURE 5.11: Trigger used to generate function calls, APIs, and expressions related to *XCreateGC*.

Name	Seed	Mined	Related APIs	Extra Specs	False	Missed
PrsTransTbl	XtParseTranslationTable	Yes	2	0	0	0
XPutImage	XPutImage	No	5	8	2	1
XSaveContext	XSaveContext	Yes	3	3	0	0
XSetFont	XSetFont	Yes	2	2	0	0

FIGURE 5.12: Statistics for the specifications mined by our framework.

our framework around the `XCreateGC` API. We use our framework to generate static traces from each client program using the Trigger shown in Figure 5.11. States $S1$ and $S2$ in the Trigger have self-transitions on *e*. *e* is any function/API invoked before/after `XCreateGC` or any expression that uses or defines the return variable and input parameters of `XCreateGC`. The Trigger causes the model checker to produce paths (as traces from `main_entry` to `main_exit`) that involve a call to `XCreateGC`. The traces contain function calls and APIs that are ancestors or descendants of `XCreateGC` in the program call graphs of each client that `XCreateGC` appears in. The model checker also produces expressions (in the program) that share a data dependency relation with `XCreateGC`'s return variable or input parameters (again, across all clients with a call site to `XCreateGC`). These traces are then fed to the partial-order miner after extracting the scenarios. The miner summarizes the traces seen from different program call graphs (from different clients) as a single partial order (for a given minimum support value, m). Our framework produces all partial orders with support s greater than or equal to m. Our framework then picks partial orders with a higher support value as likely specifications.

We next demonstrate how our framework can be used to mine specifications around those mined by Ammons et al. [11] (for convenience, we call their approach as the dynamic-trace miner). We used a minimum support value of

Specifications Mined	10
False	1
Missed	1

FIGURE 5.13: Statistics for the specifications mined around *XOpenDisplay*.

0.8 in our experiments. To select a good support value, a user should start with higher support values and lower the support value until the user starts to see patterns that are not specifications. Selecting a good support value requires user judgment. Figure 5.12 summarizes our results. An implementation limitation of our model checker is that it cannot handle function pointers or callbacks. Hence, we considered only those X11 specifications (mined by the dynamic-trace miner) that do not involve callbacks. The four specifications from dynamic-trace-miner used in our evaluation are shown in Column 1 of Figure 5.12. Our first goal was to specify an API (we call this API as the seed API) from the specification mined by the dynamic-trace miner and check if our framework can mine the same specification. Column 2 shows the seed API given to our framework. We could mine all specifications mined by dynamic-trace miner except for one (*XPutImage*) as Column 3 shows. *XPutImage* requires that the image and graphics context passed to XPutImage API must have been created on the same display. The data-flow analysis required to mine this specification was not present in the model checker that we used and hence we missed this specification.

The second goal was to mine specifications among APIs related to the specified seed, not mined by the dynamic-trace miner. Related APIs are those APIs that have simple data dependencies with the seed API. Related APIs either produce a value that the seed API consumes or consume a value produced by the seed API. Our framework first gathers the APIs related to the seed API. Column 4 displays the number of APIs that are determined by our framework to be related to the seed API. Then our framework mines frequent usage scenarios as partial orders and produces ones with high support as likely specifications. Specifications learned by our framework around the related API XOpenDisplay are shown separately later in this section because a very large number of APIs interact with XOpenDisplay. XOpenDisplay returns a display pointer, which forms an input parameter to most X11 APIs. Hence, with XOpenDisplay as the seed API, our framework mines many specifications involving X11 APIs. The statistics for the specifications mined by our framework with XOpenDisplay as the seed API are shown in Figure 5.13 separately. Column 5 shows the number of likely specifications mined by our framework, around the specification mined by the dynamic-trace miner. Column 6 shows the number of false specifications mined by our framework. As we had prior knowledge of specifications from the ICCCM manual, we noted that our framework missed a specification involving XCreateImage, a related API, owing to the data-flow-insensitivity of our model checker (Column 7).

We next present our results for specifications learned around the XOpenDisplay API. XOpenDisplay returns a pointer to the *Display* structure that serves as the connection to the X server and that contains all the information about that X server. XOpenDisplay connects the application to the X server through TCP or DECnet communication protocols, or through some local inter-process communication protocol. The pointer returned by XOpenDisplay is consumed by a large number of X11 APIs, scattered across procedure boundaries. Hence

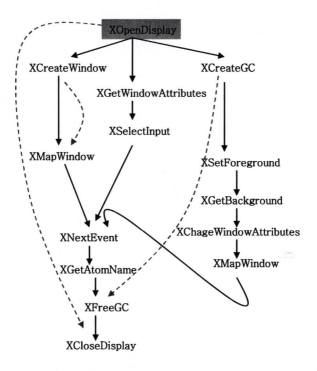

FIGURE 5.14: A usage scenario around *XOpenDisplay* API as a partial order. Lower support values produce larger partial orders. Higher support values produce smaller partial orders (specifications). Specifications are shown with dotted lines.

XOpenDisplay makes an interesting case study for our framework. Figure 5.14 shows a partial order learned by our framework, being a usage scenario. Figure 5.13 shows the statistics for the specifications learned by our framework around XOpenDisplay.

5.3 Adapting Static Trace Generation for Mining API Error-Handling Specifications

In this section, we describe how we adapt our trace generation and mining framework (presented in the previous section) for mining API error-handling specifications. The objective of the adaptations to our framework (henceforth, referred to as adaptation(s)) presented in this section is to mine error-handling specifications and identify error-handling violations. The framework presented in the previous section does not consider error paths or generate error traces. In this section, we adapt the framework presented in the previous section to generate and distinguish error traces from normal traces. Normal paths and error paths are distinguished and specifications are learned from normal paths as programmers often make mistakes along error paths [14,31,56,60].

Incorrect handling of errors incurred after API invocations can lead to serious problems such as system crashes, leakage of sensitive information, and other security compromises. API errors are usually caused by stressful environment conditions, which may occur in forms such as high computation load, memory exhaustion, process-related failures, network failures, file system failures, and slow system response. As a simple example of incorrect API error handling, a *send* procedure, which sends the content of a file across the network as packets, might incorrectly handle the failure of the `socket` API (the `socket` API can return an error value of `-1`, indicating a failure), if the *send* procedure returns without releasing system resources such as previously allocated packet buffers and opened file handlers. Unfortunately, error handling is the least understood, documented, and tested part of a system. Toy's study [56] shows that more than 50% of all system failures in a telephone switching application are due to incorrect error-handling algorithms. Cristian's survey [22] reports that up to two-thirds of a program may be devoted to error detection and recovery. Hence, correct error handling should be an important part of any reliable software system. Despite the importance of correct error handling, programmers often make mistakes in error-handling code [14, 31, 60]. Correct handling of API errors can be specified as formal specifications verifiable by static checkers at compile time. However, due to poor documentation practices, API error-handling specifications are often unavailable or imprecise.

There are three main unique challenges in automatically mining API error-handling specifications from source code. (1) Mining API error-handling specifications, which are usually temporal in nature, require identifying API *details* from source code such as (a) *critical* APIs (APIs that fail with errors), (b) different error checks that should follow such APIs (depending on different API error conditions), and (c) proper error handling or clean up in the case of API failures, indicated by API errors. Furthermore, clean up APIs might depend on the APIs called before the error is handled. Static approaches [59,60] exist for mining or checking API error-handling specifications from software repositories implemented in object-oriented languages such as Java. Java has explicit *exception-handling* support and the static approaches mainly analyze the `catch` and `finally` blocks to mine or check API error-handling specifications. Procedural languages such as C do not have explicit exception-handling mechanisms to handle API errors, posing additional challenges for automated specification mining: API details are often scattered across different procedures and files. Manually mining specifications from source code becomes hard and inaccurate. Hence, we need inter-procedural techniques to mine critical APIs, different error checks, and proper clean up from source code to automatically mine error-handling specifications. (2) As programmers often make mistakes along API error paths [14, 31, 56, 60], the proper clean up, being common among error paths and normal paths, should be mined from normal traces (i.e., static traces without API errors along normal paths) instead of error traces (i.e., static traces with API errors along error paths). Hence, we need techniques to generate and distinguish error traces and normal traces, even when the API error-handling specifications are not known *a priori*. (3) Finally, API error-handling specifications can be *conditional* – the clean up for an API might depend on the actual return value of the API. Hence, trace generation has to associate conditions along each path with the corresponding trace.

To address the preceding challenges, we adapt the trace generation framework presented in the previous section, for statically mining API error-handling specifications directly from software packages (API client code). We adapt the trace generation technique to distinguish and approximate different API run-time behaviors (e.g., error and normal behaviors), thus generating error traces and normal traces, inter-procedurally. We apply different mining techniques on the generated error traces and normal traces to identify clean up code, distinguish clean up APIs from other APIs, and mine specifications that define correct handling of API errors. To mine conditional specifications, we adapt trace generation to associate conditions along each path with the corresponding trace. We then use the mined specifications to detect API error-handling violations. Inheriting the benefits of our static framework, no user input in the form of specifications, programmer annotations, profiling, instrumentation, random inputs, or a set of relevant APIs are expected. We implement the adaptations to our framework and validate the effectiveness on 10 packages from the Redhat-9.0 distribution (52 KLOC), postfix-2.0.16 (111 KLOC), and 72 packages from the X11-R6.9.0 distribution (208 KLOC). Our adapted framework mines 62 error-handling specifications and detects 264 real error-handling defects from the analyzed packages.

The remainder of this section is structured as follows. Section 5.3.1 starts with a motivating example. Section 5.3.2 explains the adaptations to our framework in detail. Section 5.3.3 presents the evaluation results.

5.3.1 Example

In this section, we use the example code shown in Figures 5.16 and 5.17 to define several terms and notations used throughout this section (summarized in Figure 5.15). We also provide a high-level overview of our adaptation using the example code.

API errors. All APIs in the example code are shown in bold font. In Figure 5.17, InitAAText and EndAAText are *user-defined procedures*. In the figures, user-defined procedures are shown in italicized font. The user-defined procedure in which an API is invoked is called the *enclosing procedure* for the API. In Figure 5.17, EndAAText, for instance, is the enclosing procedure for

Definitions and Acronyms			
Library Application Program Interface (**API**)			
API-Error Check (**AEC**). AEC(a) is the required error check for API a.			
Error Block (**EB**). EB(a) is the error block of API a. AEC(a) precedes EB(a).			
Path (**P**)	Error Path (**ErP**)	Error Exit-Path (**ErExP**)	
		Error Return-Path (**ErRP**)	
	Normal Path (**NP**)		
Trace (**T**)	Error Trace (**ErT**)	Error Exit-Trace (**ErExT**)	
		Error Return-Trace (**ErRT**)	
	Normal Trace (**NT**)		
Specification (**S**)	Error-Check Specification (**ErCS**)		
	Multiple-API Specification (**MAS**)		
Violation (**V**)	Error-Check Violation (**ErCV**)		
	Multiple-API Violation (**MAV**)	MAV along ErExP (**MAV-ErExP**)	
		MAV along ErRP (**MAV-ErRP**)	

FIGURE 5.15: Definitions and acronyms.

the APIs `XftDrawDestroy` (Line 27), `XftFontClose` (Line 28), and `XftColorFree` (Line 29). APIs can fail because of stressful environment conditions. In procedural languages such as C, API failures are indicated through *API errors*. API errors are special return values of the API (such as `NULL`) or distinct `errno` flag values (such as `ENOMEM`) indicating failures. For example, in Figure 5.16, API `recvfrom` returns a negative integer on failures. The API error from `recvfrom` is reflected by the return variable `cc`. APIs that fail with errors are called *critical* APIs. A condition checking of API return values or `errno` flag in the source code against API errors is called *API-Error Check* (AEC); we use AEC(a) to denote the AEC of API a. For example, AEC(`recvfrom`) is `if(cc<0)`.

Error block. The block of code following an API-error check, which is executed if the API fails, is called the *error block*. Error blocks contain error-handling code to handle API failures. We use EB(a) to denote the error block of API a. For example, Lines 9-11 in Figure 5.16, and Lines 11-12 and 16-20 in Figure 5.17 represent EB(`recvfrom`), EB(`XftFontOpenName`), and EB(`XftColorAllocValue`), respectively. A given API can have multiple error blocks depending on the different ways that it can fail (not shown in the examples for simplicity).

Different paths and traces. A control-flow path exists between two program *points* if the latter is reachable from the former through some set

```
        ~/Redhat-9.0/routed/ripquery/query.c
1    #include <sys/socket.h>
2    int main(...){
3        ...
4        s = socket(...);
5        ...
6        cc = recvfrom(s, ...)
7        ...
8        if (cc < 0){
9            ...
10           close(s);
11           exit(1);
12           }
13       ...
14       close(s)
15       ...
16   }
```

FIGURE 5.16: Code snippet from *routed-0.17-14*.

of control-flow edges, i.e., Control Flow Graph (CFG) *edges*. Our adaptation identifies two types of paths – *Error Path* and *Normal Path*. There are two types of error paths. Any path from the beginning of the main procedure to an exit call (such as exit) in the error block of some API is called the Error Exit-Path. For example, all paths ending at the exit call at Line 11 in Figure 5.16 are error exit-paths (exit call inside EB(recvfrom)). Any path from the beginning of the main procedure to a return call in the error block of some API is called the Error Return-Path. For example, in Figure 5.17, all paths ending at the return call at Lines 12 (return call inside EB(XftFontOpenName)) and 20 (return call inside EB(XftColorAllocValue)) are error return-paths. Error exit-paths and error return-paths are together known as error paths. A *normal path* is any path from the beginning of the main procedure to the end of the main procedure without any API errors. For example, any path from Line 3 to Line 15 in Figure 5.16 is a normal path. For a given path, a trace is the print of all statements that exist along that path. Error paths, error exit-paths, error return-paths, and normal paths have corresponding traces: *error traces, error exit-traces, error return-traces*, and *normal traces*. Error exit-traces and error return-traces are together known as error traces. In our analysis, we restrict the traces to those that can be captured by a Finite State Machine [8]. Two APIs are said to be *related* if they manipulate at least one (or more) common variable(s). For example, in Figure 5.16, APIs recvfrom and close are related to the API socket. The socket API *produces* s, which is *consumed* by the APIs recvfrom and close. A *scenario* is a set of related APIs in a given trace. A given trace can have multiple scenarios. For example,

```
         ~/X11-R6.9.0/x11perf/do_text.c
    1    #include <X11/Xft/Xft.h>
    2    ...
    3    static XftFont *aafont;
    4    static XftDraw *aadraw;
    5    static XftColor aacolor;
    6    ...
    7    int InitAAText(XParms xp, Parms p, int reps){
    8        ...
    9        aafont = XftFontOpenName (...);
   10        if (aafont == NULL) {
   11            ...
   12            return 0;
   13            }
   14        aadraw = XftDrawCreate (...);
   15        if (!XftColorAllocValue (..., &aacolor)){
   16            ...
   17            XftFontClose (xp->d, aafont);
   18            XftDrawDestroy (aadraw);
   19            ...
   20            return 0;
   21            }
   22        ...
   23        }
   24    ...
   25    void EndAAText(XParms xp, Parms p){
   26        ...
   27        XftDrawDestroy (aadraw);
   28        XftFontClose (xp->d, aafont);
   29        XftColorFree (..., &aacolor);
   30        ...
   31        }
```

FIGURE 5.17: Code snippet from *x11perf-R6.9.0*.

if there were multiple `socket` calls in Figure 5.16, then each `socket` call, along with its corresponding related APIs, forms a different scenario.

API error-handling specifications. We identify two types of API error-handling specifications that dictate correct error handling along all paths in a program: *error-check specifications* and *multiple-API specifications*. Error-check specifications dictate that correct AEC(a)'s (API-Error Checks) exist for each API a (which can fail), before the API's return value is *used* or the `main` procedure returns. For a given API a, absence of AEC(a) causes an *error-check violation*. Multiple-API specifications dictate that the right *clean up* APIs are called along all paths. Clean up APIs are APIs called, generally before a procedure return or program exit, to free resources such as memory, sockets, pipes, and files or to *rollback* the state of a global resource such as the system registry and databases. For example, in Figure 5.17, `XftFontColose` (Line 17) and `XftDrawDestroy` (Line 18) are the clean up APIs in EB(`XftColorAllocValue`). In Figure 5.17, one error-check specification (the return value of `XftColorAllocValue` should be checked against `NULL`) and two multiple-API specifications (`XftFontOpenName` should be followed by

XftFontClose and XftDrawCreate should be followed by XftDrawDestroy) are evident. Violation of a multiple-API specification along a given path is a *multiple-API violation*. Multiple-API violations along error-exit paths could be less serious as the operating system might reclaim unfreed memory and resource handlers along program exits. However, there are several cases where explicit clean up is necessary even on program exits. For instance, unclosed files could lose recorded data along an error exit-path if the buffers are not flushed out to the disk. In addition, any user-defined procedure altering a global resource (such as the system registry or a database) should *rollback* along error exit-paths to retain the integrity of the global resource. Next, we present the high-level overview of our adaptation using the example code.

A high-level overview of our adaptation is shown in Figure 5.18. The only input to our adapted framework is the compilable source code of software package(s) implemented in C. To mine specifications, our adaptation initially distinguishes and generates API error traces and normal traces, for reasons explained later. Our adaptation then detects API error-handling violations in the source code using the mined specifications. In particular, our adaptation consists of the following three stages (shown by the three dotted boxes in Figure 5.18).

Error/normal trace generation. The trace generation stage distinguishes and generates error traces (error exit-traces and error return-traces) and normal traces, inter-procedurally. Along normal paths, it is difficult to distinguish clean up APIs from other APIs. Hence, our adaptation identifies *probable* clean up APIs from the error traces. For example, in Figure 5.16, our adaptation identifies the API close (Line 10) from the error exit-trace that goes through EB(recvfrom). In Figure 5.17, our adaptation identifies XftFontClose (Line 17) and XftDrawDestroy (Line 18) from the error return-trace that go through EB(XftColorAllocValue). Notice that, in Figure 5.17, the clean up APIs can also be invoked through the user-defined procedure EndAAText, inter-procedurally. However, even in the error block, there could be other APIs that are not necessarily clean up APIs (hence the term, *probable*). The final set of actual clean up APIs and the APIs related to them are determined during the specification mining stage.

Specification mining. The specification mining stage generates error-check specifications and multiple-API specifications. Our adaptation mines error-check specifications from error traces by determining API-error checks (AEC) for each API. For example, our adaptation determines AEC(recvfrom) to be if (cc < 0) from the error-exit trace that goes through EB(recvfrom). Programmers often make mistakes along API error paths. Hence, proper clean up, being common among error paths and normal paths, should be mined from normal traces instead of error traces. Once the probable clean up APIs are mined from error traces, our adaptation mines the APIs that might be related to the probable clean up APIs from normal traces. For example, in Figure 5.17, our adaptation determines from normal traces that XftFontClose is related to XftFontOpenName, and XftDrawDestroy is related to XftDrawCreate (Figure 5.17, however, does not show normal paths or traces for simplicity). Our adaptation generates multiple-API specifications by applying sequence mining on normal traces.

Verification. Our static verifier uses the mined specifications (error-check and multiple-API specifications) to detect violations (error-check and multiple-API violations) in the source code. Next, we present the various components of our adaptation in detail.

5.3.2   Adaptation – The Details

The algorithm presented in Figure 5.19 shows the details of our adaptations. There are 3 stages and 10 steps (numbered 1-10) in our algorithm. Section 5.3.2.1 describes the error/normal trace generation stage (Steps 1-6). Section 5.3.2.2 (Steps 7-8) explains the steps involved in mining API error-handling specifications from the static traces. Finally, Section 5.3.2.3 describes the verification stage for detecting API error-handling violations from the mined specifications (Steps 9-10).

5.3.2.1   Error/Normal Trace Generation

In this section, we explain how we adapt the trace generation technique for generating API error and normal traces from source code. As shown in Figure 5.19, the error/normal trace generation stage has six steps: generate error traces (Step 1), process error traces (Steps 2-4), identify critical APIs and probable clean up APIs from error traces (Step 5), and finally, generate normal traces (Step 6). The various steps are explained next.

Step 1 - Generate error traces. An error trace starts from the beginning of the `main` procedure and ends in some API error-block with an exit call (causing the program to exit) or a `return` call (causing the enclosing procedure to return). The trigger FSM, say $\mathbb{F}$ (Step 1, Figure 5.19), is used by our trace generator (procedure TG in the figure) to generate error traces from the program source code ($\mathcal{P}$). The procedure TG represents our trace generation technique, which adapts the push-down model checking (PDMC) process. Transitions `retValChk` and `errnoChk` in the trigger $\mathbb{F}$ (from State 2 to State 3) identify the return-value check and error-flag check, respectively, for the API. Transitions from State 3 to the final state (State `end`) in the trigger $\mathbb{F}$ capture code blocks following the `retValChk` or `errnoChk` in which the program exits or the enclosing procedure returns. The procedure TG generates all traces in $\mathcal{P}$ that satisfy the trigger $\mathbb{F}$. However, the procedure `getShortest` (Step 1, Figure 5.19) returns only the shortest trace from the set of all traces generated by TG. As we are interested only in the API-error check and the set of probable clean up APIs (PC) in the API error-block for a given API from error traces, the program statements prior to the API invocation are not needed. Hence, it suffices to generate the shortest path for each API invocation with a following `retValChk` or `errnoChk`. In case there are multiple `retValChk` or

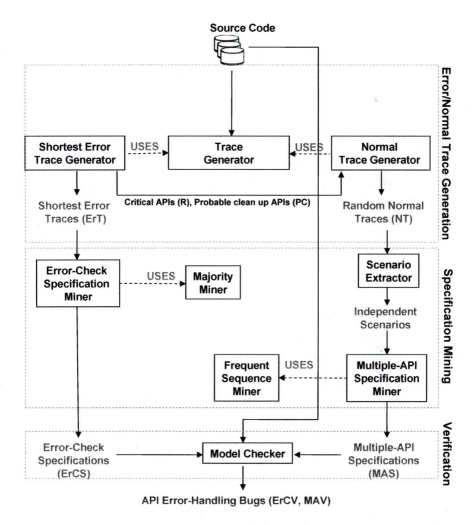

FIGURE 5.18: Adapting our static trace generation framework for mining API error-handling specifications.

// $\mathcal{P}$ = source code; $\mathbb{F}$ = FSM; **TG** = Trace-Generate; **PDMC** = Push-Down Model Check
// R = critical APIs, PC = probable clean-up APIs
// **ERROR/NORMAL TRACE GENERATION**
// Generate shortest error traces

1   ErT = **getShortest**(TG($\mathcal{P}$,));

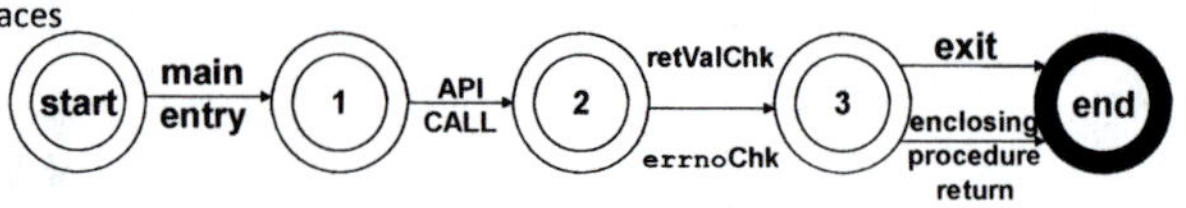

// Extract error-return traces (ErRT) and error-exit traces (ErExT) from ErT
// Note that ErT = ErExT + ErRT
2   ErExT = **getErExT**(ErT);
// Extract API-error checks (AEC) from ErExT
3   AECSet = **getAECSet**(**majorityMine**(ErExT));
// Use AECSet to extract ErRT from ErT
4   ErRT = **getErRT**(ErT, AECSet);

// Identify critical APIs and probable clean up APIs from error traces (ErT)
5   R, PC = **getRandPC**(ErT);

// Generate random normal traces (NT) up to a specified upper-bound L

6   NT = **getRandomL**(TG($\mathcal{P}$,));

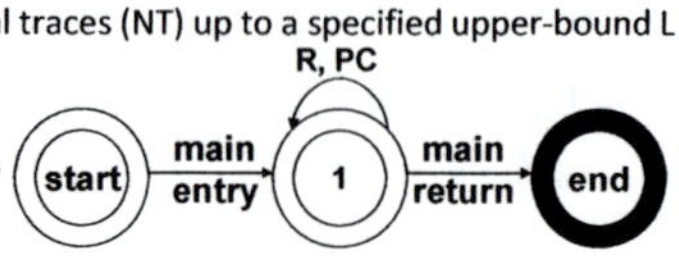

// **SPECIFICATION MINING**
// Generate error-check specifications (ErCS) as FSMs from AECSet

7   $\mathbb{F}$ ErCS = **generateErCS**(AECSet);

// Generate multiple-API specifications (MAS) as FSMs from normal traces (NT)
// Apply sequence mining with specified support on extracted scenarios

8   $\mathbb{F}$ MAS = **generateMAS**(**sequenceMine**(**extractScenarios**(NT), min_sup));

// **VERIFICATION**
// Detect error-check violations (ErCV)

9   foreach($\mathbb{F}$ in $\mathbb{F}$ ErCS) { ErCV += **getShortest**(PDMC($\mathcal{P}$, $\mathbb{F}$)); }

// Detect Multiple-API violation along error paths

10   foreach($\mathbb{F}$ in $\mathbb{F}$ MAS) {MAV += **getShortest**(PDMC($\mathcal{P}$, $\mathbb{F}$)); }

FIGURE 5.19: The algorithm for mining API error-handling specifications.

`errnoChk` for an API call site, then our adaptation generates the shortest trace for each of the checks. The trigger $\mathbb{F}$ captures the `retValChk`, `errnoChk`, and the code block after these checks, even if they are scattered across procedure boundaries. However, the traces generated by this step can also have traces where `retValChk` or `errnoChk` is followed by a normal return of the enclosing procedure. Such traces, which are not error traces, are pruned out in the next step.

Steps 2, 3, and 4 - Process error traces. Our adaptation easily extracts error exit-traces from error traces (procedure `getErExT`, Step 2, Figure 5.19): Error traces that end with an exit call are error exit-traces. We assume that the API `retValChk` or `errnoChk`, which precedes an exit call in an error-exit trace, is an API-error check. We then distinguish between the *true* and *false* branches of the API-error check. For example, in Figure 5.16, since `exit(...)` appears in the true branch of AEC(`recvfrom`) (`if(cc<0)`), we assume that `<0` is the error return value (API error) of `recvfrom`. For each API, our adaptation records API-error check with majority occurrences (procedure `majorityMine`, Step 3, Figure 5.19) among error exit-traces (procedure `getAECSet`, Step 3, Figure 5.19). As mentioned in the previous step, the traces generated in Step 1 can also have traces where `retValChk` or `errnoChk` is followed by a normal return of the enclosing procedure. Our adaptation uses the API-error check set computed from error exit-traces to prune out such traces to obtain error return-traces (procedure `getErRT`, Step 4, Figure 5.19).

Step 5 - Identify critical APIs and probable clean up APIs from error traces. Our adaptation computes the set R (critical APIs) and the set PC (probable clean up APIs) in this step (procedure `getRandPc`, Step 5, Figure 5.19). The set R of critical APIs is easily computed from error exit-traces and error return-traces. A key observation of our adaptation is that it is much easier to find clean up APIs along error paths than normal paths. It is because, on API failures, before the program exits or the enclosing procedure returns, the primary concern is clean up. Along normal paths, however, it is difficult to separate clean up APIs from other APIs. Hence, our adaptation identifies probable clean up APIs (the set PC) from the error traces. The term *probable* indicates that the APIs that occur in error blocks need not always be clean up APIs. The mining phase prunes out the non-clean-up APIs from the set PC. In the next step, we show how our adaptation identifies APIs related to the probable clean up APIs. These related APIs occur prior to API-error checks in the source code.

Step 6 - Generate normal traces. A normal trace starts from the beginning of the `main` procedure and ends at the end of the `main` procedure. The procedure `TG` uses the trigger FSM, say $\mathbb{F}$ (Step 6, Figure 5.19), to generate normal traces (NT) from the program source code ($\mathcal{P}$). The edges for State 2 in the trigger $\mathbb{F}$ are critical (set R) and probable clean up APIs (set PC). Our adaptation generates normal traces (involving critical and probable clean up APIs) randomly up to a user-specified upper bound L (procedure `getRandomL`, Step 6, Figure 5.19), inter-procedurally. An upper bound is required as the set of all possible traces could be huge in practice. Our adaptation only generates L traces randomly from the set of all possible traces in a given compilable unit. The traces contain the probable clean up APIs and the APIs related to them, if any. Finally, as API error-handling specifications can be conditional, the clean up for an API might depend on the actual return value of the API. As a simple example, for the `malloc` API, the API `free` is called only along paths in which the return value of `malloc` is not `NULL` (condition). Hence, normal paths (normal traces) are associated with their corresponding conditions involving API return values. The conditions, along with API sequences, form a part of normal traces and are used in the specification mining stage, explained next.

5.3.2.2   Specification Mining

The specification mining stage mines error-check and multiple-API specifications from the static traces (Steps 7-8). The scenario extraction and sequence mining are performed in Step 8.

Step 7 - Mine error-check specifications. Our adaptation generates error-check specifications (procedure `generateErCS`, Step 7, Figure 5.19) as Finite State Machines (FSM, $\mathbb{F}_{ErCS}$) from the computed API-error check set. The FSMs representing the error-check specifications specify that each critical API should be followed by the correct error checks.

Step 8 - Mine multiple-API specifications. Our adaptation mines multiple-API specifications from normal traces (procedure `generateMAS`, Step 8, Figure 5.19) as FSMs ($\mathbb{F}_{MAS}$). Normal traces include the probable clean up APIs (PC), APIs related to the set PC, and the conditions (involving API return values). The main observation used in mining multiple-API specifications from normal traces is that programmers often make mistakes along error paths [14,31,56,60]. Hence, our adaptation mines related APIs from only normal traces and not from error traces. However, a single normal trace generated by the trace generator might involve several API scenarios, being often interspersed. A scenario (see Section 5.3.1) is a set of related APIs in a given trace. Our adaptation separates different API scenarios from a given normal trace, so that each scenario can be fed separately to the miner. We use a scenario extraction algorithm (procedure `extractScenarios`, Step 8, Figure 5.19) 5.2.2.5 that is based on identifying *producer-consumer* chains among APIs in the trace. The algorithm is based on the assumption that an API and its corresponding clean up APIs have some form of data dependencies between them such as a producer-consumer relationship. Each producer-consumer chain is generated as an independent scenario. For example, in Figure 5.17, the API `XftFontOpenName` (Line 9) produces `aafont`, which is consumed by the API `XftFontClose` (Line 17). The APIs `XftFontOpenName` and `XftFontClose` are generated as an independent scenario.

Our adaptation mines multiple-API specifications from independent scenarios using frequent-sequence mining (procedure `sequenceMine`, Step 8, Figure 5.19). Let IS be the set of independent scenarios. We apply a frequent sequence-mining algorithm [58] on the set IS with a user-specified support min_sup ($min\_sup \in [0,1]$), which produces a set FS of frequent sequences that occur as subsequences in at least $min\_sup \times |IS|$ sequences in the set IS. Note that our adaptation can mine the different error-handling specifications for the different errors of a given API as long as the different specifications have enough support among the analyzed client code.

5.3.2.3 Verification

Our adaptation uses the specifications to find API error-handling violations (Steps 9-10).

Steps 9 and 10 - Detect error-check and multiple-API violations. In Steps 1 and 6, the push-down model checking (PDMC) process was adapted for trace generation by the procedure TG. Here we use the PDMC process for property verification. The specifications mined by our adaptation as FSMs ($\mathbb{F}_{ErCS}$ and $\mathbb{F}_{MAS}$) represent the error-handling properties to be verified at this stage. Our adaptation verifies the property FSMs in $\mathbb{F}_{ErCS}$ and $\mathbb{F}_{MAS}$ against the source code ($\mathcal{P}$). The mined specifications can also be used to verify the correct API error handling in other software packages. For verifying conditional specifications, we adapt the PDMC process to track the value of variables that take the return value of an API call along the different branches of conditional constructs. Our adaptation generates (procedure getShortest) the shortest path for each detected violation (i.e., a potential defect) in the program, instead of all violating traces, thus making bug inspection easier for the users.

5.3.3 Evaluation

To generate static traces, we adapted a publicly available model checker called MOPS [20] with procedures (Steps 1-10) shown in Figure 5.19. We used BIDE [58] to mine frequent sequences. We have applied our adaptations on 10 packages from the Redhat-9.0 distribution (52 KLOC), postfix-2.0.16 (111 KLOC), and 72 packages from the X11-R6.9.0 distribution (208 KLOC). The analyzed packages use the APIs from the POSIX and X11 libraries. We selected POSIX and X11 clients because the POSIX standard [7] and the Inter-Client Communication Conventions Manual (ICCCM) [50] from the X Consortium standard were readily available. These standards describe several rules for how well-behaved programs should use the APIs, serving as an oracle for confirming our mined results. We ran our evaluation on a machine with Redhat Enterprise Linux version 2.6.9-5ELsmp, 3 GHz Intel Xeon processor, and 4 GB RAM. For specification mining and violation detection, the analysis cost ranges from under a minute for the smallest package to under an hour for the largest one. We next explain the evaluation results (summarized in Figure 5.20) for the various stages of our adaptation.

Trace generation. The number of error exit-traces and error return-

1. Packages	2. LOC	3. ErExT					4. ErRT	5. ErCS		6. ErCV		7. MAS		8. MAV	
		Σ	Σ^op	FN = Σ-Σ^op	FP	IP		Σ	FP	Σ	FP	Σ	FP	Σ	FP
10-Redhat-9.0-pkgs	52 K	338	320	18	35	18	205	31	3	58	1	40	6	4	3
postfix-2.0.16	111 K	124	92	32	3	124	30	31	3	4	2	40	6	0	0
X11-R6.9.0	208 K	286	248	38	27	164	305	31	3	170	13	40	6	56	9
Σ	371 K	748	660	88 (12%)	65(10%)	306(41%)	540	31	3(10%)	232	16(7%)	40	6(15%)	60	12(20%)

(a) Traces and violations

Σ - Total
IP – Inter-Procedural
FP – False Positives
FN – False Negatives
ErExT – Error Exit-Traces
ErRT – Error Return-Traces
ErCS – Error-Check
Specifications

ErCV – Error-Check
Violations
MAS – Multiple-API
Specifications
MAV – Multiple-API
Violations

FIGURE 5.20: Evaluation results.

traces generated by our adaptation are shown in Columns 3 (**ErExT**) and 4 (**ErRT**) of Figure 5.20, respectively. To evaluate trace generation, we manually inspected the source code for each error exit-trace produced by our adaptation and each error exit-trace missed by our adaptation. Error exit-traces missed by our adaptation can be determined by manually identifying the exit statements in the analyzed program not found in any of the generated error exit-traces. There are five sub-columns in Column 3 (**ErExT**): Σ (total number of error exit-traces generated or missed by our adaptation), Σ^{op} (total number of error exit-traces actually generated by our adaptation), **FN** $= \Sigma - \Sigma^{op}$ (total number of error exit-traces missed by our adaptation), **FP** (false positives: generated traces that are not actually error exit-traces), and **IP** (inter-procedural: number of traces in which the API invocation, API-error check (AEC), and error blocks were scattered across procedure boundaries).

The number of false negatives (FN) and false positives (FP) were low, at 12% (88/748) and 10% (65/660), respectively. The main reason for false negatives in the traces generated by our adaptation is the lack of aliasing and pointer analysis. For example, in `xkbvleds/utils.c`, the variable `outDpy` takes the return value of the API `XtDisplay`. Then the value of `outDpy` is assigned to another variable `inDpy`, and `inDpy` is compared to `NULL`. If `inDpy` is `NULL`, a user-defined procedure `uFatalError` is called, which then calls `exit`. Our adaptation did not capture the aliasing of `outDpy` to `inDpy`, and hence the trace was missed. However, as the number of false negatives was low, our adaptation still generated enough traces for the mining process. Some of the traces generated by our adaptation were not error exit-traces, leading to false positives. For example, in `tftp/tftpd.c`, the variable `f` (process id) takes the return value of the API `fork`. The program exits on `f>0` (parent process; not an error). Although the trace was generated by our adaptation, it is not an error exit-trace (`fork` fails with a negative integer). However, as the number of false positives was low, false error exit-traces were pruned by the mining process. 41% (306/748) of all the error exit-traces were scattered across procedure boundaries, highlighting the importance of inter-procedural trace generation. Specifically, all error exit-traces from the `postfix` package crossed procedure boundaries.

Our adaptation extracts the set of probable clean up APIs from the error traces (Step 5, Figure 5.19). After discarding string-manipulating APIs (such as `strcmp` and `strlen`), printing APIs (such as `printf` and `fprintf`), and error-reporting APIs (such as `perror`), which frequently appear (but unimportant) in the error blocks, our adaptation extracted 36 APIs as probable clean up APIs. Our adaptation used probable clean up APIs in generating normal traces (NT). For each compilable unit in the analyzed packages, our adaptation randomly generated 20 normal traces, ensuring there are enough distinct traces for mining. Our adaptation discarded 14/36 APIs after mining the normal traces (NT) with one of the following reasons: (1) insufficient call sites and hence, insufficient number of traces to mine from (for example, the API `XEClearCtrlKeys` had only two traces), (2) no temporal dependencies with any

APIs called prior to the error block (for example, the API XtSetArg appears in an exit trace from xlogo/xlogo.c. However, XtSetArg does not share any temporal dependencies with APIs called prior to the exit block), or (3) insufficient support among the scenarios. Our adaptation mined 40 multiple-API specifications from the remaining 22/36 probable clean up APIs (Column 7, **MAS**).

Error-check specifications. Our adaptation mined error-check specifications for only those APIs that occur more than three times among the error traces. In all, our adaptation mined 31 error-check specifications (Column 5, **ErCS**) from the error traces across all the analyzed packages: 3 (10%) out of the 31 (subcolumn Σ) mined specifications were false positives (subcolumn **FP**). For example, the API geteuid returns the effective user ID of the current process. The effective ID corresponds to the set ID bit on the file being executed [7]. Our adaptation encounters geteuid()!=0 at least 5 times among error traces leading to a false error-check specification – "*geteuid fails by returning a non-zero integer.*" But, a non-zero return value simply indicates an unprivileged process.

Error-check violations. The error-check specifications mined from error traces are used in detecting error-check violations along the error paths in the analyzed software packages. Column 6 (**ErCV**) presents the number of error-check violations detected by our adaptation. We manually inspected the violations reported by our adaptation: 16 (7%) out of the 232 (subcolumn Σ) reported error-check violations were false positives (subcolumn **FP**). The main reason for false positives in the reported violations is, once again, the lack of aliasing and pointer analysis in our adaptation. For example, in twm/session.c and smproxy/save.c, the variable entry takes the return value of malloc. Then the variable entry is assigned to another variable pentry. The variable pentry is then checked for NULL, which was missed by our adaptation.

Multiple-API specifications. Our adaptation mines multiple-API specifications from normal traces. Our adaptation produces a pattern as a multiple-API specification if the pattern occurred in at least five scenarios, with a minimum support (*min_sup*) of 0.8 among the scenarios. Our adaptation mined 40 multiple-API specifications (Column 7, **MAS**) across all the packages, with 6 (15%) of them being false positives (subcolumn **FP**). All multiple-API specifications mined by our adaptation were conditional – the clean up APIs in conditional multiple-API specifications depend on the return value or an input parameter (that holds the return value). As an example of a conditional specification, for the API XGetVisualInfo, cleaning up through the API XFree is necessary only if the fourth input parameter of XGetVisualInfo (the number of matching *visual structures*) is non-zero. False positives among the mined specifications may occur if some patterns occuring in the analyzed source code are not necessarily specifications. This result is a limitation shared by all mining approaches, requiring human inspection and judgment to distinguish real specifications from false ones. For example, our adaptation considered the APIs XSetScreenSaver and XUngrabPointer as probable clean up APIs, as both APIs appeared in some error trace generated by our adaptation. The first parameter of both these APIs is the display pointer produced by the API XOpenDisplay. Hence the property 'XSetScreenSaver and XUngrabPointer should follow XOpenDisplay' was mined by our adaptation, leading to a false positive. The number of false specifications mined by our adaptation is low as the code base used by our adaptation for mining is sufficiently large.

Our adaptation mines the maximum number of multiple-API specifications around the clean up API XFree. From the static traces, 35 APIs from the X11 library were found to interact with the XFree API leading to 15 multiple-API specifications with sufficient support. The specifications mined around the API XFree are shown in Figure 5.21. XFree is a general-purpose X11 API that frees the specified data. XFree must be used to free any objects that were allocated by X11 APIs, unless an alternate API is explicitly specified for the object [50]. The pointer consumed by the XFree API can either be a return value or an input parameter (that holds the return value) of some X11 API. The "(R)" in (R)XGetVisualInfo, for instance, indicates that the return value of the API XGetVisualInfo should be freed through the API XFree along all paths. The "(5)" in XQueryTree(5), for instance, indicates that the fifth input parameter of the API XQueryTree should be freed through the API XFree along all paths.

Our adaptation does not handle function pointers and callbacks, an implementation limitation, inherited from the underlying model checker. The limitation decreases the number of mined specifications in some cases. We address this limitation to some extent by limiting the analysis of some procedures (reachable from the main procedure only through function pointers or callbacks) to be intra-procedural only. For example, the API XFree is one of the probable clean up APIs mined by our adaptation. XFree has six call sites in the user-defined procedure print_xprint_info(...) (xdpyinfo/xdpyinfo.c). Since print_xprint_info(...) is reachable from the main procedure only through function pointers, our adaptation does not generate any normal trace for the XFree call sites in the user-defined procedure print_xprint_info(...). However, when the procedure print_xprint_info(...) was analyzed intra-procedurally, our adaptation generated five scenarios supporting the multiple-API specification, *"The memory allocated to the return value of the API XpGetAttributes should be freed through XFree,"* and one scenario supporting the multiple-API specification, *"The memory allocated to the return value of the API XpQueryScreens should be freed through XFree."* The related APIs, XpGetAttributes and XpQueryScreens, were in the same enclosing procedure (print_xprint_info(...)) as that of XFree. In the case of XFree, only 67/135 call sites of the XFree API were reachable from the main procedure without function pointers or callbacks. With the restricted number of reachable call sites of XFree, only 19 APIs from the X11 library were found to interact with the XFree API, leading to 6 multiple-API specifications with sufficient support. With the intra-procedural heuristic, 35 APIs from the X11 library were found to interact with the XFree API resulting in 15 multiple-API spec-

(R)XGetVisualInfo	(R)XpQueryScreens	(R)XpGetAttributes
XGetWindowProperty(12)	(R)XScreenResourceString	(R)XpGetOneAttribute
XQueryTree(5)	(R)XGetAtomName	(R)glXChooseVisual
(R)XFetchBytes	(R)malloc	XGetIMValues(3)
(R)XGetKeyboardMapping	XGetWMProtocols(3)	(R)XGetWMHints

FIGURE 5.21: Multiple-API specifications mined for the clean up API *XFree*.

ifications (Figure 5.21). Our adaptation analyzes a user-defined procedure intra-procedurally only if that procedure is an enclosing procedure for some probable clean up API (such as XFree). The intra-procedural heuristic does not always result in additional specifications. For example, among the 206 call sites of another X11 API, XtFree, 184 (89%) call sites had the related API (such as XtNew, XtNewString, and XtMalloc) in a procedure different from the enclosing procedure of XtFree.

Multiple-API violations. Our adaptation uses the multiple-API specifications mined from normal traces in detecting multiple-API violations in the analyzed software packages. Column 8 (**MAV**) presents the number of multiple-API violations detected by our adaptation. We manually inspected the violations reported by our adaptation: 12 (20%) out of the 60 (subcolumn Σ) reported multiple-API violations were false positives (subcolumn **FP**). To verify conditional specifications, we adapted MOPS to track the value of variables that take the return value of an API call along the different branches of conditional constructs. Tracking API return values while verifying multiple-API specifications decreases the number of false positives, which will otherwise be reported. As a simple example, verifying conditional specifications causes false positives such as "a file is not closed before the program exits on the failure (NULL) path of the open API" not to be reported. Verifying conditional specifications by tracking return values avoided 87 false positives among the analyzed packages, which would have otherwise been reported. In all, our adaptation mines 62 error-handling specifications and detects 264 error-handling violations in the analyzed packages.

5.4   Conclusions

We begin this section by presenting the chapter summary. We end this chapter by discussing the scope and limitations of our framework, while identifying avenues for further research.

5.4.1 Summary

This chapter proposed a novel framework for addressing the main problem faced by programmers in incorporating static verification in the software development cycle: API specifications are often not documented and, hence, unavailable. When API specifications are not known, to automatically mine them from source code (API client code), we presented a framework to generate static traces from source code by adapting push-down model checking. We then presented novel applications of data mining techniques on the generated static traces for specification mining. We shared our experiences of applying our framework on several popular open-source packages to mine API specifications and detect violations, without requiring any user input. We described an implementation of our framework by adapting an open-source model checker [20] and compared our framework with an existing dynamic specification-mining technique [12] in mining X11 API specifications from the X11-R6.9.0 distribution (208 KLOC). We adapted our trace generation framework to mine API error-handling specifications and detected API error-handling violations in 10 packages from the Redhat-9.0 distribution (52 KLOC), postfix-2.0.16 (111 KLOC), and X11-R6.9.0 distribution (208 KLOC). Our framework mined 62 error-handling specifications and detected 264 real error-handling defects from the analyzed packages.

5.4.2 Scope, Limitations, and Further Research

Unlike approaches [10, 34, 61] that analyze API implementation code, our framework presented in this chapter analyzes API client code. In many cases, the third-party API implementation code might not be available and hence our framework is complementary to approaches that analyze API implementation code. While our ideas can be extended to object-oriented languages, in this chapter, our analysis is restricted to API client code implemented in procedural languages such as C. Features specific to object-oriented languages such as method overloading and overriding, dynamic binding, inheritance, and polymorphism introduce additional challenges. It is worth exploring how the basic idea of static specification mining can be extended to object-oriented languages such as Java, C++, and C#.

Dynamic approaches [12, 51, 64] exist to mine API specifications from program execution *traces* (informally, a set of program statements along a program path generated dynamically or statically, described in Section 5.2.1 in detail). Different from these approaches, our framework mines properties from the source code of API clients. The main limitation of dynamic approaches is the requirement of sufficiently high-quality system tests to exercise various API behaviors comprehensively. Hence, the API violations in the analyzed programs might not be easily exposed. Furthermore, dynamic approaches require setup of costly runtime environments and test harnesses, not required by our framework. Further research is required for synergistically combining static and dynamic trace mining approaches. Also, investigation of techniques to validate the violations discovered statically by our framework – for instance, by dynamically generating a concrete test case for exposing a reported static violation – might be useful to reduce the false positives inherent to static approaches.

Furthermore, unlike approaches [55] that analyze open-source, non-compilable, and incomplete code examples found on the web, our framework requires that the analyzed API client code is compilable and complete. An advantage of analyzing complete code is the availability of precise and inter-procedural information for specification mining and violation detection. However, a limitation of our framework surfaces when there are insufficient call sites for a given API in the analyzed source code. In such cases, we plan to explore how our framework can be complemented by approaches such as PARSEWeb [55], whose mining scope spans open-source code found in the web. Finally, like all static specification-mining approaches, we assume that the programmers correctly adhere to the API specifications in the analyzed programs most of the time and that the frequently occurring API patterns are very likely correct.

The model checker that we used does not handle function pointers and callbacks. Hence we could not mine X11 specifications that involve callbacks. Our trace generation component does not analyze loops and our miner does not handle duplicate strings; iterative patterns [42] among API specifications are not mined by our framework. However, non-iterative patterns still capture significant specifications, which are of interest to programmers [16, 17, 24, 25, 37, 48, 49]. Due to pointer- and alias-insensitive analysis, our framework might not mine all the specifications or detect all the error-checks and multiple-API violations present in the analyzed software packages, leading to false negatives. For the mined specifications and the detected violations, we have not quantified the false negatives of our framework. Quantifying the violations missed by our framework (through manual inspection of source code along all possible paths in the presence of function pointers and aliasing) is difficult and error prone. The goal of our framework, like all static specification-mining approaches [16, 25, 39, 48, 49], is to find as many specifications (and violations) as possible with low false positives. For verification, our framework adapts a compile-time model checker, MOPS [20], which is shown to be scalable in checking over 30 million lines of Linux code [19]. Static checkers [14, 31] specific to error-handling can also be used in verifying the mined specifications.

Bibliography

[1] Coverity's Static Analysis. http://www.coverity.com/products/static-analysis.html.

[2] FindBugs. http://findbugs.sourceforge.net/.

[3] GrammaTech CodeSurfer. http://www.grammatech.com/products/codesurfer/.

[4] Java PathFinder. http://javapathfinder.sourceforge.net/.

[5] Microsoft Pex. http://research.microsoft.com/en-us/projects/Pex/.

[6] Pattern Insight's Patch Miner. http://www.patterninsight.com/solutions/index.html.

[7] *IEEE Computer Society. IEEE Standard for Information Technology Portable Operating System Interface POSIX Part I: System Application Program Interface API, IEEE Std 1003.1b-1993.* 1994.

[8] Mithun Acharya, Tao Xie, Jian Pei, and Jun Xu. Mining API patterns as partial orders from source code: from usage scenarios to specifications. In *Proceedings of the 6th Joint Meeting of the European Software Engineering Conference and the ACM SIGSOFT Symposium on the Foundations of Software Engineering (ESEC/FSE)*, pages 25–34, 2007.

[9] Rakesh Agrawal and Ramakrishnan Srikant. Fast algorithms for mining association rules in large databases. In *Proceedings of the International Conference on Very Large Data Bases (VLDB)*, pages 487–499, 1994.

[10] Rajeev Alur, Pavol Cerny, P. Madhusudan, and Wonhong Nam. Synthesis of interface specifications for Java classes. In *Proceedings of the Symposium on Principles of Programming Languages (POPL)*, pages 98–109, 2005.

[11] G. Ammons, D. Mandein, R. Bodik, and J. Larus. Debugging temporal specifications with concept analysis. In *Proceedings of the Conference on Programming Language Design and Implementation (PLDI)*, pages 182–195, 2003.

[12] Glenn Ammons, Rastislav Bodik, and James Larus. Mining specifications. In *Proceedings of the Symposium on Principles of Programming Languages (POPL)*, pages 4–16, 2002.

[13] Thomas Ball and Sriram Rajamani. Automatically validating temporal safety properties of interfaces. In *Proceedings of the Workshop on Model Checking Software*, pages 103–122, 2001.

[14] Magiel Bruntink, Arie Van Deursen, and Tom Tourwe. Discovering faults in idiom-based exception handling. In *Proceedings of the International Conference on Software Engineering (ICSE)*, pages 242–251, 2006.

[15] Sagar Chaki, Edmund Clarke, Alex Groce, Somesh Jha, and Helmut Veith. Modular verification of software components in C. In *Proceedings of the International Conference on Software Engineering (ICSE)*, pages 385–395, 2003.

[16] R. Y. Chang and A. Podgurski. Finding what's not there: a new approach to revealing neglected conditions in software. In *Proceedings of the International Symposium on Software Testing and Analysis (ISSTA)*, pages 163–173, 2007.

[17] Ray-Yaung Chang, Andy Podgurski, and Jiong Yang. Discovering neglected conditions in software by mining dependence graphs. *IEEE Transactions on Software Engineering (TSE)*, pages 579–596, 2008. http://doi.ieeecomputersociety.org/10.1109/TSE.2008.24.

[18] Hao Chen. Lightweight Model Checking for Improving Software Security. Ph.D. thesis, University of California, Berkeley, 2004.

[19] Hao Chen, Drew Dean, and David Wagner. Model checking one million lines of C code. In *Proceedings of the Network and Distributed System Security Symposium (NDSS)*, pages 171–185, 2004.

[20] Hao Chen and David Wagner. MOPS: an infrastructure for examining security properties of software. In *Proceedings of the ACM Conference on Computer and Communications Security (CCS)*, pages 235–244, 2002.

[21] Edmund Clarke, Daniel Kroening, Natasha Sharygina, and Karen Yorav. SATABS: SAT-based predicate abstraction for ANSI-C. In *Proceedings of the International Conference on Tools and Algorithms for the Construction and Analysis of Systems (TACAS)*, pages 570–574, 2005.

[22] Flaviu Cristian. Exception Handling and Tolerance of Software Faults. In *Software Fault Tolerance*, Chapter 5. John Wiley and Sons, 1995.

[23] Manuvir Das, Sorin Lerner, and Mark Seigle. ESP: path-sensitive program verification in polynomial time. In *Proceedings of the Programming Language Design and Implementation (PLDI)*, pages 57–68, 2002.

[24] Dawson Engler, Benjamin Chelf, Andy Chou, and Seth Hallem. Checking system rules using system-specific, programmer-written compiler extensions. In *Proceedings of the USENIX Symposium on Operating Systems Design (SOSP)*, pages 1–16, 2000.

[25] Dawson Engler, David Yu Chen, Seth Hallem, Andy Chou, and Benjamin Chelf. Bugs as deviant behavior: a general approach to inferring errors in systems code. In *Proceedings of the ACM Symposium on Operating Systems Principles (SOSP)*, pages 57–72, 2001.

[26] Javier Esparza, David Hansel, Peter Rossmanith, and Stefan Schwoon. Efficient algorithms for model checking push down systems. In *Proceedings of the International Conference on Computer Aided Verification (CAV)*, pages 232–247, 2000.

[27] Javier Esparza, Stefan Kiefer, and Stefan Schwoon. Abstraction refinement with Craig interpolation and symbolic pushdown systems. In *Proceedings of the 12th International Conference on Tools and Algorithms for the Construction and Analysis of Systems (TACAS)*, pages 489–503, 2006.

[28] Justin Forrester and Barton P. Miller. An empirical study of the robustness of Windows NT applications using random testing. In *Proceedings of the USENIX Windows Systems Symposium*, pages 69–78, 2000.

[29] Patrice Godefroid. Model checking for programming languages using Verisoft. In *Proceedings of the Symposium on Principles of Programming Languages (POPL)*, pages 174–186, 1997.

[30] Gosta Grahne and Jianfei Zhu. Efficiently using prefix-trees in mining frequent itemsets. In *IEEE ICDM Workshop on Frequent Itemset Mining Implementations*, 2003.

[31] Haryadi Gunawi, Cindy Rubio-Gonzalez, Andrea Arpaci-Dusseau, Remzi Arpaci-Dusseau, and Ben Liblit. EIO: error handling is occasionally correct. In *Proceedings of the USENIX Conference on File and Storage Technology (FAST)*, pages 242–251, 2006.

[32] Jennifer Haddox, Gregory Kapfhammer, C. Michael, and Michael Schatz. Testing commercial-off-the-shelf software components. In *Proceedings of the 18th International Conference and Exposition on Testing (ICET)*, 2001.

[33] T. Henzinger, R. Jhala, R. Majumdar, and G. Sutre. Software verification with BLAST. In *Proceedings of the Workshop on Model Checking Software*, pages 235–239, 2003.

[34] Thomas A. Henzinger, Ranjit Jhala, and Rupak Majumdar. Permissive interfaces. In *Proceedings of the European Software Engineering Conference and the ACM SIGSOFT Symposium on the Foundations of Software Engineering (ESEC/FSE)*, pages 31–40, 2005.

[35] John Hopcroft and Jeffrey Ullman. *Introduction to Automata Theory, Languages and Computation*. Addison-Wesley, 1979.

[36] Philip Koopman and John DeVale. The exception handling effectiveness of POSIX operating systems. *IEEE Transactions on Software Engineering (TSE)*, 26(9):837–848, 2000.

156   *Mining Software Specifications: Methodologies and Applications*

[37] Ted Kremenek, Paul Twohey, Godmar Back, Dawson Engler, and Andrew Ng. From uncertainty to belief: inferring the specification within. In *Proceedings of the Symposium on Operating Systems Design and Implementation (OSDI)*, pages 161–176, 2006.

[38] Nathan Kropp, Philip J. Koopman, and Daniel P. Siewiorek. Automated robustness testing of off-the-shelf software components. In *Proceedings of the IEEE International Symposium on Fault-Tolerant Computing (FTCS)*, pages 230–239, 1998.

[39] Zhenmin Li and Yuanyuan Zhou. PR-Miner: automatically extracting implicit programming rules and detecting violations in large software code. In *Proceedings of the European Software Engineering Conference and the ACM SIGSOFT Symposium on the Foundations of Software Engineering (ESEC/FSE)*, pages 306–315, 2005.

[40] Chang Liu, En Ye, and Debra J. Richardson. Software library usage pattern extraction using a software model checker. In *Proceedings of the IEEE/ACM International Conference on Automated Software Engineering (ASE)*, pages 301–304, 2006.

[41] Benjamin Livshits and Thomas Zimmermann. DynaMine: finding common error patterns by mining software revision histories. In *Proceedings of the European Software Engineering Conference and the ACM SIGSOFT Symposium on the Foundations of Software Engineering (ESEC/FSE)*, pages 296–305, 2005.

[42] David Lo, Siau-Cheng Khoo, and Chao Liu. Efficient mining of iterative patterns for software specification discovery. In *Proceedings of the ACM SIGKDD International Conference on Knowledge Discovery and Data Mining (KDD)*, pages 460–469, 2007.

[43] Amir Michail. Data mining library reuse patterns using generalized association rules. In *Proceedings of the International Conference on Software Engineering (ICSE)*, pages 167–176, 2000.

[44] Barton Miller, Lars Fredriksen, and Bryan So. An empirical study of the reliability of UNIX utilities. *Communications of the ACM*, 33(12):32–44, December 1990.

[45] Barton Miller, David Koski, Cjin P. Lee, Vivekananda Maganty, Ravi Murthy, Ajitkumar Natarajan, and Jeff Steidl. Fuzz revisited: a re-examination of the reliability of UNIX utilities and services. *Computer Science Technical Report 1268, University of Wisconsin-Madison*, 1995.

[46] J. D. Musa, A. Iannino, and K. Okumoto. *Engineering and Managing Software with Reliability Measures.* McGraw-Hill, 1987.

[47] Jian Pei, Haixun Wang, Jian Liu, Ke Wang, Jianyong Wang, and Philip Yu. Discovering frequent closed partial orders from strings. *IEEE Transactions on Knowledge and Data Engineering (TKDE)*, 18(11):1467–1481, 2006.

[48] Murali Krishna Ramanathan, Ananth Grama, and Suresh Jagannathan. Path-sensitive inference of function precedence protocols. In *Proceedings of the International Conference on Software Engineering (ICSE)*, pages 240–250, 2007.

[49] Murali Krishna Ramanathan, Ananth Grama, and Suresh Jagannathan. Static specification inference using predicate mining. In *Proceedings of the Conference on Programming Language Design and Implementation (PLDI)*, pages 123–134, 2007.

[50] David Rosenthal. *Inter-client communication Conventions Manual (IC-CCM), Version 2.0. X Consortium, Inc.* 1994.

[51] Sriram Sankaranarayanan, Franjo Ivancic, and Aarti Gupta. Mining library specifications using inductive logic programming. In *Proceedings of the International Conference on Software Engineering (ICSE)*, pages 131–140, 2008.

[52] Matthew Schmid, Anup Ghosh, and Frank Hill. Techniques for evaluating the robustness of Windows NT software. In *Proceedings of the 2000 DARPA Information Survivability Conference and Exposition (DISCEX)*, page 1347, 2000.

[53] Benjamin Schwarz, Hao Chen, David Wagner, Geoff Morrison, Jacob West, Jeremy Lin, and Wei Tu. Model checking an entire Linux distribution for security violations. In *Proceedings of the Annual Computer Security Applications Conference (ACSAC)*, pages 13–22, 2005.

[54] Charles Shelton, Philip Koopman, and Kobey DeVale. Robustness testing of the Microsoft Win32 API. In *Proceedings of the IEEE International Conference on Dependable Systems and Networks (DSN)*, page 261, 2000.

[55] Suresh Thummalapenta and Tao Xie. PARSEWeb: a programmer assistant for reusing open source code on the web. In *Proceedings of the International Conference on Automated Software Engineering (ASE)*, pages 204–213, 2007.

[56] W.N. Toy. Fault-tolerant design of local ESS processors. In *The Theory and Practice of Reliable System Design,* Digital Press, 1982.

[57] Timothy Tsai and Navjot Singh. Reliability testing of applications on Windows NT. In *Proceedings of the IEEE International Conference on Dependable Systems and Networks (DSN)*, page 427, 2000.

[58] Jianyong Wang and Jiawei Han. BIDE: efficient mining of frequent closed sequences. In *Proceedings of the International Conference on Data Engineering (ICDE)*, pages 79–90, 2004.

[59] Westley Weimer and George C. Necula. Finding and preventing run-time error handling mistakes. In *Proceedings of the ACM SIGPLAN International Conference on Object-Oriented Programming, Systems, Languages, and Applications (OOPSLA)*, pages 419–431, 2004.

[60] Westley Weimer and George C. Necula. Mining temporal specifications for error detection. In *Proceedings of the International Conference on Tools and Algorithms for the Construction and Analysis of Systems (TACAS)*, pages 461–476, 2005.

[61] John Whaley, Michael C. Martin, and Monica S. Lam. Automatic extraction of object-oriented component interfaces. In *Proceedings of the International Symposium on Software Testing and Analysis (ISSTA)*, pages 218–228, 2002.

[62] Chadd C. Williams and Jeffrey K. Hollingsworth. Automatic mining of source code repositories to improve bug finding techniques. *IEEE Transactions on Software Engineering (TSE)*, 31(6):466–480, 2005.

[63] Tao Xie and Jian Pei. MAPO: mining API usages from open source repositories. In *Proceedings of the International Workshop on Mining Software Repositories (MSR)*, pages 54–57, 2006.

[64] Jinlin Yang, David Evans, Deepali Bhardwaj, Thirumalesh Bhat, and Manuvir Das. Perracotta: mining temporal API rules from imperfect traces. In *Proceedings of the International Conference on Software Engineering (ICSE)*, pages 282–291, 2006.

Chapter 6

Static Specification Mining Using Automata-Based Abstractions[*]

Eran Yahav

IBM T.J. Watson Research Center
and Technion – Israel Institute of Technology

Sharon Shoham

Technion – Israel Institute of Technology

Stephen Fink

IBM T.J. Watson Research Center

Marco Pistoia

IBM T.J. Watson Research Center

---

[*]This chapter is based on: S. Shoham, et al., Static specification mining using automata-based abstractions, Proceedings of the 2007 International Symposium on Software Testing and Analysis, ©2007 Association for Computing Machinery Inc. Reprinted by permission.

6.1   Introduction

> *There is only one thing more painful than learning from experience*
> *and that is not learning from experience.*
> – Archibald MacLeish

Programming is becoming more and more about using frameworks and libraries. To perform standard tasks such as parsing an XML file, or communicating with a database, programmers use existing standard frameworks and class libraries rather than writing code from scratch.

While much easier than writing code from scratch, using a library is not a trivial task. A typical library API (application programming interface) can involve thousands of classes, with tens of methods each, and specific sequences of operations that have to be invoked to perform a task. For example, sending a file over a socket using standard libraries in Java involves instantiating 4 classes, and calling 10 methods on them. More sophisticated tasks can easily span tens of classes with tens of methods to be invoked in specific sequence, also handling possible error conditions along the way.

It is common for library objects (components) to maintain an internal state, and to change their behavior and permitted operations based on this internal state. For example, a socket component may allow reading or writing when it is in its *connected* state, but may yield an error if reading or writing is attempted when it is in its *closed* state. Components often have an implicit *temporal specification*, describing what sequences of method calls are permitted on a component.

Mainstream programming languages such as Java and C# provide no support for statically checking the correct use of library APIs. To write code that uses a component correctly, programmers can rely on library documentation, on trying to understand the library code (when it is available), or on code examples of other client programs using the library.

A lot of research focused on the problem of *mining specifications* of libraries to create a higher level description of what constitutes a correct use of the library (e.g., $[1, 2, 5, 9, 10, 15, 19, 24, 30\text{--}32]$). The majority of this research has focused on *dynamic specification mining*, inferring specifications from observed behavior of representative program runs. Dynamic approaches enjoy the significant virtue that they learn from behavior that definitively occurs in a run. On the flip side, dynamic approaches can learn *only* from available representative runs; incomplete coverage remains a fundamental limitation.

In addition, *the amount of code available for inspection vastly exceeds the amount of code amenable to automated dynamic analysis.* Dynamic analysis requires someone to build, deploy, and set up an appropriate environment for a program run. These tasks, difficult and time-consuming for a human, lie far beyond the reach of today's automated technologies.

To avoid the difficulties of running a program, a tool can grab code, and apply static program analysis to approximate its behavior. For this reason, static analysis may add value as a complement or alternative to dynamic analysis for specification mining.

Static analyses for specification mining can be classified as *component-side*, *client-side*, or both. A component-side approach analyzes the implementation of an API, and uses error conditions in the library (such as throwing an exception) or user annotations to derive a specification.

In contrast, client-side approaches examine not the implementation of an API, but rather the ways client programs use that API. Thus, client-side approaches can infer specifications that represent how a particular set of clients uses a general API, rather than approximating safe behavior for all possible clients. In practice, this is a key distinction, since a specification of non-failing behaviors often drastically over-estimates the intended use cases.

This work addresses static analysis for client-side mining, applied to API specifications for object-oriented libraries. The central challenge is to accurately track sequences that represent typical usage patterns of the API. In particular, the analysis must deal with three difficult issues:

- **Aliasing.** Objects from the target API may flow through complex heap-allocated data structures.
- **Unbounded Sequence Length.** The sequence of events for a particular object may grow to any length; the static analysis must rely on a sufficiently precise yet scalable finite abstraction of unbounded sequences.
- **Noise.** The analysis will inevitably infer some spurious usage patterns, due to either analysis imprecision or incorrect client programs. A tool must discard spurious patterns in order to output intuitive, intended specifications.

We present a two-phased approach consisting of (1) an *abstract-trace collection* to collect sets of possible behaviors in client programs, and (2) a *summarization* phase to filter out noise and spurious patterns. We also suggest refinement mechanisms to make the analysis more precise. In this chapter, we present:

- a framework for client-side specification mining based on flow-sensitive, context-sensitive abstract interpretation over a combined domain abstracting both aliasing and event sequences,
- a novel family of abstractions to represent unbounded event sequences,
- novel algorithms to summarize abstract traces based on automata clusters,
- refinement that uses inspection of selected mined traces to make the framework more precise, and
- results from a prototype implementation that mines several interesting specifications from non-trivial Java programs.

The experimental results indicate that to produce reasonable specifications, the static analysis must employ sufficiently precise abstractions of aliases and event sequences. Based on experience with the prototype implementation, we discuss strengths and weaknesses of static analysis for specification mining. We conclude that this approach shows promise as a path to more effective specification mining tools.

6.2   Overview

Figure 6.1 shows a simple Java program that uses `SocketChannel` objects. Our goal is to infer the pattern of `SocketChannel` API calls the program invokes on any individual object. Figure 6.2 shows a partial specification of the `SocketChannel` API,[1] representing a desirable analysis output. The specification indicates that the program must *connect* a `SocketChannel` before using it. Connecting a channel entails a sequence of three operations: (1) configuring the channel's blocking mode, (2) requesting a connection, and (3) finishing the connection process by waiting for the connection to be established. Once the channel is connected, the program can invoke `read` and `write` in any order, and eventually, `close`.

To extract this pattern from the example code, an analysis must deal with complex heap-allocated data structures to track the state of individual objects. Note that the method `createChannels` returns a collection containing an arbitrary number of dynamically allocated `SocketChannel` objects, which flow across procedure boundaries to other API calls. To make sense of the temporal sequence of operations on any individual channel, the analysis must employ precise alias analysis to track the sequence of operations on individual objects.

---

[1]Figures use abbreviated method names.

```
class SocketChannelClient {
 void example() {
  Collection<SocketChannel> channels = createChannels();
  for (SocketChannel sc : channels) {
   sc.connect(new InetSocketAddress("tinyurl.com/23qct8",80));
   while (!sc.finishConnect()) {
    // ... wait for connection ...
   }
   if (?) {
    receive(sc);
   } else {
    send(sc);
   }
  }
  closeAll(channels);
 }
 void closeAll(Collection<SocketChannel> chnls) {
   for (SocketChannel sc : chnls) { sc.close(); }
 }
 Collection<SocketChannel> createChannels() {
  List<SocketChannel> list = new LinkedList<SocketChannel>();
  list.add(createChannel("http://tinyurl.com/23qct8", 80));
  list.add(createChannel("http://tinyurl.com/23qct8", 80));
  //...
  return list;
 }
 SocketChannel createChannel(String hostName, int port) {
  SocketChannel sc = SocketChannel.open();    // A1
  sc.configureBlocking(false);
  return sc;
 }
 void receive(SocketChannel x) {
  File f = new File("ReceivedData");
  FileOutputStream fos = new FileOutputStream(f,true);
  ByteBuffer dst = ByteBuffer.allocateDirect(1024);
  int numBytesRead = 0;
  while (numBytesRead >= 0) {
   numBytesRead = x.read(dst);
   fos.write(dst.array());
  }
  fos.close();
 }
 void send(SocketChannel x) {
  for (?) {
   ByteBuffer buf = ByteBuffer.allocateDirect(1024);
   buf.put((byte) 0xFF);
   buf.flip();
   int numBytesWritten = x.write(buf);
  }
 }
}
```

FIGURE 6.1: A simple program using APIs of interest.

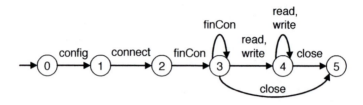

FIGURE 6.2: Partial specification for `SocketChannel`.

TABLE 6.1: Results of Mining the Running Example with Varying Heap Abstractions and Merge Algorithms

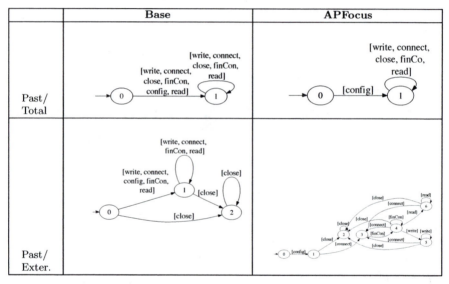

In addition to challenges with alias analysis, the specification inference must deal with a second difficult abstraction issue: tracking state related to a potentially *unbounded* sequence of events for each object. For example, the `receive` method of Figure 6.1 invokes `x.read(dst)` in a `while` loop with unknown bounds.

Our approach consists of two phases: an *abstract-trace collection* phase, which accumulates abstractions of event sequences for abstract objects, using *abstract histories*, and a *summarization* phase, which consolidates the abstract histories and reduces noise. We also suggest *refinement* mechanisms to make the analysis more precise.

6.2.1   Abstract-Trace Collection

We statically collect data regarding the event sequences for objects of a particular type. We use abstract interpretation [6], where an abstract value combines pointer information with an *abstract history*, a bounded representation of the sequence of events for a tracked object in the form of an automaton.

Our trace collection analysis is governed by two general parameters: (1) the heap abstraction and (2) the history abstraction. Table 6.1 shows the abstract histories generated for the example program, varying the choice of heap abstraction and history abstraction.

The table columns represent two heap abstractions presented previously [11]; the *Base* abstraction, which relies on a flow-insensitive Andersen's pointer analysis [3], and the *APFocus* abstraction, which employs fairly precise flow-sensitive access-paths analysis. The table rows represent variations on the history abstraction. The history abstraction relies on an *extend* operator and a *merge* operator. In the table, we fix the extend operator to one that distinguishes past behavior (the *Past* relation of Section 6.4.2.3), and vary the choice of merge operator.

The merge operator controls the *join* used to combine histories that arise at the same program point but in different execution paths. The *Total* operator joins *all* histories that occur in a particular abstract program state. The *Exterior* operator joins only histories that share a common recent past, as will be described formally later.

In the table, specifications become less permissive (and more precise) as one moves right and/or down. That is, the combination Base/Past/Total is the most permissive, and APFocus/Past/Exterior is the least permissive. The results show that the analysis requires *both a rather precise aliasing and a rather precise merge operator* to approach the desired result.

6.2.2   Summarization

Abstract trace collection generates a set of abstract histories that over-approximates possible client behavior. However, some generated histories will admit spurious behavior (noise), either due to analysis imprecision or bugs in the client corpus.

The summarization phase employs statistical approaches to consolidate the collected abstract histories. In contrast to most previous work, which summarizes either raw event traces [2, 5] or event pairs [30, 32], our "raw data" (automata) already exhibit some structure resembling a candidate specification.

Our summarization phase exploits this structure to perform effective noise elimination and consolidation. In particular, we show a clustering algorithm to partition the abstract histories into groups that represent related scenarios. The approach eliminates noise from each cluster independently, allowing it to distinguish noise from interference between independent use cases.

Returning to the running example, we note that the least permissive abstract history (APFocus/Past/Exterior) contains a few edges that look spurious, such as repeated calls to `close` (state 2 self-loop) and repeated calls to `connect` (state 6 to state 3). In fact, these transitions will occur in the example program if the same `SocketChannel` appears twice in the collection; however, most likely the programmer does not intend for this to happen, and perhaps some invariant rules out this pathological case. When this abstract history is summarized with others that do not exhibit this particular pathology, the summarization algorithm will rule out the spurious edges, resulting in the specification of Figure 6.2.

We further note that the quality of the input abstract histories limits the quality of the summarization output. It is hard to imagine any summarization algorithm producing the desired specification based on overly permissive input, such as the abstract history from Base/Past/Total.

6.2.3   Refining Mining Results via Inspection

Even after the summarization phase, the mined specification might exhibit spurious behavior. In particular, spurious behavior which is included in the mined specification due to the history abstraction sometimes eluding the statistical summarization approaches since it repeats in many of the histories.

To deal with this source of imprecision, we propose several approaches for refining the history abstraction. We can recover some of the precision lost due to merging histories by performing "inspection" of paths in the mined specifications that are ranked as *unlikely*. *Inspection* checks the absence of a specific sequence in the training-set. We distinguish between static and dynamic inspection, and between client-side and component-side inspection. We explain how inspection may be used to dismiss some paths when it is shown that they cannot occur in any execution of the code base.

6.3   Preliminaries

In this section, we provide some basic definitions that we will use in the rest of the chapter.

Definition 6.3.1. *Given a finite set Σ of input symbols, a finite automaton over* alphabet Σ *is a tuple* $\mathcal{A} = (\Sigma, \mathcal{Q}, init, \delta, \mathcal{F})$, *where $\mathcal{Q}$ is a finite set of states, $init \in \mathcal{Q}$ is the* initial state, $\delta: \mathcal{Q} \times \Sigma \to 2^{\mathcal{Q}}$ *is the* transition function, *and $\mathcal{F} \subseteq \mathcal{Q}$ is the set of* accepting states.

An automaton $\mathcal{A}$ is *deterministic* if for every $q \in \mathcal{Q}$ and $\sigma \in \Sigma$, $|\delta(q, \sigma)| \leq 1$. δ is extended to finite words in the usual way. The *language* of $\mathcal{A}$, denoted $\mathcal{L}(\mathcal{A})$, is the set of all words $\alpha \in \Sigma^*$ such that $\delta(init, \alpha) \cap \mathcal{F} \neq \emptyset$.

For an automaton state $q \in \mathcal{Q}$, we define $in_k(q) = \{\alpha \in \Sigma^k \mid \exists q' \in \mathcal{Q} : q \in \delta(q', \alpha)\}$. Similarly, $out_k(q) = \{\alpha \in \Sigma^k \mid \exists q' \in \mathcal{Q} : q' \in \delta(q, \alpha)\}$. In particular, for every $q \in \mathcal{Q}$, $in_0(q) = out_0(q) = \{\epsilon\}$, where ϵ denotes the empty sequence. To ensure that for every $q \in \mathcal{Q}$ and every $k \geq 1$, $in_k(q), out_k(q) \neq \emptyset$, we extend Σ by some $\perp \notin \Sigma$ and view each state that has no predecessor (resp. successor) as having an infinite ingoing (resp. outgoing) sequence $\perp^\omega$.

Definition 6.3.2 (Quotient). *Let* $\mathcal{A} = (\Sigma, \mathcal{Q}, init, \delta, \mathcal{F})$ *be an automaton, and* $\mathcal{R} \subseteq \mathcal{Q} \times \mathcal{Q}$ *an equivalence relation on* $\mathcal{Q}$, *where* $[q]$ *denotes the equivalence class of* $q \in \mathcal{Q}$. *Then the* quotient automaton *is* $Quo_\mathcal{R}(\mathcal{A}) = (\Sigma, \{[q] \mid q \in \mathcal{Q}\}, [init], \delta', \{[q] \mid q \in \mathcal{F}\})$, *where* $\delta'([q], \sigma) = \{[q'] \mid \exists q'' \in [q] : q' \in \delta(q'', \sigma)\}$.

The quotient automaton is an automaton whose states consist of the equivalence classes of states of the original automaton. The outgoing transitions are then defined as the union of the outgoing transitions of all the states in the equivalence class (this might result in nondeterministic automata even if $\mathcal{A}$ is deterministic). It is easy to show that $\mathcal{L}(\mathcal{A}) \subseteq \mathcal{L}(Quo_\mathcal{R}(\mathcal{A}))$.

In the following, the alphabet Σ consists of method calls (observable events) over the objects of the tracked type.

6.4 Abstract Trace Collection

Our trace collection analysis produces "abstract histories," which summarize the event sequences of many possible concrete executions. The analysis propagates a sound approximation of program state that tracks alias information and histories for each abstract object.

In the following, we describe the analysis in terms of a sound abstraction of an instrumented concrete semantics.

6.4.1 Concrete Instrumented Semantics

We define an instrumented concrete semantics that tracks the concrete trace of events for each concrete object. We refer to the concrete trace of events as the *concrete history* of the concrete object. We start with a standard concrete semantics for an imperative object-oriented language, defining a program state and evaluation of an expression in a program state.

Restricting our attention to reference types, the semantic domains are defined in a standard way as follows:

$$
\begin{aligned}
L^\natural &\in 2^{objects^\natural} \\
v^\natural &\in Val = objects^\natural \cup \{null\} \\
\rho^\natural &\in Env = VarId \to Val \\
\pi^\natural &\in Heap = objects^\natural \times FieldId \to Val \\
state^\natural = \langle L^\natural, \rho^\natural, \pi^\natural \rangle &\in States = 2^{objects^\natural} \times Env \times Heap
\end{aligned}
$$

where $objects^\natural$ is an unbounded set of dynamically allocated objects, $VarId$ is a set of local variable identifiers, and $FieldId$ is a set of field identifiers.

A *program state* keeps track of the set $L^\natural$ of allocated objects, an *environment* $\rho^\natural$ mapping local variables to values, and a mapping $\pi^\natural$ from fields of allocated objects to values.

In our instrumented semantics, each concrete object is mapped to a "concrete history" that records the sequence of events that has occurred for that object. Technically, we define the notion of a *history* which captures a regular language of event sequences.

Definition 6.4.1. *A* history *h is a finite automaton $(\Sigma, \mathcal{Q}, init, \delta, \mathcal{F})$, where $\mathcal{F} \neq \emptyset$. $\mathcal{F}$ is also called the set of* current states. *We define the* traces *represented by h, $Tr(h)$, to be the language $\mathcal{L}(h)$.*

A *concrete history* $h^\natural$ is a special case of a history that encodes a single finite trace of events, that is, where $Tr(h^\natural)$ consists of a single finite trace of events. In Section 6.4.2 we will use the general notion of a history to describe a regular language of event sequences. We refer to a history that possibly describes more than a single trace of events as an *abstract history*.

Example 6.4.2. *Figure 6.3 shows examples of concrete histories occurring for a* SocketChannel *object of the example program at various points of the program. Figure 6.6 and Figure 6.7 show examples of abstract histories describing regular languages of events. In all figures, current states are depicted as double circles. Note that the automaton corresponding to an abstract history may be non-deterministic (e.g., as shown in Figure 6.7).*

We denote the set of all concrete histories by $\mathcal{H}^\natural$. We augment every concrete state $\langle L^\natural, \rho^\natural, \pi^\natural \rangle$ with an additional mapping $his^\natural \colon L^\natural \rightharpoonup \mathcal{H}^\natural$ that maps an allocated object of the tracked type to its concrete history. A state of the instrumented concrete semantics is therefore a tuple $\langle L^\natural, \rho^\natural, \pi^\natural, his^\natural \rangle$.

Given a state $\langle L^\natural, \rho^\natural, \pi^\natural, his^\natural \rangle$, the semantics generates a new state $\langle L^{\natural'}, \rho^{\natural'}, \pi^{\natural'}, his^{\natural'} \rangle$ when evaluating each statement. We assume a standard interpretation for program statements updating $L^\natural$, $\rho^\natural$, and $\pi^\natural$. The $his^\natural$ component changes when encountering object allocations and observable events:

- *Object Allocation:* For a statement x = new T() allocating an object of the tracked type, a new (fresh) object $l_{new} \in objects^\natural \setminus L^\natural$ is allocated, and $his^{\natural'}(l_{new}) = h_0^\natural$, where $h_0^\natural = (\Sigma, \{init\}, init, \delta_0, \{init\})$ and δ_0 is

Statement	Concrete History
sc = open()	
sc.config	
sc.connect	
sc.finCon	
...	
sc.finCon	
x.read	
...	
x.read	
sc.close	

FIGURE 6.3: Example of concrete histories for an object of type SocketChannel in the example program.

a transition function that maps every state and event to an empty set. That is, the newly allocated object is mapped into the empty-sequence history.

- *Observable Events:* For a statement x.m() where $\rho^\natural(x)$ is of the tracked type T, the object $\rho^\natural(x)$ is mapped to a new concrete history $extend^\natural(h^\natural, m)$, where $h^\natural = his^\natural(\rho^\natural(x))$ and $extend^\natural : \mathcal{H}^\natural \times \Sigma \to \mathcal{H}^\natural$ is the concrete *extend transformer* that adds exactly one new state to $h^\natural$, in the natural way, to reflect the call to $m()$.

Figure 6.3 shows the evolution of concrete histories for an object in the example program. Each concrete history records the sequence of observable events (method calls) upon the SocketChannel during a particular execution. Note that the length of a concrete history is a priori unknown, as events may occur in loops.

6.4.2 Abstract Semantics

The instrumented concrete semantics uses an unbounded description of the program state, resulting from a potentially unbounded number of objects, each with a potentially unbounded history. In this section, we describe an abstract semantics that conservatively represents the instrumented semantics with various degrees of precision and cost.

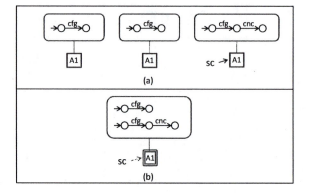

FIGURE 6.4: Example of concrete and abstract states: (a) concrete state with three `SocketChannel` objects with the same instance key *A*1; (b) abstract state with a single abstract object representing multiple concrete objects allocated at *A*1.

6.4.2.1   Abstract States

Following [11], we base the abstraction on a global *heap graph*, obtained through a flow-insensitive, partially context-sensitive subset-based may points-to analysis [3]. This provides a partition of the *objects*[h] set into abstract objects; each partition represents the set of all objects allocated at some allocation site, and is assigned a unique name called an *instance key*.

The partition based on instance keys is a *fixed* partition of the heap into abstract objects, and may be too coarse. For example, the heap graph representation of our motivating example contains a single instance key for type `SocketChannel`, representing *all* the objects allocated in `createChannel`. To simplify presentation, we treat the static call to `open` as an allocation site denoted by *A*1. The actual allocation site, as observed by our implementation, is inside this library call.

Example 6.4.3. *Figure 6.4(a) shows an example of a partial concrete state for the program of Figure 6.1. In the figure, we only show objects of type* SocketChannel. *A heap-allocated object is shown as a small rectangle labeled with an instance key (A1 in this case). For each object of type* SocketChannel, *we show the concrete history associated with it inside a round-rectangle connected to the object. We use an arrow from the variable name* sc *to denote that the object is pointed to by the program variable* sc. *In this example program, all objects of type* SocketChannel *are allocated at the same allocation site, and therefore have the same instance key.*

Figure 6.4 (b) shows an abstract state that represents the concrete state of Figure 6.4 (a). In this abstract state, there is a single abstract object, shown as a rectangle with double-edge boundaries. The abstract object (potentially) represents multiple concrete objects. Since the abstract object A1 represents all concrete objects allocated at A1, it has to represent all possible histories associated with these objects, and thus in this case has two histories associated with it. Because a pointer can only point to a single object, it does not point to all the objects represented by the abstract object, and we lose the information on which of the represented objects is pointed to by sc. *We use a dashed arrow to denote the fact that* sc *may point to some object represented by the abstract object.*

The abstract object A1 may represent multiple concrete objects. As a result, further operations applied to this abstract object will have to conservatively perform weak updates, *as the single representative has to represent all possible states of all possible concrete objects it represents.*

The heap abstraction we use refines the fixed partition and uses a *dynamic* partition. The partition changes based on the properties of objects. In particular, the partition changes based on the references that point to an object, and based on the history of an object. This is a form of "lightweight shape analysis."

An abstract program state consists of a set of tuples, called "factoids." Each factoid represents an abstract object (instance key) within the abstract program state. It summarizes the heap properties of the abstract object, as well as its history. More precisely, a factoid is a tuple $\langle o, \textit{heap-data}, h \rangle$, where

- o is an instance key.
- *heap-data* consists of multiple components describing heap properties of o (described below).
- h is the abstract history representing the traces observed for o until the corresponding execution point.

An abstract state can contain multiple factoids for the same instance key o, representing different alias contexts and abstract histories. This reflects the dynamic nature of the heap partition we use.

The *heap-data* component of the factoid is crucial for precision; we adopt the *heap-data* abstractions of [11]. Intuitively, the heap abstraction relies on the combination of a preliminary scalable (e.g., flow-insensitive) pointer analysis and selective predicates indicating access-path aliasing, and information on object uniqueness. Technically, the *heap-data* component of the factoid uses tuples of the form $\langle unique, AP_{must}, May, AP_{mustNot} \rangle$ where:

- *unique* indicates whether the corresponding instance key has a single concrete live object.
- AP_{must} is a set of access paths that must point to o.
- *May* is true indicating that there are additional access paths (not in the AP_{must} set) that may point to o.
- $AP_{mustNot}$ is a set of access paths that do not point to o.

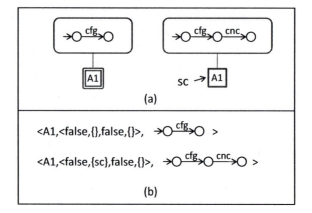

FIGURE 6.5: Example of an abstract state with access path information: (a) shown pictorially; (b) shown as a set of tuples.

For example, a factoid with instance key o, and with *heap-data* $= \langle unique = true, AP_{must} = \{x.f\}, AP_{mustNot} = \{y.g\}, May = true \rangle$ represents a program state in which there is exactly one object named o, such that $x.f$ must evaluate to point to o, $y.g$ must *not* evaluate to point to o, and there *may* be other pointers to o not represented by the must access path $x.f$ (nor by the must-not access path $y.g$).

Example 6.4.4. *Figure 6.5(a) shows an abstract state abstracting the concrete state of Figure 6.4(a). The same abstract state is shown as a set of tuples in Figure 6.5(b). In contrast to the abstract state of Figure 6.4(b), the abstract state in Figure 6.5 represents the object pointed to by* sc *separately from the representation of the other objects allocated at A1.*

A conservative representation of the concrete program state must obey the following properties:

(a) An instance key can be indicated as unique if it represents a single object for this program state.

(b) The access path sets (the must and the must-not) do not need to be complete. This does not compromise the soundness of the analysis due to the indication of the existence of other possible aliases (the *May* indication).

(c) The instance keys induce a static heap partition based on the syntactic program location in which an object has been allocated. The must and must-not access path sets refine this partition by separating objects that are known to be must-pointed (and must-not-pointed) by specific access paths. If the must point-to set is non-empty, the must-pointed partition represents a single concrete object.

(d) If $May = false$, the must access path is complete; it contains all access paths to this object.

The *Base* abstraction does not make use of the *heap-data* components, meaning that $AP_{must} = AP_{mustNot} = \emptyset$, $unique = false$, and $May = true$ in all factoids. The *APFocus* abstraction, on the other hand, uses these components to obtain better precision. Crucially, the tracking of *must point-to* information, as well as *uniqueness*, allows *strong updates* [4] when propagating dataflow information through a statement. For more details on the heap abstraction we refer the reader to [11, 12].

While a concrete history describes a unique trace, an abstract history typically encodes multiple traces as the language of the automaton. Different abstractions consider different history automata (e.g., deterministic versus non-deterministic) and different restrictions on the current states (e.g., exactly one current state versus multiple current states). We denote the set of abstract histories by $\mathcal{H}$. The remainder of this section considers semantics and variations of history abstractions.

6.4.2.2 Abstract Semantics

An abstract semantics for the history is defined via the following:
- An abstraction for the empty-sequence history, denoted h_0,
- An abstract extend transformer, $extend : \mathcal{H} \times \Sigma \to \mathcal{H}$, and
- A merge operator $\bigsqcup : 2^{\mathcal{H}} \to 2^{\mathcal{H}}$ which generates a new set of abstract histories that overapproximates the input set.

In the abstract semantics, the abstract history component for a fresh object is initialized to h_0. When an observable event occurs, the semantics updates the relevant histories using the *extend* operator.

As long as the domain of abstract histories is bounded, the abstract analysis is guaranteed to terminate. However, in practice, it can easily suffer from an exponential blowup due to branching control flow. The merge operator will mitigate this blowup, accelerating convergence. Specifically, at control flow join points, all factoids that represent the same instance key and have identical heap-data are merged. Such factoids differ only in their abstract histories, i.e., they represent different execution paths of the same abstract object in the same aliasing context.

Soundness. We design the abstraction to keep track of (at least) all the traces, or concrete histories, produced by the code base. We denote the set of all concrete histories possibly generated by a code base C by $\mathcal{H}_C^\natural$. Similarly, we denote the set of all abstract histories generated by the analysis of C by $\mathcal{H}_C$. The analysis is *sound* if for every concrete history $h^\natural$ in $\mathcal{H}_C^\natural$ there exists some abstract history in $\mathcal{H}_C$ whose set of traces includes the single concrete trace represented by $h^\natural$, i.e.,

$$\bigcup_{h^\natural \in \mathcal{H}_C^\natural} Tr(h^\natural) \subseteq \bigcup_{h \in \mathcal{H}_C} Tr(h)$$

Soundness is achieved by making sure that every reachable (instrumented) concrete state $istate^{\natural}$ is represented by some reachable abstract state $istate$, meaning that for every object $o^{\natural} \in L^{\natural}$ there exists a factoid $\langle o, heap\text{-}data, h \rangle$ in $istate$ that provides a sound representation of $o^{\natural}$. This is a factoid whose *heap-data* component fulfills the conditions described in [11], and in addition h is a sound representation of $his^{\natural}(o^{\natural})$, i.e., $Tr(his^{\natural}(o^{\natural})) \subseteq Tr(h)$. Soundness of h_0, the extend transformer, and of the merge operator ensures that the analysis is sound.

Definition 6.4.5. *An abstract extend transformer extend is* sound, *if whenever $Tr(h^{\natural}) \subseteq Tr(h)$ then for every $\sigma \in \Sigma$, $Tr(extend^{\natural}(h^{\natural}, \sigma)) \subseteq Tr(extend(h, \sigma))$.*

Definition 6.4.6. *A merge operator $\bigsqcup$ is* sound, *if for every set of abstract histories $H \subseteq \mathcal{H}$, $\bigcup_{h \in H} Tr(h) \subseteq \bigcup_{h \in \bigsqcup H} Tr(h)$.*

Precision. The analysis is *precise* when it does not introduce additional behaviors to those that are permitted by the code base, i.e.,

$$\bigcup_{h^{\natural} \in \mathcal{H}_C^{\natural}} Tr(h^{\natural}) = \bigcup_{h \in \mathcal{H}_C} Tr(h)$$

Remark. In practice, instead of considering the traces represented by *all* the abstract histories generated by the analysis, we consider the *prefix-closures* of the history automata at the exit points of the program, obtained by setting $\mathcal{F}' = \mathcal{Q}$ (i.e., all the states are considered accepting). The set of observed traces is maintained when we restrict ourselves to the prefix-closures of these automata since all other traces are prefixes of the traces represented by them.

6.4.2.3 History Abstractions

We present a parameterized framework for history abstractions, based on intuition regarding the structure of API specifications.

Quotient-Based Abstractions. In practice, automata that characterize API specifications are often simple, and further admit simple characterizations of their states (e.g., their ingoing or outgoing sequences). Exploiting this intuition, we introduce abstractions based on quotient structures of the history automata, which provide a general, simple, and often precise framework to reason about abstract histories.

Informally, given an equivalence relation $\mathcal{R}$ and some *merge criterion*, the quotient-based abstraction generalizes histories based on their quotient structures w.r.t. $\mathcal{R}$. The merge criterion is used to determine which abstract histories are merged by the merge operator. More precisely, we define the quotient-based abstraction of $\mathcal{R}$ as follows.

- The abstraction h_0 of the empty-sequence history is $Quo_{\mathcal{R}}(h_0^{\natural}) = h_0$, i.e., the empty-sequence history.

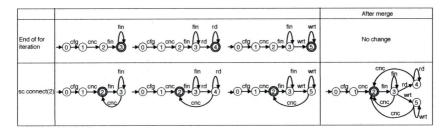

				After merge
End of for iteration				No change
sc.connect(2)				

FIGURE 6.6: Abstract interpretation with past abstraction (exterior merge).

- The *extend transformer* appends the new event σ to the current states, and constructs the quotient of the result. More formally, let $h = (\Sigma, Q, init, \delta, \mathcal{F})$. For every $q_i \in \mathcal{F}$ we introduce a fresh state, $n_i \notin Q$. Then $extend(h, \sigma) = Quo_{\mathcal{R}}(h')$, where $h' = (\Sigma, Q \cup \{n_i \mid q_i \in \mathcal{F}\}, init, \delta', \{n_i \mid q_i \in \mathcal{F}\})$ with $\delta'(q_i, \sigma) = \delta(q_i, \sigma) \cup \{n_i\}$ for every $q_i \in \mathcal{F}$, and $\delta'(q', \sigma') = \delta(q', \sigma')$ for every $q' \in Q$ and $\sigma' \in \Sigma$ such that $q' \notin \mathcal{F}$ or $\sigma' \neq \sigma$. Moreover, $\delta'(n_i, \sigma) = \emptyset$ for every new state n_i and for every $\sigma \in \Sigma$.

- The *merge operator* first partitions the set of histories based on the given *merge criterion*. Next, the merge operator constructs the union of the automata in each partition, and returns the quotient of the result.

It can be shown that for every equivalence relation $\mathcal{R}$ and merge criterion, the quotient-based abstraction w.r.t. $\mathcal{R}$ is sound.

To instantiate a quotient-based abstraction, we next consider options for the requisite equivalence relation and merge criteria.

Past-Future Abstractions. In many cases, API usages have the property that certain sequences of events are always preceded or followed by the same behaviors. For example, a `connect` event of `SocketChannel` is always followed by a `finishConnect` event. This means that the states of the corresponding automata are characterized by their ingoing and/or outgoing behaviors. As such, we consider quotient abstractions w.r.t. the following parametric equivalence relation.

Definition 6.4.7 (Past-Future Relation). *Let q_1, q_2 be history states, and $k_1, k_2 \in \mathbb{N}$. We write $(q_1, q_2) \in R[k_1, k_2]$ iff $in_{k_1}(q_1); out_{k_2}(q_1) \cap in_{k_1}(q_2); out_{k_2}(q_2) \neq \emptyset$, i.e., q_1 and q_2 share both an ingoing sequence of length k_1 and an outgoing sequence of length k_2.*

For example, consider the abstract history depicted in Figure 6.8(a). States 2 and 4 (marked by arrows) are equivalent w.r.t. $R[1, 0]$ since $in_1(2) = in_1(4) = \{cnc\}$ and $out_0(2) = out_0(4) = \{\epsilon\}$.

We will hereafter focus attention on the two extreme cases of the past-future abstraction, where either k_1 or k_2 is zero. Recall that $in_0(q) = out_0(q) =$

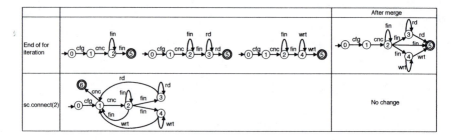

FIGURE 6.7: Abstract interpretation with future abstraction (exterior merge).

$\{\epsilon\}$ for every state q. As a result, $R[k, 0]$ collapses to a relation that considers ingoing sequences of length k. We refer to it as $\mathcal{R}^k_{past}$, and to the abstraction as the *k-past abstraction*. Similarly, $R[0, k]$ refers to outgoing sequences of length k, in which case we also refer to it as $\mathcal{R}^k_{future}$. We refer to the corresponding abstraction as the *k-future abstraction*. Intuitively, analysis using the k-past abstraction will distinguish patterns based only on their recent past behavior, and the k-future abstraction will distinguish patterns based only on their near future behavior. These abstractions will be effective if the recent past (near future) suffices to identify a particular sequence.

Merge Criteria. Having defined equivalence relations, we now consider merge criteria to define quotient-based abstractions. A merge criterion will determine when the analysis should collapse abstract program states, thus potentially losing precision, but accelerating convergence.

We consider the following merge schemes.

- *None:* Each history comprises a singleton set in the partition. This scheme is most precise, but is impractical, as it results in an exponential blowup.

- *Total:* The partition consists of a single set that contains all histories, i.e., all histories are merged into one.

- *Exterior:* The histories are partitioned into subsets in which all the histories have compatible initial states and compatible current states. Namely, histories h_1 and h_2 are merged only if (a) $(init_1, init_2) \in \mathcal{R}$; and (b) for every $q_1 \in \mathcal{F}_1$ there exists $q_2 \in \mathcal{F}_2$ s.t. $(q_1, q_2) \in \mathcal{R}$, and vice versa.

Intuitively, the total criterion forces the analysis to track exactly one abstract history for each "context" (i.e., alias context, instance key, and program point).

The exterior criterion provides a less aggressive alternative, based on the intuition that the distinguishing features of a history can be encapsulated by the features of its initial and current states, which we refer to as the "exterior" of the history. The thinking follows that if history states differ only on the characterization of intermediate (inner) states, merging them may be an attractive option to accelerate convergence without undue precision loss.

Example 6.4.8. *Figure 6.6 presents abstract histories produced during the analysis of the single instance key in our running example, using the 1-past abstraction with exterior merge. The first row describes the histories observed at the end of the first iteration of the* for *loop of* example() *, in which a channel is connected, and either the* receive *procedure, reading bytes from the channel, or the* send *procedure, writing bytes on the channel, is invoked. These all hold abstract histories for the same instance key at the same abstract state. Each history tracks a possible execution path of the abstract object.*

Although these histories refer to the same instance key and alias context, exterior merge does not apply since their current states are not equivalent. The second row shows the result of applying the extend transformer on each history after observing a connect *event at the beginning of the next iteration of the* for *loop. The intermediate step, before the quotient construction, for the automaton on the left is depicted in Figure 6.8(a). There, and in all other cases as well, the new state is equivalent to an existing state according to the 1-past relation; a state with* connect *as its incoming event already exists in each automaton. As a result, extend simply adds the new transitions and adds no new states.*

After observing this event, the resulting three histories meet the exterior merge criterion, and are therefore combined. The analysis discards the original histories and proceeds with the merged one which overapproximates them.

Figure 6.7 presents the corresponding abstract histories using the 1-future abstraction with exterior merge (in fact, in this case total merge behaves identically). Unlike the case under the past abstraction, merge applies at the end of the first loop iteration, since the initial and current states are equivalent under the 1-future relation. As a result, the analysis continues with the single merged history. The second row shows the result of applying the extend transformer on it after observing a connect *event.*

Figure 6.8(b) presents the intermediate step in which the merged abstract history is extended by connect*, before the quotient is constructed. An outgoing transition labeled* connect *is added from state 5 (the previous current state) to a new state, making state 5 share a future with state 1. Thus states 1 and 5 are merged, resulting in the abstract history depicted in the second row of Figure 6.7.*

Nondeterminism. It is easy to verify that the quotient structure of a deterministic automaton w.r.t. $\mathcal{R}_{past}^k$ is deterministic. This ensures that the k-past abstraction always produces deterministic automata, as demonstrated by Figure 6.6. On the other hand, when the future parameter is nontrivial (i.e., $k_2 \neq 0$), nondeterminism can result during the quotient construction. For example, in Figure 6.7, all the automata are non-deterministic.

Precision. If automata satisfy the following structural property, then we can prove that the past-future abstraction is precise.

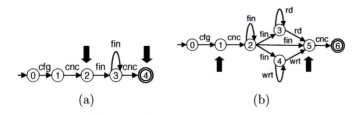

(a)   (b)

FIGURE 6.8: (a) Past abstraction step; and (b) future abstraction step, before quotient construction.

Definition 6.4.9. *An automaton $\mathcal{A}$ has the (k_1, k_2)-past-future property if for every $q_1 \neq q_2 \in \mathcal{Q}$, $in_{k_1}(q_1); out_{k_2}(q_1) \cap in_{k_1}(q_2); out_{k_2}(q_2) = \emptyset$. This implies that every sequence of length $k_1 + k_2$ is linked to a unique automaton state.*

Proposition 6.4.10 (Precision Guarantee). *If $\bigcup_{h^\natural \in \mathcal{H}_C^\natural} Tr(h^\natural)$ is accepted by some automaton that has the (k_1, k_2)-past-future property, then the (k_1, k_2)-past-future abstraction with exterior merge is precise.*

When the precision precondition is not met, different choices of k_1, k_2 in the past-future abstraction can lead to different results:

Example 6.4.11. *The first row of Figure 6.9 presents two histories produced while using the 1-past abstraction to track an abstract object that uses the Signature API. The history on the left uses the verify feature of the API, while the history on the right uses sign. The current states of these two histories, states 2 and 2′, are compatible ($in_1(2) = in_1(2') = \{update\}$), and the histories are therefore merged into the history presented in Figure 6.9 on the right. In particular, states 2 and 2′ are merged. As a result, the relation between an invocation of initVerify (resp. initSign) and a later invocation of verify (resp. sign) is lost.*

When using the 1-future abstraction, on the other hand, the corresponding abstract histories, depicted in the second row of Figure 6.9, are not compatible since their initial states are not compatible ($out_1(0) = \{initVerify\}$,

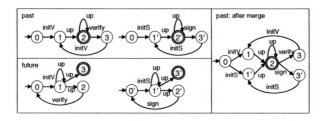

FIGURE 6.9: Past abstraction versus future abstraction.

while $out_1(0') = \{initSign\}$), and are therefore not merged, preventing the precision loss.

Of course, increasing the parameters k_1 and k_2 makes the abstraction more precise, but may negatively impact convergence.

6.5   Summarization Using Statistical Approaches

The abstract trace collection produces automata that overapproximate the actual behavior. However, the trace collection output may represent spurious behavior due to at least three sources of noise:

- **Analysis Imprecision:** The output of the abstract interpretation is an over-approximation that may include behavior from infeasible paths.
- **Bugs in Training Corpus:** Programs in the training corpus may contain a (hopefully small) number of incorrect usages.
- **Unrestricted Methods:** Some API methods (e.g., side-effect free methods) may not play a role in the intended API specification, but may still appear in the collected abstract traces.

To deal with unrestricted methods, one could leverage *component-side* techniques to analyze the API implementation, identify side-effect-free methods, and exclude them from consideration [27]. Similarly, we could apply component-side analysis to exclude spurious patterns which lead to violations of simple safety or liveness properties. We elide further discussion of such techniques as they fall outside the scope of this work, which focuses on client-side techniques.

To deal with the other sources of noise, we turn to statistical techniques inspired by approaches such as z-ranking [9] and the ranking of [30]. Statistical techniques distinguish signal from noise according to sample frequency. A crucial factor concerns what relative weight to assign to each sample.

We observe that each static occurrence of a usage pattern represents some thought and work by a programmer, while each dynamic occurrence typically represents an iteration of a loop counter. We assign weights to patterns based on a conjecture that the *number of times an API usage pattern appears in the code* provides a more meaningful metric than the number of times that code executes.[2]

Most previous work on statistical trace analyses considered raw traces consisting of raw event streams [2, 5] or event pairs [30, 32]. In contrast, our work summarizes samples that already represent summarized abstract traces, rep-

---

[2]An empirical evaluation of this conjecture falls outside the scope of this work, but would be an interesting direction for future work.

resented as automata. In this section, we present new approaches to statistical summarization that exploit the structure already present in these automata.

Our Summarization phase combines the results produced during the analysis of the clients in the code base. It can also consider a number of different client code bases. Due to its statistical nature, summarization does not maintain the soundness guarantee of the trace collection phase. Namely, it might erroneously identify correct behaviors as spurious ones, and remove them.

In the sequel, we assume without loss of generality that the observed traces are given via a set $\mathcal{I}$ of deterministic finite automata (if nondeterministic automata were produced, we would add a determinization step). The output of summarization consists of a ranked set of $k \leq |\mathcal{I}|$ automata, where each of the k represents a candidate API specification.

6.5.1   Union Methods

Naive Union. The naive approach outputs the union of all the automata in $\mathcal{I}$ as the API specification, without any noise reduction. This approach treats all traces uniformly, regardless of their frequency. Moreover, it does not distinguish between different ways in which the API is used.

Weighted Union. A better straightforward statistical approach uses a weighted union of the input automata to identify and eliminate infrequent behaviors. Specifically, we form the union automaton for all input automata, labeling each transition with the count of the number of input automata which contain it. Given this labeled automaton, one can apply any number of heuristics to discard transitions with low weights. Our implementation takes a threshold parameter f ($0 \leq f \leq 1$) and discards any transitions whose weight is less than f times the number of input automata.

6.5.2   Clustering

When a code base contains several independent patterns of API usage, these patterns may interfere to defeat union-based noise reduction. Instead, we partition the input into clusters of "similar" automata, and eliminate noise in each cluster independently.

We use a simple clustering algorithm based on a notion of automata *inclusion*. Automaton A *includes* automaton B iff $\mathcal{L}(A) \supseteq \mathcal{L}(B)$. The *include* relation induces a partial order on the set of automata. Each "maximal" element (automaton) w.r.t. this order represents a cluster consisting of all the automata included in it. Our algorithm forms clusters based on inclusion, and then applies the weighted union technique independently in each cluster.

Example 6.5.1. *Consider Figure 6.10. Each of the automata (a) and (b) represents a possible usage of the* Signature *API in some code base. Assume that each of them was observed numerous times. A weighted union of them with any reasonable threshold will return the right-most automaton in Figure 6.10,*

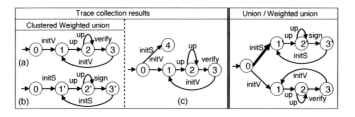

FIGURE 6.10: Summarization: clustered weighted union versus weighted union.

where the two usage patterns are combined. A clustered union, on the other hand, will identify that these are two different usage patterns, and will return (a) and (b) as two clusters.

Assume further that the code base also produced the automaton (c) of Figure 6.10. Automaton (c) refers to the same usage pattern as (a), but contains an additional transition from the initial state, which represents an invocation of initSign. *This transition is erroneous in this particular usage pattern, although it is not erroneous in the global view of the API, since an invocation of* initSign *from the initial state is a legal behavior in another context – that of pattern (b). In the weighted union, this transition simply increases the weight of the bold edge by 1, but it is not recognized as an error. Our clustered weighted union, on the other hand, recognizes that (c) belongs to the cluster of (a), and as a result it identifies and removes the erroneous transition.*

Note that after transitions are removed, the *include* relation can change as disparate clusters sometimes converge. As such, we iterate the entire process, starting from the clustering, until reaching a fixpoint. As a post-pass, an entire cluster can be removed as noise based on further statistical analysis.

6.6   Refining Mining Results Using Inspection

When performing mining, some of the loss of precision is due to the (essential) abstraction of the history. Spurious behavior that is included in the mined automata due to the history abstraction sometimes eludes the statistical summarization approaches since it repeats itself in multiple automata. Thus, other techniques are needed to deal with such noise.

In this section, we describe a number of approaches for refining the results obtained through mining. These approaches are based on making the history abstraction more precise. Our refinement is based on the observation that the mined automata indicate where more analysis effort could help make the results more precise. Namely, we select candidate paths from the mined automata and use *inspection* to check if those paths represent correct usage patterns of the API. If a path turns out to be spurious, we refine the abstraction to eliminate that path.

6.6.1   Static Inspection

Static inspection can be performed from the client side and the component side.

6.6.1.1   Static Client Inspection

Static client inspection statically checks whether a given scenario is present in the code base. Checking for the absence of a scenario is also known as *typestate verification* (e.g., [11]). Since checking for a specific scenario only requires recording the current state of the typestate property, and not a more elaborate abstraction of the history, it is generally cheaper than mining. Therefore, the checking procedure can use more precise (and thus costly) heap abstractions and be used to prune spurious scenarios that are observed as absent from the code base.

6.6.1.2   Static Component Inspection

Static component inspection statically checks whether a given scenario might produce an error when executed over the component.

The extreme case of static component inspection is that of [1] and [24], which exhaustively (and conservatively) explore all client scenarios and the resulting component behaviors.

6.6.2   Dynamic Inspection

While static inspection is limited, as it still requires some heap abstraction, dynamic inspection has the advantage that it can also identify imprecision that results from the heap abstraction.

Similarly to static inspection, dynamic inspection also comes in two flavors: client side and component side.

- Dynamic client-side inspection checks whether a given usage-scenario may exist in a given code base (under-approximation). This can be implemented by instrumenting client-code to record various events. This approach is applied by dynamic mining tools such as Daikon [10].

- Dynamic component side inspection checks whether a given usage-scenario may execute without failure over the component. This is an under-approximation, as the component may fail this sequence only on specific environment conditions (e.g., only fail the sequence on Mondays). It can be performed without the code of the component, but requires an ability to execute it. This is commonly referred to as unit-testing.

6.6.3   Selection of Paths for Inspection

When a scenario is identified as spurious, the abstraction used for mining can be locally refined to eliminate the spurious scenario. The question remaining is how to identify spurious paths, namely, how to select paths for inspection.

There are a number of approaches for selecting paths for inspection. The naive approach is to simply try all acyclic paths in the mined automaton, or some bounded unrolling of the cyclic paths. When the final result of mining is a weighted automaton, spurious paths/edges may be identified as the ones that have a relatively low weight.

Example 6.6.1. *Consider the* `Signature` *API. Suppose that the mined automaton, mined with the past abstraction, is the one depicted in Figure 6.11(a). We now enumerate all acyclic paths in the mined automaton of Figure 6.11(a):*

(i)	`initSign; update; sign; initSign`
(ii)	`initSign; update; verify; initVerify`
(iii)	`initVerify; update; verify; initVerify`
(iv)	`initVerify; update; sign; initSign`

We now run inspection, say static client-side inspection (typestate verification), to verify the absence of each one of the sequences (i)-(iv). This is done by specifying the sequence itself as an input typestate property for the verifier.

Since the typestate verifier does not need to record histories, we can employ the solver with more precise abstractions, and observe the fact that both (ii) and (iv) are sequences that cannot occur in the client program.

Based on this information, we can locally increase the context for the past abstraction such that it is able to distinguish the valid sequences (i) and (iii) from the invalid ones (ii) and (iv).

6.6.4   Refinement Based on Abstraction Merge Points

A more sophisticated approach for refinement, which also uses inspection, is based on the merge points of the abstraction. Recall that our past-future abstractions merge automata states based on their ingoing/outgoing sequences. These merge points are responsible for the over-approximation of the specification. As such, we aim at identifying merge points which are potentially responsible for the inclusion of spurious behaviors.

Consider the past abstraction. Similar ideas are applicable for the future abstraction as well. In the k-past abstraction, an automaton state q that has (at least) two ingoing paths of length k labeled with the same sequence represents a merge point. The joint suffix of length k of the two ingoing paths is responsible for the merge of the states that resulted in q. For example, in Figure 6.11(a), state 2 is a merge point of the past abstraction as it has two ingoing sequences (`initSign; update, initVerify; update`). The suffix `update` of these sequences is responsible for the merge.

If the state q that represents a merge point also has (at least) two different outgoing behaviors, then this means that one originated while tracking the first ingoing sequence and the second originated when tracking the other. The merge introduced the additional two combinations of ingoing and outgoing sequences.

For example, in Figure 6.11(a), state 2 has two outgoing sequences: `sign` which originated after tracking the ingoing sequence `initSign; update`, and `verify` which originated after tracking the ingoing sequence `initVerify; update`. The merge introduced the (erroneous) combinations of `initSign; update` and `verify` and of `initVerify; update` and `sign`.

States that have multiple ingoing and outgoing sequences are therefore considered *suspicious* merge points and are candidates for inspection. When a suspicious merge point q is encountered, the validity of the merge is inspected by checking if all the combinations of an ingoing sequence and an outgoing sequence are legitimate.

If one of these combinations turns out to be illegal, refinement of q is needed. This can be achieved by increasing the context of the past abstraction to reflect the difference between the two ingoing sequences of q.

Example 6.6.2. *Consider the* `Signature` *API. Suppose that the mined automaton, mined with the past abstraction, is the one depicted in Figure 6.11(a). In this case, state 2 is a suspicious merge point as it has both two different ingoing sequences (`initSign; update, initVerify; update`) and two outgoing sequences (`sign, verify`). Indeed, inspection shows that the concatenation of `initSign; update` and `verify`, as well as the concatenation of `initVerify; update` and `sign`, results in a spurious path. Thus, refinement increases the context of the past abstraction to 2, as length 2 reflects the difference between the ingoing sequences of state 2. This prevents the spurious merge and the resulting automaton is depicted in Figure 6.11(b).*

Note, however, that this kind of refinement does not guarantee that the "bad" state q will be split in the next iteration of mining (with the extended context), since there can be other ingoing sequences of the increased length that will cause q to be merged again. For example, if in the `Signature` example state 2 has a selfloop with the `update` event (i.e., the code base allows any number of `update` events before `verify` or `sign`), then no finite context will prevent the merge.

Suspicious merge points are found as follows. First, an automaton state that has (at least) two ingoing paths labeled with the same sequence of length k is found by a BFS from the initial state. Whenever a new state is encountered, we check if it has at least two ingoing transitions. If it does, then it has

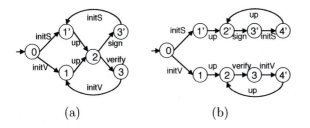

(a)   (b)

FIGURE 6.11: (a) 1-Past abstraction; and (b) 2-Past abstraction.

(at least) two ingoing paths labeled with the same suffix of length k (due to the past-property). For example, in Figure 6.11(a), state 2 has two ingoing transitions, and indeed these represent two ingoing paths labeled with the same suffix of length 1.

Note that the full sequences that label the ingoing paths that lead from the initial state to such a state cannot be identical, although they end with an identical suffix. This is because at latest the ingoing paths collide at the initial state, and since the automaton is deterministic, the transitions where the paths collide must be labeled by different events. In the above example the ingoing paths of state 2 collide at the initial state and the corresponding transitions are indeed labeled by different events: `initSign` and `initVerify`. Moreover, the two different ingoing sequences can be found by a backward traversal of the BFS tree until the initial state is encountered.

Let q be such an automaton state that has two different ingoing sequences. To check if q also has at least two different outgoing behaviors (and find them), another BFS is applied, starting from q. There are three possibilities.

(1) The search ends without finding any state with more than one outgoing transition. In this case, no inspection is needed since q has only one outgoing behavior, thus the merge did not add any behavior.

(2) The search reaches a state q' (possibly q itself) that has at least two outgoing transitions. In this case, the path from q to q' followed by the two outgoing transitions of q' defines two different outgoing behaviors of q. This is the case in Figure 6.11(a), where state 2 itself has two outgoing transitions: one labeled `sign` and one labeled `verify`.

(3) The search reaches a previously visited state q'. This means that a simple loop was encountered, one that has no outgoing transitions (except for the ones along the loop). In this case different unwindings of the loop define different behaviors that originate in q.

Similar ideas can be used on the nondeterministic automata returned by future merge.

6.7   Experimental Results

We have implemented a prototype of our analysis based on the WALA analysis framework [28] and the typestate analysis framework of [11]. Our analysis builds on a general Reps-Horwitz-Sagiv (RHS) IFDS tabulation solver implementation [26]. We extended the RHS solver to support dynamic changes and merges in the set of dataflow facts. The pointer analysis adds one level of call-string context to calls to various library factory methods, `arraycopy`, and `clone` statements, which tend to badly pollute pointer flow precision if handled without context-sensitivity. The system uses a substantial library of models of native code behavior for the standard libraries.

6.7.1   Benchmarks

Table 6.2 lists the benchmarks used in this study. Each of the benchmarks bobalice, js-chap13, and j2ns is a set of examples taken from a book on Java security [25]. flickrapi is an open source program providing a wrapper over flickr APIs, as well as some utilities using it. ganymed is a library implementing the SSH-2 protocol in pure Java; the library comes with examples and utility programs that use it. javacup and jlex are a parser generator and lexical analyzer, respectively, for Java. jbidwatcher is an online auction tool. jfreechart is a Java chart library. tinysql is a lightweight Java SQL engine. tvla is a static analysis framework.

The table reports size characteristics restricted to methods discovered by on-the-fly call-graph construction. The call graph includes methods from both the application and the libraries; for many programs the size of the program

TABLE 6.2: Benchmarks

Num	Benchmark	Classes	Methods	Bytecodes	Contexts	Clients
1	aamfetch	635	2544	246284	3316	2
2	bobalice	259	1318	71048	1917	2
3	crypty	450	2138	127130	2794	1
4	flickrapi	123	423	26607	527	2
5	ganymed	121	649	49232	919	4
6	j2ns	944	4817	399402	6570	5
7	javacup	373	2000	122592	2981	2
8	javasign	111	473	45670	740	11
9	jbidwatcher	64	525	18717	269	9
10	jfreechart	654	2644	250718	3457	18
11	jlex	89	317	25261	382	2
12	jpat-p	374	2043	141649	5570	1
13	JPDStore	109	359	23040	418	2
14	js-chap13	661	2795	259273	3770	6
15	privatray	175	665	56543	876	1
16	tinysql	701	3019	277881	3980	2
17	tvla	643	2572	249243	3355	3

analyzed is dominated by the standard libraries. The table also reports the number of (method) contexts in the call graph (the context-sensitivity policy models some methods with multiple contexts). The last column shows the number of client programs for each benchmark.

Using these clients, we applied our prototype to mine specifications for a number of APIs, as described in more detail in the next section. Our implementation employs standard automata minimization, and our results always refer to minimized automata.

Our most precise solvers (APFocus/Past/Exterior and APFocus/Future/Exterior) run in less than 30 minutes per benchmark. Our less precise solvers run in about half the time. This performance seems reasonable for non-interactive mining of a code base.

6.7.2   Results

Our evaluation focuses first on three dimensions for abstract trace collection:

- The heap abstraction (Section 6.4.2.1): Base versus APFocus
- The history abstraction (Section 6.4.2.3): Past versus Future
- The merge criteria (Section 6.4.2.3): Total versus Exterior Merge

Table 6.3 characterizes the specifications generated by our analysis, varying the abstractions along these three dimensions. Each row summarizes the result for a specific API across a number of benchmarks.

Some APIs appear in several separate benchmarks, while others appear in several programs contained within the same benchmark. The `Auth` and `Photo` APIs are used in benchmark 4. `Channel`, `ChannelManager`, `Connection`, `Session`, and `TransportManager` are used in benchmark 5. `Cipher` is used in benchmarks 1, 3, 14, and 15. `KeyAgreement` is used in benchmark 2. `LineAndShapeRenderer` is used in benchmark 10. `MessageDigest` is used in benchmarks 1, 13, and 15. `PrintWriter` is used in benchmarks 7 and 11. `Signature` is used in 6 and 8. `URLConnection` is used in benchmark 9.

Each column of the table corresponds to a combination of a heap abstraction, history abstraction, and merge criterion. When using Total merge, we only show results for Past history abstraction; results for Future would be similar under this aggressive merge criterion. All results in the table reflect the Naive Union summarization (Section 6.5.1), which preserves all information collected by the trace collectors. This allows to compare the quality of different abstract trace collectors without interference from summarization effects.

The table reports, for each mined specification, the number of states and transitions, and the average degree (number of outgoing edges) of states in the specification. Intuitively, the degree of a node represents the number of possible legal operations from a given state. Since all specifications in the table over-approximate client behavior, a smaller degree represents a better specification since it admits fewer spurious behaviors. Note that the different

TABLE 6.3: Characteristics of Our Mined Specifications with Varying Data Collectors

API	Base/Past /Total			Base/Past /Ext			Base/Future /Ext			APF/Past /Total			APF/Past /Ext			APF/Future /Ext		
	states	edges	avg. degree	states	edges	avg. degree	states	edges	avg. degree	states	edges	avg. degree	states	edges	avg. degree	states	edges	avg. degree
Auth	2	3	1.50	2	3	1.5	2	3	1.5	2	2	1.00	2	2	1.00	2	2	1.00
Channel	2	6	3.00	3	6	2.00	3	6	2.00	3	3	1.00	3	3	1.00	3	3	1.00
ChannelMgr	2	11	5.50	5	18	3.60	6	19	3.17	4	7	1.75	5	9	1.80	5	9	1.80
Cipher	1	5	5.00	4	14	3.50	6	12	2.00	7	10	1.43	7	10	1.43	7	10	1.43
Connection	3	12	4.00	4	12	3.00	4	12	3.00	5	7	1.40	5	7	1.40	5	7	1.40
KeyAgreement	2	5	2.50	4	6	1.50	4	6	1.5	4	3	0.75	4	3	0.75	4	3	0.75
LineAndShape	3	12	4.00	6	15	2.50	6	15	2.50	6	8	1.33	6	8	1.33	6	8	1.33
MsgDigest	1	2	2.00	2	2	1.00	2	2	1.00	2	2	1.00	2	2	1.00	2	2	1.00
Photo	1	12	12.00	1	12	12.00	1	8	8.00	8	8	1.00	8	8	1.00	8	8	1.00
PrintWriter	1	3	3.00	2	3	1.50	2	3	1.50	6	11	1.83	3	5	1.67	3	5	1.67
Session	2	7	3.50	5	10	2.00	5	10	2.00	5	4	0.80	5	4	0.80	5	4	0.80
Signature	2	8	4.00	5	12	2.40	5	12	2.40	4	6	1.50	4	6	1.50	4	6	1.50
TransportMgr	9	24	2.67	2	19	9.50	8	27	3.38	9	26	2.89	9	24	2.67	9	24	2.67
URLConnection	2	9	4.50	4	10	2.5	3	6	2	4	7	1.75	-	-	-	-	-	-
Average			4.08			3.46			2.57			1.39			1.33			1.33
Std dev			2.54			3.22			1.71			0.56			0.52			0.52

Note: For every mined specification DFA, we show the number of states, edges, and the density of the DFA. APIs for which the most precise analysis generated the ideal specification appear in bold.

over-approximations may be incomparable in terms of the languages they accept; that is, we cannot, in general, rank the mined specifications based on a simulation ordering. Note also that average degree is a relative metric; its absolute value depends on the number of observable events in the specification.

The results show across the board that precise alias analysis is significant; the mined specifications appear significantly more permissive under Base aliasing than under APFocus. Exterior merge improves over total merge frequently when using Base aliasing, and occasionally under APFocus aliasing. When using the most precise APFocus aliasing and exterior merge, the distinction between past and future abstractions vanishes in these experiments, although they behave significantly different under Base aliasing.

For some specifications, we were able to track the usage pattern manually by inspecting the client code. For others, the complexity of the client code (or even lack of Java source code) prevented us from understanding the client API usage based on inspection. Based on manual inspection, we were able to verify that for 5 out of the 14 APIs, the most precise analysis generated the ideal specification, even with the naive union summarization. These APIs appear in bold in the table.

We additionally collected specifications with weighted summarization for each benchmark. We do not report densities obtained by weighted summarization, as the specification density will depend directly on the threshold parameter provided as input. We note based on inspection that a user-provided threshold of 1/2 for the weighted union algorithm yields improved specifications for several APIs. In practice, we expect a user would provide feedback to iteratively tune the threshold as desired.

We also ran the cluster-based summarization for all specifications. For several APIs, clustering correctly identified a number of independent usage patterns of the API in our code base. In particular, the specification obtained for Cipher using the naive union collector was polluted by calls to irrelevant methods. Using the combination of clustering and weighted algorithms, we obtained the "ideal" specification expected by a human.

Figure 6.12 shows the output of our tool for the Signature API. This API was mined using APFocus/Past/Exterior collector, and summarized us-

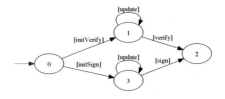

FIGURE 6.12: Mined specification for java.security.Signature, obtained with APFocus/Past/Exterior.

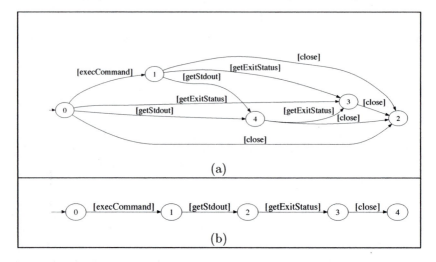

FIGURE 6.13: Session API with Past/Exterior merge and (a) Base aliasing; and (b) APFocus aliasing.

ing the naive union summarization. Note that the specification correctly disambiguates two use cases, *verify* and *sign*. An approach based on event pairs (e.g., [30, 32]) could not distinguish these two cases.

Figure 6.13 shows the output of our tool for the ganymed Session API under two collector settings, and summarized using the naive union summarization. This figure shows a typical qualitative difference between Base aliasing and APFocus. Figure 6.14 shows a similar comparative output of our tool for the KeyAgreement API.

A small gallery of mined specifications appears in an informal online supplement [13].

6.7.3 Discussion

Generally, the mined specifications are useful in many settings. For example, we suggest the following usage scenarios:

- program understanding: understanding a component by the way it is used by a client, and understanding an unknown client by the way it is using known components.

- regression: where new code added to a code-base has to conform to the way the code-base is using key APIs.

- identifying deviant behaviors that do not comply with the specification as likely bugs, and possibly even used for automatically fixing code by making it conform to common usage patterns.

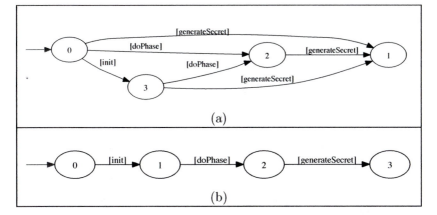

FIGURE 6.14: KeyAgreement API with Past/Exterior merge and (a) Base aliasing; and (b) APFocus aliasing.

- finding existing code fragments that bring the program to a specified desired state (a natural, more powerful, extension of [22]).

The quality of the mined specification should be evaluated with respect to its particular usage. For example, a specification mined for the purpose of program understanding should be human-readable, where a specification mined for identifying deviant behaviors may ignore such a requirement.

Our experiments indicate that having both a precise-enough heap abstraction and a precise-enough history abstraction is required to be able to mine a reasonable specification for either of the aforementioned usage scenarios.

Without such precise abstractions, the collected abstract histories might deteriorate to a point in which no summarization algorithm will recover the lost information. For example, the specification mined for the Photo API using the Base heap abstraction has a single state. This means that the specification does not contain any temporal information on the ordering of events (similarly for PrintWriter under Base/Past/Total.)

6.7.3.1 Soundness

All of the results in Table 6.3 were obtained when our analysis was run to completion, and are therefore guaranteed to be an over-approximation of the behavior present in the analyzed code base. In contrast, it is also possible to employ our analysis with a predetermined timeout (or with, e.g., a small limited heap size). In such cases, the specification obtained using the analysis will not over-approximate code base behavior, but may still help understand some behaviors. For example, when running on TVLA, we mined a partial but interesting description of the way tvla.Engine is used in the code base.

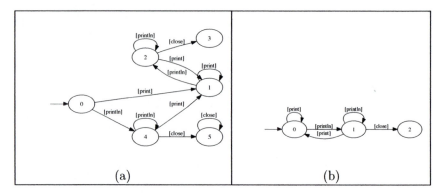

FIGURE 6.15: `PrintWriter` API with APFocus aliasing, and past (a) total merge; and (b) exterior merge.

6.7.3.2   Limitations

Our prototype shows encouraging results, but due to several limitations, does not yet suffice for deployment in an industrial tool.

Our implementation currently considers all methods of an API as equally interesting. In general, this pollutes specifications with calls to pure methods that do not change the state of the component. When library code is available, one might analyze the library to identify pure methods and treat them specially in both abstract trace collection and summarization. In the absence of library code, we envision a feedback loop involving user input, specifying methods that should be ignored.

In some cases, the specifications mined by our approach are too detailed, and track distinctions that hold no interest to the end user. For example, the specification we mine for `PrintWriter`, shown in Figure 6.15, records some artificial temporal ordering between `print` and `println`. We'd expect these problems to resolve themselves with a larger input corpus; if not, a practical tool would probably resort to user feedback to refine results.

Our current implementation does not scale to code bases larger than roughly a few tens of thousands of lines in reasonable time and space (depending on properties of the dataflow solution). The scaling problem is fundamental to all whole program analyses, and does not stem primarily from our particular history abstractions. In the future, we plan to explore how this technique could be turned into a modular one in the spirit of [33], which we believe is a crucial step for a practical implementation.

Our current prototype restricts itself to specifications involving a single object; however, many interesting specifications involve multiple types and objects. The ideas we presented can apply to components that involve multiple objects, but the scalability and precision questions remain open.

Despite these limitations, we are encouraged by the results obtained with our current implementation, which show the strength of our heap and history abstractions, as well as our summarization algorithms. We also expect these abstractions to be useful in the context of other analyses that track temporal sequences.

6.8   Related Work

Dynamic Analysis. When it is feasible to run a program with adequate coverage, dynamic analysis represents the most attractive option for specification mining, since dynamic analysis does not suffer from the difficulties inherent to abstraction.

Cook and Wolf [5] consider the general problem of extracting a FSM model from an event trace, and reduce the problem to the well-known *grammar inference* [14] problem. Cook and Wolf discuss algorithmic, statistical, and hybrid approaches, and present an excellent overview of the approaches and fundamental challenges. This work considers mining automata from uninterpreted event traces, attaching no semantic meaning to events.

Ammons et al. [2] infer temporal and data dependence specifications based on dynamic trace data. This work applies sophisticated probabilistic learning techniques to boil traces down to collections of finite automata which characterize the behavior. Lo and Khoo [20] extend Ammons' work, and employ machine learning techniques to mine probabilistic temporal specifications from dynamic execution traces.

Whaley et al. [31] present a two-phased approach to mining temporal API interfaces, combining a static component-side safety check with a dynamic client-side sequence mining. The static analysis is extremely simple, and used primarily to restrict the dynamic search of temporal sequences, rather than to directly infer specifications. This work presents several insights on how to refine results, based on side-effect free methods, and partitioning methods based on how they access fields. We plan to incorporate these insights into a future version of our analysis.

The Perracotta tool [32] addressed challenges in scaling dynamic mining of temporal properties to large code bases. This tool mines traces for two-event patterns with an efficient algorithm, and relies on heuristics to help identify interesting patterns.

Livshits and Zimmermann [19] mine a software repository revision history to find small sets of methods whose usage may be correlated. This analysis is simple and scalable; in contrast to ours, it does not consider temporal ordering nor aliasing. In a second (dynamic) phase, the system checks whether candidate temporal patterns actually appear in representative program traces. Our analysis technology could perhaps be employed in a similar architecture to provide a more effective first phase of mining.

Demsky and Rinard [8] present a dynamic mining approach and tool based on the concept of *roles*. As in Kuncak et al. [16], this work starts with the hypothesis that aliasing relationships between objects define roles, or relevant typestates. Based on this observation, they present a graphical tool which allows the user to navigate role relationships derived by analysis of a dynamic trace. The user can guide the tool with respect to role separation criteria and other heuristics, to navigate to a meaningful specification. This work also incorporates the notion of state changes based solely on method calls on a particular object, similar to traces presented in our concrete semantics.

Dallmeier et al. [7] use a dynamic analysis to extract object behavior models (similar to our temporal specifications) from program executions. Their approach uses a preceding static analysis that classifies each method as a mutator (modifies object state) or an inspector (does not affect object state). The mutator methods are then instrumented to record the resulting object state.

Mariani and Pezzè [23] use dynamic analysis to detect COTS component incompatibilities. They dynamically analyze component behavior to extract interaction models between components in the form of finite-state automata representing the sequences of interactions triggered by invoking services. The automata are extracted by an inference algorithm which works incrementally on a set of positive samples (traces). Their algorithm identifies subsequences of a new trace in the current automaton and connects the identified subsequences to include the new trace in the automaton. It thus resembles our past abstraction.

In [21], the authors use annotated FSMs to represent individual failure executions of enterprise applications encountered at run time (as a part of a self-protecting technique). The annotated FSMs are augmented with weights that indicate the relevance of the transitions with respect to the identification of a failure. A failure context is then generated from the weighted FSM.

Several projects mine specifications in the form of *dynamic invariant detection*. Daikon [10] instruments a running program and infers invariants based on values of variables in representative program traces, typically discovering method preconditions, postconditions, and loop invariants. Daikon does not explicitly target temporal sequences, but may apply to temporal properties that are reflected by variable invariants at particular program points. DIDUCE [15] combines invariant detection and checking in a single tool, aimed to help diagnose failures. As a program runs, DIDUCE maintains a set of hypothesized invariants, and reports violations of these invariants as they occur.

Component-Side Static Analysis. In component-side static analysis, a tool analyzes a component's implementation, and infers a specification that ensures the component does not fail in some predetermined way, such as by raising an exception. In contrast, client-side mining produces a specification that represents the usage scenarios in a given code-base. The two approaches are complementary, as demonstrated in [31].

Alur et al. [1] use Angluin's algorithm together with a model-checking procedure to learn a permissive interface of a given component. Nandi et al. [24] use static mining to learn a permissive first-order specification involving objects, their relationships, and their internal states.

Client-Side Static Analysis. A few papers have applied static analysis to client-side specification mining.

Engler et al. [9] use various static analyses to identify common program behaviors, and consider deviations from these behaviors as bugs. Their approach automatically establishes certain invariants as likely *beliefs*, and the tool searches for bugs by finding code sequences that violate these invariants. The tool searches for invariants based on a set of standard templates, and filters potential specifications with a statistical measure (z-ranking). Their approach has been highly effective in finding bugs in system code.

Weimer and Necula [30] use a simple, lightweight static analysis to infer simple specifications from a given codebase. Their insight is to use exceptional program paths as negative examples for correct API usage. We believe that our approach could also benefit from using exceptional paths as negative examples. Weimer and Necula learn specifications that consist of pairs of events $\langle a, b \rangle$, where a and b are method calls, and do not consider larger automata. They rely on type-based alias analysis, and so their techniques should be much less precise than ours. On the other hand, their paper demonstrates that even simple techniques can be surprisingly effective in finding bugs.

Mandelin et al. [22] use static analysis to infer a sequence of code (*jungloid*) that shows the programmer how to obtain a desired target type from a given source type (a *jungloid query*). This code-sequence is only checked for type-safety and does not address the finer notion of typestate. In contrast, our approach focuses on mining temporal specifications.

Wasylkowski et al. [29] use an intraprocedural static analysis to automatically mine object usage patterns and identify usage anomalies. Their approach is based on identifying usage patterns. In contrast, our approach mines temporal specifications that over-approximate the usage scenarios in a code-base.

Other Static Analyses. [17] presents a model-extraction technique and extracts both the object relationships and a model of their interactions. This approach requires user annotation that associates a "token" with every object of interest and uses static analysis to infer the relationships and interactions between tokens. In contrast, our approach currently focuses only on typestate specifications, but is fully automatic.

Lie et al. [18] present an approach to extract state transition models using an extensible compiler, xg++. In this work, the user specifies patterns corresponding to state variables and operations relevant to a particular protocol. Based on this specification, the compiler slices the program to elide irrelevant statements, and then performs a simple user-guided translation to output the model in a desired form, suitable for input to a model-checker. This work targets low-level cache coherency protocols implemented in C.

6.9   Conclusion

We presented a technique for client-side temporal API mining with static analysis beyond trivial alias analysis and history abstractions. Static analysis improves coverage over dynamic analysis both by exploring all paths for a single program, and by expanding the corpus of code amenable to automated analysis. We plan to conduct further research into modular analysis techniques and improved summarization heuristics, to move closer to practical application of this technology.

Bibliography

[1] Rajeev Alur, Pavol Černý, P. Madhusudan, and Wonhong Nam. Synthesis of interface specifications for java classes. In *POPL '05: Proceedings of the 32nd ACM SIGPLAN-SIGACT Symposium on Principles of Programming Languages*, pages 98–109, ACM Press, New York, 2005.

[2] Glenn Ammons, Rastislav Bodik, and James R. Larus. Mining specifications. In *POPL '02: Proceedings of the 29th ACM SIGPLAN-SIGACT Symposium on Principles of Programming Languages*, pages 4–16, ACM Press, New York, 2002.

[3] L.O. Andersen. Program Analysis and Specialization for the C Programming Language. Ph.D. thesis, DIKU, University of Copenhagen, May 1994. (DIKU report 94/19).

[4] D.R. Chase, M. Wegman, and F. Zadeck. Analysis of pointers and structures. In *Proc. ACM Conf. on Programming Language Design and Implementation*, pages 296–310, ACM Press, New York, 1990.

[5] Jonathan E. Cook and Alexander L. Wolf. Discovering models of software processes from event-based data. *ACM Transactions Software Engineering and Methodology*, 7(3):215–249, 1998.

[6] Patrick Cousot and Radhia Cousot. Abstract interpretation: a unified lattice model for static analysis of programs by construction or approximation of fixpoints. In *POPL '77: Proceedings of the 4th ACM SIGACT-SIGPLAN Symposium on Principles of Programming Languages*, pages 238–252, ACM Press, New York, 1977.

[7] Valentin Dallmeier, Christian Lindig, Andrzej Wasylkowski, and Andreas Zeller. Mining object behavior with adabu. In *WODA '06: Proceedings*

of the 2006 International Workshop on Dynamic Systems Analysis, pages 17–24, ACM Press, New York, 2006.

[8] Brian Demsky and Martin Rinard. Role-based exploration of object-oriented programs. In *ICSE '02: Proceedings of the 24th International Conference on Software Engineering*, pages 313–324, ACM Press, New York, 2002

[9] Dawson Engler, David Yu Chen, Seth Hallem, Andy Chou, and Benjamin Chelf. Bugs as deviant behavior: a general approach to inferring errors in systems code. In *SOSP '01: Proceedings of the Eighteenth ACM Symposium on Operating Systems Principles*, pages 57–72, ACM Press, 2001.

[10] Michael D. Ernst, Jake Cockrell, William G. Griswold, and David Notkin. Dynamically discovering likely program invariants to support program evolution. *IEEE Transactions on Software Engineering*, 27(2):99–123, February 2001.

[11] Stephen Fink, Eran Yahav, Nurit Dor, G. Ramalingam, and Emmanuel Geay. Effective typestate verification in the presence of aliasing. In *ISSTA '06: Proceedings of the 2006 International Symposium on Software Testing and Analysis*, pages 133–144, ACM Press, New York, 2006.

[12] Stephen J. Fink, Eran Yahav, Nurit Dor, G. Ramalingam, and Emmanuel Geay. Effective typestate verification in the presence of aliasing. *ACM Transactions on Software Engineering and Methodology*, 17(2):1–34, 2008.

[13] Gallery of mined specification. http://tinyurl.com/23qct8 or http://docs.google.com/View?docid=ddhtqgv6_10hbczjd.

[14] E.M. Gold. Language identification in the limit. *Information and Control*, 10:447–474, 1967.

[15] Sudheendra Hangal and Monica S. Lam. Tracking down software bugs using automatic anomaly detection. May 2002.

[16] Viktor Kuncak, Patrick Lam, and Martin Rinard. Role analysis. In *Proc. ACM Symp. on Principles of Programming Languages*, Portland, January 2002.

[17] Patrick Lam and Martin Rinard. A type system and analysis for the automatic extraction and enforcement of design information. In *ECOOP*, 2003.

[18] David Lie, Andy Chou, Dawson Engler, and David L. Dill. A simple method for extracting models for protocol code. In *ISCA '01: Proceedings of the 28th Annual International Symposium on Computer Architecture*, pages 192–203, ACM Press, New York, 2001.

[19] V. Benjamin Livshits and Thomas Zimmermann. Dynamine: finding common error patterns by mining software revision histories. In *Proceedings of the 13th ACM SIGSOFT International Symposium on the Foundations of Software Engineering (FSE-13)*, pages 296–305, September 2005.

[20] David Lo and Siau-Cheng Khoo. SMArTIC: towards building an accurate, robust and scalable specification miner. In *SIGSOFT '06/FSE-14: Proceedings of the 14th ACM SIGSOFT International Symposium on Foundations of Software Engineering*, pages 265–275, ACM Press, New York, 2006.

[21] Davide Lorenzoli, Leonardo Mariani, and Mauro Pezzè. Towards self-protecting enterprise applications. In *18th IEEE International Symposium on Software Reliability Engineering (ISSRE 2007)*, November 2007.

[22] David Mandelin, Lin Xu, Rastislav Bodik, and Doug Kimelman. Jungloid mining: helping to navigate the API jungle. In *PLDI '05: Proceedings of the 2005 ACM SIGPLAN Conference on Programming Language Design and Implementation*, pages 48–61, ACM Press, New York, 2005.

[23] L. Mariani and M. Pezzè. Dynamic detection of COTS components incompatibility. *IEEE Software*, 24(5):76–85, September/October 2007.

[24] Mangala Gowri Nanda, Christian Grothoff, and Satish Chandra. Deriving object typestates in the presence of inter-object references. In *OOPSLA '05: Proceedings of the 20th annual ACM SIGPLAN Conference on Object Oriented Programming, Systems, Languages, and Applications*, pages 77–96, ACM Press, New York, 2005.

[25] Marco Pistoia, Duane Reller, Deepak Gupta, Milind Nagnur, and Ashok K. Ramani. *Java 2 Network Security*. Prentice Hall PTR, Upper Saddle River, NJ, August 1999.

[26] T. Reps, S. Horwitz, and M. Sagiv. Precise interprocedural dataflow analysis via graph reachability. In *Proc. ACM Symposium on Principles of Programming Languages*, pages 49–61, 1995.

[27] Alexandru Salcianu and Matin Rinard. Purity and side effect analysis for Java programs. In *VMCAI'05: Proceedings of the 6th International Conference on Verification, Model Checking, and Abstract Interpretation*, 2005.

[28] WALA: The T. J. Watson Libraries for Analysis. http://wala.sourceforge.net.

[29] Andrzej Wasylkowski, Andreas Zeller, and Christian Lindig. Detecting object usage anomalies. In *ESEC-FSE '07: Proceedings of the 6th Joint Meeting of the European Software Engineering Conference and the ACM*

SIGSOFT Symposium on the Foundations of Software Engineering, pages 35–44, ACM Press, New York, 2007.

[30] Westley Weimer and George Necula. Mining temporal specifications for error detection. In *TACAS*, 2005.

[31] John Whaley, Michael C. Martin, and Monica S. Lam. Automatic extraction of object-oriented component interfaces. In *Proceedings of the International Symposium on Software Testing and Analysis*, pages 218–228, ACM Press, New York, July 2002.

[32] Jinlin Yang, David Evans, Deepali Bhardwaj, Thirumalesh Bhat, and Manuvir Das. Perracotta: mining temporal API rules from imperfect traces. In *ICSE '06: Proceeding of the 28th International Conference on Software Engineering*, pages 282–291, ACM Press, New York, 2006. ACM Press.

[33] Greta Yorsh, Eran Yahav, and Satish Chandra. Generating precise and concise procedure summaries. In *POPL '08: Proceedings of the 35th Annual ACM SIGPLAN-SIGACT Symposium on Principles of Programming Languages*, pages 221–234, ACM Press, New York, 2008.

Chapter 7

DynaMine: Finding Usage Patterns and Their Violations by Mining Software Repositories

Benjamin Livshits

Microsoft Research–Redmond

Thomas Zimmermann

Microsoft Research–Redmond

7.1 Introduction

A great deal of attention has been given lately to addressing application-specific software bugs such as errors in operating system drivers [4,14], security errors [24,43], or errors in reliability-critical embedded software in domains like avionics [7,8]. These represent critical errors in widely used software and tend to get fixed relatively quickly when found. A variety of static and dynamic analysis tools have been developed to address these high-profile bugs.

However, many other errors are specific to individual applications or platforms. This is especially true when it comes to extensible development platforms such as J2EE, .NET, and others that have a variety of programmers at all skill levels writing code to use the same sets of APIs. Violations of these application-specific coding rules, referred to as *error patterns*, are responsible for a multitude of errors. Error patterns tend to be re-introduced into the code over and over by multiple developers working on a project and are a common source of software defects. While each pattern may be only responsible for a few bugs in a given project snapshot, when taken together over the project's lifetime, the detrimental effect of these error patterns is quite serious and they can hardly be ignored in the long term if software quality is to be expected.

However, finding the error patterns to look for with a particular static or dynamic analysis tool is often difficult, especially when it comes to legacy code, where error patterns either are recoded as comments in the code or not documented at all [15]. Moreover, while well-aware of certain types of behavior that cause the application to crash or well-publicized types of bugs such as buffer overruns, programmers often have difficulty formalizing or even expressing API invariants. In addition to a handful of patterns that can be collected from the literature, newsgroups, and previous bug reports, application programmers are rarely able to tell which invariants the APIs they use have. The situation is only slightly better when it comes to software architects and API designers who are generally much more aware of application-specific patterns.

In this chapter we propose an automatic way to extract likely error patterns by mining software revision histories. Moreover, in order to ensure that all the errors we find are relatively easy to confirm and fix, we pay particular attention in our experiments to errors that can be fixed with a *one-line change*. It is worth pointing out that many well-known error patterns such as memory leaks, double-`free`'s, mismatched locks, open and close operations on operating system resources, buffer overruns, and format string errors can often be addressed with a one-line fix. Looking at incremental changes between revisions as opposed to complete snapshots of the source allows us to better focus our mining strategy and obtain more precise results. Our approach uses revision history information to infer likely error patterns. We then experimentally evaluate the patterns we extracted by checking for them dynamically.

We have performed experiments on Eclipse and jEdit, two large, widely used open-source Java applications. Both Eclipse and jEdit have many many-years of software development behind them and, as a collaborative effort of hundreds of people across different locations, are good targets for revision history mining. By mining CVS, we have identified 56 high-probability patterns in Eclipse and jEdit APIs, all of which were previously unknown to us. Out of these, 21 were dynamically confirmed as valid patterns and 263 pattern violations were found.

7.1.1 Contributions

This chapter makes the following contributions:

- We present DynaMine,[1] a *tool for discovering usage patterns and detecting their violations* in large software systems [28, 29]. All of the steps involved in mining and running the instrumented application are accessible to the user from within an Eclipse plugin: DynaMine automates the task of collecting and pre-processing revision history entries and mining for common patterns. Likely patterns are then presented to the user for review; runtime instrumentation is generated for the patterns that the user deems relevant. Results of dynamic analysis are also presented to the user in an Eclipse view.

- We propose a *data mining strategy* that detects common usage patterns in large software systems by analyzing software revision histories. Our strategy is based on a classic Apriori data mining algorithm, which we

---

[1]The name DynaMine comes from the combination of <u>Dyna</u>mic analysis and <u>Min</u>ing revision histories.

augment in a number of ways to make it more scalable, reduce the amount of noise, and provide a new, effective ranking of the resulting patterns.

- We present a *categorization of patterns* found in large modern object-oriented systems. Our experience with two large Java projects leads us to believe that similar pattern categories will be found in most other systems of similar size and complexity.

- We propose a *dynamic analysis approach* for validating usage patterns and finding their violations. DynaMine currently utilizes an off-line approach that allows us to match a wider category of patterns. DynaMine supplies default handlers for analyzing most common categories of patterns.

- We present a *detailed experimental study* of our techniques as applied to finding errors in two large, mature open-source Java applications with many years of development behind them. We have identified 56 patterns in both and found 263 pattern violations with our dynamic analysis approach. Furthermore, 21 patterns were experimentally confirmed as valid.

- Finally, we provide an overview of the possible design options that combine revision history mining and program analysis techniques. We also give justifications of our design choices.

7.1.2   Chapter Organization

The rest of the chapter is organized as follows. Section 11.2 provides an informal description of DynaMine, our pattern mining and error detection tool. Section 7.3 describes our revision history mining approach. Section 7.4 describes our dynamic analysis approach. Section 7.5 summarizes our experimental results for (a) revision history mining and (b) dynamic checking of the patterns. In Sections 7.6 and 7.7, we discuss the design choices that we made for DynaMine and possible extension. Sections 7.8 and 7.9 present related work and conclude with future work.

7.2   DynaMine

It is common for today's large software systems to support mechanisms such as plugins, extension modules, or drivers that allow expanding applications functionality. Successful software platforms such as Apache, Eclipse

TABLE 7.1: Number of Extensions for Commonly Used Software Platforms

Application	Version	Type of Extensions	Count
Linux	2.4.xx	drivers	1,739
Apache	2.0.53	modules	385
Eclipse	3.1	plugins	317
jEdit	4.2	plugins	277
Mozilla	1.7.6	plugins	56
Trillian	3.1	plugins	36

rich client platform, Mozilla Firefox, and others support dozens of plugins. Table 7.1 summarizes approximate numbers of available plugins, extension modules, or drivers for various software platforms. Extensions are written by programmers who develop code according to a set of predefined APIs.

It is generally recognized that plugins typically consist of lower quality code, in part because plugin writers are usually less aware of the requirements of the APIs they need to use. Inadvertently violating invariants of these APIs may take the form of forgetting to call a function such as `close` or `free` to release a resource or performing an action unnecessarily in an effort to maintain consistency leading to the same action performed multiples times. Many such programming mistakes in plugin code lead to subtle runtime errors that often occur *outside of the plugin* because of violated program invariants later in the program execution; this makes the cause of the error difficult to diagnose and fix.

A great deal of research has been done in the area of checking and enforcing specific coding rules, the violation of which leads to well-known types of errors. However, these rules are not very easy to come by; much time and effort has been spent by researchers looking for worthwhile rules to check [37] and some of the best efforts in error detection come from people intimately familiar with the application domain [14, 41]. As a result, lesser known types of bugs and applications remain virtually unexplored in error detection research. A better approach is needed if we want to attack "unfamiliar" applications with error detection tools. This chapter proposes a set of techniques that automate the step of application-specific pattern discovery through revision history mining.

7.2.1 Motivation

Our approach hinges on the following observation:

Observation 7.2.1 Given multiple software components that use the same API, there are usually *common errors* specific to that API.

In fact, much of research done on bug detection so far can be thought of as focusing on specific classes of bugs pertaining to particular APIs: studies of operating-system bugs provide synthesized lists of API violations specific to operating system drivers resulting in rules such as "do not call the interrupt disabling function `cli()` twice in a row" [14]. In order to locate common errors, we mine for frequent usage patterns in revision histories, as justified by the following observation.

Observation 7.2.2 Method calls that are frequently added to the source code simultaneously often represent a pattern.

Looking at incremental changes between revisions as opposed to full snapshots of the sources allows us to better focus our mining strategy. However, it is important to notice that not every pattern *mined* by considering revision histories is an actual *usage* pattern.

Example 1. Table 7.2 lists sample method calls that were added to revisions of files `Foo.java`, `Bar.java`, `Baz.java`, and `Qux.java`. All these files contain a usage pattern that says that methods

$$\{\texttt{addListener}, \texttt{removeListener}\}$$

must be precisely matched. However, mining these revisions yields additional patterns like

$$\{\texttt{addListener}, \texttt{println}\}$$

and

$$\{\texttt{addListener}, \texttt{iterator}\}$$

that are definitely *not* usage patterns. Furthermore, we have to take into account the fact that in reality some patterns may be inserted incompletely, e.g., by mistake or to fix a previous error. In Table 7.2 this occurs in file `Qux.java`, where `addListener` and `removeListener` were inserted independently in revisions 1.41 and 1.42. □

The observation that follows gives rise to an effective ranking strategy used in DynaMine.

Observation 7.2.3 Small changes to the repository such as one-line additions often represent bug fixes.

TABLE 7.2: Method Calls Added across Different Revisions

File	Revision	Added method calls
Foo.java	1.12	o1.addListener
		o1.removeListener
Bar.java	1.47	o2.addListener
		o2.removeListener
		System.out.println
Baz.java	1.23	o3.addListener
		o3.removeListener
		list.iterator
		iter.hasNext
		iter.next
Qux.java	1.41	o4.addListener
	1.42	o4.removeListener

This observation is supported in part by anecdotal evidence and also by recent research into the nature of software changes [36] and is further discussed in Section 7.3.3. To make the discussion in the rest of this section concrete, we present the categories of patterns discovered with our mining approach.

- **Matching method pairs** represent two method calls that must be precisely matched on all paths through the program.

- **State machines** are patterns that involve calling more than two methods on the same object and can be captured with a finite automaton.

- **More complex patterns** are all other patterns that fall outside the categories above and involve multiple related objects.

The categories of patterns above are listed in the order of frequency of high-likelihood pattern in our experiments.

7.2.2 System Overview

We conclude this section by summarizing how the various stages of DynaMine processing work when applied to a new application. All of the steps involved in mining and dynamic program testing are accessible to the user from within custom Eclipse views. A diagram representing the architecture of DynaMine is shown in Figure 7.1.

(a) Pre-process revision history, compute method calls that have been inserted, and store this information in a database.

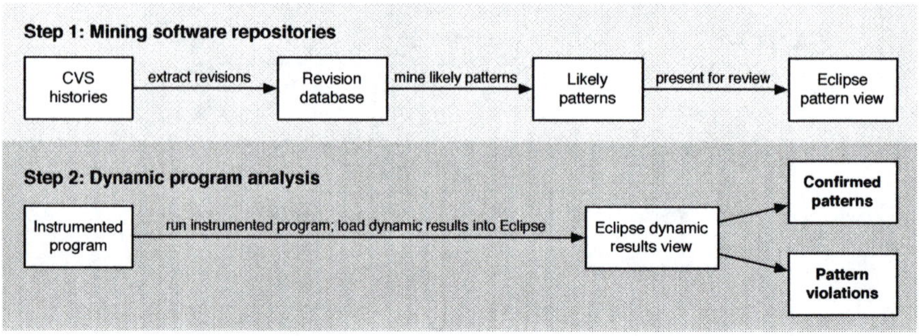

FIGURE 7.1: Architecture of DynaMine. The first row represents revision history mining. The second row represents dynamic analysis.

(b) Mine the revision database for likely usage and error patterns.

(c) Present mining results to the user in an Eclipse plugin for assessment.

(d) Generate instrumentation for patterns deemed relevant and selected by the user through DynaMine's Eclipse plugin.

(e) Run the instrumented program and dynamic data are collected and post-processed by dynamic checkers.

(f) Dynamic pattern violation statistics are collected and presented to the user in Eclipse.

Steps (d)–(f) above can be performed in a loop; once dynamic information about patterns is obtained, the user may decide to augment the patterns and re-instrument the application.

7.3   Mining Usage Patterns

In this section we describe our mining approach. We start by providing the terms we use in our discussion of mining. Next we lay out our general algorithmic approach that is based on the Apriori algorithm [1, 30] that is commonly used in data mining for applications such as market basket analysis. The algorithm uses a set of *transactions* such as store item purchases as its input and produces as its output (a) frequent purchasing patterns ("items X, Y, and Z are purchased together") and (b) strong association rules ("a person who bought item X is likely to buy item Y").

However, the classical Apriori algorithm has a serious drawback. The algorithm runtime can be exponential in the number of items. Our "items" are names of individual methods in the program. For Eclipse, which contains 59,929 different methods, calls to which are inserted, scalability is a real concern. To improve the scalability of our approach and to reduce the amount of noise, we employ a number of filtering strategies described in Section 7.3.2 to reduce the number of viable patterns Apriori has to consider. Furthermore, Apriori does not rank the patterns it returns. Since even with filtering, the number of patterns returned is quite high, we apply several ranking strategies described in Section 7.3.3 to the patterns we mine. We start our discussion of the mining approach by defining some terminology used in our algorithm description.

Definition 7.3.1 A *usage pattern* $U = \langle M, S \rangle$ is defined as a set of methods M and a specification S that defines how the methods should be invoked. A *static usage pattern* is present in the source if calls to all methods in M are located in the source and are invoked in a manner consistent with S. A *dynamic usage pattern* is present in a program execution if a sequence of calls to methods M is made in accordance with the specification S.

The term "specification" is intentionally open-ended because we want to allow for a variety of pattern types to be defined. Revision histories record method calls that have been inserted together and we shall use these data to mine for method sets M. The fact that several methods are correlated does not define the nature of the correlation. Therefore, even though the exact pattern may be obvious given the method names involved, it is generally quite difficult to *automatically* determine the specification S by considering revision history data only and human input is required.

Definition 7.3.2 For a given source file revision, a *transaction* is a set of methods, calls to which have been inserted.

Definition 7.3.3 The *support count* of a usage pattern $U = \langle M, S \rangle$ is the number of transactions that contains all methods in M.

In the example in Table 7.2 the support count for {addListener, removeListener} is 3. The changes to Qux.java do not contribute to the support count because the pattern is distributed across two revisions.

Definition 7.3.4 An *association rule* $A \Rightarrow B$ for a pattern $U = \langle M, S \rangle$ consists of two non-empty sets A and B such that $M = A \cup B$.

For a pattern $U = \langle M, S \rangle$ there exist $2^{|M|} - 2$ possible association rules. An association rule $A \Rightarrow B$ is interpreted as follows: Whenever a programmer inserts calls to all methods in A, she also inserts the calls of all methods in B. Obviously, such rules are not always true. They have a probabilistic meaning.

Definition 7.3.5 The *confidence* of an association rule $A \Rightarrow B$ is defined as the conditional probability $P(B|A)$ that a programmer inserts the calls in B, given the condition she has already inserted the calls in A.

The confidence indicates the *strength* of a rule. However, we are more interested in the patterns than in association rules. Thus, we rank patterns by the confidence values of their association rules.

7.3.1   Basic Mining Algorithm

A classical approach to computing patterns and association rules is the Apriori algorithm [1, 30]. The algorithm takes a *minimum support count* and a *minimum confidence* as parameters. We call a pattern *frequent* if its support is above the minimum support count value. We call an association rule *strong* if its confidence is above the minimum confidence value. Apriori computes (a) the set P of all frequent patterns and (b) the set R of all strong association rules in two phases:

(a) The algorithm iterates over the set of transactions and forms patterns from the method calls that occur in the same transaction. A pattern can only be frequent when its subsets are frequent and patterns are expanded in each iteration. Iteration continues until a fixed point is reached and the final set of frequent patterns P is produced.

(b) The algorithm computes association rules from the patterns in P. From each pattern $p \in P$ and every method set $q \subseteq p$ such that $p, q \neq \emptyset$, the algorithm creates an association rule of the form $p \setminus q \Rightarrow q$. All rules for a pattern have the same support count, but different confidence values. Strong association rules $p \setminus q \Rightarrow q$ are added to the final set of rules R.[2]

In Sections 7.3.2 and 7.3.3 we describe how we adapt the classic Apriori approach to improve its scalability and provide a ranking of the results.

7.3.2   Pattern Filtering

The running time of Apriori is greatly influenced by the number of patterns it has to consider. While the algorithm uses thresholds to limit the number of patterns that it outputs in P, we employ some filtering strategies that are specific to the problem of revision history mining. Another problem is that these thresholds are not always adequate for keeping the amount of noise down. The filtering strategies described below greatly reduce the running time of the mining algorithm *and* significantly reduce the amount of noise it produces.

7.3.2.1   Considering a Subset of Method Calls Only

Our strategy to deal with the complexity of frequent pattern mining is to ignore method calls that either lead to no usage patterns or only lead to obvious ones such as {hasNext, next}.

---

[2]We use \ in the rest of the chapter to denote set difference.

TABLE 7.3: Most Frequently Inserted Method Calls

Method name	Number of additions
equals	9,054
add	6,986
getString	5,295
size	5,118
get	4,709
toString	4,197
getName	3,576
append	3,524
iterator	3,340
length	3,339

- **Ignoring initial revisions.** We do not treat initial revisions of files as additions. Although they contain many usage patterns, taking initial check-ins into account introduces more incidental patterns, i.e., noise, than patterns that are actually useful.

- **Last call of a sequence.** Given a call sequence $c_1().c_2()\ldots c_n()$ included as part of a repository change, we only take the final call $c_n()$ into consideration. This is due to the fact that in Java code, a sequence of "accessor" methods is common and typically only the last call mutates the program environment. Calls like

$$\texttt{ResourcesPlugin.getPlugin().getLog().log()}$$

in Eclipse are quite common and taking intermediate portions of the call into account will contribute to noise in the form of associating the intermediate getter calls. Such patterns are not relevant for our purposes; however, they are well-studied and are best mined from a snapshot of a repository rather than from its history [32, 33, 38].

- **Ignoring common calls.** To further reduce the amount of noise, we ignore some very common method calls, such as the ones listed in Table 7.3; in practice, we ignore method calls that were added more than 100 times. These methods tend to get intermingled with real usage patterns, essentially causing noisy, "overgrown" ones to be formed.

7.3.2.2 Considering Small Patterns Only

Generally, patterns that consist of a large number of methods are created due to noise. Another way to reduce the complexity and the amount of noise is to reduce the scope of mining to *small* patterns only. We employ a combination of the following two strategies.

- **Fine-grained transactions.** As mentioned in Section 7.3.1, Apriori relies on transactions that group related items together. We generally have a choice between using *coarse-grained* or *fine-grained* transactions. Coarse-grained transactions consist of all method calls added in a single revision. Fine-grained transactions additionally group calls by the access path. In Table 7.2, the coarse-grained transaction corresponding to revision 1.23 of Baz.java is further subdivided into three fine-grained transactions for objects o3, list, and iter. An advantage of fine-grained transactions is that they are smaller, and thus make mining more efficient. The reason for this is that the runtime heavily depends on the size and number of frequent patterns, which are restricted by the size of transactions. Fine-grained transactions also tend to reduce noise because processing is restricted to a common prefix. However, we may miss patterns containing calls with different prefixes, such as pattern {iterator, hasNext, next} in Table 7.2.

- **Mining method pairs.** We can reduce the complexity even further if we mine the revision repository only for method pairs instead of patterns of arbitrary size. This technique has frequently been applied to software evolution analysis and proved successful for finding evolutionary coupling, etc. [19,20,53]. While very common, method pairs can only express relatively simple usage patterns.

7.3.3   Pattern Ranking

Even when filtering is applied, the Apriori algorithm yields many frequent patterns. However, not all of them turn out to be good usage patterns in practice. Therefore, we use several ranking schemes when presenting the patterns we discovered to the user for review.

7.3.3.1   Standard Ranking Approaches

Mining literature provides a number of standard techniques we use for pattern ranking. Among them are the pattern's (1) support count, (2) confidence, and (3) strength, where the strength of a pattern is defined as following.

Definition 7.3.6 The *strength* of pattern p is the number of strong association rules in R of the form $p \setminus q \Rightarrow q$ where $q \subset p$, both p and q are frequent patterns, and $q \neq \emptyset$.

For our experiments, we rank patterns lexicographically by their strength and support count. However, for matching method pairs $\langle a, b \rangle$ we use the product of confidence values $conf(a \Rightarrow b) \times conf(b \Rightarrow a)$ instead of the strength because the continuous nature of the product gives a more fine-grained ranking than the strength; the strength only takes the values of 0, 1, and 2 for pairs. The advantage of products over sums is that pairs where both confidence values are high are favored. In the rest of the chapter we refer to the ranking that follows classical data mining techniques as *regular ranking*.

7.3.3.2 Corrective Ranking

While the ranking schemes above can generally be applied to any data mining problem, we have come up with a measure of a pattern's importance that is specific to mining revision histories. Observation 7.2.3 is the basis of the metric we are about to describe. A check-in may only add *parts* of a usage pattern to the repository. Generally, this is a problem for the classic Apriori algorithm, which prefers patterns, all parts of which are "seen together." However, we can leverage these incomplete patterns when we realize that they often represent bug fixes.

A recent study of the dynamic of small repository changes in large software systems performed by Purushothaman et al. sheds a new light on this subject [36]. Their paper points out that almost 50% of all repository changes were small, involving less than 10 lines of code. Moreover, among one-line changes, less than 4% were likely to cause a later error. Furthermore, only less than 2.5% of all one-line changes were *perfective* changes that add functionality, rather than *corrective* changes that correct previous errors. These numbers imply a very strong correlation between one-line changes and bug corrections or fixes.

We use this observation to develop a *corrective ranking* that extends the ranking that is used in classical data mining. For this, we identify one-line fixes and mark method calls that were added at least once in such a fix as *fixed*. In addition to the measures used by regular ranking, we then additionally rank by the number of fixed methods calls which is used as the first lexicographic category. As discussed in Section 7.5, patterns with a high corrective rank result in more dynamic violations than patterns with a high regular rank.

7.3.4 Locating Added Method Calls

In order to speed up the mining process, we pre-process the revision history extracted from CVS and store this information in a general-purpose database; our techniques are further described in Zimmermann et al. [52]. The database stores method calls that have been inserted for each revision. To determine the calls inserted between two revisions r_1 and r_2, we build abstract syntax trees (ASTs) for both r_1 and r_2 and compute the set of all calls C_1 and C_2, respectively, by traversing the ASTs. $C_2 \setminus C_1$ is the set of inserted calls between r_1 and r_2.

Unlike Williams and Hollingsworth [46, 47] our approach does not build snapshots of a system. As they point out such interactions with the build environment (compilers, makefiles) are extremely difficult to handle and result in high computational costs. Instead we analyze only the differences between single revisions. As a result our preprocessing is cheap and platform- and compiler-independent; the drawback is that types cannot be resolved because only one file is investigated. In order to avoid noise that is caused by this, we additionally identify methods by the count of arguments.

7.4   Checking Patterns at Runtime

In this section we describe our dynamic approach for checking the patterns discovered through revision history mining.

7.4.1   Pattern Selection and Instrumentation

To aid with the task of choosing the relevant patterns, the user is presented with a list of mined patterns in an Eclipse view such as the one shown in Figure 7.2. The list of patterns may be sorted and filtered based on various ranking criteria described in Section 7.3.3 to better target user efforts. Human involvement at this stage, however, is optional, because the user may decide to dynamically check *all* the patterns discovered through revision history mining.

After the user selects the patterns of interest, the list of relevant methods for each of the patterns is generated and passed to the instrumenter. We use JBoss AOP [9], an aspect-oriented framework to insert additional "bookkeeping" code at the method calls relevant for the patterns. However, the task of pointcut selection is simplified for the user by using a graphical interface. In addition to the method being called and the place in the code where the call occurs, values of all actual parameters are also recorded.

Our instrumenter inserts Java bytecode at call sites to each relevant method that outputs a *dynamic event descriptor* $\langle T, E, L \rangle$ each time a relevant call site is hit at runtime, where:

(a) T is a unique timestamp for the method call.

First method	Second method	Score	LR confidence	RL confidence
registerErrorSource	unregisterErrorSource	5	0.4545	0.6250
contentInserted	insert	3	0.4286	0.6000
start	stop	33	0.5882	0.5156
addToolBar	removeToolBar	6	0.6000	0.3000
expandFold	narrow	5	0.4167	0.3571
elementAt	size	95	0.7787	0.1766
append	toString	148	0.4790	0.2686
isRunning	stop	11	0.7333	0.1719
charAt	length	124	0.5905	0.1928
length	substring	135	0.2100	0.5315
JTextField	addHelpFor	8	0.1860	0.5714

FIGURE 7.2: DynaMine pattern selection view.

(b) *E* is the environment that contains values of each object passed into or returned by the method call.

(c) *L* is the source code locations of the relevant call site.

7.4.2 Post-Processing Dynamic Traces

The trace produced in the course of a dynamic run are post-processed to produce the final statistics about the number of times each pattern is followed and the number of times it is violated. We decided in favor of off-line post-processing because some patterns are rather difficult and sometimes impossible to match with a fully online approach. In order to facilitate the task of post-processing in practice, DynaMine is equipped with checkers to look for matching method pairs and state machines. Users who wish to create checkers for more complex patterns can do so through a Java API exposed by DynaMine that allows easy access to runtime events.

Dynamically obtained results for matching pairs and state machines are exported back into Eclipse for review. The user can browse through the results and ascertain which of the patterns she thought must hold do actually hold at runtime. Often, examining the dynamic output of DynaMine allows the user to correct the initial pattern and re-instrument.

7.4.2.1 Dynamic Interpretation of Patterns

While it may be intuitively obvious what a given coding pattern means, what kind of *dynamic behavior* is valid may be open to interpretation, as illustrated by the following example.

Example 2. Consider a matching method pair ⟨beginOp, endOp⟩ and a dynamic call sequence

$$seq = \text{o.beginOp}()\ldots\text{o.beginOp}()\ldots\text{o.endOp}()$$

Obviously, a dynamic execution consisting of a sequence of calls o.beginOp()...o.endOp() follows the pattern. However, execution sequence *seq* probably represents a pattern violation.

While declaring *seq* a violation may appear quite reasonable on the surface, consider now an implementation of method beginOp that starts by calling super.beginOp(). Now *seq* is the dynamic call sequence that results from a static call to o.beginOp followed by o.endOp; the first call to beginOp comes from the static call to beginOp and the second comes from the call to super. However, in this case *seq* may be a completely reasonable interpretation of this coding pattern. □

As this example shows, there is generally no obvious mapping from a coding pattern to a dynamic sequence of events. As a result, the number of dynamic pattern matches and mismatches is interpretation-dependent. Errors found by DynaMine at runtime can only be considered such with respect to a particular dynamic interpretation of patterns. Moreover, while violations of application-specific patterns found with our approach represent *likely* bugs, they cannot be claimed as definite bugs without carefully studying the effect of each violation on the system.

In the implementation of DynaMine, to calculate the number of times each pattern is validated and violated we match the unqualified names of methods applied to a given dynamic object. Fortunately, complete information about the object involved is available at runtime, thus making this sort of matching possible. For patterns that involve only one object, we do not consider method arguments when performing a match: Our goal is to have a dynamic matcher that is as automatic as possible for a given type of pattern, and it is not always possible to automatically determine which arguments have to match for a given method pair. For complex patterns that involve more than one object and require user-defined checkers, the trace data saved by DynaMine contain information that allows the relevant call arguments to be matched.

7.4.2.2   Dynamic versus Static Counts

A single pattern violation at runtime involves one or more objects. We obtain a *dynamic count* by counting how many object combinations participated in a particular pattern violation during program execution. Dynamic counts are highly dependent on how we use the program at runtime and can be easily influenced by, for example, recompiling a project in Eclipse multiple times.

Moreover, dynamic error counts are not representative of the work a developer has to do to fix an error, as many dynamic violations can be caused by the same error in the code. To provide a better metric on the number of errors found in the application code, we also compute a *static count*. This is done by mapping each method participating in a pattern to a static call site and counting the number of unique call site combinations that are seen at runtime. Static counts are computed for validated and violated patterns.

7.4.2.3   Pattern Classification

We use runtime information on how many times each pattern is validated and how many times it is violated to classify the patterns. Let v be the number of validated instances of a pattern and e be the number of its violations. The constants used in the classification strategy below were obtained empirically to match our intuition about how patterns should be categorized. However, clearly, ours is but one of many potential classification approaches.

We define an error threshold $\alpha = min(v/10, 100)$. Based on the value of α, patterns can be classified into the following categories:

Method Pairs   Dynamic Events   Static Events

First method	Second method	Validated	Violated	Validated	Violated
beginTask	done	334	642	42	21
addWidget	removeWidget	1264	16	5	2
preValueChange	postValueChange	63	2	11	2
addPropertyChangeListener	removePropertyChangeListener	1789	478	55	25
annotationAdded	annotationRemoved	0	8	0	2
preReplaceChild	postReplaceChild	40	0	26	0
OpenEvent	fireOpen	0	3	0	1
addElementChangedListener	removeElementChangedListener	5	2	1	1
addResourceChangeListener	removeResourceChangeListener	25	4	19	4
preRemoveChildEvent	postAddChildEvent	0	172	0	3

Writable   Smart Insert   1 : 1

FIGURE 7.3: DynaMine dynamic results view. Error patterns are shown in red (medium gray). Usage patterns are shown in blue (dark gray). Unlikely patterns are grayed out.

(a) **Likely usage patterns**: patterns with a sufficiently high support that are mostly validated with relatively few errors.
$(e < \alpha \wedge v > 5)$

(b) **Likely error patterns**: patterns that have a significant number of validated cases as well as a large number of violations.
$(\alpha \le e \le 2v \wedge v > 5)$

(c) **Unlikely patterns**: patterns that do not have many validated cases or cause too many errors to be usage patterns.
$(e > 2v \vee v \le 5)$

In DynaMine, a categorization of patterns is presented to the user in an Eclipse view, as shown in Figure 7.3. The patterns are color-coded in the Eclipse view to represent their type, with blue (dark gray) being a likely usage pattern, red (medium gray) being a likely error pattern, and gray being an unlikely pattern.

7.5 Experimental Results

In this section we discuss our practical experience of applying DynaMine to real software systems. Section 7.5.1 describes our experimental setup; Section 7.5.2 evaluates the results of both our patterns mining and dynamic analysis approaches.

TABLE 7.4: Summary Statistics about the Evaluation Subjects

	Eclipse	JEdit
Lines of code	2,924,124	714,715
Source files	19,115	3,163
Java classes	19,439	6,602
CVS revisions	2,837,854	144,495
Method calls inserted	465,915	56,794
Unique methods called in inserts	59,929	10,760
Developers checking into CVS	122	92
CVS history since	2001-05-02	2000-01-15

7.5.1   Experimental Setup

We have chosen to perform our experiments on Eclipse [11] and jEdit [35], two very large open-source Java applications; in fact, Eclipse is one of the largest Java projects ever created. A summary of information about the benchmarks is given in Table 7.4. For each application, the number of lines of code, source files, and classes is shown in rows 2–4. Both applications are known for being highly extensible and having a large number of plugins available; in fact, much of Eclipse itself is implemented as a set of plugins. In addition to these standard metrics that reflect the size of the benchmarks, we show the number of revisions in each CVS repository in row 5, the number of inserted calls in row 6, and the number of distinct methods that were called in row 7. Both projects have a significant number of individual developers working on them, as evidenced by the numbers in row 8. The date of the first revision is presented in row 9.

7.5.1.1   Mining Setup

When we performed the pre-processing on Eclipse and jEdit, it took about four days to fetch all revisions over the Internet because the complete revision data are about 6 GB in size and the CVS protocol is not well-suited for retrieving large volumes of history data. Computing inserted methods by analyzing the ASTs and storing this information in a database takes about a day on a Powermac G5 2.3 Ghz dual-processor machine with 1 GB of memory.

Once the pre-processing step was complete, we performed the actual data mining. Without any of the optimizations described in Sections 7.3.2 and 7.3.3, the mining step does not complete even in the case jEdit, not to mention Eclipse. Among the optimizations we apply, the biggest time improvement and noise reduction are achieved by disregarding common method calls, such as `equals`, `length`, etc. With *all* the optimizations applied, mining becomes orders of magnitude faster, usually only taking several minutes.

7.5.1.2 Dynamic Setup

Because the incremental cost of checking for additional patterns at runtime is generally low, when reviewing the patterns in Eclipse for inclusion in our dynamic experiments, we were fairly liberal in our selection. We would usually either just look at the method names involved in the pattern or briefly examine a few usage cases. We believe that this strategy is realistic, as we cannot expect the user to spend hours poring over the patterns. To obtain dynamic results, we ran each application for several minutes on a Pentium 4 machine running Linux, which typically resulted in several thousand dynamic events being generated.

7.5.2 Discussion of the Results

Overall, 32 out of 56 (or 57%) patterns were hit at runtime. Furthermore, 21 out of 32 (or 66%) of these patterns turned out to be either usage or error patterns. The fact that two thirds of all dynamically encountered patterns were likely patterns demonstrates the power of our mining approach.

In this section we discuss the categories of patterns briefly described in Section 11.2 in more detail.

7.5.2.1 Matching Method Pairs

The simplest and most common kind of a pattern detected with our mining approach is one where two different methods of the same class are supposed to match precisely in execution. Many of known error patterns in the literature such as ⟨fopen, fclose⟩ or ⟨lock, unlock⟩ fall into the category of function calls that require exact matching: failing to call the second function in the pair or calling one of the functions twice in a row is an error.

Table 7.5 and 7.6 list matching pairs of methods discovered with our mining technique for corrective and regular ranking, respectively. The methods of a pair ⟨a, b⟩ are listed in the order they are supposed to be executed, e.g., a should be executed before b. For brevity, we only list the names of the method; full method names that include package names should be easy to obtain. A quick glance at the table reveals that many pairs follow a specific naming strategy such as pre–post, add–remove, begin–end, and enter–exit. These pairs could have been discovered by simply pattern matching on the method names. Moreover, looking at method pairs that use the same prefixes or suffixes is an obvious extension of our technique.

However, a significant number of pairs have less than obvious names to look for, including ⟨HLock, HUnlock⟩, ⟨progressStart, progressEnd⟩, and ⟨blockSignal, unblockSignal⟩. Finally, some pairs are very difficult to recognize as matching method pairs and require a detailed study of the API to confirm, such as ⟨stopMeasuring, commitMeasurements⟩, ⟨suspend, resume⟩, etc.

TABLE 7.5: Effectiveness of Corrective Ranking

	Method pair (a,b)		Confidence			Support	Dynamic		Static		Type
	Method a	Method b	$conf$	$conf_{ab}$	$conf_{ba}$	$count$	v	e	v	e	
	CORRECTIVE RANKING										
Eclipse (16 pairs)	NewRgn	DisposeRgn	0.76	0.92	0.82	49					
	kEventControlActivate	kEventControlDeactivate	0.69	0.83	0.83	5					
	addDebugEventListener	removeDebugEventListener	0.61	0.85	0.72	23	4	1	4	1	Unlikely
	beginTask	done	0.60	0.74	0.81	493	332	759	41	28	Unlikely
	beginRule	endRule	0.60	0.80	0.74	32	7	0	4	0	Usage
	suspend	resume	0.60	0.83	0.71	5					
	NewPtr	DisposePtr	0.57	0.82	0.70	23					
	addListener	removeListener	0.57	0.68	0.83	90	143	140	35	29	Error
	register	deregister	0.54	0.69	0.78	40	2,854	461	17	90	Error
	malloc	free	0.47	0.68	0.68	28					
	addElementChangedListener	removeElementChangedListener	0.42	0.73	0.57	8	6	1	1	1	Error
	addResourceChangeListener	removeResourceChangeListener	0.41	0.90	0.46	26	27	1	21	1	Usage
	addPropertyChangeListener	removePropertyChangeListener	0.40	0.54	0.73	140	1,864	309	54	31	Error
	start	stop	0.39	0.59	0.65	32	69	18	20	9	Error
	addDocumentListener	removeDocumentListener	0.36	0.64	0.56	29	38	2	14	2	Usage
	addSyncSetChangedListener	removeSyncSetChangedListener	0.34	0.62	0.56	24					
jEdit (8 pairs)	addNotify	removeNotify	0.60	0.77	0.77	17	3	0	3	0	Unlikely
	setBackground	setForeground	0.57	0.67	0.86	12	75	175	5	5	Unlikely
	contentRemoved	contentInserted	0.51	0.71	0.71	5	17	11	7	5	Error
	setInitialDelay	start	0.40	0.80	0.50	4	0	32	0	2	Unlikely
	registerErrorSource	unregisterErrorSource	0.28	0.45	0.62	5					
	start	stop	0.20	0.39	0.52	33	83	98	10	13	Error
	addToolBar	removeToolBar	0.18	0.60	0.30	6	24	43	5	5	Error
	init	save	0.09	0.40	0.24	31					
(24 pairs)	Subtotals for the corrective ranking scheme:						5,546	2,051	241	222	3 U, 8 E

Note: Matching method pairs discovered through CVS history mining. The support count is *count*. The confidence for $\{a\} \Rightarrow \{b\}$ is $conf_{ab}$, for $\{b\} \Rightarrow \{a\}$ it is $conf_{ba}$. The pairs are ordered by $conf = conf_{ab} \times conf_{ba}$. In the last column, usage and error patterns are abbreviated as "U" and "E", respectively. Empty cells represent patterns that have not been observed at runtime.

TABLE 7.6: Effectiveness of Regular Ranking

	Method pair (a,b)		Confidence			Support	Dynamic		Static		Type
	Method a	Method b	$conf$	$conf_{ab}$	$conf_{ba}$	count	v	e	v	e	
	REGULAR RANKING										
Eclipse (15 pairs)	createPropertyList	reapPropertyList	1.00	1.00	1.00	174	40	0	26	0	Usage
	preReplaceChild	postReplaceChild	1.00	1.00	1.00	133					
	preLazyInit	postLazyInit	1.00	1.00	1.00	112	63	2	11	2	Usage
	preValueChange	postValueChange	1.00	1.00	1.00	46	2,507	16	26	6	Usage
	addWidget	removeWidget	1.00	1.00	1.00	35					
	stopMeasuring	commitMeasurements	1.00	1.00	1.00	15					
	blockSignal	unblockSignal	1.00	1.00	1.00	13					
	HLock	HUnLock	1.00	1.00	1.00	9					
	addInputChangedListener	removeInputChangedListener	1.00	1.00	1.00	9	0	171	0	3	Unlikely
	preRemoveChildEvent	postAddChildEvent	1.00	1.00	1.00	8					
	progressStart	progressEnd	1.00	1.00	1.00	8					
	CGContextSaveGState	CGContextRestoreGState	1.00	1.00	1.00	7					
	addInsert	addDelete	1.00	1.00	1.00	7					
	annotationAdded	annotationRemoved	1.00	1.00	1.00	7	0	10	0	4	Unlikely
	OpenEvent	fireOpen	1.00	1.00	1.00	7	3	0	1	0	Unlikely
jEdit (13 pairs)	readLock	readUnlock	1.00	1.00	1.00	16	8,578	0	14	0	Usage
	setHandler	parse	1.00	1.00	1.00	6	12	0	8	0	Usage
	addTo	removeFrom	1.00	1.00	1.00	5					
	execProcess	ssCommand	1.00	1.00	1.00	4					
	freeMemory	totalMemory	1.00	1.00	1.00	4	95	0	2	0	Usage
	lockBuffer	unlockBuffer	1.00	1.00	1.00	4					
	writeLock	writeUnlock	0.85	0.85	1.00	11	38	0	8	0	Usage
	allocConnection	releaseConnection	0.83	1.00	0.83	5					
	getSubregionOfOffset	xToSubregionOfOffset	0.80	0.80	1.00	4					
	initTextArea	uninitTextArea	0.80	0.80	1.00	4					
	undo	redo	0.69	0.83	0.83	5	0	4	0	1	Unlikely
	setSelectedItem	getSelectedItem	0.37	0.50	0.73	11	7	17	7	7	Unlikely
	addToSelection	setSelection	0.29	0.57	0.50	4	12	27	1	9	Unlikely
(28 pairs)	Subtotals for the regular ranking scheme:						11,355	247	104	32	7 U
(52 pairs)	Overall totals:						16,901	2,298	245	254	10 U, 8 E

Tables 7.5 and 7.6 also summarize dynamic results for matching pairs. The tables provide dynamic and static counts of validated and violated patterns as well as a classification into usage, error, and unlikely patterns. Below we summarize some observations about the data. About a half of all method pair patterns that we selected from the filtered mined results were confirmed as likely patterns, out of those 10 were usage patterns and 8 were error patterns. Many more potentially interesting matching pairs become available if we consider lower support counts; for the experiments we have only considered patterns with a support of four or more.

Several characteristic pairs are described below. Both locking pairs in jEdit ⟨writeLock, writeUnlock⟩ and ⟨readLock, readUnlock⟩ are excellent usage patterns with no violations. ⟨contentInserted, contentRemoved⟩ is not a good pattern despite the method names: The first method is triggered when text is added in an editor window; the second when text is removed. Clearly, there is no reason why these two methods have to match. Method pair ⟨addNotify, removeNotify⟩ is perfectly matched, however, its support is not sufficient to declare it a usage pattern. A somewhat unusual kind of matching methods that at first we thought was caused by noise in the data consists of a constructor call followed by a method call, such as the pair ⟨OpenEvent, fireOpen⟩. This sort of pattern indicates that all objects of type OpenEvent should be "consumed" by passing them into method fireOpen. Violations of this pattern may lead to resource and memory leaks, a serious problem in long-running Java programs such as Eclipse, which may be open at a developer's desktop for days.

Overall, corrective ranking was significantly more effective than regular ranking schemes that are based on the product of confidence values. The top half of the table that addresses patterns obtained with corrective ranking contains 24 matching method pairs; the second half that deals with the patterns obtained with regular ranking contains 28 pairs. Looking at the subtotals for each ranking scheme reveals 241 static validating instances versus only 104 for regular ranking; 222 static error instances are found versus only 32 for regular ranking. Finally, 11 pairs found with corrective ranking were dynamically confirmed as either error or usage patterns versus 7 for regular ranking. This confirms our belief that corrective ranking is more effective.

7.5.2.2   State Machines

In many of cases, the order in which methods are supposed to be called *on a given object* can easily be captured with a finite state machine. Typically, such state machines must be followed precisely; omitting or repeating a method call is a sign of error. The fact that state machines are encountered often is not surprising; state machines are the simplest formalism for describing the object life-cycle [40]. Matching method pairs are a specific case of state machines, but there are other prominent cases that involve *more that two methods*, which are the focus of this section.

An example of state machine usage comes from class `Scribe` from the package `org.eclipse.jdt.internal.formatter` in Eclipse responsible for pretty-printing Java source code. Method `exitAlignment` is supposed to match an earlier `enterAlignment` call to preserve consistency. Typically, method `redoAlignment` that tries to resolve an exception caused by the current `enterAlignment` would be placed in a `catch` block and executed optionally, only if an exception is raised. The regular expression

o.enterAlignment o.redoAlignment? o.exitAlignment

summarizes how methods of this class are supposed to be called on an object o of type `Scribe`. In our dynamic experiments, the pattern matched 885 times with only 17 dynamic violations that correspond to 9 static violations, which makes this an excellent usage pattern.

Another interesting state machine below is found based on mining jEdit. Methods `beginCompoundEdit` and `endCompoundEdit` are used to group editing operations on a text buffer together so that undo or redo actions can be later applied to them at once.

$$\begin{aligned} &\texttt{o.beginCompoundEdit()}\\ &\quad \texttt{(o.insert(...) | o.remove(...))}^{+}\\ &\texttt{o.endCompoundEdit()} \end{aligned}$$

A dynamic study of this pattern reveals that (1) methods `beginCompoundEdit` and `endCompoundEdit` are *perfectly* matched in all cases; (2) 86% of calls to `insert/remove` are *within* a compound edit; (3) there are three cases of several ⟨begin−, endCompoundEdit⟩ pairs that have no `insert` or `remove` operations between them. Since a compound edit is established for a reason, this shows that our regular expression most likely does not fully describe the life-cycle of a `Buffer` object. Indeed, a detailed study of the code reveals some other methods that may be used within a compound edit. Subsequently adding these methods to the pattern and re-instrumenting the jEdit led to a new pattern that fully describes the `Buffer` object's life-cycle.

Precisely following the order in which methods must be invoked is common for C interfaces [14], as represented by functions that manipulate files and sockets. While such dependency on call order is less common in Java, it still occurs in programs that have low-level access to OS data structures. For instance, methods `PmMemCreateMC`, `PmMemFlush`, and `PmMemStop`, `PmMemReleaseMC` declared in `org.eclipse.swt.OS` in Eclipse expose low-level memory context management routines in Java through the use of JNI wrappers. These methods are supposed to be called in an order described by the regular expression below:

$$\begin{aligned} &\texttt{OS.PmMemCreateMC}\\ &\quad \texttt{(OS.PmMemStart OS.PmMemFlush OS.PmMemStop)?}\\ &\texttt{OS.PmMemReleaseMC} \end{aligned}$$

The first and last lines are mandatory when using this pattern, while the middle line is optional. Unfortunately, this pattern only exhibits itself at runtime on certain platforms, so we were unable to confirm it dynamically.

Another similar JNI wrapper found in Eclipse that can be expressed as a state machine is responsible for region-based memory allocation and can be described with the following regular expression:

$$(\texttt{OS.NewPtr} \mid \texttt{OS.NewPtrClear}) \;\texttt{OS.DisposePtr}$$

Either one of functions `NewPtr` and `NewPtrClear` can be used to create a new pointer; the latter function zeroes-out the memory region before returning.

Another commonly used pattern that can be captured with a state machine has to do with hierarchical allocation of resources. Objects request and release system resources in a way that is perfectly nested. For instance, one of the patterns we found in Eclipse suggests the following resource management scheme on objects of type component:

```
o.createHandle()
o.register()
o.deregister()
o.releaseHandle()
```

The call to `createHandle` requests an operating system resource for a GUI widget, such as a window or a button; `releaseHandle` frees this OS resource for subsequent use. `register` associates the current GUI object with a `display` data structure, which is responsible for forwarding GUI events to components as they arrive; `deregister` breaks this link.

7.5.2.3   More Complex Patterns

More complicated patterns, that are concerned with the behavior of more than one object or patterns for which a finite state machine is not expressive enough, are quite widespread in the code base we have considered as well. Notice that approaches that use a restrictive model of a pattern, such as matching function calls [15], would not be able to find these complex patterns.

Due to space restrictions, we only describe one complex pattern in detail here, which is motivated by the code snippet in Figure 7.4. The lines relevant to the pattern are highlighted in bold. Object `workspace` is a runtime representation of an Eclipse workspace, a large complex object that has a specialized transaction scheme for when it needs to be modified. In particular, one is supposed to start the transaction that requires workspace access with a call to `beginOperation` and finish it with `endOperation`.

Calls to `beginUnprotected()` and `endUnprotected()` on a `WorkManager` object obtained from the `workspace` indicate "unlocked" operations on the workspace: The first one releases the workspace lock that is held by default and the second one re-acquires it; the `WorkManager` is obtained for a `workspace` by calling `workspace.getWorkManager`. Unlocking operations should be precisely matched if no error occurs; in case an exception is raised,

```
try {
    monitor.beginTask(null, Policy.totalWork);
    int depth = -1;
    try {
        workspace.prepareOperation(null, monitor);
        workspace.beginOperation(true);
        depth = workspace.getWorkManager().beginUnprotected();
        return runInWorkspace(Policy.subMonitorFor(monitor,
            Policy.opWork,
            SubProgressMonitor.PREPEND_MAIN_LABEL_TO_SUBTASK));
    } catch (OperationCanceledException e) {
        workspace.getWorkManager().operationCanceled();
        return Status.CANCEL_STATUS;
    } finally {
        if (depth >= 0)
            workspace.getWorkManager().endUnprotected(depth);
        workspace.endOperation(null, false,
        Policy.subMonitorFor(monitor, Policy.endOpWork));
    }
    } catch (CoreException e) {
        return e.getStatus();
} finally {
    monitor.done();
}
```

FIGURE 7.4: Example of workspace operations and locking discipline usage in class `InternalWorkspaceJob` in Eclipse.

method `operationCanceled` is called on the `WorkManager` of the current workspace. As can be seen from the code in Figure 7.4, this pattern involves error handling and may be quite tricky to get right. We have come across this pattern by observing that pairs ⟨beginOperation, endOperation⟩ and ⟨beginUnprotected, endUnprotected⟩ are both highly correlated in the code. This pattern is easily described as a context-free language that allows nested matching brackets, whose grammar is shown below.[3]

$$S \rightarrow O^\star$$
$$O \rightarrow \text{w.prepareOperation()}$$
$$\text{w.beginOperation()}$$
$$U^\star$$
$$\text{w.endOperation()}$$

---

[3]S is the grammar start symbol and $\star$ is used to represent 0 or more copies of the preceding non-terminal; ? indicates that the preceding non-terminal is optional.

$$U \quad \rightarrow \quad \text{w.getWorkManager().beginUnprotected()}$$
$$S$$
$$\text{w.getWorkManager().operationCanceled() ?}$$
$$\text{w.getWorkManager().beginUnprotected()}$$

This is a very strong usage pattern in Eclipse, with 100% of the cases we have seen obeying the grammar above. The nesting of `Workspace` and `WorkManager` operations was usually 3–4 levels deep in practice.

As this example shows, characterizing the pattern with a grammar or some other specification is not an easy task. In DynaMine, this task is delegated to the user. However, restricting the formalism used for describing the pattern such as state machines in Whaley et al. [45] may make it possible to determine the pattern automatically.

7.6   Design Decisions

In this section we discuss some of the design choices we made when working on DynaMine. Our approach for the rest of the section is to outline where our technique stands with respect to several design dimensions:

- Static versus dynamic analysis

- Amount of user involvement

- Granularity of mined information

Each of these dimensions is discussed in an individual section below.

7.6.1   Static versus Dynamic Analysis

Our approach is to look for pattern violations at runtime, as opposed to using a static analysis technique. This is justified by several considerations outlined below.

- **Scalability.** Our original motivation when starting the DynaMine project was to be able to analyze Eclipse, which is one of the largest Java applications ever created. The code base of Eclipse is comprised of more than 2,900,000 lines of code and 31,500 classes. Most of the patterns we are interested in are spread across multiple methods and need an interprocedural approach to analyze. Given the substantial size of the application under analysis, precise whole-program flow-sensitive static analysis is expensive. Moreover, static call graph construction presents a challenge for applications that use dynamic class loading [27]. In contrast, dynamic analysis does not require call graph information.

- **Validating discovered patterns.** A benefit of using dynamic analysis is that we are able to "validate" the patterns we discover through CVS history mining as real usage patterns by observing how many times they occur at runtime. Patterns that are matched a large number of times with only a few violations represent likely patterns with a few errors. The advantage of validated patterns is that they increase the degree of assurance in the quality of mined results. With static analysis, validating patterns would not generally be possible unless flow-sensitive "must" information is available.

  In contrast to a static technique, runtime analysis does not suffer from false positives because all pattern violations detected with our system actually *do* occur at the time of execution.

- **Opportunity for automatic repair.** Finally, only dynamic analysis provides the opportunity to fix the problem on the fly without any user intervention. This is especially appropriate in the case of a matching method pair when the second method call is missing. While we have not implemented automatic "pattern repair" in DynaMine, we believe it to be a fruitful future research direction. However, care must be taken not to perform the repair action more than once, as most such actions are not idempotent.

While we believe that dynamic analysis is more appropriate than static analysis for the problem at hand, a serious shortcoming of dynamic analysis is its lack of coverage.

In fact, in our dynamic experiments, we have managed to find runtime use cases for some, but not all, of our mined patterns. Another concern is that a workload selection may significantly influence how patterns are classified by DynaMine. In our experiments with Eclipse and jEdit we were careful to exercise common functions of both applications that represent hot paths through the code and thus contain errors that may manifest at runtime often. However, we likely have missed error patterns that occur on exception paths that were not hit at runtime.

In addition to the inherent lack of coverage, another factor that reduced the number of patterns available for checking at runtime was that Eclipse contains quite a bit of platform-specific code. This code is irrelevant unless the pattern is located in the portion of the code specific to the execution platform.

Another way to gain some insight into which pattern is more likely is by resorting to static analysis. One approach is to look at flow-sensitive information that is computed statically. If we can conclude that there is a dominance or a post-dominance relation between a set of method calls, that will help us in establishing a pattern. However, doing so interprocedurally is a difficult task.

Another possibility is to use a static checker and examine its results. The intuition is that a pattern that results in a large number of violations is somewhat unlikely.

Williams et al. [47] propose a different interaction between the mining and analysis stages. They mine information from CVS histories to determine what functions have been "fixed" and use this information to propagate those functions to the top in the static analysis stage. The notion of "being fixed" is pretty rigid, however: They developed a heuristic for the return value checker that does simple syntactic analysis of the relevant change. Notice that unless bug database information can be easily correlated with revision history data, detecting whether a change is a bug fix is a difficult task in general. While "one-line change" heuristic seems to work pretty well in practice, many bug fixes are missed.

7.6.2   Amount of User Involvement

Our system currently requires user involvement at the following two stages: First, the candidate patterns need to be formulated by the user based on the methods mined from revision history repositories. Most of the patterns considered in this chapter are relatively simple and can be captured with a state machine or, in the more complex cases, a grammar.

However, the need for human involvement can be reduced if we fix the paradigm, i.e., "state machines only." Then, at runtime, we can consider all potential state machines and rank them based on how many times each machine reaches a success state.

For example, for the pair {addListener, removeListener} the two machines that are ordered versions of this pair are possible. Of course, other machines, such as the one that requires addListener to be called three times, followed by removeListener, followed by another call to addListener is possible. While an infinite number of potential machines exist, based on our experience, we can often just limit ourselves to permutations of the methods involved.

7.6.3   Granularity of Mined Information

Our approach to interpreting source code information found in revision repositories can be further improved. We are currently oblivious to type information found in the program, relying only on the syntactic notion of what a method call is. We also use the notion of a common prefix, as described in Section 7.3.2.2, which is fully oblivious to aliasing information.

In other words, if we have two methods calls, p_1.foo and p_2.bar, and we know that p_1 and p_2 are aliases for the same heap object, as determined by a pointer analysis, the information we mine will be more complete. However, it will also be more noisy because of pointer analysis imprecision.

Even though we have access to parsed abstract syntax trees, the amount

```
C1.java:
            class C1 {
                void foo(){
                    ...
+                   workspace.getWidget().addListener();
                    ...
                }
            }


C2.java:
            class C2 {
                void bar(){
                    ...
+                   widget.removeListener();
                    ...
                }
            }
```

FIGURE 7.5: Cross-file check-in containing of two lines spread across two different files. Inserted lines are marked with '+'.

of analysis that can be done locally within a single file is somewhat limited (pointer analysis is typically global). Having aliasing information as well as parse trees for all revisions of a particular project would enable us to consider patterns that span multiple files. For instance, for the pattern {addListener, removeListener}, the check-in shown in Figure 7.5 will contribute to the pattern, assuming access paths workspace.getWidget() in class C1 and widget in class C2 may refer to the same object.

Finally, another option for the mining strategy is to pay attention to *deletions* as well as additions. It is likely, however, that the number of deletions observed will be fewer.

7.7 Extensions

While the patterns DynaMine discovers can be fed into bug detection tools to detect coding effects in code after it has been written, it would be even better to prevent problems from happening before the coding phase is finished. In this section we outline one such extension where mined patterns are translated into coding templates supported by the developer's editor. As a result, common coding mistakes are avoided from the start.

```
            try {
                ...
                A(...);
                ...
            } finally {
                B(...);
            }
```

FIGURE 7.6: A typical `try − finally` block involving a matching method pair.

As we observed earlier, matching method pairs represent one of the most commonly used temporal patterns in software. While pairs such as ⟨fopen, fclose⟩ are widespread in C, as this chapter has shown, similar method pairs are present in large Java code bases as well. Eclipse APIs have a number of such methods pairs scattered throughout the code, including ⟨register, unregister⟩, ⟨beginCompoundEdit, endCompoundEdit⟩, etc.

A common coding idiom pertaining to using method pairs consists of making sure that the second method is placed within a `finally` block so that the "closing bracket" method is always executed. Given a pair of methods ⟨A, B⟩, the coding pattern shown in Figure 7.6 is quite common. To ensure that method B is called on *all* execution paths, the call to B is placed within the `finally` block. Placing it outside the `finally` block may lead to B not being called when an exception is thrown. This coding idiom in Java is explored in more detail in [44].

We take this concept further by creating a set of *coding templates* common to plugin development. According to the Eclipse documentation, "templates are a structured description of coding patterns that reoccur in source code," and thus represent a perfect mechanism for our purposes: Whenever the user introduces a call to method A, the machinery built into Eclipse is responsible for expanding the template to build the structure shown in Figure 7.7.

7.8   Related Work

A vast amount of work has been done in bug detection. C and C++ code in particular is prone to buffer overrun and memory management errors; tools such as PREfix [10] and Clouseau [23] are representative examples of systems designed to find specific classes of bugs (pointer errors and object ownership violations, respectively). Dynamic systems include Purify [22], which traps

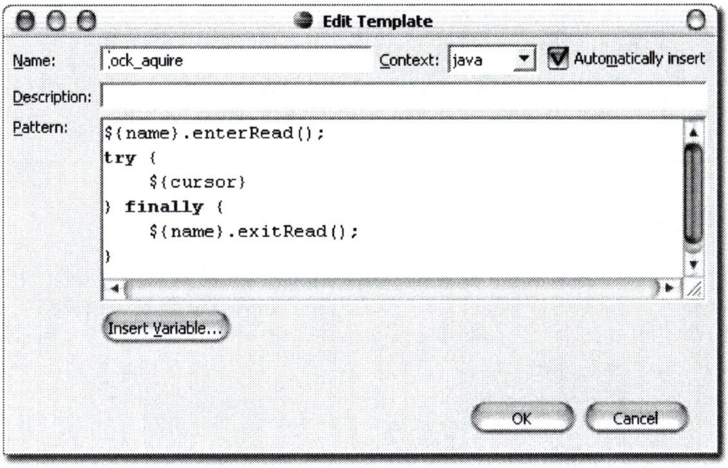

FIGURE 7.7: Template creation for ⟨`acquireRead`, `exitRead`⟩ pattern.

heap errors, and Eraser [39], which detects race conditions. Both of these analyses have been implemented as standard uses of the Valgrind system [34]. Much attention has been given to detecting high-profile software defects in important domains such as operating system bugs [21, 23], security bugs [41, 43], bugs in firmware [25] and errors in reliability-critical embedded systems [7, 8].

Space limitations prohibit us from reviewing a vast body of literature of bug-finding techniques. Engler et al. are among the first to point out the need for extracting rules to be used in bug-finding tools [15]. They employ a static analysis approach and statistical techniques to find likely instantiations of pattern templates such as matching function calls. Our mining technique is not a priori limited to a particular set of pattern templates; however, it is powerless when it comes to patterns that are never added to the repository after the first revision.

Several projects focus on application-specific error patterns, including SABER [37] that deals with J2EE patterns. Their work was motivated by the desire to analyze really large Java systems such as WebSphere. Based on the experience of IBM's developers, they have identified a range of usage patterns in Java AWT, Swing, and EJB code and analyses created to find violations of these patterns. The Metal system [21] addresses the types of bugs in OS code.

PQL is a language that allows one to express and enforce API usage patterns [31]. PQL supports both runtime and static checking as well as a hybrid mode when static analysis removes superfluous runtime checks to reduce the overhead. The need to come up with useful patterns for PQL served as the original inspiration for our work.

Certain categories of patterns can be gleaned from AntiPattern literature [13, 42], although many AntiPatterns tend to deal with high-level architectural concerns than with low-level coding issues. In the rest of this section, we review literature pertinent to revision history mining and software model extraction.

7.8.1   Revision History Mining

One of the most frequently used techniques for revision history mining is co-change. The basic idea is that two items that are changed together are related to one another. These items can be of any granularity; in the past co-change has been applied to changes in modules [19], files [5], classes [6, 20], and functions [51]. Recent research improves on co-change by applying data mining techniques to revision histories [49, 53]. Michail used data mining on the source code of programming libraries to detect reuse patterns, but not for revision histories only for single snapshots [32, 33]. Our work is the first to apply co-change and data mining based on method calls. While Fischer et al. were the first to combine bug databases with dynamic analysis [18], our work is the first that combines the mining of revision histories with dynamic analysis.

The work most closely related to ours is that by Williams and Hollingsworth [46]. They were the first to combine program analysis and revision history mining. Their paper proposes error ranking improvements for a static return value checker with information about fixes obtained from revision histories. Our work differs from theirs in several important ways: They focus on prioritizing or improving existing error patterns and checkers, whereas we concentrate on discovering new ones. Furthermore, we use dynamic analysis and thus do not face high false positive rates their tool suffers from.

Recently, Williams and Hollingsworth also turned toward mining function usage patterns from revision histories [47]. In contrast to our work, they focus only on pairs and do not use their patterns to detect violations.

7.8.2   Model Extraction

Most work on automatically inferring state models on components of software systems has been done using dynamic analysis techniques. The Strauss system [3] uses machine learning techniques to infer a state machine representing the proper sequence of function calls in an interface.

Dallmeier et al. trace call sequences and correlate sequence patterns with test failures [12]. Whaley et al. [45] hardcode a restricted model paradigm so that probable models of object-oriented interfaces can be easily automatically extracted. Alur et al. [2] generalize this to automatically produce small, expressive finite state machines with respect to certain predicates over an object. Lam and Rinard use a type system-based approach to statically extract interfaces [26]. Their work is more concerned with high-level system structure rather than low-level life-cycle constraints [40].

Daikon is able to validate correlations between values at runtime and is therefore able to validate patterns [16]. Weimer and Necula use exception control flow paths to guide the discovery of temporal error patterns with considerable success [44]; they also provide a comparison with other ing specification mining work.

Perracota uses a runtime analysis to propose a set of temporal properties [48] in a manner similar to Daikon [17]. The resulting properties can then be verified using a theorem prover. In contrast to Perracota, our approach is designed to be much more lightweight, sidestepping costly static analysis or theorem proving and only requiring dynamic analysis for validation of the candidate properties.

PR-Miner relies on parsing code snapshots and frequent itemset mining to detect common patterns that may include functions, variables, and files [50]. Rules with a low threshold are removed and additional pruning techniques are used to reduce the number of rules used for error checking further. A combination of intra- and interprocedural analysis is then used to find bugs. However, generating a lot of "candidate" rules does not help in a real-life setting unless the noise is very low. Moreover, PR-Miner reports a total of 23 bugs and 75 false positives, suggesting that runtime analysis lacking false positives is a good way to proceed.

7.9 Conclusions

In this chapter we presented DynaMine, a tool for learning common usage patterns from the revision histories of large software systems. Our method can learn both simple and complicated patterns, scales to millions of lines of code, and has been used to find more than 250 pattern violations. Our mining approach is effective at finding coding patterns: Two thirds of all dynamically encountered patterns turned out to be likely patterns.

DynaMine is the first tool that combines revision history information with dynamic analysis for the purpose of finding software errors. Our tool largely automates the mining and dynamic execution steps and makes the results of both steps more accessible by presenting the discovered patterns as well as the results of dynamic checking to the user in custom Eclipse views.

Optimization and filtering strategies that we developed allowed us to reduce the mining time by orders of magnitude and to find high-quality patterns in millions of lines of code in a matter of minutes. Our ranking strategy that favored patterns with previous bug fixes proved to be very effective at finding error patterns. In contrast, classical ranking schemes from data mining could only locate usage patterns. Dynamic analysis proved invaluable in establishing trust in patterns and finding their violations.

DynaMine is one of the first crossover projects between the areas of revision history mining and bug detection. We see many potential extensions for our work, some of which are listed below:

- Patterns discovered by DynaMine can be used in a variety of bug-finding tools. While whole-program static analysis is expensive, applying a lightweight intraprocedural static approach to the patterns confirmed using dynamic analysis will likely discover interesting errors on rarely executed exceptional paths.

- Extends the set of patterns discovered with DynaMine by simple textual matching. For example, if ⟨blockSignal, unblockSignal⟩ is known to be a strong pattern, then perhaps all pairs of the form ⟨X, unX⟩ are good patterns to check.

- As with other approaches to pattern discovery, there are ample opportunities for programmer assistant tools. For example, if a developer types blockSignal in a Java code editor, then a call to unblockSignal can be suggested or automatically inserted by the editor.

Acknowledgments. We would like to thank Wes Weimer, Ted Kremenek, Chris Unkel, Christian Lindig, and the anonymous reviewers for providing useful feedback on how to improve this chapter. We are especially grateful to Michael Martin for his assistance with dynamic instrumentation and last-minute proofreading. This work is based on an earlier work: "DynaMine: Finding Common Error Patterns by Mining Software Revision Histories", in ESEC/FSE-13: Proceedings of the 10th European Software Engineering Conference held jointly with 13th ACM SIGSOFT International Symposium on Foundations of Software Engineering. © ACM, 2005. http://doi.acm.org/10.1145/1081706.1081754

Bibliography

[1] R. Agrawal and R. Srikant. Fast algorithms for mining association rules. In *Proceedings of the 20th Very Large Data Bases Conference*, pages 487–499, Morgan Kaufmann, 1994.

[2] Rajeev Alur, Pavol Černý, P. Madhusudan, and Wonhong Nam. Synthesis of interface specifications for Java classes. In *Proceedings of the 32nd ACM Sysposium on Principles of Programming Languages*, pages 98–109, Long Beach, CA, 2005.

[3] G. Ammons, R. Bodik, and J. Larus. Mining specifications. In *Proceedings of the 29th ACM Symposium on Principles of Programming Languages*, pages 4–16, 2002.

[4] Thomas Ball, Byron Cook, Vladimir Levin, and Sriram K. Rajamani. SLAM and static driver verifier: technology transfer of formal methods inside Microsoft. Technical Report MSR-TR-2004-08, Microsoft, 2004.

[5] Jennifer Bevan and James Whitehead. Identification of software instabilities. In *Proceedings of the Working Conference on Reverse Engineering*, pages 134–143, Victoria, British Columbia, Canada, November 2003.

[6] James M. Bieman, Anneliese A. Andrews, and Helen J. Yang. Understanding change-proneness in OO software through visualization. In *Proceedings of the 11th International Workshop on Program Comprehension*, pages 44–53, Portland, OR, May 2003.

[7] B. Blanchet, P. Cousot, R. Cousot, J. Feret, L. Mauborgne, A. Miné, D. Monniaux, and X. Rival. A static analyzer for large safety-critical software. In *Proceedings of the ACM Conference on Programming Language Design and Implementation*, pages 196–207, San Diego, CA, June 2003.

[8] Guillaume Brat and Arnaud Venet. Precise and scalable static program analysis of NASA flight software. In *Proceedings of the 2005 IEEE Aerospace Conference*, Big Sky, MT, 2005.

[9] Bill Burke and Adrian Brock. Aspect-oriented programming and JBoss. http://www.onjava.com/pub/a/onjava/2003/05/28/aop_jboss.html, 2003.

[10] W.R. Bush, J.D. Pincus, and D.J. Sielaff. A static analyzer for finding dynamic programming errors. *Software Practice Experience (SPE)*, 30(7):775–802, 2000.

[11] David Carlson. *Eclipse Distilled*. Addison-Wesley Professional, 2005.

[12] Valentin Dallmeier, Christian Lindig, and Andreas Zeller. Lightweight defect localization for java. In *Proceedings of the 19th European Conference on Object-Oriented Programming*, Glasgow, Scotland, July 2005.

[13] Bill Dudney, Stephen Asbury, Joseph Krozak, and Kevin Wittkopf. *J2EE AntiPatterns*. Wiley, 2003.

[14] D. Engler, B. Chelf, A. Chou, and S. Hallem. Checking system rules using system-specific, programmer-written compiler extensions. In *Proceedings of the Fourth Symposium on Operating Systems Design and Implentation*, pages 1–16, 2000.

[15] Dawson R. Engler, David Yu Chen, and Andy Chou. Bugs as deviant behavior: a general approach to inferring errors in systems code. In *Symposium on Operating Systems Principles*, pages 57–72, 2001.

[16] Michael D. Ernst, Jake Cockrell, William G. Griswold, and David Notkin. Dynamically discovering likely program invariants to support program evolution. *IEEE Transactions on Software Engineering*, 27(2):99–123, 2001.

[17] Michael D. Ernst, Jeff H. Perkins, Philip J. Guo, Stephen McCamant, Carlos Pacheco, Matthew S. Tschantz, and Chen Xiao. The Daikon system for dynamic detection of likely invariants. *Science of Computer Programming*, 2006.

[18] Michael Fischer, Martin Pinzger, and Harald Gall. Analyzing and relating bug report data for feature tracking. In *Proceedings of the Working Conference on Reverse Engineering*, pages 90–101, Victoria, British Columbia, Canada, November 2003.

[19] Harald Gall, Karin Hajek, and Mehdi Jazayeri. Detection of logical coupling based on product release history. In *Proceedings of the International Conference on Software Maintenance*, pages 190–198, Washington, D.C., November 1998.

[20] Harald Gall, Mehdi Jazayeri, and Jacek Krajewski. CVS release history data for detecting logical couplings. In *Proceedings International Workshop on Principles of Software Evolution*, pages 13–23, Helsinki, Finland, September 2003.

[21] S. Hallem, B. Chelf, Y. Xie, and D. Engler. A system and language for building system-specific, static analyses. In *Proceedings of the Conference on Programming Language Design and Implementation*, pages 69–82, Berlin, Germany, 2002.

[22] R. Hastings and B. Joyce. Purify: fast detection of memory leaks and access errors. In *Proceedings of the Winter USENIX Conference*, pages 125–138, San Francisco, CA, December 1992.

[23] David Heine and Monica Lam. A practical flow-sensitive and context-sensitive C and C++ memory leak detector. In *Conference on Programming Language Design and Implementation (PLDI)*, pages 168–181, San Diego, CA, June 2003.

[24] Yao-Wen Huang, Fang Yu, Christian Hang, Chung-Hung Tsai, Der-Tsai Lee, and Sy-Yen Kuo. Securing web application code by static analysis and runtime protection. In *Proceedings of the 13th Conference on World Wide Web*, pages 40–52, New York, May 2004.

[25] Sanjeev Kumar and Kai Li. Using model checking to debug device firmware. *SIGOPS Operating Systems Review*, 36(SI):61–74, 2002.

[26] Patrick Lam and Martin Rinard. A type system and analysis for the automatic extraction and enforcement of design information. In *Proceedings of the 17th European Conference on Object-Oriented Programming*, pages 275–302, Darmstadt, Germany, July 2003.

[27] Benjamin Livshits, John Whaley, and Monica S. Lam. Reflection analysis for Java. In *LNCS 3780*, pages 139–160, November 2005.

[28] Benjamin Livshits and Thomas Zimmermann. DynaMine: finding common error patterns by mining software revision histories. In *Proceedings of the 13th ACM SIGSOFT International Symposium on the Foundations of Software Engineering (FSE-13)*, pages 296–305, September 2005.

[29] Benjamin Livshits and Thomas Zimmermann. Locating matching method calls by mining revision history data. In *Proceedings of the Workshop on the Evaluation of Software Defect Detection Tools*, June 2005.

[30] Heikki Mannila, Hannu Toivonen, and A. Inkeri Verkamo. Efficient algorithms for discovering association rules. In *Proceedings of the AAAI Workshop on Knowledge Discovery in Databases*, pages 181–192, Washington, D.C., July 1994.

[31] Michael Martin, Benjamin Livshits, and Monica S. Lam. Finding application errors and security flaws using PQL: a program query language. In *OOPSLA '05: Proceedings of the 20th Annual ACM SIGPLAN Conference on Object Oriented Programming Systems Languages and Applications*, pages 365–383, 2005.

[32] Amir Michail. Data mining library reuse patterns in user-selected applications. In *Proceedings of the 14th International Conference on Automated Software Engineering*, pages 24–33, IEEE, Cocoa Beach, FL, October 1999.

[33] Amir Michail. Data mining library reuse patterns using generalized association rules. In *Proceedings of the International Conference on Software Engineering*, pages 167–176, Limerick, Ireland, June 2000.

[34] Nicholas Nethercote and Julian Seward. Valgrind: a program supervision framework. *Electronic Notes in Theoretical Computer Science*, 89:1–23, 2003.

[35] Slava Pestov. jEdit user guide. http://www.jedit.org/, 2005.

[36] Ranjith Purushothaman and Dewayne E. Perry. Towards understanding the rhetoric of small changes. In *Proceedings of the International Workshop on Mining Software Repositories*, pages 90–94, Edinburgh, Scotland, May 2004.

[37] Darrell Reimer, Edith Schonberg, Kavitha Srinivas, Harini Srinivasan, Bowen Alpern, Robert D. Johnson, Aaron Kershenbaum, and Larry Koved. SABER: Smart Analysis Based Error Reduction. In *Proceedings of the International Symposium on Software Testing and Analysis*, pages 243–251, Boston, MA, July 2004.

[38] Filip Van Rysselberghe and Serge Demeyer. Mining version control systems for FACs (frequently applied changes). In *Proceedings of the International Workshop on Mining Software Repositories*, pages 48–52, Edinburgh, Scotland, May 2004.

[39] Stefan Savage, Michael Burrows, Greg Nelson, Patrick Sobalvarro, and Thomas Anderson. Eraser: a dynamic data race detector for multi-threaded programs. *ACM Transactions on Computer Systems*, 15(4):391–411, 1997.

[40] Stephen R. Schach. *Object-Oriented and Classical Software Engineering*. McGraw-Hill Science/Engineering/Math, 2004.

[41] Umesh Shankar, Kunal Talwar, Jeffrey S. Foster, and David Wagner. Detecting format string vulnerabilities with type qualifiers. In *Proceedings of the 2001 Usenix Security Conference*, pages 201–220, Washington, D.C., 2001.

[42] Bruce Tate, Mike Clark, Bob Lee, and Patrick Linskey. *Bitter EJB*. Manning Publications, 2003.

[43] D. Wagner, J. Foster, E. Brewer, and A. Aiken. A first step towards automated detection of buffer overrun vulnerabilities. In *Proceedings of Network and Distributed Systems Security Symposium*, pages 3–17, San Diego, CA, February 2000.

[44] Westley Weimer and George Necula. Mining temporal specifications for error detection. In *Proceedings of the 11th International Conference on Tools and Algorithms for the Construction and Analysis of Systems*, pages 461–476, April 2005.

[45] J. Whaley, M. Martin, and M. Lam. Automatic extraction of object-oriented component interfaces. In *Proceedings of the International Symposium of Software Testing and Analysis*, pages 218–228, Rome, Italy, July 2002.

[46] Chadd C. Williams and Jeffrey K. Hollingsworth. Automatic mining of source code repositories to improve bug finding techniques. *IEEE Transactions on Software Engineering*, 31(6):466–480, June 2005.

[47] Chadd C. Williams and Jeffrey K. Hollingsworth. Recovering system specific rules from software repositories. In *Proceedings of the International Workshop on Mining Software Repositories*, pages 7–11, May 2005.

[48] Jinlin Yang, David Evans, Deepali Bhardwaj, Thirumalesh Bhat, and Manuvir Das. Perracotta: mining temporal API rules from imperfect traces. In *Proceedings of the International Conference on Software Engineering*, May 2006.

[49] Annie T.T. Ying, Gail C. Murphy, Raymond Ng, and Mark C. Chu-Carroll. Predicting source code changes by mining change history. *IEEE Transactions on Software Engineering*, 30(9):574–586, September 2004.

[50] Li, Zhenmin and Zhou, Yuanyuan. PR-Miner: Automatically extracting implicit programming rules and detecting violations in large software code. *Proceedings of the 10th European Software Engineering Conference held jointly with 13th ACM SIGSOFT International Symposium on Foundations of Software Engineering*, pages 306–315, New York, NY, USA, 2005.

[51] Thomas Zimmermann, Stephan Diehl, and Andreas Zeller. How history justifies system architecture (or not). In *Proceedings International Workshop on Principles of Software Evolution*, pages 73–83, Helsinki, Finland, September 2003.

[52] Thomas Zimmermann and Peter Weißgerber. Preprocessing CVS data for fine-grained analysis. In *Proceedings of the International Workshop on Mining Software Repositories*, pages 2–6, Edinburgh, Scotland, May 2004.

[53] Thomas Zimmermann, Peter Weißgerber, Stephan Diehl, and Andreas Zeller. Mining version histories to guide software changes. In *Proceedings of the 26th International Conference on Software Engineering*, pages 563–572, Edinburgh, Scotland, May 2004.

Chapter 8

Automatic Inference and Effective Application of Temporal Specifications*

Jinlin Yang

Microsoft—Redmond

David Evans

University of Virginia

---

*This chapter is partly based on [84–88].

8.1   Introduction

For many years, researchers have claimed that software specifications can be used to improve many software development activities. A formal specification documents important properties and hence is useful in understanding programs [41,67]. Formal specifications can be used to automatically generate test inputs [14,21,60]. Program verification needs a formal specification that defines the correct behaviors of a program [34,41,67]. Other uses include refining a specification into a correct program [1] and protecting a programmer from making changes that violate important invariants [26].

Despite these benefits, formal specifications are rarely available for real systems [42,52,54]. To help realize the benefits of formal specifications, this work develops techniques for automatically inferring formal specifications and investigates the uses of inferred specifications in software development.

This work focuses on temporal properties. Temporal properties constrain the order of a program's states [53, 67]. For example, acquiring a lock should always be followed by releasing the lock. Temporal properties are important in many types of systems such as network protocols. Satisfying temporal properties is crucial for establishing a program's correctness properties.

8.1.1 Prior Work on Inferring Specifications

Several researchers have recognized the unavailability of specifications as an important problem and studied specification inference and its application to software development [2, 3, 26, 28, 40, 79, 81]. A *specification inference technique* automatically discovers a formal specification of a target program by analyzing program artifacts. A specification inference tool is often called a *specification miner* [3], *specification synthesizer* [2], or *specification prospector* [59]. A program's source code or execution traces are the most common artifacts used by specification miners, though it is also possible to analyze other artifacts including design documents, bug reports, and revision history [12, 58].

A static inference technique analyzes source code. In addition to eliminating the need to execute the target program, a static inference technique can theoretically examine all execution paths of a program and therefore can infer precise specifications of a program. However, features common in modern programming languages, such as pointers, branches, loops, threads, inheritance, and polymorphic interfaces, can be too expensive to analyze precisely from source code.

In contrast, a dynamic inference technique analyzes execution traces that have precise information about pointers, branches, threads, and the other features of programming executions. However, dynamic analysis only sees execution paths present in the traces and therefore might infer specifications that are stronger than the program itself when the executions do not cover all possible scenarios.

We take the dynamic inference approach in our work for several reasons. The temporal specifications we aim to infer typically involve objects and threads that are difficult to analyze statically. In addition, we want to apply our techniques to large real systems that typically have complex control flow structures for which static techniques do not scale well.

Previous dynamic specification inference techniques have shown promising results in many areas, including bug detection [38, 58, 62, 68], test case selection [36, 39, 83], and program steering [57]. However, all of the results to date have been on relatively small execution traces. For example, the largest execution traces analyzed by Daikon have only hundreds of variables, whereas a large system usually has thousands of variables [26, 65].

Scaling dynamic inference to handle large real systems involves several important challenges. The inference technique must effectively deal with imperfect execution traces. An *imperfect execution trace* is a trace that contains event sequences that violate a property specification that is necessary for the correctness of a system. Suppose we want to learn the temporal specification of a type of lock. If our target program neglects to release this type of lock during some executions (due to bugs), running this program would produce an imperfect trace that fails to exhibit the rule for correctly using the lock. A dynamic inference technique needs to effectively deal with such imperfect execution traces; otherwise it would risk missing important specifications in the inference results. For example, the Strauss specification miner requires human guidance to tune an imperfect trace so that it can discover important specifications that would otherwise be missing [3]. Daikon requires 100% satisfaction of a pattern [26], which might exclude important specifications if the execution trace is imperfect. Although we aim to handle imperfect traces, we assume that our traces are mostly correct – our target program should exhibit the desirable behavior most of the time.

Our inference technique must be able to select interesting specifications. An *interesting specification* is a specification whose violation would produce bad consequences. For example, we consider specifications about using critical system resources such as locks and transactions to be interesting. Such properties are important because violating them can have serious consequences such as causing system crashes [5,19] and opening security vulnerabilities [10]. Selecting interesting specifications is important because for a large program thousands of properties may be inferred, only a small fraction of which are interesting. We present several techniques that can effectively increase the percentage of interesting properties in the results.

8.1.2   Contributions

We describe dynamic inference techniques for automatically inferring temporal specifications and experimentally evaluate our techniques on real systems, as well as several different applications of the inferred properties. Our dynamic inference techniques address three limitations of prior inference work described in the previous section:

(a) The inference algorithms scale poorly with the size of the program and the execution traces.

(b) Previous dynamic inference techniques do not work well in situations where perfect traces are not available.

(c) A significant portion of the inferred properties are uninteresting. For small programs, it is feasible to manually select the interesting properties; for large programs, property selection must be mostly automated.

In particular we make the following contributions in the area of scaling dynamic inference techniques:

(a) We develop a scalable inference algorithm that can analyze large execution traces (Section 8.2).

(b) We create a statistical inference algorithm that can deal with imperfect execution traces (Section 8.2.5).

(c) We develop two heuristics for eliminating uninteresting properties (Section 8.2.6). These heuristics increase the percentage of interesting properties in the inference results and are crucial for the approach to be useful in practice.

(d) We present a chaining method for constructing large finite state automata out of a set of smaller ones (Section 8.2.7). This method is useful for presenting a large number of inferred properties in a more readable way.

In order to evaluate our approach, we built a prototype tool called Perracotta and applied it to several real systems including Microsoft Windows and the JBoss Application Server. The results demonstrate that the dynamic analysis technique is useful in several different software development activities. Section 8.3 presents the inference results on real systems with a focus on helping program understanding. Section 8.4 describes other uses of the inferred properties. Section 8.4.1 describes combining Perracotta with two program verification tools. Section 8.4.2 presents the experiments of using Perracotta in program differencing. We show that the technique can aid in program differencing by discovering important differences among multiple versions of real systems.

8.2 Specification Inference

To illustrate our dynamic temporal specification inference approach we use a simple Producer-Consumer program as a running example (Section 8.2.1). Our inference approach follows the steps shown in Figure 8.1. An *instrumentor* instruments the program to monitor information of interest (Section 8.2.2). Then, the instrumented program is executed against a set of test cases to

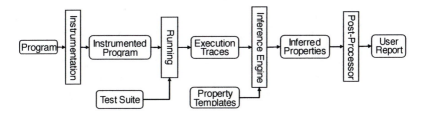

FIGURE 8.1: Overview of our approach.

produce execution traces (Section 8.2.3). Next, the inference engine matches the traces against a set of predefined property templates (Section 8.2.4). A post-processor selects the interesting properties out of the matched properties using several heuristics (Section 8.2.6). The chaining method aims to condense the inferred properties so that users can better comprehend them (Section 8.2.7). Section 8.2.8 describes Perracotta, a prototype implementation of our inference approach.

8.2.1   A Running Example: Producer-Consumer

The Java program in Figure 8.2 implements a simplified version of the Producer-Consumer problem. The Producer and Consumer classes implement a Producer and a Consumer, respectively. Only one Producer and one Consumer object exist at any time. The Producer interacts with the Consumer through a global Buffer object, buf, which is a static member of the Heap class. At any time, a Buffer object can only hold one integer element, queue, whose value can be retrieved through the take method and updated through either the add method or the stop method. The buffer is empty when the value of queue is −1. The Producer inserts a new integer into buf by calling its add method and the Consumer removes an integer from buf by calling its take method. The Producer iteratively inserts integers from 1 to n (as designated by program arguments) into buf, while the Consumer takes those numbers from buf and prints them out. After the Producer calls the stop method that writes 0 to buf, the Consumer reads 0, exits the run loop, and terminates.

All three methods of the Buffer class, take, add, and stop, are declared with the Java synchronized keyword to ensure mutual exclusion among multiple threads that access a same Buffer object. We implement synchronization among multiple threads using the commonly used Java wait-notify idiom.

This program exhibits two interesting properties: (1) Inserting an integer to buf alternates with removing an integer from buf. Hence, the Producer cannot overwrite a new element before the Consumer retrieves it. Furthermore, the Consumer cannot take an element from an empty buffer. (2) Once the Producer calls the stop method, the Consumer must eventually stop.

8.2.2   Instrumentation

A program execution involves a great deal of information: values of parameters and object fields, thread contexts, branches taken, exceptions raised, etc. Some information represents state (e.g., object fields), whereas other information captures control flow (e.g., branches taken, exceptions raised).

Ideally we would record every detail of a program's execution. This is impractical for several reasons. Instrumenting everything without affecting a program's normal behavior is difficult. In a real-time system, the overhead introduced by the instrumentation code might prevent a process from meeting its deadline. Furthermore, collecting all information does not scale to long-

```
class Buffer {
  int queue = -1;
  public synchronized int take() {
    int value;
    while (queue < 0)
      try { wait(); } catch(InterruptedException ex) {}
    value = queue;
    queue = -1;
    notifyAll();
    return value;
  }
  public synchronized void add(int x) {
  while (queue != -1)
      try { wait(); } catch(InterruptedException ex) {}
      queue = x;
      notifyAll();
  }
  public synchronized void stop() {
    while (queue != -1)
      try { wait (); } catch (InterruptedException ex) {}
    queue = 0; notifyAll ();
  }
}

class Heap { static Buffer buf; }

class Producer {
  static public void main(String[] args) {
    Heap.buf = new Buffer();
    (new Consumer()).start();
    for(int i = 1; i < Integer.valueOf(args[0]).intValue(); i++)
      Heap.buf.add(i);
    Heap.buf.stop();
  }
}

class Consumer extends Thread {
  public void run () {
    int tmp = -1;
    while ((tmp = Heap.buf.take ()) != 0)
      System.err.println ("Result: " + tmp);
  }
}
```

FIGURE 8.2: A Java implementation of the simplified Producer-Consumer problem.

```
Enter:Producer.main():[main]
Enter:Buffer.add():[main]
Enter:Consumer.run():[Thread-1]
Exit:Buffer.add():[main]
Enter:Buffer.take():[Thread-1]
Enter:Buffer.add():[main]
Exit:Buffer.take():[Thread-1]
Exit:Buffer.add():[main]
Enter:Buffer.add():[main]
Enter:Buffer.take():[Thread-1]
Exit:Buffer.take():[Thread-1]
Exit:Buffer.add():[main]
Enter:Buffer.take():[Thread-1]
Enter:Buffer.add():[main]
Exit:Buffer.take():[Thread-1]
Exit:Buffer.add():[main]
Enter:Buffer.take():[Thread-1]
Enter:Buffer.stop():[main]
Exit:Buffer.take():[Thread-1]
Exit:Buffer.stop():[main]
Enter:Buffer.take():[Thread-1]
Exit:Producer.main():[main]
Exit:Buffer.take():[Thread-1]
Exit:Consumer.run():[Thread-1]
```

FIGURE 8.3: A trace of running the Producer-Consumer program. Each line corresponds to a single event that represents the entrance or exit of a method. We omit the method's signature, argument values, and return values to simplify presentation. For example, Enter:Producer.main():[main] indicates that the main thread enters the main method in the Producer class.

running systems as the size of the data becomes too large to be efficiently stored and processed.

Our instrumentor instruments a program at the method level and records the thread contexts, argument values, and return values (Section 8.2.8.1). Our instrumentor instruments the entrance and exit events of all the methods in the Producer-Consumer program. For example, executing the instrumented Producer-Consumer program with 5 as its input produces the execution trace shown in Figure 8.3. To simplify presentation, we do not include the argument values and return values in this trace.

Each line in the trace corresponds to a single event. An event starts with either Enter or Exit corresponding to the entrance and exit events, respectively. The middle part of an event is a method's name. The last part of an event includes the thread context information and, optionally, argument values. For example, Enter:Producer.main():[main] indicates that the main thread enters the main method in the Producer class.

8.2.3 Running

The executions affect the results of any dynamic analysis. Our goal is to develop a dynamic inference technique that works with readily available or easily produced execution traces. Hence, we run a target system's regression test suite if one is available. Furthermore, when generating inputs is necessary, we either randomly select inputs from a program's input domain [22, 80] or exhaustively generate all inputs within certain bounds [8, 14, 51].

For the example, we run the Producer-Consumer program with 100 randomly selected integers between 1 and 10000.

8.2.4 Inference Engine

The inference engine produces a set of properties from a trace. Here, we introduce the predefined property templates in Section 8.2.4.1 and describe our inference algorithm that scales to large execution traces.

8.2.4.1 Property Templates

A property template abstracts a set of concrete properties. Our property templates have two parameters that can be substituted with values to generate concrete properties. Property templates determine the properties that can be inferred. It is essential that these templates capture properties users care about.

Dwyer et al. developed a temporal property pattern library after surveying hundreds of temporal property specifications checked by program verification tools [23]. One pattern in their library is the Response pattern, which constrains the cause-effect relationship between two events P and S so that P's occurrence must be followed by S's occurrence. We use regular expressions to represent these patterns. For example, $[\neg P]^*(P[\neg S]^*S[\neg P]^*)^*$ is the regular expression for the Response pattern. After removing all events other than P and S, the Response pattern can be simplified as $S^*(PP^*SS^*)^*$. The Response pattern does not constrain the number of P events, the number of S events, or whether the S event can occur before the P event. As a result, knowing that two events satisfy the Response pattern does not give us precise information about their relationship.

We use the seven property patterns based on the Response pattern shown in Table 8.1. For example, the MultiEffect pattern is $(PSS^*)^*$; PSS is a string that satisfies the MultiEffect pattern. Furthermore, the MultiEffect pattern only allows one P event to occur between two S events and also requires that the first P event to occur before the first S event. Hence, PPS and SPS do not satisfy the MultiEffect pattern. Another pattern is Alternating that requires a strictly alternating relationship between two events. Its regular expression is $(PS)^*$. We use the notation $P \rightarrow S$ to indicate that P and S satisfy the Alternating pattern.

The Alternating pattern is *stricter* than the MultiEffect pattern because all

TABLE 8.1: Temporal Property Templates

Name	Regular Expression	Satisfying Example	Violating Examples
Response	$S^*(PP^*SS^*)^*$	*SPPSS*	*SPPSSP, PSP*
Alternating	$(PS)^*$	*PSPS*	*PSS, PPS, SPS*
MultiEffect	$(PSS^*)^*$	*PSS*	*PPS, SPS*
MultiCause	$(PP^*S)^*$	*PPS*	*PSS, SPS*
EffectFirst	$S^*(PS)^*$	*SPS*	*PSS, PPS*
CauseFirst	$(PP^*SS^*)^*$	*PPSS*	*SPSS, SPPS*
OneCause	$S^*(PSS^*)^*$	*SPSS*	*PPSS, SPPS*
OneEffect	$S^*(PP^*S)^*$	*SPPS*	*PPSS, SPSS*

Note: For example, the regular expression of the MultiEffect pattern is $(PSS^*)^*$; hence, PSS is a string that satisfies the MultiEffect template, whereas PPS or SPS do not satisfy the template.

strings that satisfy the Alternating pattern must also satisfy the MultiEffect pattern but not vice versa. Formally, we say a pattern A is stricter than another pattern B if $L(A) \subset L(B)$, where $L(A)$ is the set of strings accepted by A. The seven new patterns form a partial order in terms of their strictness as illustrated in Figure 8.4. Alternating is the strictest pattern among the seven patterns. In addition, these patterns have internal logic relationship as illustrated by the logical $\wedge$ operators among them. For example, a string satisfies the MultiEffect pattern if and only if it satisfies the OneCause and CauseFirst patterns.

We can derive the strictest pattern a string satisfies by exploring the logical relationship among the patterns. Our algorithm first determines which of the three primitive patterns a string satisfies and then deduces the strictest pattern. For example, if a string satisfies all three primitive patterns, then the strictest pattern it satisfies is Alternating.

In addition to the patterns with two parameters, we also derive two Alternating patterns that have three parameters. The two-effect-alternating pattern, $P \rightarrow S \mid T$, allows P to alternate with either S or T. The two-cause-alternating pattern, $P \mid S \rightarrow T$, requires either P or S to alternate with T. These patterns correspond to properties of real programs. For example, a file, after being successfully opened, can be either read or written, and finally be closed.

8.2.4.2 Pattern Matching Algorithm

All the patterns described in the previous section have only two or three parameters (e.g., P, S, and T). We present our pattern matching algorithm using the Alternating template as an example, although the essential ideas of the algorithm also work for other templates. Given a trace with N distinct

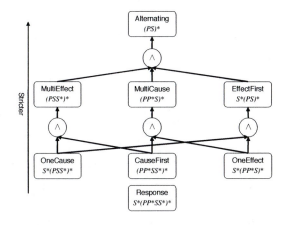

FIGURE 8.4: Partial order of property templates. Each box shows a property template and its regular expression representation. A pattern A is stricter than another pattern B if $L(A) \subset L(B)$, where $L(A)$ means all the strings accepted by A. The eight patterns form a partial order in terms of their strictness. For example, Alternating is the strictest pattern among them. In addition, these patterns have an internal logical relationship as illustrated by the logical $\wedge$ operators among them. For example, a string satisfies the MultiEffect pattern if and only if it satisfies the OneCause and CauseFirst patterns.

events and L events total, we want to infer which pairs of events can satisfy the Alternating pattern. For example, a hypothetical trace $ABCACBDC$ has four distinct events: A, B, C, and D. Hence, there are 12 ways to instantiate the Alternating template: $(AB)^*$, $(AC)^*$, $(AD)^*$, $(BA)^*$, ..., $(DC)^*$. Of these, the only Alternating property that string satisfies is $A \rightarrow B$.

A brute force algorithm would check the string against all 12 instantiations of the property one by one. However, this algorithm does not scale when the number of distinct events becomes large. For N distinct events, there are $N(N-1)$ instantiations of a pattern with two parameters. Checking the string against each instantiation needs to traverse the string once. Hence, the naïve algorithm has running time in $\Theta(N^2 L)$.

Next, we introduce a more efficient inference algorithm with time complexity in $\Theta(NL)$ and space complexity in $\Theta(N^2)$.

The algorithm encodes a property template as a table. Figure 8.5(a) shows a finite state machine representation of the Alternating template. State 0 is both the initial state and the accepting state. State 2 is the error state. We can encode the transitions in this FSM as the table shown in Figure 8.5(b). The column header is the current state of the FSM. The row header is the current event in the trace. Given the current state and the current event, our

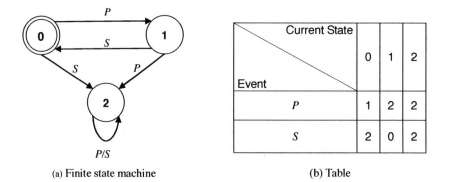

(a) Finite state machine   (b) Table

FIGURE 8.5: Representing the Alternating template in different forms.

algorithm determines the next state by looking it up in the table. For example, if the current state is state 0 and the event is P, the next state is state 1.

Figure 8.6 shows our inference algorithm. Figure 8.7 shows how our inference algorithm infers which of the 12 instantiations of the Alternating template the trace $ABCACBDC$ satisfies.

The algorithm scans a trace twice. In the first pass, it identifies all the distinct events and creates a mapping between the event names and integer index numbers (lines 3-13). After scanning the whole trace, the algorithm creates state, an $N \times N$ array, for keeping track of the states of the instantiations of the Alternating pattern (line 17). The value of state[i][j] corresponds to the FSM state of the instantiation in which P is $Event_i$ and S is $Event_j$. The elements of this array, except the diagonal ones, are initialized to 0 since all FSMs start in the initial state (lines 18-23). The diagonal elements are initialized to 2 (i.e., the error state) because the two events cannot be equal (line 21). In the second pass, our algorithm rescans the execution trace (line 27). When it reads an event from the trace, it updates the state array (lines 28-34). Here the key observation is that an event, $Event_k$, could be either the P event or the S event. If $Event_k$ is the P event, our algorithm updates the k-th row of the state array (line 32). If $Event_k$ is the S event, our algorithm updates the k-th column of the state array (line 34). Our algorithm updates the state by looking up the pre-encoded tables of the FSMs (Figure 8.5). After scanning the trace twice, if state[i][j] is in an accepting state, our algorithm outputs $Event_i \rightarrow Event_j$ as a satisfied Alternating property (lines 37-41).

This algorithm has time complexity in $\Theta(NL)$ and space complexity in $\Theta(N^2)$. The loop from line 11 to 13 has running time in $\Theta(L)$: it scans the trace once, updating the event2index mapping for each element. The loop from line 18 to 23 has running time in $\Theta(N^2)$. The loop from line 28 to 34 updates one row and one column of the state array for each event in the trace. Hence, the time complexity of the loop is in $\Theta(NL)$. Finally, the loop from line 37

```
1     void Infer( RandomAccessFile tracefile )
2
3         byte[ ][ ] ALTERNATING = { {1, 2}, {2, 0}, {2, 2} };
4         // A mapping between an event to its index
5         Hashtable event2index = new Hashtable();
6         // The number of distinct events
7         int n = 0;
8         String current_event = null;
9
10        // First pass: create event table
11        while( ( current_event = tracefile.readLine() ) != null )
12            if( !event2index.contains( current_event ) )
13                event2index.add( current_event, n++ );
14
15        // Create a table for keeping track of the states
16        // state[ i ][ j ] records the current state of the "Event i → Event j" template
17        byte state[ ][ ] = new byte[ n ][ n ];
18        for( int i = 0; i < n; i++ )
19            for( int j = 0; j < n; j++)
20                if( i == j )
21                    state[ i ][ j ] = 2;
22                else
23                    state[ i ][ j ] = 0;
24
25        // Second pass
26        // restart from the beginning of the trace file
27        tracefile.seek( 0 );
28        while( ( current_event = tracefile.readLine() ) != null )
29            k = event2index.get( current_event );
30            for( int i = 0; i < n; i++ )
31                // Update the state when current_event is the P event
32                state[ k ][ i ] = ALTERNATING[ state[ k ][ i ] ][ 0 ];
33                // Update the state when current_event is the S event
34                state[ i ][ k ] = ALTERNATING[ state[ i ][ k ] ][ 1 ];
35
36        // Check final state
37        for( int i = 0; i < n; i++ )
38            for( int j = 0; j < n; j++ )
39                // Is the state in an accepting state?
40                if( state[ i ][ j ] == 0 )
41                    System.out.println( i + "→" + j );
```

FIGURE 8.6: The inference algorithm for the Alternating pattern.

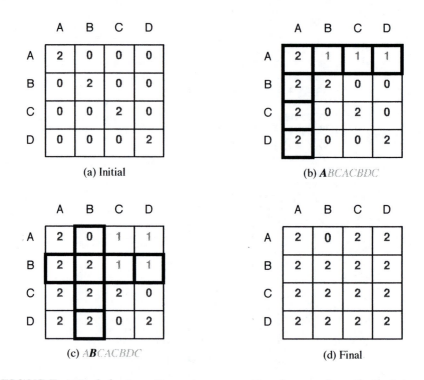

FIGURE 8.7: Inferring Alternating properties from a hypothetical trace *ABCACBDC*.

Enter:Buffer.stop():[main] → Exit:Consumer.run():[Thread-1]
Exit:Buffer.stop():[main] → Exit:Consumer.run():[Thread-1]

Enter:Buffer.add():[main] → Exit:Buffer.add():[main]
Enter:Consumer.run():[Thread-1] → Exit:Consumer.run():[Thread-1]
Enter:Producer.main():[main] → Exit:Producer.main():[main]
Enter:Buffer.stop():[main] → Exit:Buffer.stop():[main]
Enter:Buffer.take():[Thread-1] → Exit:Buffer.take():[Thread-1]

Enter:Producer.main():[main] → Enter:Consumer.run():[Thread-1]
Enter:Producer.main():[main] → Enter:Buffer.stop():[main]
Enter:Producer.main():[main] → Exit:Buffer.stop():[main]
Enter:Producer.main():[main] → Exit:Consumer.run():[Thread-1]
Enter:Consumer.run():[Thread-1] → Enter:Buffer.stop():[main]
Enter:Consumer.run():[Thread-1] → Exit:Buffer.stop():[main]
Enter:Consumer.run():[Thread-1] → Exit:Producer.main():[main]
Enter:Buffer.stop():[main] → Exit:Producer.main():[main]
Exit:Buffer.stop():[main] → Exit:Producer.main():[main]
Exit:Producer.main():[main] → Exit:Consumer.run():[Thread-1]

FIGURE 8.8: Alternating properties inferred from the trace in Figure 8.3.

to 41 has time complexity in $\Theta(N^2)$. Because $L \geqslant N$, the time complexity of the algorithm is in $\Theta(NL)$. The algorithm requires creating an $N \times N$ array. Therefore, its space complexity is in $\Theta(N^2)$.

The Producer-Consumer trace in Figure 8.3 has 10 distinct events. Hence, there are 90 candidate Alternating properties. The inference algorithm determines that the trace satisfies the 17 Alternating properties shown in Figure 8.8. The two properties in boldface represent the property that whenever the Producer sends out the stop signal, the Consumer will stop execution eventually. The next five properties are uninteresting because they correspond to the trivial fact that entering and exiting a method always alternate. The remaining properties reflect the static call graph and are not very interesting either (e.g., Producer.main() calls Consumer.run()). Section 8.2.6 describes the post-processing component that selects interesting properties, eliminates redundant and uninteresting properties, and better presents the results.

8.2.4.3 Handling Context Information

A major advantage of dynamic analysis over static analysis is the ready availability of precise context information including threads, objects, argument values, and return values. This section presents our techniques for using context information to infer more precise properties.

We use three general approaches: *context-neutral*, *context-sensitive*, and *context-slicing*. The context-neutral approach treats two events with same static signature but different context information as the same event, whereas the context-sensitive approach considers them as two distinct events.

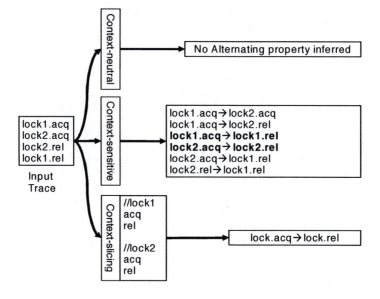

FIGURE 8.9: Context handling techniques. *Context-neutral* does not differentiate between *lock1.acq/rel* and *lock2.acq/rel* and does not infer any Alternating property. *Context-sensitive* differentiates between the methods of *lock1* and *lock2* and infers six Alternating properties. However, only two of the six properties shown in boldface correspond to the property that acquiring a lock should alternate with releasing a lock. *Context-slicing* slices the original trace by the identity of the lock and produces two subtraces. Hence, *context-slicing* infers lock.acq → lock.rel.

For example, consider the example trace in Figure 8.9. The context-neutral approach sees two distinct events (lock.acq and lock.rel), but the context-sensitive approach sees four events (lock1.acq, lock1.rel, lock2.acq, and lock2.rel). Context-neutral analysis does not infer lock.acq → lock.rel. On the other hand, context-sensitive analysis infers six Alternating properties, only two of which are useful (shown in boldface in Figure 8.9). Neither context-sensitive nor context-neutral analysis infers that lock.acq and lock.rel alternate for a same lock object. To infer this property, we need to generalize the results of the context-sensitive analysis by slicing the original trace into separate traces based on object identity. We call this the *context-slicing* approach. Context-slicing produces two traces from which our inference algorithm infers lock.acq → lock.rel. In addition to slicing on object identities, context-slicing can also slice thread identities, argument values, and return values.

The results of context-sensitive analysis are the most complete, but are not useful without generalization. Context-slicing is a simple way to generalize the results of context-sensitive analysis. A limitation of context-slicing is that it cannot detect properties that involve more than one context. For example, if slicing is done by threads, an Alternating pattern between P in one thread and S in another thread would not be detected.

8.2.5 Approximate Inference

The algorithm in Figure 8.6 only infers properties that are completely satisfied by the trace. For example, P and S satisfy the Alternating template in $PSPSPSPSPSPSPSPS$ but not in $PSPSPSPSPSPSPSPSP$ because the last P does not have a corresponding S. This 100% satisfaction requirement is a big limitation of the original algorithm when applied to traces from real systems. This algorithm would miss many interesting properties because the traces are imperfect.

8.2.5.1 Imperfect Traces

An *imperfect trace* is a trace that contains event sequences that violate a property specification that is necessary for the correctness of a system.

Bugs in a program are the most insurmountable reason for imperfect execution traces. The hypothetical buggy program in Figure 8.10 illustrates this. Suppose the code on line 5 has no side effect on either i or *lock*. The while loop exits when i becomes greater than 10. During each iteration except the last one, the loop body acquires a lock, does some work, and releases the lock. On the last iteration, however, the program does not release the lock. As a result, executing the program produces the trace $PSPSPSPSPSPSPSPSP$, where P represents lock.acquire and S represents lock.release. Although this trace does not satisfy the $P \rightarrow S$ property, $P \rightarrow S$ is the predominant pattern in the trace.

In addition to buggy programs, sampling can also cause imperfect traces. Monitoring the complete execution of long running programs such as operating systems is impractical. In practice, traces typically sample partial execution by recording either the complete run-time data for a short period or randomly selected data for the whole execution. In either case, the trace does not capture the whole execution.

```
1       int i=0;
2       while(true){
3           lock.acquire();
4           // do something here
5           ......
6           if(++i>10)
7               break;
8           lock.release();
9       }
```

FIGURE 8.10: A hypothetical program that forgets to release a lock.

```
1    while (not at the end of the trace)
2        read the next event from the trace
3        update the property FSMs
4        update the monitor FSM
5        if (the monitor FSM is in an accepting state)
6            Increase the counter of the monitor FSM by one
7            for each property FSM
8                if (the property FSM is in an accepting state)
9                    increase the counter of the property FSM by one
10                reset the property FSM to its start state
```

FIGURE 8.11: The approximate inference algorithm.

Finally, instrumentation tools have some limitations on the data they can capture. For example, an instrumentor might not be able to record argument values and return values. So, the execution trace can miss information such as the identity of a lock. When there are multiple instances of a lock, the identity serves as a way to differentiate operations on the locks. If a trace does not have the identity of a lock or other ways to distinguish different locks, all calls to acquire or release different locks will appear to be the same events and may violate the Alternating property.

8.2.5.2   Detecting the Dominant Behavior

To deal with the imperfect traces, we adapt the algorithm from Figure 8.6. The new algorithm decides what fraction of an execution trace satisfies a property template instead of just determining satisfaction of a property template. The new algorithm partitions the original trace into subtraces, decides whether each subtrace satisfies a pattern, and computes the fraction of the subtraces that satisfy a pattern.

We define a subtrace using a regular expression. We call this regular expression the *monitor template* and its finite state machine the *monitor FSM*. We call the finite state machine of a property template (e.g., Alternating) the *property FSM*. We use $P_{property\ template}$ to represent the percentage of a trace that satisfies a property template. For example, P_{AL} indicates the percentage of the subtraces that satisfy the Alternating template.

One intuitive definition of a subtrace is P^+S^+. In addition, the leading S events form a subtrace and so do the trailing P events. For example, we partition $PSPSPSPSPSPSPSPSP$ into 10 subtraces $PS, PS, PS, PS, PS, PS, PS, PS, PS, P$. The first nine subtraces satisfy the $P \rightarrow S$ property, whereas the last one does not. Therefore, 90% of the subtraces satisfy $P \rightarrow S$ and $P_{Alternating}$ is 0.90.

The new algorithm tracks one monitor FSM and one or more property FSMs. As with the original algorithm, it scans the execution trace twice. The two algorithms differ in how they update the states during the second scan. Figure 8.11 shows the pseudo-code of the new algorithm. When the new algorithm reads an event (line 2), it first updates all the property FSMs (line 3) in the same way as the original algorithm (lines 25-34 in Figure 8.6). Then the new algorithm updates the state of the monitor FSM (line 4). If the monitor FSM reaches one of its accepting states (line 5), this indicates the end of a subtrace. The new algorithm increases the counter of the monitor FSM by one (line 6) and then checks whether the property FSMs reach their accepting states (line 7-8). If a property FSM is in an accepting state, this subtrace satisfies the property FSM and hence the new algorithm increases the property FSM's counter by one (line 9). Finally, the new algorithm resets the property FSMs to their starting states (line 10) before analyzing the next subtrace. Like the original algorithm, this algorithm has running time in $\Theta(NL)$ and space complexity in $\Theta(N^2)$.

8.2.6   Property Selection

When processing a large trace that has many distinct events, our inference technique typically infers thousands of properties, which are too many to be effectively used in practice. Hence, one big challenge is to select a subset of the properties that are mostly interesting. An *interesting* property is a property for which developers are likely to make mistakes and violation of which would produce bad consequences. For example, we consider properties of critical system resources such as locks and transactions to be interesting. Such properties are important because violating them can have serious consequences such as causing system crashes [5, 19] and opening security vulnerability [10]. Next, we describe two heuristics for selecting interesting properties.

8.2.6.1   Static Call Graph Based Heuristic

One way to identify interesting properties is based on a program's static call graph [35]. The key observation is that a property is more likely to be interesting when the two events it involves are not reachable in the static call graph.

Figure 8.12(a) illustrates this idea. Suppose our inference technique infers two Alternating properties: KeSetTimer → KeSetTimerEx and ExAcquireFast-MutexUnsafe → ExReleaseFastMutexUnsafe. In the first property, KeSetTimer is a wrapper of KeSetTimerEx. Therefore, whenever KeSetTimer is called, KeSet-TimerEx must also be called. In the second property, ExAcquireFastMutexUnsafe and ExReleaseFastMutexUnsafe do not call each other. Thus, their executions are asynchronous.

Figure 8.12(b) shows an abstract form of the two scenarios. $A \rightarrow B$ and $C \rightarrow D$ are Alternating properties. The second property is usually more interesting than the first one for two reasons. The first property represents a trivial relationship that can be easily discovered by constructing a static call graph. On the other hand, the second property captures two events that do not have an obvious static relationship. In addition, the second property cap-

```
void KeSetTimer( ) {                void X( ) {
   KeSetTimerEx( );                    ...
}                                      ExAcquireFastMutexUnsafe(&m);
                                       ...
                                       ExReleaseFastMutexUnsafe(&m);
                                       ...
                                    }
```

(a) A concrete example

```
A( ) {                              X( ) {
   ...                                 ...
   B ( );                              C ( );
   ...                                 ...
}                                      D ( );
                                       ...
                                    }
```

(b) Abstract form

FIGURE 8.12: Two scenarios of static call graph.

tures a protocol between two functions, which developers are more likely to forget. The developers are obligated to call the pair of functions together. In contrast, the first property represents a delegation relationship between the two functions, which does not suggest any obligation on the developers.

8.2.6.2   Naming Similarity Heuristic

The second heuristic exploits the naming conventions used in many real systems. For example, Microsoft uses the Hungarian Notation [73]. The key observation behind the naming similarity heuristic is that a property is more likely to be interesting if the events it involves have similar names. For example, KeAcquireInStackQueuedSpinLock and KeReleaseInStackQueuedSpinLock only differ by one word and clearly appear to represent a desirable locking discipline relationship.

The naming similarity heuristic partitions the two events' names into words and then computes a similarity score of the two names. For a property $A \rightarrow B$, where A has w_A words, B has w_B words, and A and B have w words in common, this heuristic computes the similarity score of A and B as

$$Similarity_{AB} = \frac{2w}{w_A + w_B}$$

We distinguish words by capital letters or underscores. For example, KeAcquireInStackQueuedSpinLock has seven words, and so does KeReleaseInStackQueuedSpinLock (i.e., Ke, Acquire/Release, In, Stack, Queued, Spin, and Lock). Therefore, $w_A = w_B = 7$. There are six common words and so $w = 6$. As a result, the similarity score of these two names is 85.7%.

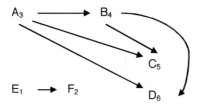

FIGURE 8.13: Alternating chains.

The naming similarity heuristic is especially effective for selecting properties that tend to involve events with similar function names. For example, locking disciplines and resource allocation/deletion protocols usually have a pair of functions with similar names. Although this heuristic does eliminate some interesting properties that involve events with very different names, our goal is to increase the density of interesting properties in the results. The experimental results (Section 8.3.3) demonstrate that the naming heuristic is effective for achieving this goal.

8.2.7 Chaining Method

The chaining method presents the inferred Alternating properties in a condensed form so that users can gain a better picture of how a system works. Next, we introduce a *property graph* that is a graph representation of a set of Alternating properties, prove several important properties of the property graph, and define the *chaining problem*. We prove the chaining problem is in NP-complete, and describe a brute force algorithm for solving the chaining problem. Despite being exponential in general, this algorithm performs well in our experiments due to the low density of property graphs for real programs.

8.2.7.1 Property Graph

We map a set of Alternating properties to a directed graph $G = < V, E >$, where V is a set of nodes and E is a set of edges. Each distinct event corresponds to a node in V. Therefore, $|V| = N$. An edge from node i to node j corresponds to an Alternating property $Event_i \rightarrow Event_j$. We call G the *property graph*. Figure 8.13 shows a property graph involving six events and six Alternating properties (the subscripts correspond to the topological numbers explained later in this subsection).

If all the Alternating properties in a property graph have $P_{AL} = 1.0$, the property graph is a directed acyclic graph (DAG). In other words, for any i and j, if there is a path from node i to node j, there does not exist a path from node j to node i. To prove this, we first prove the following lemma: If there is a path from node i to node j, the first $Event_i$ must occur before the first $Event_j$ in the trace.

We prove the lemma by induction on l, the length of a path from node i to node j. The base case is $l = 1$. In this case there is an edge from node i to node j. According to the definition of the property graph, $Event_i \rightarrow Event_j$ is true. Therefore, according to the definition of the Alternating property, the first $Event_i$ must occur before the first $Event_j$ in the trace. For $k > 1$, assume that the lemma holds for all l where $1 \leqslant l < k$. Next, we prove the lemma when $l = k$. Suppose there is a path from node i to node j and this path's length is k. If the next to last node on this path is node p, there is a path from node i to node p and this path's length is $k - 1$. According to the induction hypothesis, the first $Event_i$ must occur before the first $Event_p$ in the trace. In addition, there is an edge from node p to node j. According to the induction hypothesis, the first $Event_p$ must occur before the first $Event_j$ in the trace. As a result, the first $Event_i$ must occur before the first $Event_j$ in the trace.

Using the above lemma, we prove by contradiction that a property graph is a DAG. If a property graph G is not a DAG, then G contains a cycle. There must exist two nodes, i and j, such that there exists a path P from i to j and a path P' from j to i. According to the above lemma, the existence of P implies that the first $Event_i$ must occur before the first $Event_j$ in the trace. In addition, the existence of P' implies the first $Event_j$ must occur before the first $Event_i$ in the trace, which is a contradiction. Hence, a property graph is a DAG.

When a property graph includes Alternating properties with $p_{AL} < 1.0$, it might still be a DAG. As explained later, our chaining algorithm first checks if a property graph (with properties whose $p_{AL} < 1.0$) has any cycles. Our algorithm only performs the chaining operation when the property graph is a DAG. The rest of this section assumes a property graph is a DAG.

A *topological number* of a node in a DAG is an integer such that if there exists an edge from node i to node j, then the topological number of node i is less than the topological number of node j [15]. Because a property graph is a DAG, we can sort the nodes based on their topological numbers. The subscript of each node in Figure 8.13 indicates its topological number.

An *alternating chain* is a subgraph $G' = < V', E' >$ of a property graph $G = < V, E >$, where $V' \subseteq V$ and $E' = \{(i, j) \mid i, j \in V' \text{ and } (i, j) \in E\}$, such that if the topological number of node i is less than the topological number of node j, then $(i, j) \in E'$. By definition, an edge in a property graph is a trivial alternating chain. For example, in Figure 8.13, the subgraph consisting of A and B is a trivial alternating chain. In addition, the subgraph consisting of A, B, and C is an alternating chain, while the subgraph consisting of A, B, C, and D is not an alternating chain.

A maximal alternating chain is an alternating chain $G' = < V', E' >$ of a property graph $G = < V, E >$ such that $\forall i \in V - V'$, $G'' = < V'', E'' >$ is not an alternating chain, where $V'' = V' \cup \{i\}$ and $E'' = E' \cup \{(i, j) \mid j \in V' \text{ and } (i, j) \in E\} \cup \{(j, i) \mid j \in V' \text{ and } (j, i) \in E\}$. For example, in Figure

8.13, the subgraph consisting of A, B, and C and the subgraph consisting of E and F are maximal alternating chains.

The *chaining problem* is the problem of, given a property graph G and an integer k, determining whether there exists an alternating chain of k nodes in G. The *chain enumeration problem* is the problem of, given a property graph G, identifying all the maximal alternating chains of G.

8.2.7.2 Chaining Is in NP-Complete

Given any subgraph of a property graph, we can easily verify in polynomial time whether the subgraph is an alternating chain. Hence, the chaining problem is in NP.

We prove the NP-hardness of the chaining problem by reducing the clique problem to the chaining problem. The *clique problem* in graph theory states "for an undirected graph G and an integer k, does G have a complete subgraph that has k nodes" [50]. The clique problem is a well-known NP-Complete problem. Next we construct a polynomial-time reduction from the clique problem to the chaining problem.

Given an undirected graph G, we can convert all of its undirected edges to directed edges in polynomial time. We call the resulting directed graph G'. The conversion works by following the standard black-gray-white color depth-first-search (DFS) algorithm [15]. Figure 8.14 shows the transformation algorithm. Initially, all the nodes are marked as white (lines 7-8). Next, the algorithm checks each node and performs DFS for white nodes (lines 9-11). DFS is a recursive function that takes a node i to be explored as its argument (line 13). The node that is currently being explored is marked as gray (line 14). Next, all the adjacent nodes of i are explored (lines 16-17). If the adjacent node j is a white node, the algorithm converts the corresponding edge to a directed edge from i to j and continues to explore j (lines 19-22); if j is a gray node, the algorithm converts the corresponding edge to a directed edge from j to i (lines 23-25); if j is a black node, the algorithm does not do anything (lines 26-27). After all the adjacent nodes of i have been explored, node i is marked as black (line 29). The time complexity of the conversion algorithm is polynomial because DFS is in $\Theta(|V| + |E|)$.

Now we prove by contradiction that the resulting graph G' is a DAG. Suppose there is a cycle, $i, ..., j, i$, in G'. Without loss of generality, let us assume that i is the first node in the cycle that is explored during the conversion process. In other words, when i changes color from white to gray, the other nodes on the cycle are still white. According to the algorithm, there are two ways the edge from j to i can be created. First, when the adjacent nodes of j are explored (hence, j is gray), i (one of j's adjacent nodes) is white (lines 19-22). This case is impossible due to our assumption that i is the first node on the cycle that has gray color. Second, when the adjacent nodes of i are explored, j is gray, too (lines 23-25). So the algorithm creates an edge from j to i (line 24). This also contradicts our assumption that j is white when i

```
1    int total;              // the number of nodes
2    int undirected[ ][ ];   // total x total, an undirected graph with no self-loop
3    int directed[ ][ ];     // total x total
4    int color[ ];           // total
5
6    void undirected2directed ( )
7      for ( int i = 0; i < total; i++ )
8        color[ i ] = WHITE;
9      for ( int i = 0; i < total; i++ )
10       if (color [ i ] == WHITE)
11         DFS ( i );
12
13   void DFS ( int i )
14     color [ i ] = GRAY;
15
16     for ( int j = 0; j < total; j++ )
17       if ( undirected [ i ][ j ] == CONNECTED )
18         switch ( color [ j ] )
19           case WHITE:
20             directed [ i ][ j ] = CONNECTED;
21             DFS ( j );
22             break;
23           case GRAY:
24             directed [ j ][ i ] = CONNECTED;
25             break;
26           case BLACK:
27             break;
28
29     color [ i ] = BLACK;
```

FIGURE 8.14: Algorithm for transforming an undirected graph to a DAG.

is gray. Therefore, it is impossible to have an edge from j to i in G', which contradicts the last edge on the cycle.

Given an instance of the clique problem (determining whether an undirected graph G has a complete subgraph with k nodes), the above transformation converts the clique problem to an instance of the chaining problem (determining whether the resulted DAG G' has an alternating chain with k nodes). Next we show that if we have a solution to the chaining problem, we can use it to solve the clique problem. We use $[i, j]$ to represent a directed edge from i to j and (i, j) to represent an undirected edge between i and j. Suppose our algorithm determines that G' has an alternating chain, $X' = < V_{X'}, E_{X'} >$ with k nodes. The counterpart of X' in G is $X = < V_X, E_X >$, where $V_X = V_{X'}$ and $E_X = \{(i, j) | i, j \in V_X, [i, j] \text{ or } [j, i] \in E_{X'}\}$. According to the definition of Alternating Chain, $\forall i, j \in V_{X'}, [i, j]$ or $[j, i] \in E_{X'}$. Therefore, $\forall i, j \in V_X$, $(i, j) \in E_X$. Hence, X is a clique with k nodes in G.

Thus, the clique problem reduces to the chaining problem so the chaining problem is also in NP-hard. We already proved the chaining problem is in NP, so the chaining problem is NP-Complete.

8.2.7.3 The Chaining Algorithm

Assume $P \neq NP$, no algorithm can have a better asymptotic worst-case performance than a brute force algorithm. The performance of a brute force algorithm is highly dependent on the structure of the property graph. For a directed graph with n nodes and m edges, we compute its edge density as $2m/n^2$. Intuitively, a brute force algorithm generally performs better on a sparse property graph than a dense property graph because there are fewer edges (and so much fewer combinations of edges) to try in a sparse property graph. In our experiments, all of our property graphs are very sparse with densities around 10%. Next we present a brute force algorithm whose worst-case performance is exponential. The running time scales with the edge density, which we have found to be low in practice. We have applied our chaining algorithm to analyze a property graph with 91 nodes and 490 edges in less than one minute.

Given a property graph G, we can convert all its directed edges to be undirected. We call the resulted graph $G_{undirected}$. If a subgraph C of G is an alternating chain, then the corresponding subgraph $C_{undirected}$ of $G_{undirected}$ must be a clique, and vice versa. Finding all the maximal alternating chains in G, therefore, can be solved by finding all the maximal cliques in $G_{undirected}$.

Our chaining algorithm first identifies all the connected components in $G_{undirected}$ using a depth-first-search [15]. Then the algorithm identifies the maximal cliques in each connected component. To convert a maximal clique to an alternating chain, we output the clique in topological order. Figure 8.15 shows the chaining algorithm.

The chaining algorithm is a work-list algorithm. The algorithm first creates a worklist (line 5). The worklist stores the cliques that will be examined.

```
1     for each cc in Gundirected
2         chaining ( cc );
3
4     chaining ( cc )
5         Vector worklist = new Vector();
6         add all the edges of cc to worklist;
7         while ( worklist is not empty )
8             clq = worklist.remove ( 0 );
9             boolean cannotExpand = true;
10            for each node i of cc
11                if ( i is in clq )
12                    continue;
13                if ( there is an edge between i and each node of clq )
14                    newclq = clq U { i };
15                    cannotExpand = false;
16                    for each element x of worklist
17                        if ( x is a subset of newclq )
18                            remove x from worklist;
19                    insert newclq to the beginning of worklist;
20                    break;
21            if ( cannotExpand )
22                print out clq in topological order;
```

FIGURE 8.15: The chaining algorithm.

Each clique is represented as a set of nodes. The worklist is a set of sets of nodes, initially containing one set for each edge in the graph consisting of the endpoints of that edge (line 6). The algorithm removes the first clique, clq, from the worklist (line 8). For each node of the current connected components, the algorithm first tests if it is in clq (lines 11-12). For a node i that is not in clq, the algorithm tests if there is an edge between i and each node of clq (line 13). If so, the algorithm expands clq to newclq (line 14), removes all the cliques in worklist that are subsets of newclq (lines 15-18), and inserts newclq to the beginning of worklist (line 19). The boolean variable, cannotExpand, indicates whether clq can be expanded (lines 9 and 15). If cannotExpand is true after processing clq, the algorithm outputs clq according to the topological order in the directed property graph (lines 21-22).

Next we analyze the complexity of our chaining algorithm. Suppose a connected component, cc, has n nodes and m maximal cliques. Suppose the ith maximal clique has n_i nodes. In order to construct the maximal cliques, the while loop (lines 8-22) executes $\sum_{i=1}^{m} n_i$ times because the clique grows one node in each loop. The for loop (lines 11-20) executes n_i times. During each for loop, the algorithm needs to check up to n_i edges (line 13). In addition, when a larger clique, newclq, is formed, the algorithm needs to remove redundant cliques from the worklist (lines 16-18). A clique, x, is redundant if it is a subset of newclq. When newclq has p nodes, in worst case,

Chain #1
Enter:Buffer.add():[main] →
Exit:Buffer.add():[main]

Chain #2
Enter:Buffer.take():[Thread-1] →
Exit:Buffer.take():[Thread-1]

Chain #3
Enter:Producer.main():[main] →
Enter:Consumer.run():[Thread-1] →
Enter:Buffer.stop():[main] →
Exit:Buffer.stop():[main] →
Exit:Producer.main():[main] →
Exit:Consumer.run():[Thread-1]

FIGURE 8.16: Alternating chains for the Producer-Consumer program.

the number of redundant cliques is in $\Theta(C_{n_i}^{p-1})$. Therefore, the for loop is in $\Theta(n_i(n_i + C_{n_i}^{p-1}))$. To construct the *ith* maximal clique, the algorithm's complexity is in $\Theta(\sum_{p=1}^{n_i}(n_i(n_i + C_{n_i}^{p-1}))) = \Theta(n_i 2^{n_i} + n_i^3)$. Therefore, the worst-case complexity of our chaining algorithm is still exponential. The complexity of the chaining algorithm varies by the density of the property graph. In practice, the density of the property graph tends to be small (typically around 10% in our experiments). Therefore, the performance of our algorithm is acceptable in practice.

Figure 8.16 shows the three chains constructed for the Producer-Consumer program. The longest chain (#3) has six events and represents an important property: After the Producer calls the stop method, the Consumer eventually stops. Each of the other two chains has only two events and is uninteresting because these Alternating properties correspond to the trivial fact that entering a method alternates with exiting the method.

8.2.8 Perracotta

We adapted a Java instrumentation tool and implemented the inference engine in a prototype tool called Perracotta. In addition to implementing the inference algorithm, Perracotta also implements the two selection heuristics, the chaining method, and the context-handling techniques.

8.2.8.1 Instrumentation

To instrument Java programs, we adapted the Java Runtime Analysis Toolkit (JRat) [48]. JRat has two important components: an instrumentor and a runtime system. The instrumentor component uses the Byte Code Engineering Library (BCEL) to parse and insert hooks into Java bytecode [6]. When an instrumented Java application executes, the hooks generate events for method entrances, method exits, and exceptions. The JRat runtime system processes the events by delegating them to one or more handlers. Different handlers process the events in different ways. JRat provides an event handler Service Provider Interface (SPI). Users can develop their own handlers by implementing this SPI and can configure the handlers that the JRat runtime system uses by either setting an environment variable or supplying a configuration file. We developed an event handler for collecting method execution traces. For each Java method, our handler records its entrance, exit, signature, arguments, return value, and any exceptions generated. If an argument is of a primitive type, the handler outputs its value. If an argument is of an object type, the handler outputs its hashcode as its object ID.

For small C programs, we manually instrument the source code to monitor function calls. For Windows kernel, we use a Vulcan-based instrumentor [76]. This instrumentor works on x86 binaries and can monitor function calls and thread information. However, this instrumentor cannot monitor argument values and return values.

8.2.8.2   Inference Engine

Perracotta implements the inference engine and post-processing components. Perracotta is implemented in 12000 lines of Java code. Perracotta can be run in two modes: the strictest pattern mode for inferring the strictest pattern and the approximate mode for inferring properties whose satisfaction ratio is greater than a threshold between 0.0 and 1.0. In addition, it also has an interface that accepts user-specified templates and determines the satisfaction ratios. To implement the static call graph based heuristic for Java, Perracotta has a module for computing the static call graph. For C/C++, it accepts static call graph as a textual file. In addition, Perracotta can eliminate uninteresting properties based on the naming similarity based heuristic. Furthermore, Perracotta implements the chaining method for the Alternating properties as presented in Section 8.2.7.3.

Perracotta also provides several utility programs that slice traces as described in Section 8.2.4.3. The *ThreadSlicer* slices the trace into subtraces based on the thread identities. Similarly, the *ObjectSlicer* slices the trace into subtraces based on the object identities.

8.3   Inference Experiments

This section presents experiments applying Perracotta to several programs. We evaluate the usefulness of the inferred properties in revealing important information of a program. Section 8.4 investigates other uses of the inferred properties including program verification (Section 8.4.1) and program differencing (Section 8.4.2).

Complex systems are hard to understand in that it is challenging to recognize delocalized plans [55]. *Delocalized plans* are "programming plans realized by lines scattered in different parts of the program." [55] We hypothesize that our dynamic temporal specification inference technique can effectively detect certain delocalized plans.

To test the hypothesis and also evaluate the scalability, accuracy, and cost of our technique, we conducted several case studies on a wide range of programs:

(a) *Bus Simulator*, a collection of student submissions for an assignment of implementing a multi-threaded C program in a graduate course taught at the University of Virginia.

(b) *Daisy*, a prototype implementation of a Unix-like file system in Java. Daisy was developed as a common testbed for different program verification tools [18].

(c) *OpenSSL*, a C implementation of the Secure Sockets Layer (SSL) specification [63, 74]. Our experiment focuses on its handshake protocol.

(d) *JBoss*, a Java application server conforming to the J2EE specification [45, 47]. Our experiment focuses on its transaction management module.

(e) *Microsoft Windows kernel APIs*, a set of about 1800 functions written in C or C++. These functions are the foundation of the Windows operating system. Our experiment is on Windows Vista.

Table 8.2 summarizes the characteristics of these five testbeds. Bus Simulator and Daisy are small prototype programs. They are good for proof-of-concept experiments. The other three programs are complex and widely used. They are valuable for understanding the strength and weakness of our technique when it is applied to real systems. Our testbeds differ in the quality of specification available. The Bus Simulator comes with instructor's English description of a list of properties a valid implementation ought to have. Daisy does not have any temporal specification except a list of properties in English provided by one of its developers. OpenSSL has an extensive specification, the SSL specification [63, 74]. The SSL specification includes a detailed description as well as a finite state automaton of the handshake protocol. The JBoss application server implements the J2EE specification [45, 47]. In particular, its transaction management module implements the Java Transaction API (JTA) specification [49], which has an extensive English description and an object interaction diagram illustrating the temporal behavior of the components participating in a transaction. For the Windows kernel APIs, some of their temporal rules are documented either publicly in the MSDN library or privately in some internal documents. These documented rules are, however,

TABLE 8.2: Characteristics of Testbeds

Name	Category	Language	Size	Maturity	Temporal Specifications Available?	Additional Experiments
Bus Simulator	Student multi-threaded program	C/C++	259	Prototype	Yes, in English	Program differencing
Daisy	Unix-like file system	Java	2K	Prototype	Limited	Program verification
OpenSSL (Handshake Protocol)	Network protocol	C	32K (418)[1]	Production	Yes, SSL specification in English and FSM	Program differencing
JBoss (Transaction Management)	Network middleware	Java	1M (7K)[2]	Production	Yes, JTA specification in English and FSM	
Windows Vista Kernel APIs	OS kernel	C/C++	50M (1800 APIs)	Production	Limited, MSDN and MS internal document including SLAM	Program verification

1. In OpenSSL version 0.9.7d, the implementation of the SSL specification (i.e., *.c* and *.h* files in the *ssl* directory) has 32,000 lines and the implementation of the SSL handshake protocol on the server's side (i.e., the *ssl3_accept* function in the *s3_srvr.c* file) has 418 lines.

2. In JBoss version 4.0.2, all the *.java* files have one million lines. The transaction management module (i.e., all the *.java* files belonging to the *org.jboss.tm* package) has 7000 lines.

```
┌─────────────────────────────────┐
│        Files, Directories       │
└─────────────────────────────────┘
                 ↑
┌─────────────────────────────────┐
│  Inodes, Blocks, Allocation Bits │
└─────────────────────────────────┘
                 ↑
┌─────────────────────────────────┐
│           Byte Streams          │
└─────────────────────────────────┘
                 ↑
┌─────────────────────────────────┐
│            Hard Drive           │
└─────────────────────────────────┘
```

FIGURE 8.17: Daisy's System Architecture. Daisy emulates the hard drive through a Java RandomAccessFile object.

by no means complete as our experiment discovered many undocumented important rules. We include two systems with extensive specifications (OpenSSL and JBoss) so that we can compare the inferred properties against the existing specifications. These existing specifications serve as a guideline of what properties are important and interesting, without which it would be much more difficult to tell whether the inference approach produces useful results.

Next, Sections 8.3.1 to 8.3.3 present the inference results for all the testbeds except OpenSSL and Bus Simulator. We defer the presentation of the experiments on OpenSSL and Bus Simulator to Section 8.4.2 because the focus of these experiments is on evaluating the usefulness of the inferred properties in program differencing. Our experimental results strongly support that Perracotta can be useful for program understanding. Perracotta discovered interesting temporal properties for all the testbeds. For the Windows kernel, Perracotta inferred 56 interesting properties, many of which were undocumented. For JBoss, Perracotta inferred a 24-event finite state machine that was consistent with the JTA specification. Many of the JBoss properties represent delocalized plans as the events cross multiple "distant" modules of the target systems. Discovering these delocalized plans is valuable because they can be hard to discover by manual inspection and violating them when modifying the system could introduce serious errors.

8.3.1 Daisy

Daisy is a prototype Unix-like file system implemented in 2000 lines of Java code [18]. Daisy's architecture has four layers as shown in Figure 8.17. At the bottom, Daisy emulates the hard drive using a RandomAccessFile (RAF) object. Above it, the disk layer abstracts the hard drive into byte streams. The next layer abstracts the byte streams into blocks. The top layer provides an interface for files and directories.

We used JRat to monitor the invocation of all Daisy methods except those inherited from the Object class (e.g., toString). We created a wrapper for the Java RandomAccessFile class so that JRat can monitor its methods. JRat recorded a method's signature, thread, this object, and arguments.

To execute Daisy, we adapted the test harness in the Daisy distribution.

Our test harness, DaisyTest, takes four parameters: F, the number of files to be created initially; T, the number of threads to be created; N, the number of iterations each thread executes; and R, the seed for the random number generator. The main thread of DaisyTest first creates F files and T threads. Next, each child thread makes a sequence of N calls to randomly selected methods of the DaisyDir class (one of read, write, set_attr, or get_attr). These methods are invoked with arguments randomly selected within the valid range.

8.3.1.1   Inference Results

We ran DaisyTest with $F = 5$, $T = 5$, $N = 15$, and $R = 0$. This execution produced a trace of about 70000 events. We used Perracotta to slice the original trace by threads and obtained six subtraces (five for the child threads and one for the main thread). We ran Perracotta in approximate mode with 0.70 as the acceptance threshold for p_{AL}. Our analysis only considered the 40 distinct events that occurred more than 10 times in the trace. Perracotta inferred 70 properties, 52 of which had a satisfaction ratio less than one. We applied Perracotta's chaining method to infer nine Alternating Chains.

The six shortest chains, with length from one to three events, are uninteresting because they correspond to wrapper functions. The other three chains also contain uninteresting edges due to wrapper functions. Next we applied Perracotta's call graph based heuristic to eliminate these wrapper properties and got eight properties.

Several properties provide insight into the temporal behaviors of Daisy. For example, DaisyDisk.readAllocBit $\rightarrow$ DaisyLock.relb ($p_{AL} = 0.97$) indicates that reading the allocation bit of a block (DaisyDisk.readAllocBit) often alternates with releasing the lock on the block (DaisyLock.relb). Because these two methods are not eliminated by the call graph based heuristic, they represent an interesting pair of asynchronous operations. These two methods do not necessarily alternate because DaisyLock.relb is called in several places (e.g., Daisy.read and Daisy.write) where DaisyDisk.readAllocBit is not called. Another interesting property is LockManager.acq $\rightarrow$ LockManager.rel ($p_{AL} = 0.86$) that captures an important locking relationship. The satisfaction ratio of this property is less than 1.0 because the traces are not sliced by objects.

Next, we used Perracotta to slice the this object and a method's first argument. Perracotta inferred two properties with $p_{AL} = 1.0$: Mutex.acq $\rightarrow$ Mutex.rel and LockManager.acq $\rightarrow$ LockManager.rel. Slicing on other arguments did not lead Perracotta to infer more properties. Object slicing missed some useful properties that involve more than one object such as LockManager.acq $\rightarrow$ Mutex.rel.

We also ran Perracotta with the two-effect-alternating and the two-cause-alternating patterns (Section 8.2.4.1). Perracotta inferred an important property: RAF.seek $\rightarrow$ RAF.readByte | RAF.writeByte. We found a race condition in Daisy that violates this property using the Java PathFinder model checker (Section 8.4.1.1).

In summary, the inferred properties represent interesting temporal behaviors of Daisy. Several of the inferred properties such as DaisyDisk.readAllocBit → DaisyLock.relb involve more than one class, which indicates delocalized plans that would be useful to aid programmers in understanding the system.

8.3.2 JBoss Application Server

An *application server (AS)* is middleware that provides important services such as transactions, security, and caching for running web applications [45]. A web application built upon an application server reuses these well-tested services and components.

A *Java application server* is an application server that runs on a Java virtual machine [45]. The J2EE specification defines the interface between a web application and a Java application server [45]. JBoss is open-source and is currently one of the most widely used Java application servers [47].

We are particularly interested in the APIs of the transaction management service because a transaction occurs in multiple stages with certain temporal ordering constraints. The Java Transaction API (JTA) specification defines the interfaces between a transaction manager and the other participants in a distributed transaction system: the application, the resource manager, and the application server [49]. The JTA specification has an object interaction diagram [31] as an illustration of how an application server may handle a transactional connection request from an application (note that the diagram is just one typical scenario, but not a specification) [49]. An application server starts a transaction by first calling the begin method of the transaction manager (TM). Next the AS tries to get a transactional resource from the resource adapter (RA). The AS calls the enlistResource method to declare its ownership of a resource. Then the application does its work. To finish a transaction, the AS calls the delistResource method to release its ownership of the corresponding resource and then commits the transaction. The transaction commission follows a two-stage commit protocol that first prepares and then commits the transaction.

8.3.2.1 Inference Results

We obtained the source code of the JBoss Application Server version 4.0.2 from *www.jboss.org* (the latest one at the time of our experiments). The source code distribution included about 4000 fully automated regression test cases. We used JRat to instrument all method invocations of the transaction management module (i.e., all classes in the org.jboss.tm package) and ran the regression test suite. After dropping events that occurred fewer than 10 times, the execution trace contained 2.5 million events with 91 distinct events (we only monitored the entrance events). Perracotta analyzed the trace in 80 seconds on a machine with one 3GHz CPU, 1GB RAM, and Windows XP Professional.

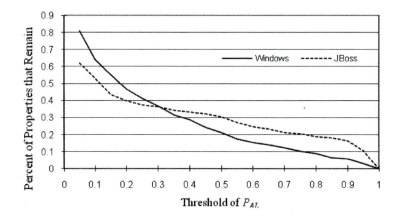

FIGURE 8.18: Inferred properties versus the acceptance threshold for p_{AL}.

Figure 8.18 shows the percentage of all instantiations of the Alternating pattern with p_{AL} greater than an acceptance threshold that increases from 0 to 1. The other line is for the Windows experiments described in Section 8.3.3. We arbitrarily picked 0.9 as the acceptance threshold to select properties. The initial result had 490 properties, too many to inspect manually. Next, the chaining method converted the properties to 17 chains. We applied the chaining method before applying other heuristics because other heuristics might prevent a long chain from being formed. Then we pruned the results by applying the static call graph based heuristic, which reduced the number of chains to the 15 chains shown in Table 8.3.

8.3.2.2   Comparison with JTA Specification

The longest chain (Figure 8.19) has 24 events including not only the public methods declared in the JTA specification but also private methods internal to the implementation of JBoss. After omitting the private methods, we obtain the shorter chain shown in Figure 8.20. The *TxManager* and *Transaction-Impl* classes implement the JTA *TransactionManager* and *Transaction* interfaces respectively. This chain is almost identical to the object interaction diagram in the Java Transaction API (JTA) specification except that Perracotta does not infer the alternating relationship between enlistResource and delistResource. This is because whenever enlistResource is called, either delistResource or commitResources must be called. Therefore, a resource does not have to be delisted. As shown in Figure 8.20, Perracotta incorrectly infers enlistResource → commitResources as it is the dominant behavior in the trace.

The longest chain reveals more than just how the public APIs interact. It also provides insight into the internal implementation such as starting and committing a transaction, which would help new developers understand JBoss.

TABLE 8.3: The JBoss AS TM Alternating Chains

No	JBoss Transaction Management Module Alternating Chains
1	org.jboss.tm.TransactionImpl.lock org.jboss.tm.TransactionImpl.unlock
2	org.jboss.tm.TxManager.setRollbackOnly org.jboss.tm.TxManager.rollback
3	org.jboss.tm.TxManager.setTransactionTimeout org.jboss.tm.TxManager.suspend
4	org.jboss.tm.TxUtils.isActive org.jboss.tm.TxManager.commit
5	org.jboss.tm.usertx.server.UserTransactionSessionImpl.getInstance org.jboss.tm.usertx.server.UserTransactionSessionImpl.getTransactionManager
6	org.jboss.tm.GlobalId.computeHash org.jboss.tm.XidFactory.extractLocalIdFrom
7	org.jboss.tm.XidImpl.getLocalId org.jboss.tm.TransactionImpl.getGlobalId
8	org.jboss.tm.TransactionLocal.storeValue org.jboss.tm.TxManager.storeValue
9	org.jboss.tm.XidImpl.getFormatId org.jboss.tm.XidImpl.getGlobalTransactionId org.jboss.tm.XidImpl.getBranchQualifier
10	org.jboss.tm.TransactionImpl.checkWork org.jboss.tm.TransactionImpl.rollbackResources org.jboss.tm.TxManager.incRollbackCount
11	org.jboss.tm.TransactionLocal.getValue org.jboss.tm.TxManager.getValue
12	org.jboss.tm.TransactionPropagationContextUtil.getTPCFactoryClientSide org.jboss.tm.TxManager.getTransactionPropagationContext org.jboss.tm.TxManager.getTransaction
13	org.jboss.tm.TransactionLocal.initialValue org.jboss.tm.TransactionLocal.set org.jboss.tm.TransactionLocal.containsValue org.jboss.tm.TxManager.containsValue
14	org.jboss.tm.TransactionImpl.associateCurrentThread org.jboss.tm.TransactionImpl.commit org.jboss.tm.TxManager.resume org.jboss.tm.TxManager.suspend
15	See Figure

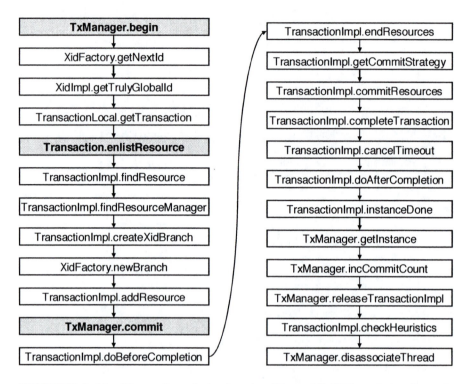

FIGURE 8.19: Alternating chain for the JBoss AS TM module. Grayed events are public methods.

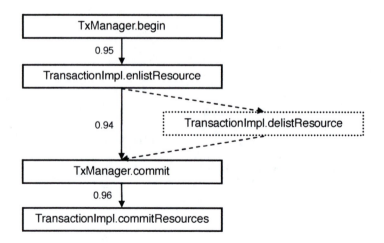

FIGURE 8.20: Alternating chain for the public APIs of the JBoss AS TM module.

In summary, Perracotta successfully infers a complex finite state machine that is consistent with the JTA specification. This demonstrates that Perracotta can help programmers understand a real legacy system. Suppose there is no specification available for the transaction management module; it would have been a great challenge for programmers to discover its temporal behaviors by hand because these properties cross the boundary of many modules and represent a non-trivial delocalized plan. These properties would also be difficult for static analysis to infer because JBoss extensively uses polymorphic interfaces, pointers, and exception handlers. Precisely handling all these features is still beyond the state-of-the-art of static analysis. In addition, the static call graph based heuristic and the chaining method are helpful for reducing the number of properties and presenting the results. On the other hand, the naming similarity based heuristic is not very useful in the experiment since being a Java program, JBoss has few methods that implement basic resource management and locking disciplines.

8.3.3 Windows

In this experiment, we applied Perracotta to infer API rules for the latest (as of summer 2005) kernel (*ntoskrnl.exe*) and core components (*hal.dll* and *ntdll.dll*) of Windows Vista. Perracotta not only inferred many documented properties, but also found several important but undocumented properties. We checked 10 arbitrarily selected properties using the ESP verifier, which found a serious deadlock bug in the NTFS file system (see Section 8.4.1.2).

8.3.3.1 Inference Results

We obtained 17 execution traces from a developer in the Windows core development team. This developer instrumented APIs of the Windows kernel and core components and collected these traces by running some typical Windows applications (e.g., Windows MediaPlayer, Windows MovieMaker). He collected these traces mainly for performance tuning and debugging. We did not have any control of generating execution traces because these traces had already been generated before we started our experiments. In particular, the execution traces included the thread context information, but did not include the values of function arguments.

The lengths of the traces ranged from about 300,000 to 750,000 events, for about 5.8 million total events. The number of distinct events in each trace varied from around 30 to 1300. On average, each execution trace had about 500 distinct events. Perracotta analyzed all traces in 14 minutes on a machine running Windows XP Professional with one 3GHz CPU and 1GB RAM. As with JBoss, we set the acceptance threshold for p_{AL} to 0.90. Perracotta inferred 7611 properties, too many to manually inspect. We randomly selected 200 inferred properties and found that only 2 of them are interesting. So we applied the call graph and naming similarity heuristics to select the interesting

TABLE 8.4: Impact of Selection Heuristics

Prop	Name Similarity (>0.5)		Call Graph Only				Both	
	Prop	Reduction	Unreachable	Unknown	Total	Reduction	Prop	Reduction
7611	185	97.6%	3280	3326	6606	23.5%	142	98.13%

properties. We used the static call graph of ntoskrnl.exe generated by ESP [19]. After using both selection heuristics, 142 properties remained.

Table 8.4 summarizes the impact of the two heuristics. The naming similarity based heuristic alone reduces the number of properties from 7611 to 185, which is a 97.6% reduction. Although the static call graph based heuristic has a smaller reduction rate than the naming similarity, it is still very helpful for reducing the number of properties as indicated by the 23.5% reduction.

We manually inspected the 142 properties and identified the 56 (40%) interesting ones shown in Table 8.5. The properties we deemed interesting are relevant to either resource allocation/deallocation or locking discipline. The heuristics increased the density of interesting properties and therefore were effective. The approximation algorithm is essential for detecting useful properties such as ObpCreateHandle → ObpCloseHandle and ExCreateHandle → ExDestroyHandle that otherwise would be missing.

We compared the 56 inferred properties against those checked by the Static Driver Verifier (SDV), and found that Perracotta inferred four of the 16 sequencing properties that the SDV checked [75]. For example, KeAcquireQueuedSpinLock → KeReleaseQueuedSpinLock is one of the four properties. Perracotta missed seven properties such as KeAcquireSpinLock → KeReleaseSpinLock that the SDV checked because our execution traces did not include those events. Perracotta missed five other properties that the SDV checked because the property templates could not express them. For example, our property templates cannot represent the property that an event only happens once. Therefore, Perracotta cannot infer the property that IoInitializeTimer is called only once.

Perracotta also inferred two important properties KiAcquireSpinLock → KiReleaseSpinLock and KfAcquireSpinLock → KfReleaseSpinLock that the SDV did not check because these functions were internal to Windows and therefore were invisible to the device driver developers.

The Windows experimental results are encouraging. The inferred properties capture critical rules which Windows developers are expected to follow when using the Windows kernel and other core components. Perracotta's approximate inference algorithm effectively handles imperfect traces. In all the experiments, Perracotta inferred interesting properties whose p_{AL} was below 1.0. These properties involve operations on key system resources such as locks and file handles.

Violating these rules could result in system crashes that would be difficult

TABLE 8.5: Selected Properties Inferred for Windows

P_{AL}	Property
1.00	ExAcquireFastMutex →ExReleaseFastMutex
1.00	ExAcquireRundownProtectionCacheAwareEx → ExReleaseRundownProtectionCacheAwareEx
1.00	HMFreeObject →HMAllocObject
1.00	HvpGetCellMapped →HvpReleaseCellMapped
1.00	IoAcquireVpbSpinLock →IoReleaseVpbSpinLock
1.00	KeAcquireQueuedSpinLock →KeReleaseQueuedSpinLock
1.00	KefAcquireSpinLockAtDpcLevel →KefReleaseSpinLockFromDpcLevel
1.00	KeInitThread →KeStartThread
1.00	KeSuspendThread →KeResumeThread
1.00	KfAcquireSpinLock →KfReleaseSpinLock
1.00	KiAcquireSpinLock →KiReleaseSpinLock
1.00	LdrLockLoaderLock →LdrUnlockLoaderLock
1.00	MiMapPageInHyperSpace →MiUnmapPageInHyperSpace
1.00	MiSecureVirtualMemory →MiUnsecureVirtualMemory
1.00	MmSecureVirtualMemory →MmUnsecureVirtualMemory
1.00	NtfsAcquireFileForCcFlush →NtfsReleaseFileForCcFlush
1.00	NtGdiDdGetDC →NtGdiDdReleaseDC
1.00	NtUserBeginPaint →NtUserEndPaint
1.00	ObpAllocateObjectNameBuffer →ObpFreeObjectNameBuffer
1.00	PopAcquirePolicyLock →PopReleasePolicyLock
1.00	RtlAcquirePebLock →RtlReleasePebLock
1.00	RtlAcquireSRWLockExclusive →RtlReleaseSRWLockExclusive
1.00	RtlActivateActivationContext →RtlDeactivateActivationContext
1.00	RtlDeleteTimer →RtlCreateTimer
1.00	RtlLockHeap →RtlUnlockHeap
1.00	RtlpAllocateActivationContextStackFrame →RtlpFreeActivationContextStackFrame
1.00	RtlpAllocateUserBlock →RtlpFreeUserBlock
1.00	RtlpFindFirstActivationContextSection →RtlFindNextActivationContextSection
1.00	RtlValidSid →RtlCopySid
1.00	SeCaptureSid →SeReleaseSid
1.00	SeLockSubjectContext →SeUnlockSubjectContext
1.00	xxxBeginPaint →xxxEndPaint
0.99	ObpCreateHandle →ObpCloseHandle
0.99	_GetDC → _ReleaseDC
0.99	RtlpRemoveListLookupEntry →RtlpAddListLookupEntry
0.99	GreLockDisplay →GreUnlockDisplay
0.99	RtlActivateActivationContextUnsafeFast → RtlDeactivateActivationContextUnsafeFast
0.98	CmpRemoveFromDelayedClose →CmpAddToDelayedClose
0.98	KeAcquireInStackQueuedSpinLock →KeReleaseInStackQueuedSpinLock
0.98	SeCreateAccessState →SeDeleteAccessState
0.98	KeAcquireInStackQueuedSpinLockRaiseToSynch → KeReleaseInStackQueuedSpinLockFromDpcLevel
0.97	IoAllocateIrp →IoFreeIrp
0.96	CmpLockRegistry →CmpUnlockRegistry
0.96	ObAssignSecurity →ObDeassignSecurity
0.96	VirtualAllocEx →VirtualFreeEx
0.95	ExCreateHandle →ExDestroyHandle
0.95	ExpAllocateHandleTableEntry →ExpFreeHandleTableEntry
0.95	CmpFreeDelayItem →CmpAllocateDelayItem
0.94	ExInitializeResourceLite →ExDeleteResourceLite
0.94	RtlEnterCriticalSection →RtlLeaveCriticalSection
0.93	MiGetPreviousNode →MiGetNextNode
0.92	RtlValidAcl →RtlCreateAcl
0.92	ObFastReferenceObject →ObFastDereferenceObject
0.92	PsChargeProcessPoolQuota →PsReturnSharedPoolQuota
0.91	EtwpInitializeDll →EtwpDeinitializeDll
0.90	IoFreeMdl →IoAllocateMdl

Note: Properties in gray shade are neither documented anywhere in MSDN nor checked by SDV.

to diagnose. Furthermore, many of the inferred properties are not properly documented. In our personal communication with several Windows developers, they expressed the need for a tool to help them learn the important rules of Windows such as the ones Perracotta infers. For example, two summer interns in the Windows group were assigned a task of writing a program using a type of queue in Windows kernel. Unfortunately they could not find any documentation about this queue. As a result, they had to manually look at programs to distill the rules about how to use the queue, which was very time-consuming.

8.4   Using Inferred Properties

This section presents experiments using the inferred properties. Section 8.4.1 describes experiments using a verification tool to check the inferred properties. Section 8.4.2 describes experiments using the inferred properties to identify differences among multiple versions of a program.

8.4.1   Program Verification

Program verification techniques try to decide whether or not a program conforms to a specification. Although verifying any non-trivial property is undecidable [72], recently researchers have achieved much practical success in verifying important generic safety properties [9] as well as application-specific properties [5, 19, 27, 78]. For example, Microsoft uses the Static Driver Verifier (also known as the SLAM project) to check device drivers against a list of driver-related rules. The adoption of such tools, however, is limited by the unavailability of property specifications.

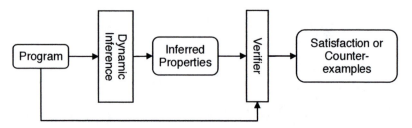

FIGURE 8.21: Use inferred properties in program verification.

We present two case studies on the Daisy file system and the Microsoft Windows kernel respectively. Figure 8.21 illustrates this process. In particular, we used the ESP verifier to check the Windows kernel, properties and the Java PathFinder model checker to verify the Daisy properties [19, 78].

```
1   public class Alt {
2       private final static byte[ ][ ] rule = { { 1, 2 }, { 2, 0 }, { 2, 2 } };
3       private byte currState;
4       public Alt() {
5           currState = 0;
6       }
7       public synchronized void update(int event) {
8           Verify.beginAtomic();
9           currState = rule[currState][event];
10          assert (currState != 2);
11          Verify.endAtomic();
12      }
13      public synchronized void checkExitState() {
14          assert (currState == 0);
15      }
16  }
```

FIGURE 8.22: The Java code for monitoring Alternating properties.

8.4.1.1 Daisy

Section 8.3.1 introduced Daisy, a prototype Unix-like file system [18]. We applied Java PathFinder (JPF) [78] to verify the 22 inferred properties shown in Table 8.6. Java PathFinder is an explicit-state model checker for Java programs [78]. It checks deadlocks, race conditions, unhandled exceptions, and user-specified assertions. It can scale to a program of about 10,000 lines. Upon finding a violation of a property, it produces an execution path illustrating the problem. It has been used to find complex concurrent bugs in real systems [78].

Setup. We developed a Java class, Alt, for checking the Alternating template (Figure 8.22). We encode a safety property as an assertion on the FSM's state, which says the current state cannot be an error state (line 10). Our instrumentor instruments Daisy so that it calls the update method whenever the P or S event occurs. Our instrumentor also inserts a call to the checkExitState method (line 13-15) to ensure that the current state is in an accepting state before the program terminates (to catch bugs such as when a lock is not released).

JPF did not support many Java native classes such as RandomAccessFile (RAF). We created an array to emulate RAF. We also created a simpler test harness, DaisyTestSimple, which creates one file and two threads. Each thread either reads from or writes to the created file once. We used JPF's Verify.random in place of Java's random number generator so that JPF would automatically explore all possible results of the random number generator.

In our preliminary experiments, JPF did not finish analyzing several properties within 24 hours. JPF allows users to indicate a sequence of statements as an atomic segment by enclosing the statements between Verify.beginAtomic and Verify.endAtomic. This significantly reduces the number of states JPF

TABLE 8.6: Results of Checking Daisy Properties with Java PathFinder

No	Causing Event (*P*)	Effect Event (*S* or *S|T*)	JPF Found Violation?
1	Daisy.alloc()	DaisyDisk.writeAllocBit(blockno, ...)	
2	Daisy.creat()	Daisy.alloc()	
3	Daisy.creat()	Daisy.ialloc()	
4	Daisy.creat()	DaisyDisk.writeAllocBit(blockno, ...)	
5	Daisy.get_attr(inodeno, ...)	Daisy.get_attr(inode, ...)	
6	Daisy.ialloc()	Daisy.alloc()	
7	Daisy.ialloc()	DaisyDisk.writeAllocBit(blockno, ...)	
8	Daisy.iget(inodeno)	DaisyDisk.readi(inodeno, inode)	✓
9	Daisy.iget(inodeno)	DaisyLock.acqi(inodeno)	✓
10	Daisy.iget(inodeno)	DaisyLock.reli(inodeno)	✓
11	Daisy.read(inodeno, ...)	Daisy.read(inode, ...)	✓
12	Daisy.write(inodeno, ...)	Daisy.write(inode, ...)	✓
13	DaisyDir.writeLong(inodeno, ...)	Utility.longToBytes(...)	
14	DaisyDisk.readi(inodeno, inode)	DaisyLock.reli(inodeno)	
15	DaisyLock.acqb(blockno)	DaisyLock.relb(blockno)	
16	DaisyLock.acqi(inodeno)	DaisyDisk.readi(inodeno, inode)	✓
17	DaisyLock.acqi(inodeno)	DaisyLock.reli(inodeno)	✓
18	LockManager.acq(lockno)	LockManager.rel(lockno)	✓
19	Mutex.acq()	Mutex.rel()	✓
20	Petal.read(location, ...)	RAF.length()	
21	Petal.write(location, ...)	RAF.writeByte(...)	
22	RAF.seek(location)	RAF.readByte() | RAF.writeByte(...)	✓

has to check. To improve performance, we enclosed the initialization code of DaisyTestSimple and the monitoring code in atomic segments (line 8-11 in Figure 8.22).

Results. When JPF finds a counterexample, it might be a bug. For example, consider the RAF.seek → (RAF.read | RAF.write) property (number 22 in Table 8.6), which says whenever RAF.seek is called, RAF.read or RAF.write must be called before the next invocation of RAF.seek. JPF detected a violation of this property, where RAF.seek was called twice without a call to either RAF.read or RAF.write in-between. Diagnosing this problem revealed a race condition in Daisy that was also detected by several other verification tools [18]. After one thread moves the file pointer to location A, another thread starts executing and moves the file pointer to location B. If the first thread is scheduled to execute again, it would write to an incorrect position.

A counterexample can also result from a faulty property inferred from inadequate execution. For example, Perracotta inferred DaisyLock.acqi(inodeno) → DaisyLock.reli(inodeno) (number 17 in Table 8.6). These two methods operate on the lock of the inode whose inode number equals inodeno. Although this property appears to be valid, JPF found a counterexample. Inspecting the code revealed a subtle and interesting aspect of Daisy. DaisyLock.acqi(inodeno) calls LockManager.acq(lockno) that calls Mutex.acq() corresponding to the Mutex object that has the lockno. Similarly, DaisyLock.reli(inodeno) calls LockManager.rel(lockno) that calls Mutex.rel() corresponding to the Mutex object that has the lockno. Therefore, as long as the implementation of Mutex guarantees synchronized access to an inode, an upper level class (e.g., DaisyLock) does not have to ensure synchronization. JPF detected counterexamples to properties 8 to 12 and 16 to 19 in Table 8.6 for a similar reason. Although such counterexamples do not reveal bugs, they provide insight into some important yet subtle properties of Daisy.

Furthermore, the counterexample of Mutex.acq() → Mutex.rel() (number 19 in Table 8.6) revealed a limitation of our inference technique. Figure 8.23 shows the implementation of the two methods. Recall that our instrumentor monitors the entrance of a method. Hence, the Mutex.acq() event corresponds to entry of the acq() method of the Mutex class (line 4). Similarly, Mutex.rel() event corresponds to entry of the rel() method of the Mutex class (line 14). Therefore, Mutex.acq() does not have to alternate with Mutex.rel() because Mutex.acq() does not correspond to the start of the critical section (line 12).

8.4.1.2 Windows

We use the ESP verifier [19] to verify the inferred properties of the Windows kernel from Section 8.3.3. ESP is a validation tool for typestate properties [77]. Typestates are more expressive than ordinary types: for an object created during program execution, its ordinary type is invariant through the lifetime of the object, but its typestate may be updated by certain operations. ESP allows a user to write a custom specification encoded in a finite state

```
1   class Mutex {
2       boolean locked;
3       ......
4       synchronized void acq() {
5          while (locked) {
6             try {
7                this.wait();
8             } catch (Exception e) {
9                System.out.println(e);
10            }
11         }
12         locked = true;
13      }
14      synchronized void rel() {
15         locked = false;
16         this.notify();
17      }
18 }
```

FIGURE 8.23: The Mutex class in Daisy.

machine to describe typestate transitions. Based on the specification, ESP instruments the target program with the state-changing events. It then employs an inter-procedural data-flow analysis algorithm to compute the typestate behavior at every program point [70]. ESP handles inter-procedural analysis through the use of partial transfer functions via function summaries.

From the 56 inferred properties (see Table 8.5), we randomly selected 10 locking properties and checked them using ESP. ESP found one previously unknown deadlock bug in the NTFS file system. The property is a typical locking discipline property: Acquiring a specific type of kernel Mutex must be followed by releasing the same Mutex. Figure 8.24 shows a snippet of the buggy code (the function names have been changed to protect Microsoft's proprietary information). Whenever GetData is called from PushNewInfo, the Mutex will be acquired twice (line 3 and 13), causing the system to deadlock. ESP clearly showed this execution path. To fix it, the second argument on line 6 should be changed to TRUE. The Windows development team confirmed that this was a real bug and subsequently fixed the problem.

For all 10 properties, ESP produced false positives. The number of false positives was large for some properties. For example, ESP found 600 counterexamples of one property. We manually examined several counterexamples that all turned out to be false positives due to known limitations of ESP. Manually examining all counterexamples would take too much time and might not be worthwhile as previous experience indicated the false positive rate could be high. Instead, we wrote a simple Perl script to recognize the syntactical pattern of known false positives, ran the script on the counterexamples, and only manually examined those counterexamples that the script did not rec-

```
1    void PushNewInfo ( struct1 s1, struct2 s2 ) {
2        ...
3        acquire ( s1.mutex);
4        ...
5        if ( s2.flag )
6            GetData ( s1, FALSE );
7        ...
8    }
9
10   void GetData ( struct1 s1, boolean locked ) {
11       ...
12       if ( !locked ) {
13           acquire ( s1.mutex );
14       ...
15   }
```

FIGURE 8.24: The NTFS bug in Windows Vista.

ognize. This process helped us eliminate those cases that were highly likely false positives. For this property, the script matched all 600 counterexamples mentioned earlier with known false positive patterns.

One common type of false positive we observed was caused by the imprecision of pointer analysis. For example, ESP does not precisely analyze the target of a function pointer and therefore might consider infeasible paths. About half of the 600 false positives were caused by the imprecision of function pointer analysis. Another type of false positive we observed was caused by the imprecision in modeling non-linear arithmetic operators. ESP uses a theorem prover to decide whether a branch should be taken. Because its theorem prover cannot precisely model the effect of non-linear arithmetic operators such as shift, ESP might explore infeasible paths.

Diagnosing the counterexamples of a property took at least a day of human effort. Some types of false positives are very difficult to diagnose. For example, one counterexample caused by the imprecise modeling of the shift operator took four people including two ESP developers and one Windows developer eight hours to diagnose. Initially, three of the four people believed it was a bug in Windows until the fourth person found it to be a false positive after careful inspection of the code.

Even though diagnosis of the counterexamples was very time-consuming, it increased our confidence in the correctness of the Windows code. In addition, some of the false positives motivated the ESP developers to enhance ESP to reduce the false positives and to make diagnosis of counterexamples easier.

8.4.2 Program Differencing

Inferring the differences between two versions of a program is an important problem in program evolution [7,43,44,46,61]. We hypothesize that Perracotta can infer useful properties for differentiating programs. In particular, compar-

Bus waiting for trip 1
Passenger 0 gets in
Bus drives around Charlottesville
Passenger 0 gets off
Bus waiting for trip 2
Passenger 1 gets in
Bus drives around Charlottesville
Passenger 1 gets off
Bus stops for the day

FIGURE 8.25: Sample output of Bus Simulator with $n = 2$, $C = 1$, and $T = 2$.

ing the inferred properties can increase users' confidence that desirable temporal properties are preserved by modifications. Furthermore, inconsistencies among the inferred properties can reveal interesting facts such as bug fixes or program enhancement.

This section presents experiments applying Perracotta to two families of programs: student implementations of a multi-threaded programming assignment in a graduate software systems course and archived versions of OpenSSL [63]. Because all programs in each case implement the same informal specification, any differences in the inferred temporal properties are likely to be interesting. For these experiments, we use the acceptance threshold of 1.0 for all the properties, thus only consistently true properties are considered. We use Perracotta to infer the strictest properties for each version of a program. We call the inferred properties the *signature* of each version and compare the signatures of program versions.

8.4.2.1   Tour Bus Simulator

The first experiment used submissions for an assignment in a graduate software systems course taught at the University of Virginia in fall 2003. The assignment was a multi-threaded program simulating the operation of city bus with an informal specification, paraphrased below:

Write a program that takes three inputs: n, the number of passengers, C, the maximum number of passengers the bus can hold (C must be $\leq$ n), and T, the number of trips the bus takes, and simulates a tour bus transporting passengers around town. The passengers repeatedly wait to take a tour of town in the bus, which can hold a maximum of C passengers. The bus waits until it has a full load of passengers, and then drives around town. After finishing a trip, each passenger gets off the bus and wanders around before returning to the bus for another trip. The bus makes up to T trips in a day and then stops.

The assignment also specified the format of input and output. Figure 8.25 shows the output of a typical execution when $n = 2$, $C = 1$, and $T = 2$.

Because the outputs corresponded to events of interest to us, we did not

TABLE 8.7: Bus Simulator Properties

P	S	Property in Correct Versions	Property in Faulty Version
wait	drives	Alternating	MultiEffect
wait	gets off	MultiEffect	CauseFirst
drives	gets off	MultiEffect	CauseFirst
wait	gets in	MultiEffect	MultiEffect
gets in	drives	MultiCause	MultiCause
gets in	gets off	CauseFirst	CauseFirst
drives	stops	MultiCause	N/A
gets in	stops	MultiCause	N/A
wait	stops	MultiCause	N/A
gets off	stops	MultiCause	N/A

need to instrument the programs. Instead, we mapped the output logs directly to event sequences. In the mapping, we considered these five events:

1 wait (*Bus waiting for trip n*)

2 drives (*Bus drives around Charlottesville*)

3 stops (*Bus stops for the day*)

4 gets in (*A passenger gets in*)

5 gets off (*A passenger gets off*)

Note that the numbers of the trip and passenger were ignored in our event mapping to reduce the number of distinct events.

A correct solution must satisfy several temporal properties:

(a) The bus always drives with exactly C passengers.

(b) No passenger jumps off or on the bus while it is running.

(c) No passenger starts another trip before getting off the bus.

(d) All passengers get off the bus before passengers for the next trip begin getting on.

We analyzed eight different submissions, all of which were previously evaluated as correct by a grader.

Inference Results. We executed each solution 100 times with randomly generated parameters ($20 \leq C \leq 40$, $C + 1 \leq n \leq 2C$, and $1 \leq T \leq 10$). We used Perracotta to infer the strictest pattern the execution traces satisfy (Section 8.2.4.1). Perracotta inferred the same set of temporal properties for seven out of the eight submissions. Table 8.7 summarizes the results.

Perracotta inferred the Alternating pattern, wait $\rightarrow$ drives, for seven of the programs. In the other program, the strictest pattern inferred for wait and

```
1    void go_for_drive() {
2        pthread_mutex_lock (&mutex[mutex_lock]);
3        if (num_riders < capacity) {
4            printf ("Bus waiting for trip %d\n", num_trips);
5            pthread_cond_wait (&cond[cond_shuttle_full], &mutex[mutex_lock]);
6        }
7        printf ("Bus drives around Charlottesville\n");
8        sleep (3);
9        pthread_cond_broadcast (&cond[cond_ride_over]);
10       num_riders = 0;
11       num_trips--;
12       pthread_mutex_unlock (&mutex[mutex_lock]);
13   }
```

FIGURE 8.26: A synchronization bug in one bus implementation.

drives was MultiEffect. Recall that the regular expression of the MultiEffect pattern is $(PSS^*)^*$. The result indicates multiple drives events corresponded to one wait event. This led us to find the bug shown in Figure 8.26. At the end of function go_for_drive, the bus thread releases the lock (line 12). This effectively allows the passenger threads to compete for the lock (line 2) and to possibly "get in" the bus before the bus starts waiting for passengers. In most cases, the bus thread can successfully obtain the lock (line 2) before it has been filled to capacity (i.e., num_riders < capacity on line 3), so it can generate the wait event (line 4). However, the bus can be already full when the bus thread obtains the lock (i.e., num_riders ⩾ capacity on line 3), in which case it does not produce the wait event. In such situations, wait and drives do not alternate. One way to fix this bug would be to use a conditional variable to synchronize the bus thread and the passenger threads and make sure the bus thread generates the wait event before it broadcasts that condition.

Another difference concerned the property between drives and gets off. In seven of the implementations, drives and gets off satisfied MultiEffect, but in the other implementation the strictest property satisfied is CauseFirst $((PP^*SS^*)^*)$, which meant it was possible for the bus to drive around Charlottesville more than once without allowing passengers to get off between these trips. This turned out to be another bug of missing synchronization between the bus thread and the passenger threads. As shown in Figure 8.26, the bus thread broadcasts that the ride is over to all passenger threads after driving around the city (line 9). Then it should wait for all the passengers to get off before starting the next trip. If the bus thread runs before any passengers depart, it will still be full and will begin the next trip. The third difference in the property between wait and gets off was caused by the same bug.

8.4.2.2   OpenSSL

Our second experiment considered six versions of OpenSSL [63], a widely used open source implementation of the Secure Sockets Layer (SSL) specifica-

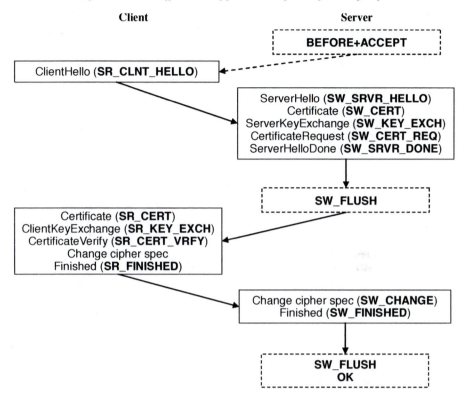

FIGURE 8.27: SSL handshake protocol states.

tion. The SSL protocol provides secure communication over TCP/UDP using public key cryptography [74]. We focused on the *handshake* protocol that performs authentication and establishes important cryptographic parameters before data transmission starts.

Figure 8.27 illustrates the handshake protocol (derived from the SSL specification) [74]. The three boxes with dashed outlines contain internal events introduced by the OpenSSL implementation but not specified in the SSL specification. The remaining boxes contain sequences of events corresponding to messages defined by the SSL handshake protocol. We gave each server event a more descriptive name and showed the original server event in the parentheses.

The handshake protocol begins when the server receives a ClientHello message from a client. Then the server sends out five messages consecutively (ServerHello, Certificate, ServerKeyExchange, CertificateRequest, and ServerHelloDone). Next, the server enters the SR_CERT state in which it tries to read certificate from the client (whether or not the client sends its certificate depends on the server's certificate request message). Then the server reads four consecutive messages from the client (Certificate, ClientKeyExchange, CertificateV-

BEFORE+ACCEPT → SR_CLNT_HELLO → SW_SRVR_HELLO → SW_CERT →
SW_KEY_EXCH → SW_CERT_REQ → SW_SRVR_DONE → SR_CERT →
SR_KEY_EXCH → SR_CERT_VRFY → SR_FINISHED → SW_CHANGE →
SW_FINISHED → OK

FIGURE 8.28: A server event trace of normal handshake process.

erify, and Finished). If no error occurs, the server sends out its ChangeCipherSpec message and wraps up the handshake by sending its Finished message.

As shown in the dash lined boxes in Figure 8.27, the server implements several additional internal states which are also monitored. First, the server always initializes its state to BEFORE+ACCEPT at the beginning of the handshake. After sending each batch of messages, the server flushes the socket by entering the SW_FLUSH state. In addition, OK is another internal state indicating that the server cleans things up and is ready for data transmission. Figure 8.28 shows a typical event trace.

In the OpenSSL server implementation, the handshake process is encapsulated in the function, ssl3_accept. This function implements the protocol state machine as an infinite loop that checks the current protocol state, sends or receives messages, and advances the state accordingly. We manually instrumented this function to monitor the 15 events shown in Figure 8.27.

Running OpenSSL. We adapted the OpenSSL client to generate OpenSSL server traces. We were particularly interested in analyzing the server's behavior when the client does not follow the protocol correctly, since this is often a source of errors. Therefore, we modified the OpenSSL client so that it transitioned to some randomly selected state different from the original one with 5% probability.

Our test harness was based on a simple OpenSSL-based implementation of the HTTPS protocol: wclient and wserver (version 20020110) originally developed by Eric Rescorlia [71]. We added one more command-line option to wclient so that we could seed the random number generator with a specific integer to reproduce of the experiments. We modified wserver so that it only accepted one connection and exited after that. We also added handler functions to print out SIGSEGV and SIGPIPE signals.

We selected six versions of OpenSSL: 0.9.6, 0.9.7, 0.9.7a, 0.9.7b, 0.9.7c, and 0.9.7d. For each version, we executed both wclient and wserver in tandem 1000 times on two machines, which produced 1000 server traces. We used the default keys and certificates supplied in the example program's package and the default choice of cryptographic algorithm.

Results. We first applied Perracotta to all traces. Then we partitioned the traces into four groups: (1) correct client (i.e., the client neither changes to any unintended state nor generates segmentation faults); (2) faulty client (i.e., the client changes its state to some unintended one at least once) but no errors generated in traces; (3) segmentation fault; (4) faulty client generating

TABLE 8.8: Alternating Properties Satisfied by Six Versions of OpenSSL

	0.9.6	0.9.7	0.9.7a	0.9.7b	0.9.7c	0.9.7d
SW_CERT→SW_KEY_EXCH		✓	✓	✓	✓	✓
SR_KEY_EXCH→SR_CERT_VRFY	✓	✓	✓	✓		
SW_SRVR_DONE→SR_CERT		✓				

errors other than segmentation faults. We applied Perracotta to each group of traces.

Table 8.8 highlights three key differences among the inferred Alternating properties. In the first row, Perracotta inferred SW_CERT → SW_KEY_EXCH, for all versions except 0.9.6. Investigating the traces revealed that the server sometimes crashed after entering SW_CERT state with a SIGPIPE signal. We found this was caused by a documented critical bug in earlier versions of OpenSSL [63].

In the second row, Perracotta inferred SR_KEY_EXCH → SR_CERT_VRFY, for all versions up to 0.9.7b but not for 0.9.7c and 0.9.7d. This was caused by a change to version 0.9.7c in order to make the implementation conform to the SSL 3.0 specification (documented in the change log of version 0.9.7c [63]). Starting from version 0.9.7c, a server did not process any certificate message it received from a client if it did not previously request authentication of that client. The condition of whether the server requested client authentication was recorded in a variable, which could be set using a command line option. The server checked this variable to determine its next state after entering the receiving certificate state (SR_CERT). If the server did not request client authentication, it directly advanced to receiving key exchange state (SR_KEY_EXCH). Otherwise, it first read and examined the client's certificate before changing to that state. Our faulty client may send its certificate even if the server did not request one. A server earlier than 0.9.7c noticed this as an error and stopped the handshake immediately: The SR_KEY_EXCH state was not entered at all. In contrast, a server of version 0.9.7c or 0.9.7d ignored the client's certificate, continued to change its state to SR_KEY_EXCH, and then stopped the handshake because of the wrong type of message the client sends (it expected the ClientKeyExchange message, but got the Certificate message).

In the third row, Perracotta inferred SW_SRVR_DONE → SR_CERT, only for version 0.9.7. Using the log messages we identified the cause to be a race condition present in all versions. When the client changed to a false state and got some unexpected message from the server, it tried to send an alert message to the server to stop the handshake process. After that, the client disconnected the socket with the server. If the client had disconnected the socket during the sending of messages by the server, the server would have gotten a sending error message. The server had not and would not get the alert message from the client now because the socket had been disconnected. The server would only be able to get the alert message if it had already finished sending messages to

BEFORE+ACCEPT → SR_CLNT_HELLO → SW_SRVR_HELLO → SW_CERT →
SW_KEY_EXCH → SW_CERT_REQ → SW_SRVR_DONE → SR_CERT →
SR_KEY_EXCH → SR_CERT_VRFY → SR_FINISHED → SW_CHANGE →
SW_FINISHED → OK

FIGURE 8.29: Inferred alternating chains for correct OpenSSL clients.

client and entered a receiving state. In the experiment, this receiving state was
SR_CERT. If the server was able to enter this state before the client sent the
alert message, this event and an alert message would both be printed out at
the server. Therefore, there was no guarantee that an alert message would be
received after sending. Perracotta discovered this important design decision
that was not documented in the specification.

Correct clients. Perracotta inferred an Alternating Chain as shown in Figure 8.29 from the server traces in which the client behaves correctly (i.e., the
5% probability of switching to a random state is never selected). All versions
agree on the same Alternating Chain. This result is desirable because the pattern
in Figure 8.29 conforms exactly to the SSL specification as shown in Figure
8.27. This demonstrates that the server implementation of the handshake protocol conforms to the specification as OpenSSL evolves.

Faulty clients without errors generated. Next, we considered the set
of traces corresponding to faulty clients that, surprisingly, did not generate
any error event on either the server or client. For all six versions, Perracotta
inferred the two Alternating Chains shown in Figure 8.30. These two chains
closely follow the normal handshake. However, there are a few key distinctions
between the patterns in Figure 8.29 and Figure 8.30.

Two of the Alternating properties that are present in Figure 8.29 do
not appear in Figure 8.30. Instead, those event pairs satisfy weaker patterns. SR_CERT and SR_KEY_EXCH satisfy the MultiCause pattern, and BE-
FORE+ACCEPT and SR_CLNT_HELLO satisfy the MultiEffect pattern. Figure
8.31(a) shows a trace that violates the expected Alternating properties. The key
distinction between this trace and the traces produced using correctly behaving clients is that the eight-event sequence appears twice (shown in boldface
in Figure 8.31(a)). Figure 8.31(b) shows the corresponding client events. The
faulty client falsely changes its state to renegotiate (an internal state in the implementation of the client, not shown in Figure 8.27 since it is not part of the

SR_CLNT_HELLO → SW_SRVR_HELLO → SW_CERT → SW_KEY_EXCH →
SW_CERT_REQ → SW_SRVR_DONE → SR_CERT

BEFORE+ACCEPT → SR_KEY_EXCH → SR_CERT_VRFY → SR_FINISHED →
SW_CHANGE → SW_FINISHED → OK

FIGURE 8.30: Inferred alternating chains for non-error faulty OpenSSL
clients.

BEFORE+ACCEPT, OK+ACCEPT,
SR_CLNT_HELLO, SW_SRVR_HELLO, SW_CERT, SW_KEY_EXCH,
SW_CERT_REQ, SW_SRVR_DONE, SW_FLUSH,SR_CERT,
SR_CLNT_HELLO, SW_SRVR_HELLO, SW_CERT, SW_KEY_EXCH,
SW_CERT_REQ, SW_SRVR_DONE, SW_FLUSH,SR_CERT,
SR_KEY_EXCH, SR_CERT_VRFY, SR_FINISHED, SW_CHANGE, SW_FINISHED,
SW_FLUSH, OK

(a) Server trace

BEFORE+CONNECT, OK+CONNECT, CW_CLNT_HELLO,
CR_SRVR_HELLO,CR_CERT, CR_KEY_EXCH, CR_CERT_REQ,CR_SRVR_DONE,
RENEGOTIATE,
BEFORE, CONNECT, BEFORE+CONNECT, OK+CONNECT, CW_CLNT_HELLO,
CR_SRVR_HELLO, CR_CERT, CR_KEY_EXCH, CR_CERT_REQ, CR_SRVR_DONE,
CW_KEY_EXCH, CW_CHANGE, CW_FINISHED, CW_FLUSH, CR_FINISHED, OK

(b) Client trace

FIGURE 8.31: Traces generated with a faulty OpenSSL client.

normal handshake process) instead of CW_CERT after reading the five messages from server (ServerHello, Certificate, ServerKeyExchange, CertificateRequest, and ServerHelloDone). Then, the client starts the handshake again by sending the ClientHello message, which causes the server to repeat the hello stage of the handshake again. If a client always changes its state to renegotiate after receiving the ServerHelloDone message, the server and the client will enter an infinite loop.

Suspecting this could be exploited in a denial of service (DOS) attack, we contacted the OpenSSL developers. They argued that it did not indicate a serious DOS vulnerability because the server looped infinitely only when an ill-behaved client kept sending renegotiation requests. This was similar to too many clients attempting to connect to a server, which was a scenario that could not really be prevented at the server. Although this was not a real vulnerability, it did reveal an interesting aspect of OpenSSL, which was not documented in the SSL specification and was not obvious from code inspection.

Segmentation faults. There were three traces that included segmentation faults in all versions prior to 0.9.7d. These traces were from the faulty client that sent a change_cipher_spec instead of the normal client hello message at the beginning of the handshake process. We examined the change log for version 0.9.7d and found that this was due to a critical update [64], where an assignment to a null-pointer in the do_change_cipher_spec function caused the server to crash. Although this finding did not result from comparing the inferred temporal properties, it shows that using randomly behaving clients to test a server is powerful enough to uncover important problems.

Faulty clients with other errors. For all versions, Perracotta inferred the same temporal properties for traces within this category. This demonstrated that the server handled misbehaving clients consistently with respect to the properties Perracotta inferred.

8.5   Related Work

This section surveys related work. Section 8.5.1 describes the grammar inference problem and its complexity, which provides the theoretical context of the specification inference problem. Section 8.5.2 classifies other inference work based on its underlying techniques and describes the representative work in each category. Finally, Section 8.5.3 presents previous work on using the inferred specifications.

8.5.1   Grammar Inference

A grammar G describes a language L if and only if $L(G)$ (the language generated by G) equals to L. The grammar inference problem can be informally stated as: "given some sample sentences in a language (positive samples), and perhaps some sentences specifically not in the language (negative samples), infer a grammar that describes the language." [12] Inferring temporal specifications from a program's execution traces is a concrete example of the grammar inference problem, where the specifications inferred comprise the grammar and the execution traces are the sample sentences. Gold developed the first theoretical framework for analyzing the grammar inference problem [32]. Gold proved that it is NP-hard to infer a deterministic finite-state automaton (DFA) with a minimum number of states from positive and negative sample sentences [33]. In addition, Gold showed that it is impossible to infer such a DFA given only positive samples because an algorithm has no way to determine whether it is overgeneralizing. Cook and Wolf survey the grammar inference problem, its theoretical complexity, and several practical inference techniques [12].

Gold's results indicate that it is very difficult to infer the exact grammar (e.g., a DFA with minimal number of states) even for relatively simple languages such as regular languages. This explains why earlier specification inference approaches to extract a complete finite-state machine do not scale well.

8.5.2   Property Inference

We classify other property inference work into two main categories: *template-based inference techniques* that have a set of pre-defined templates and try to match either execution traces or static program paths against these templates [24,25,28,37,38,66,79] and *arbitrary model inference techniques* that do not have a set of pre-defined templates and can discover arbitrary models that execution traces or static program paths satisfy [3,13,30,58,69,81]. The major difference between a template-based inference technique and an arbitrary model inference technique is that a template-based technique tries to detect whether and how a program fits in a specific pattern, whereas an arbitrary model inference technique tries to create the best model that fits the target program or its execution traces.

We can further classify techniques in each of the two main categories into two subcategories: machine learning-based techniques that use statistical machine learning to infer patterns [3, 13, 24, 25, 38, 58, 69, 79, 81], and dataflow analysis-based techniques that infer properties by either symbolically executing a program [30, 37, 66] or using a verification tool as an oracle [28]. Following subsections compare our work with the work in each category.

8.5.2.1 Template-Based Inference

Template-based inference techniques have a set of pre-defined templates that can capture pre-condition, post-condition, and invariants [26, 28, 38], temporal constraints [24, 79], or very specific program features such as locks [66] or buffers [37].

Daikon is a tool that automatically infers likely program invariants from a program's execution traces [25, 26, 65]. The technique uses a set of pre-defined invariant patterns that are matched against the values observed in the traces; invariants that are violated are dropped. Invariants that survive are ranked in order of confidence. Only invariants that are above a specified confidence threshold are reported. The original Daikon inference algorithm is limited by its scalability because the algorithm is cubic in the number of variables monitored [26]. Several new optimizations recently developed by Perkins and Ernst greatly improve Daikon's performance, but performance remains an impediment to applying Daikon to large-scale programs [65]. Our work is distinct from Daikon in that our approach infers specifications of the temporal behaviors of a system, which Daikon does not infer. Our technique also scales much better to large-scale real systems such as Windows. In addition, Daikon requires 100% satisfaction of templates and therefore is less robust to imperfect traces than our approximate inference algorithm.

Diduce is a run-time anomaly detection tool that is based on invariant inference [38]. Diduce infers data invariants as a program executes and generates alarms whenever the execution violates the current invariants. The invariants Diduce infers are bit field patterns (e.g., the last bit of a byte at certain address is always 0) and therefore are useful for detecting memory usage errors at runtime. Our work is different from Diduce in that our work focuses on API level invariants. In addition, the properties Perracotta infers can be used for several other purposes other than run-time monitoring.

Engler et al. proposed a method for extracting properties by statically examining source code based on a set of pre-defined templates [24]. Like our approach, their technique scales well by targeting simple property templates. Our chaining method can build more complex properties that their technique does not infer. To deal with the imprecision of static analysis, they use statistics to prioritize their results. Similarly, our approximate inference algorithm is also statistical. Furthermore, they use a set of specific names to reduce the number of candidate events [24]. In order to infer a property, Engler's technique requires that an event (e.g., a function foo) occurs frequently enough in the code base (e.g., foo is called at many different places). In contrast, our dynamic technique can still infer a property as long as an event occurs frequently enough in the trace. The limitation of Engler's work is that it often produces too many false positives. To lower the rate of false positives, Weimer et al. improved Engler's work by developing an approach that examines a program's exception handling routines [79]. The intuition is that programs often make mistakes on exceptional paths, even when they are mostly correct on the normal paths. On one hand, Weimer's approach mainly focuses on local properties, while our technique can identify relationships among events that are far removed from each other in program text. On the other hand, Weimer's work and our work complement each other because it is usually very hard to generate test inputs for exception handling routines.

Houdini is an annotation inference tool for ESC [28, 29]. The annotations are in the standard Hoare-style logic that includes pre-condition, post-condition, and invariants [41]. Houdini first generates a set of candidate annotations and then feeds these candidates to ESC. ESC either proves or refutes a property. The main problem of Houdini is that it does not scale well because the underlying ESC is slow.

Other static inference techniques focus on certain program features and are very effective. LockSmith is a tool for automatically inferring locking discipline annotations that are later used to check for deadlocks and race conditions [66]. SALInfer is a tool for inferring annotations for function arguments that are related to buffer usages [37]. SALInfer has been successfully used to help annotate the whole Windows code-base. Both LockSmith and SALInfer use dataflow analysis. Compared to LockSmith, Perracotta infers a similar type of property using a regular expression inference from execution traces. Compared to SALInfer, our work focuses on a different class of properties that SALInfer does not infer. Furthermore, our underlying technique is based on regular expression matching instead of dataflow analysis.

8.5.2.2   Arbitrary Model Inference

Arbitrary model inference techniques try to discover a model that fits the target program or its execution traces. Most of the related work in this category analyzes program execution traces [3,13,69,81]. Other artifacts analyzed include revision history [58] and source code [30].

Ammons et al. used an off-the-shelf probabilistic finite state automaton learner to mine temporal and data-dependence specifications for APIs or abstract data structures from dynamic traces [3, 4]. In addition to handling of traces containing bugs (i.e., imperfect traces as defined in our work), their approach required non-trivial human guidance. In contrast, our techniques can automatically tolerate imperfect traces without guidance. Their machine learning algorithm has a high computational cost, whereas our algorithm scales better to larger traces than theirs.

Whaley et al. proposed a static and a dynamic approach for inferring what protocols clients of a Java class must follow [81]. The protocols their approach found are mainly typestate properties that involve one component and are small. In contrast, our approach is able to discover useful properties involving more than one component. In addition, our chaining method is able to construct large finite state machines efficiently.

Cook et al. developed a statistical dynamic analysis for extracting thread synchronization models from a program's execution traces [13]. Our work differs from theirs in that our approach focuses on detecting API rules and assumes the trace already has the thread information.

Reiss and Renieris developed a technique to compact large volumes of execution traces [69]. Their tool uses the sequencing properties on individual objects, while Perracotta detects rules across multiple objects.

DynaMine extracts error patterns from a system's CVS revision histories and dynamically validates inferred patterns [58]. This approach is complementary to our work in that examining a CVS history is a way to select events to monitor at run-time. Their mining algorithm has to filter out a fixed set of frequent events to scale to large scenarios, which is not as general as our heuristics. The patterns their approach infers tend to focus only on methods within a class, whereas our approach can infer properties involving more than one class.

8.5.3 Use of Inferred Specifications

This section presents related work on using the inferred specifications to improve a variety of software development activities, including defect detection [11, 16, 17, 24, 28, 30, 37, 38, 58, 62, 66, 79, 81], test case generation [17, 39, 83], program evolution [26], program understanding [13, 59], theorem proving [82], bug localization [56], and data structure repairing at runtime [20].

8.5.3.1 Defect Detection

Defect detection is the application to which inferred specifications are most widely applied. We can further divide the related work into several groups: using a separate verification tool [28, 37, 58, 62, 81], statistical defect detection [11, 24, 38, 79], context-free language reachability analysis [30, 66], combining static analysis and test generation [16, 17].

The work in the first group simply feeds the inferred properties to a separate program verification tool [28, 37, 58, 62, 81]. This is similar to our work on checking the inferred properties using Java PathFinder and ESP. The benefits of such an approach are that inferred specifications can be easily checked by different verification tools.

The work using statistical defect detection integrates specification inference tightly with defect detection [11,24,38,79]. Engler et al. pioneered work in statistical defect detection [24]. Their technique examined a program's source code to observe common behavioral patterns (called *belief*) and detected violations of the common behavioral patterns based on statistics. Weimer and Necula tried to reduce the false positive rate by focusing the analysis on exception handling routines [79]. The Diduce tool used a similar idea as Engler's work except that Diduce detected abnormal program behavior at runtime [38]. Chilimbi and Ganapathy were inspired by Diduce and aimed to detect abnormal memory usage patterns [11]. Statistical defect detection works well in practice because real world programs, even though not perfectly correct, behave correctly most of the time and therefore only expose abnormal behaviors occasionally. Its drawback is that the defects that can be detected are hardcoded and therefore extending existing tools to check new defects requires significant effort. Our approximate inference algorithm bears a similar spirit as the statistical defect detection work. Instead of detecting bugs, our approximate inference algorithm tries to use a statistical approach to tolerate imperfect program behaviors.

Foster's Ph.D. dissertation on type qualifiers introduced the idea of using constraint-based context-free language reachability analysis to infer type annotations and detect bugs [30]. More recent work applied this idea to infer correlation between data and locks [66]. The inferred correlations were checked for race conditions. This work also tightly combined the inference of specifications (type qualifiers or data-lock correlations) with the detection of their violation.

Recent work by Csallner and Smaragdakis opened an interesting direction of combining dynamic inference, static analysis, and automated test generation for bug detection [16, 17]. Their work used dynamic inference to infer intended program behaviors so that users did not have to provide the specifications, static verification tool to detect violations of inferred invariants, and test generation to check the validity of the errors reported by the static analysis. One advantage of this approach compared to a purely static analysis was that the test generation eliminated the false positives in the results. Compared to this work, our work of checking the inferred specifications still produced too many false positives to be practical.

8.5.3.2   Other Uses

Inferred specifications were used to augment and minimize test suite [39]. The idea was to use inferred properties as a test coverage criterion. Test cases were selected until the set of inferred properties stabilized. Harder's work, however, did not automatically generate new test cases. Xie and Notkin used inferred properties to automatically generate unit-test cases [83]. In our future work, we plan to investigate how to use the inferred temporal specification to select and generate test cases.

Ernst et al. studied using the invariants inferred by Daikon to aid programmers in modifying programs [26]. In their experiments, programmers were supplied with the inferred invariants, as they added a new feature to an existing program. The programmers found the inferred invariants useful. Our work on using inferred invariants in differencing programs was inspired by Ernst's work. Compared to Ernst's work, our work focused more on automatically detecting the semantic difference of multiple versions of a program, whereas Ernst's work aimed to evaluate whether the inferred specification could be useful for programmers.

Naturally, inferred specifications can be used to help programmers gain more insights into the target program. Cook et al. developed a technique for inferring thread interaction models from execution traces [13]. Their technique used a statistical approach. Mandelin et al. developed a technique for discovering the sequence of APIs that were needed to accomplish some tasks [59]. They called their tool *specification prospector* and the inferred API sequence *jungloid*. Our work on inferring Alternating Chains bore a similar motivation as Mandelin's work.

Another representative use of inferred specifications is in guiding theorem prover to verify distributed programs [82].

Liblit et al. showed the inferred specifications can be used to debug a program [56]. Their work monitored a set of program predicates and compared the observed properties of a successful execution against the ones of a failed execution. Their technique used a statistical approach to eliminate irrelevant predicates and rank inferred predicates. One big advantage of this work compared to previous work on bug localization is that it can effectively handle programs that have more than one bug. We also plan to investigate whether the temporal specifications inferred by Perracotta can be useful in debugging.

Much work has been on using inferred specifications to detect bugs, Demsky et al. showed that the inferred specification can also be used to let a program continue its execution in face of data structure corruption [20]. Their technique used Daikon to infer invariants for data structures and automatically detected and restored corrupted data structures to behave normally with regard to the invariants.

8.6 Conclusion

Software specifications are the foundation of many software development activities including maintenance, testing, and verification. We have presented Perracotta, a tool that automatically infers temporal specifications of programs by analyzing execution traces. Perfect, fully automatic specification inference for industrial programs remains an elusive goal, well beyond the state-of-the-art. We have shown, however, that by targeting simple properties that can be efficiently discovered and by using approximation inference techniques along with heuristics for pruning the set of inferred properties, it is possible to obtain useful results even for programs as large and complex as JBoss and Windows.

Limitations. Our approach, being a dynamic analysis, shares the limitations of any dynamic analysis. In particular, most real systems have an infinite number of execution paths. It is impossible to execute such a system on all of its paths. Dynamic analysis only examines a subset of all paths of a target program and might produce results that are false for some paths. Therefore manual or machine validation is required before they can be used as specifications. In addition, dynamic analysis needs to instrument a target program to observe its behaviors. This instrumentation can affect the normal behavior of a target program. The extra computation introduced by the instrumentation might cause a thread in a real-time system to miss its deadline. The extra memory used by the instrumentation might affect cache locality. Hence, dynamic analysis is impractical to analyze properties that can be affected by the instrumentation.

Our approach uses a set of pre-defined property templates. This limits the properties that can be inferred to those that can be expressed using these templates. Even though we can introduce a new template to express new properties, a new template will also introduce many uninteresting properties that require new heuristics to filter. Developing a good heuristic for distinguishing interesting properties from uninteresting ones requires much effort and may not always be possible. Without a good heuristic, inferred properties can be useless if the density of interesting properties is very low. Furthermore, if a new template is complex (i.e., templates with many parameters), it might be very inefficient to infer properties that satisfy it.

To reduce the effort required to analyze the inference results, our approach relies heavily on the effectiveness of heuristics for selecting interesting properties. The effort required to analyze the remaining properties after applying the heuristics sometimes can still be quite high even for users familiar with the target system. In addition, heuristics, no matter how good they are, can mis-classify interesting properties as uninteresting ones. Therefore, interesting properties may be missing in the final results.

One of our assumptions is that a target program is well tested and exhibits desirable specifications most of the time. To tolerate imperfection in the traces, our technique uses a very simple statistical approach. Even though our experimental results show that this assumption is valid for typical real systems, our approach can hardly be applicable to systems that do not satisfy this assumption.

Summary. We have presented a dynamic analysis approach for inferring interesting temporal properties. Through experiments on several real systems, we have shown that our approach is scalable, effective, and useful in aiding a variety of software development activities. There are many exciting opportunities for further work in both automatic inference of program properties and ways to use inferred program properties. Our current templates are very limited in the kinds of properties they can express. Developing richer templates with more parameters and conditional relationships can capture more important program properties, but poses challenges for scalability. Currently we only infer properties from a fixed set of test cases. We still don't understand how the inferred properties change as we vary the test cases, when the inferred properties stabilize as we add new test cases, and what size of test suite is required to produce a stable set of properties. Such knowledge can guide users in selecting test cases for inferring properties.

The experimental results of applying Perracotta to a diverse range of real systems provide strong evidence that our approach is useful in aiding several different software development tasks: program understanding, program differencing, and program verification. In particular, the experimental results demonstrate that our approach is able to automatically identify important temporal properties, identify interesting behavioral differences among multiple versions of programs, and help find bugs.

Acknowledgments

The work described here was partly funded by the National Science Foundation and Air Force Office of Scientific Research.

Bibliography

[1] J. R. Abrial. *The B-Book: Assigning Programs to Meanings*. Cambridge University Press, October 1996.

[2] R. Alur, P. Cerny, P. Madhusudan, and W. Nam. Synthesis of interface specifications for Java classes. In *Symposium on Principles of Programming Languages*, January 2005.

[3] G. Ammons, R. Bodik, and J. R. Larus. Mining specifications. In *Symposium on Principles of Programming Languages*, January 2002.

[4] G. Ammons, D. Mandelin, R. Bodik, and J. R. Larus. Debugging temporal specifications with concept analysis. In *Conference on Programming Language Design and Implementation*, June 2003.

[5] T. Ball and S. K. Rajamani. Automatically Validating temporal safety properties of interfaces. In *International SPIN Workshop on Model Checking of Software*, May 2001.

[6] The Byte Code Engineering Library. http://jakarta.apache.org/bcel/.

[7] D. Binkley, R. Capellini, L. Raszewski, and C. Smith. An implementation of and experiment with semantic differencing. In *International Conference on Software Maintenance*, November 2001.

[8] C. Boyapati, S. Khurshid, and D. Marinov. Korat: Automated Testing based on java predicates. In *International Symposium on Software Testing and Analysis*, July 2002.

[9] W. R. Bush, J. D. Pincus, and D. J. Sielaff. A static analyzer for finding dynamic programming errors. *Software – Practice and Experience*, Volume 20, 2000.

[10] H. Chen and D. Wagner. MOPS: an infrastructure for examining security properties of software. In *Conference on Computer and Communications Security*, November 2002.

[11] T. M. Chilimbi and V. Ganapathy. HeapMD: identifying heap-based bugs using anomaly detection. In *Conference on Architectural Support for Programming Languages and Operating Systems*, October 2006.

[12] J. E. Cook and A. Wolf. Discovering models of software processes from event-based data. *ACM Transactions on Software Engineering and Methodology*, Volume 7, 1998.

[13] J. E. Cook, Z. Du, C. Liu, and A. L. Wolf. Discovering models of behavior for concurrent workflows. *Computers in Industry*, April 2004.

[14] D. Coppit, J. Yang, S. Khurshid, W. Le, and K. Sullivan. Software assurance by bounded exhaustive testing. *IEEE Transactions on Software Engineering*, Volume 31, April 2005.

[15] T. H. Cormen, C. E. Leiserson, R. L. Rivest, and C. Stein. *Introduction to Algorithms, Second Edition*. MIT Press and McGraw-Hill, 2001.

[16] C. Csallner and Y. Smaragdakis. Check 'n' crash: combining static checking and testing. In *International Conference on Software Engineering*, May 2005.

[17] C. Csallner and Y. Smaragdakis. DSD-crasher: a hybrid analysis tool for bug finding. In *International Symposium on Software Testing and Analysis*, July 2006.

[18] Joint CAV/ISSTA Special Event on Specification, Verification, and Testing of Concurrent Software, July 2004.

[19] M. Das, S. Lerner, and M. Seigle. ESP: path-sensitive program verification in polynomial time. In *Conference on Programming Language Design and Implementation*, June 2002.

[20] B. Demsky, M. D. Ernst, P. J. Guo, S. McCamant, J. H. Perkins, and M. Rinard. Inference and enforcement of data structure consistency specifications. In *International Symposium on Software Testing and Analysis*, July 2006.

[21] J. Dick and A. Faivre. Automating the generation and sequencing of test cases from model-based specifications. In *International Symposium of Formal Methods Europe on Industrial-Strength Formal Methods*, April 1993.

[22] J. W. Duran and S. C. Ntafos. An evaluation of random testing. *IEEE Transactions on Software Engineering*, July 1984.

[23] M. Dwyer, G. Avrunin, and J. Corbett. Patterns in property specifications for finite-state verification. In *International Conference on Software Engineering*, May 1999.

[24] D. Engler, D. Y. Chen, S. Hallem, A. Chou, and B. Chelf. Bugs as deviant behavior: a general approach to inferring errors in systems code. in *Symposium on Operating Systems Principles*, October 2001.

[25] M. D. Ernst. Dynamically Discovering Likely Program Invariants. Ph.D. dissertation, University of Washington, Department of Computer Science and Engineering, August 2000.

[26] M. Ernst, J. Cockrell, W. Griswold, and D. Notkin. Dynamically discovering likely program invariants to support program evolution. *IEEE Transactions on Software Engineering*, February 2001.

[27] D. Evans. Static detection of dynamic memory errors. In *Conference on Programming Language Design and Implementation*, May 1996.

[28] C. Flanagan, R. Joshi, K. Rustan, and M. Leino. Annotation inference for modular checkers. *Information Processing Letters*, February 2001.

[29] C. Flanagan, K. R. M. Leino, M. Lillibridge, G. Nelson, J. B. Saxe, and R. Stata. Extended static checking for Java. In *Conference on Programming Language Design and Implementation*, June 2002.

[30] J. S. Foster. Type Qualifiers: Lightweight Specifications to Improve Software Quality. Ph.D. thesis. University of California, Berkeley, December 2002.

[31] M. Fowler. *UML Distilled: A Brief Guide to the Standard Object Modeling Language, Third Edition.* Addison-Wesley Professional, September 2003.

[32] E. Gold. Language identification in the limit. *Information and Control*, Volume 10, 1967.

[33] E. Gold. Complexity of automatic identification from given data. *Information and Control*, Volume 37, 1978.

[34] D. Gries. *The Science of Programming*. Springer Verlag, New York, 1981.

[35] D. Grove and C. Chambers. A framework for call graph construction algorithms. *ACM Transactions on Programming Languages and Systems.* Volume 23, November 2001.

[36] N. Gupta. Generating test data for dynamically discovering likely program invariants. In *Workshop on Dynamic Analysis*, May 2003.

[37] B. Hackett, M. Das, D. Wang, and Z. Yang. Modular checking for buffer overflows in the large. In *International Conference on Software Engineering*, May 2006.

[38] S. Hangal and M. S. Lam. Tracking down software bugs using automatic anomaly detection. In *International Conference on Software Engineering*, May 2002.

[39] M. Harder, J. Mellen, and M. D. Ernst. Improving test suites via operational abstraction. In *International Conference on Software Engineering*, May 2003.

[40] J. Henkel. Discovering and Debugging Algebraic Specifications for Java Classes. Ph.D. Dissertation, University of Colorado at Boulder, May 2004.

[41] C. A. R. Hoare. An axiomatic basis for computer programming. *Communications of the ACM*, October 1969.

[42] C. M. Holloway and R. W. Butler. Impediments to industrial use of formal methods. *IEEE Computer*, April 1996.

[43] S. Horwitz. Identifying the semantic and textual differences between two versions of a program. In *Conference on Programming Language Design and Implementation*, June 1990.

[44] S. Horwitz and T. Reps. The use of program dependence graphs in software engineering. In *International Conference on Software Engineering*, May 1994.

[45] J2EE. http://java.sun.com/j2ee.

[46] D. Jackson and D. Ladd. Semantic Diff: a tool for summarizing the effects of modifications. In *International Conference on Software Maintenance*, October 1994.

[47] JBoss. http://www.jboss.org.

[48] JRat. http://jrat.sourceforge.net.

[49] Java Transaction API specification. http://java.sun.com/products/jta.

[50] R. Karp. Reducibility among combinatorial problems. In *Complexity of Computer Computations*. 1972.

[51] S. Khurshid and D. Marinov. TestEra: a novel framework for automated testing of Java programs. *Automated Software Engineering Journal*, December 2002.

[52] J. C. Knight, C. L. DeJong, M. S. Gibble, and L. G. Nakano. Why are formal methods not used more widely? In *NASA Langley Formal Methods Workshop*, September 1997.

[53] F. Kröger. *Temporal Logic of Programs*. Springer-Verlag, New York, 1987.

[54] A. Lamsweerde. Formal specification: a roadmap. In *International Conference on Software Engineering*, May 2000.

[55] S. Letovsky and E. Soloway. Delocalized plans and program comprehension. *IEEE Software*, May 1986.

[56] B. Liblit, M. Naik, A. X. Zheng, A. Aiken, and M. I. Jordan. Scalable statistical bug isolation. In *Conference on Programming Language Design and Implementation*, June 2005.

[57] L. Lin and M. D. Ernst. Improving adaptability via program steering. In *International Symposium on Software Testing and Analysis*, July 2004.

[58] B. Livshits and T. Zimmermann. DynaMine: finding common error patterns by mining software revision histories. In *Symposium on the Foundations of Software Engineering*, September 2005.

[59] D. Mandelin, L. Xu, R. Bodik, and D. Kimelman. Mining jungloids: helping to navigate the API jungle. In *Conference on Programming Language Design and Implementation*, June 2005.

[60] A. M. Memon, M. E. Pollack, and M. L. Soffa. Hierarchical GUI test case generation using automated planning. *IEEE Transactions on Software Engineering*. Volume 27, February 2001.

[61] W. Miller and E. W. Myers. A file comparison program. *Software – Practice and Experience*, Volume 15, 1985.

[62] J. W. Nimmer and M. D. Ernst. Invariant inference for static checking: an empirical evaluation. In *Symposium on the Foundations of Software Engineering*, November 2002.

[63] OpenSSL. http://www.openssl.org.

[64] OpenSSL security advisory, 17 March 2004. http://www.openssl.org/news/secadv_20040317.txt.

[65] J. Perkins and M. Ernst. Efficient incremental algorithms for dynamic detection of likely invariants. In *International Symposium on Foundations of Software Engineering*, November 2004.

[66] P. Pratikakis, J. S. Foster, and M. Hicks. Context-sensitive correlation analysis for detecting races. In *ACM Conference on Programming Language Design and Implementation*, June 2006.

[67] A. Pnueli. The temporal logic of programs. In *Symposium on Foundations of Computer Science*, October/November 1977.

[68] B. Pytlik, M. Renieris, S. Krishnamurthi, and S. Reiss. Automated fault localization using potential invariants. In *International Symposium on Automated and Analysis-Driven Debugging.* September 2003.

[69] S. P. Reiss and M. Renieris. Encoding program executions. In *International Conference on Software Engineering*, May 2001.

[70] T. Reps, S. Horwitz, and M. Sagiv. Precise inter-procedural dataflow analysis via graph reachability. In *Symposium on Principles of Programming Languages*, January 1995.

[71] E. Rescorla. An Introduction to OpenSSL Programming, Part One. http://www.rtfm.com/ openssl-examples/, October 2001.

[72] H. G. Rice. Classes of recursively enumerable sets and their decision problems. *Transactions of the American Mathematics Society*, Volume 74, 1953.

[73] C. Simonyi. Hungarian notation. MSDN library. *http://msdn.microsoft.com/library/default.asp?url=/library/en-us/dnvs600/html/HungaNotat.asp.*

[74] SSL Specification, Third Version. http://wp.netscape.com/eng/ssl3.

[75] Static driver verifier: finding bugs in device drivers at compile-time. In *Windows Hardware Engineering Conference*, April 2004.

[76] A. Srivastava, A. Edwards, and H. Vo. Vulcan: Binary Transformation in a Distributed Environment. Microsoft Research Technical Report, MSR-TR-2001-50, April 2001.

[77] R. E. Strom and S. Yemini. Typestate: a programming language concept for enhancing software reliability. *IEEE Transactions on Software Engineering*, Volume 12, January 1986.

[78] W. Visser, K. Havelund, G. Brat, S. Park, and F. Lerda. Model checking programs. *Automated Software Engineering Journal*, April 2003.

[79] W. Weimer and G. Necula. Mining temporal specifications for error detection. In *International Conference on Tools and Algorithms for the Construction and Analysis of Systems*, April 2005.

[80] E. J. Weyuker and T. J. Ostrand. Theories of program testing and the application of revealing subdomains. *IEEE Transactions on Software Engineering*, May 1980.

[81] J. Whaley, M. C. Martin, and M. S. Lam. Automatic extraction of object-oriented component interfaces. In *International Symposium on Software Testing and Analysis*, July 2002.

[82] T. N. Win, M. D. Ernst, S. J. Garland, D. Kirli, and N. Lynch. Using simulated execution in verifying distributed algorithms. *Software Tools for Technology Transfer*, July 2004.

[83] T. Xie and D. Notkin. Tool-assisted unit-test generation and selection based on operational abstractions. *Automated Software Engineering Journal*, Volume 13, July 2006.

[84] J. Yang and D. Evans. Dynamically inferring temporal properties. In *Workshop on Program Analysis for Software Tools and Engineering*, June 2004.

[85] J. Yang and D. Evans. Automatically inferring temporal properties for program evolution. In *International Symposium on Software Reliability Engineering*, November 2004.

[86] J. Yang and D. Evans. Automatically Discovering Temporal Properties for Program Verification. Technical Report, Department of Computer Science, University of Virginia, 2005.

[87] J. Yang, D. Evans, D. Bhardwaj, T. Bhat, and M. Das. Perracotta: mining temporal API rules from imperfect traces. In *International Conference on Software Engineering*, May 2006.

[88] J. Yang. Automatic Inference and Effective Application of Temporal Specifications. Ph.D. dissertation, University of Virginia, Department of Computer Science, May 2007.

Chapter 9

Path-Aware Static Program Analyses for Specification Mining[*]

Muralikrishna Ramanathan

Coverity, Inc.

Ananth Grama

Purdue University

Suresh Jagannathan

Purdue University

---

[*]This chapter is based on: M. Ramanathan et al., "Static specification inference using predicate mining," Proceedings of the 2007 ACM SIGPLAN Conference on Programming Language Design and Implementation, ©2007 Association for Computing Machinery Inc. Reprinted by permission.

9.1   Introduction

In this chapter, we address issues pertaining to improving software reliability by exploring static program analysis methodologies that permit the efficient *mining* of useful and pertinent specifications. Our techniques help answer the following two important questions: (1) What are the specifications and invariants a program execution is expected to follow? (2) When specifications are not followed, what are the root causes for failure?

The reason these questions are important is because well-defined specifications can significantly enhance the reliability and correctness of complex software systems. When available, they can be used to verify correctness of libraries and device drivers [4, 9, 25, 44], enable modular reuse [35], and guide testing mechanisms toward bugs [15, 21]. When specifications are provided by the user, type systems [13, 18, 19], model checking [9, 25], typestate interpretation [24, 29], and other related static analyses [44] can be used to check whether implementations satisfy necessary invariants. Often, specifications are easy to define (e.g., procedure p must always be called after data structure d is initialized), or are well-documented (e.g., `pthread_mutex_init` must be present on all program paths reaching a call to `pthread_mutex_lock`). In many cases, though, specifications are not known, and even when available, are often informal, imprecise, or incomplete. This is especially true for complex system software libraries. Therefore, if the process of generating specifications is automated, the efficiency and utility of verification and testing can be improved. While specifications (or assertions) have been shown to be useful for enhancing software reliability and maintainability, understanding *why* an assertion fails (or succeeds) is an equally important problem. Such knowledge directly contributes to understanding program behavior, improving documentation, and aids program transformation and refactoring.

9.1.1   Path-Aware Analyses

For the analyses discussed in this chapter, we assume the presence of control flow graphs corresponding to the procedures in the program. A node in a control flow graph represents a statement in the program and an edge between two nodes (u and v) represents possible control flow between the statements associated with nodes u and v, respectively. A *path* in a program corresponds to the sequence of statements in a program (e.g., s1, s2, s4 is a path in the program shown below). In realistic programs, there are potentially many paths (e.g., there are four paths in the program shown below). Any program analysis technique that takes paths into account is considered to be *path-aware*.

```
void main(int argc, char *argv[]) {
  /* assume argv[0] = "prog" */
    int x;
    char *str = NULL;
    if(argc > 2) {
        str = (char *)malloc(strlen(argv[2])+1);
        strcpy(str, argv[2]);  /* s1 */
    }
    x = atoi(argv[1]);
    if(x > 0)
        write(1, "positive",9);  /* s2 */
    else
        write(1, "not positive",13);  /* s3 */
    write(1, str, strlen(str));  /* s4 */
}
```

To see why path-awareness is important for deriving useful specifications and localizing specification violations, consider the code fragment shown above, which takes two arguments and characterizes the first argument as positive(s2) or not positive(s3) and simply prints(s4) the second argument after storing(s1) it in a local variable str. The above fragment is obviously erroneous (at statement s4) if there is exactly one argument provided. Any analysis technique that considers statement s4 in the context of statement s1 not being executed can only conclude the error associated with statement s4.

If we define a simple analysis to detect whether str is assigned some value before statement s4 after the NULL assignment, a path-unaware analysis will collect all the statements preceding statement s4 and detect the assignment at statement s1. Conversely, a path-aware analysis will consider each program path separately and determine that str is not assigned a value *always*. It is this precision associated with path-aware analysis that dictates improved accuracy with respect to software reliability.

9.1.2 Dynamic versus Static Path Generation

Even when a program analysis is path-aware, the paths analyzed can be generated dynamically or statically. Dynamic path-aware analyses work by running a program on a set of test inputs, deriving traces of the execution, subsequently analyzing these traces to determine salient properties. In a static analysis, the program source is analyzed to determine the properties of the program. While dynamic analysis is precise with respect to the data analyzed, the quality of the analysis is critically dependent on the completeness of the test inputs. On the other hand, static analysis is totally independent of the test inputs. However, due to program abstractions, static analysis cannot always provide the same precision as dynamic analysis.

Thus, dynamic techniques suffer from the problem of *under approximation*, i.e., a set of predicates $\Theta_u = \{\pi_1, \pi_2, \ldots \pi_n\}$ is declared to hold before a call to procedure p even when only a subset of the predicates found in Θ_u are valid elements of p's precondition set; this is possible because not all possible paths to the call may have been examined, and these unexamined paths may invalidate the inclusion of some of the π_i in Θ_u.

Similarly, static techniques suffer from the problem of *over approximation*, i.e., a set of predicates Θ_o is considered to hold before a call to procedure p, even though other predicates (not present in Θ_o) should also be included; this is possible because a particular predicate that cannot be proven to hold along a certain path may result in its omission from Θ_o, even if that path is infeasible (e.g., the path follows a branch that could never be taken) or erroneous.

We elaborate on these points using the example shown in Figure 9.1. Before every call to procedure p, there are certain predicates that hold. For example, in Figure 9.1(a), there are two call-sites to p. There are two paths, labeled 1 and 2, to one of the call-sites; on path 1, predicate π_1 holds and on path 2, predicates π_1 and π_2 hold. There are three paths leading to the other call-site to p (the call-site on the right of Figure 9.1(a)); these paths are labeled 3, 4, and 5, with predicates π_1 and π_2 valid on paths 3 and 4, and π_2 valid on path 5. In a dynamic analysis scheme, if the paths 2, 3, and 4 are the only ones traversed, we may erroneously conclude that both π_1 and π_2 hold always before a call to procedure p. Note that this case is difficult to distinguish from the scenario illustrated in Figure 9.1(b) where π_1 and π_2 *indeed* form the precondition for p. Ensuring that the paths 1 and 5 in Figure 9.1(a) are traversed depends upon the comprehensiveness of the test suite.

The problem of *over approximation* is illustrated in Figure 9.1(c). Here, there is one infeasible path (path 5) to a call-site of p. A typical static analysis would conclude that one call to p (through paths 1 and 2) has a set of predicates that include π_1 and π_2. Because of the absence of π_2 on the infeasible path 5, the analysis would conclude that the other call to p (accessed through paths 3, 4, and 5) does not include π_1 and π_2.

9.1.3 Specification Inference

The process of inferring specifications from complex software systems forms the focus of this chapter. We describe a static inference mechanism for identifying the preconditions that must hold whenever a procedure is called. These preconditions may reflect both dataflow properties (e.g., whenever p is called, variable x must be non-null) as well as control-flow properties (e.g., every call to p must be preceded by a call to q). We derive these preconditions using a static inter-procedural path-sensitive dataflow analysis that gathers predicates at each program point. We apply mining techniques to these predicates to make specification inference robust to errors. This technique also allows us to derive higher-level specifications that abstract structural similarities

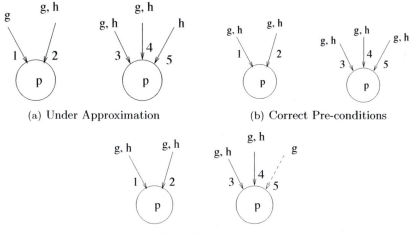

(a) Under Approximation   (b) Correct Pre-conditions

(c) Over Approximation

FIGURE 9.1: An example illustrating under- and over-approximation of predicates. (With kind permission from Springer Science + Business Media: Protocol Inference Using Static Path Profiles, SAS, 2008, pp. 78–92, M. Ramanthan et al., Figure 1.)

among predicates (e.g., procedure p is called immediately after a conditional test that checks whether *some* variable v is non-null). We describe an implementation of these techniques, and validate the effectiveness of the approach on a number of large open-source benchmarks. Experimental results confirm that our mining algorithms are efficient, and that the specifications derived are both precise and useful – the implementation discovers several critical, yet previously undocumented, preconditions for well-tested libraries.

9.1.4 Path Profiles

We also discuss a specification inference approach that typically mine commonalities among states at relevant program points. For example, to infer the invariants that must hold at all calls to a procedure p requires examining the state abstractions found at all call-sites to p. Unfortunately, existing approaches to building these abstractions require being able to explore all paths (either static or dynamic) to all of p's call-sites to derive specifications with any measure of confidence. Because programs that have complex control-flow structure may induce a large number of paths, naive path exploration is impractical. We examine a specification inference technique that allows us to efficiently explore *statically* all paths to a program point. Our approach builds *static path profiles*, profile information constructed by a static analysis that accumulates predicates valid along different paths to a program point. These profiles aim to combine the accuracy afforded by dynamic path analyses with the completeness guarantees available to static analysis.

To make our technique tractable, we employ a summarization scheme to merge predicates at join points based on the frequency with which they occur on different paths. For example, predicates present on a *majority* of static paths to *all* call-sites of any procedure p forms the pre-condition of p. Qualitative analysis indicates that it is more accurate than existing static mining techniques, can be used to derive useful specification even for APIs that occur infrequently (statically) in the program, and is robust against imprecision that may arise from examination of infeasible or infrequently occurring dynamic paths. A comparison of the specifications generated using this strategy with a dynamic specification inference engine indicates that static path profiles generate comparably precise specifications with smaller cost.

9.2   Specification Inference

Specifications for large software applications are often not known, or even when available, are often informal, imprecise, or incomplete. This is especially true for complex system software libraries. Clients must therefore either examine a library implementation to determine the appropriate constraints on arguments, or proactively perform error checks before making the call. Both approaches have obvious drawbacks, and neither work if the client is not even aware that a potential issue exists.

Ideally, we wish to statically infer specifications *transparently* without requiring programmer annotations. Specifically, we consider the problem of generating specifications that define *preconditions* for procedures – predicates that must always hold when the procedure is called. We consider two important classes of preconditions: control-flow predicates that define precedence properties among procedures (e.g., a call to `fgets` is always preceded by a call to `fopen`), and data-flow predicates that capture dataflow properties associated with variables (e.g., whenever `fgets` is called, pointer `fp` must not be null).

We define an inter-procedural, path-sensitive static analysis that identifies a collection of constraints whose solution defines potential preconditions. If procedure p has precondition π, it means that π holds on all *calls* to p. To compute preconditions, our analysis collects a predicate set along each distinct path to each call-site. To manage the size of this set, intersections of predicate sets are constructed at join points where distinct paths merge. Predicates computed within a procedure are memoized and are used to compute preconditions that capture inter-procedural control and dataflow information. To compute the preconditions of a procedure p, we consider the intersection of the predicate sets at each call-site to p.

There are several significant design issues that need to be resolved for the derived preconditions to have any practical significance. We observe that using simple set intersection on predicates is too fragile to yield interesting specifications in general. This is because the predicates generated are insufficiently abstract (e.g., "at a call to procedure p, variable x bound in p is read, and the contents of locations a and b allocated in p are compared"). The intersection of any set S with a set containing just these predicates would be non-empty only if S contained *identical* predicates, reflecting the same operations on the same variables and locations. To relax this limitation, we examine techniques that allow us to define *structural similarities* among predicate sets. Such similarities enable preconditions that specify properties which are abstracted over variable names, references, and values. We are thus able to define preconditions that define more abstract properties such as "procedure q is called whenever *some* integer variable v is greater than zero, and the contents of *some* pair of locations l_1 and l_2 holding a value of type τ are equal."

While the use of intersection guarantees safety by ensuring that derived preconditions for a procedure hold at all call-sites, it is not a robust mechanism in the presence of errors. An error that causes a predicate to be omitted along some path leading to a call to procedure p would result in the predicate not being included as part of p's preconditions. To address this concern, we employ frequent itemset and sequence mining on the predicates computed at each call-site to p, and use the predicates that are most frequently occurring as the preconditions for p. Like other mining-based approaches, we assume that errors violating invariants occur *infrequently*, thus making mining a feasible strategy to filter such deviations from the generated specifications.

9.2.1 Precedence Protocols

A particular important class of specifications is that which defines precedence protocols, a protocol that dictates the order in which different program components (such as functions) are executed. For example, a call to function pthread_mutex_init must be present upstream on any program path from a call to pthread_mutex_lock, since the former initializes data structures associated with the mutex into an initially unlocked state.[1] The precedence relation between pthread_mutex_init and pthread_mutex_lock forms a part of a precedence protocol that defines how these functions can be used in programs.

In some cases, precedence protocols are well specified. Certain groups of library functions,[2] (e.g., a call to accept should always be preceded by a call to bind and socket, a call to pthread_mutex_lock must always be preceded by

---

[1] Note that this precedence relation does not imply that every call to pthread_mutex_lock is preceded by a unique corresponding call to pthread_mutex_init; rather, it states that there must be some pthread_mutex_init upstream from the call-site.

[2] Our presentation throughout this chapter applies to both functions and procedures, and we use the two terms interchangeably.

a call to pthread_mutex_init, etc.), have well-understood relationships with one another. When precedence protocols are known, a variety of techniques can be employed to check that they are faithfully obeyed in programs [9,25,44]. In general, however, the relationships that exist among most functions in a program (especially non-library ones) are known only to the designers of those functions, and are rarely documented precisely.

Existing research on specification inference [3, 4, 8, 15, 16, 22, 28, 31, 33, 42, 43, 46] is based on the premise that commonly occurring patterns in analyzed programs are indicative of a likely specification. We further qualify this notion by deriving procedure call patterns that reflect call precedence relations. Like previous specification mining efforts, we assume that most programs are well written, and that call patterns which occur often are likely to be correct. Given these assumptions, we can define an inter-procedural path-sensitive static analysis that computes a collection of constraints whose solution defines potential precedence relations among procedure calls. These relations are of the form, "*a call to procedure q must always be preceded by a call to procedure p.*" The generated sequences can then be mined [2] based on a user-defined confidence level to obtain a set of precedence protocols.

```
181 RI_FKey_check(PG_FUNCTION_ARGS)
182 {
199    ri_CheckTrigger(...);
210    pk_rel = heap_open(...);
248    if (tgnargs == 4)
249    {
              // match_type not checked
250       ri_BuildQueryKeyFull(...);
294    }
296    match_type = ri_DetermineMatchType(...);
298    if (match_type == RI_MATCH_TYPE_PARTIAL)
299       ereport(...);
303    ri_BuildQueryKeyFull(...);
437 }
```

FIGURE 9.2: Extract from RI_FKey_check in postGreSQL-8.1.3.

To motivate the problem, consider the code fragment in Figure 9.2. This fragment shows part of procedure RI_FKey_check from postGreSQL, version 8.1.3. Observe that the call to ri_BuildQueryKeyFull at line 303 is preceded by calls to ri_DetermineMatchType, heap_open, and ri_CheckTrigger in this order. This pattern occurs at several other locations in the program. However, in one specific instance of the call to ri_BuildQueryKeyFull at line 250, the rule is not satisfied, as there is no call to ri_DetermineMatchType preceding it. The absence of this call is significant; if the match_type is

RI_MATCH_TYPE_PARTIAL, the call to `ri_BuildQueryKeyFull` is erroneous because the procedure does not handle arguments of this type. Path-aware analysis is *critical* to deriving these inferences.

9.2.2   Preceded-By and Followed-By Relations

In this chapter, we focus only on precedence properties ("a call to q must be *preceded* by a call to p"). Notably, our implementation does not consider constraints of the form "a call to p is *followed-by* a call to q." While useful in certain contexts, we observe that protocols of this form are less precise than precedence protocols, especially in the presence of non-local jumps, errors, and exceptions. A *precedence* relation captures the set of antecedent constraints (e.g., initialization invariants) that must be satisfied before a procedure call can be made; a *follows* relation captures the set of consequent actions (e.g., finalization invariants) that must occur after a procedure call is executed.

A precedence relation captures behavior that is guaranteed to occur if the protocol is properly obeyed (e.g., a call to `pthread_mutex_lock` must be preceded by a call to `pthread_mutex_init`). On the other hand, the fact that a forward relation is not satisfied does not necessarily imply that program behavior is incorrect. Consider the following snippet from some procedure p:

```
if((id = user_open(...)) == err) {
   print("error");
   return;
}
user_close(id);
```

Here, we cannot assert that every call to `user_open` will always be followed by a call to `user_close` because an error condition that occurs in the interim may lead to an abnormal exit from procedure p. On the other hand, if a call to `user_close` does take place, it is guaranteed that a preceding call to `user_open` would have occurred if the protocol were properly followed. This is a key insight that enables us to infer precise precedence protocols whose violation may signal the presence of a bug.

9.2.3   Dataflow Predicates

The other class of specifications we consider here are those involving *dataflow* properties. A dataflow property indicates value flow relationships among executed statements. These properties define constraints on the set of values a particular variable may contain at a specific program point (e.g., whenever f is called, pointer `fp` must not be null, or x is true whenever y > 10).

We motivate the issues using a real-world example – deriving a specification for the `bind` system call in the Linux `socket` library. While the application of our approach is in deriving specifications for undocumented procedures, it is

```
 main(...)
883    struct addrinfo *ai;
918    initialize_server_options(&options);
1075   fill_default_server_options(&options);
1272   for (ai=options.listen_addrs; ai;ai=ai->ai_next) {
1273     if(ai->ai_family != AF_INET && ai->ai_family != AF_INET6)
1274       continue;
1275     if (num_listen_socks >= MAX_LISTEN_SOCKS)
         . . .
1278     if ((ret = getnameinfo(...))) {
         . . .
1287     listen_sock = socket(ai->ai_family,...);
1289     if (listen_sock < 0) {
         . . .
1294     if (set_nonblock(listen_sock) == -1) {
         . . .
1302     if (setsockopt(...) == -1)
1304       error(''setsockopt SO_REUSEADDR: ...'');
1309     if (bind(listen_sock, ai->ai_addr, ai->ai_addrlen) < 0) {
         . . .
```

(a) `sshd.c`

```
}
991 ssh_control_listener(void)
993    struct sockaddr_un addr;
997    if (options.control_path == NULL ||
998      options.control_master == SSHCTL_MASTER_NO)
999        return;
1003   memset(&addr, 0, sizeof(addr));
1004   addr.sun_family = AF_UNIX;
1005   addr_len = offsetof(...)
1008   if (strlcpy(addr.sun_path, options.control_path,
1009   sizeof(addr.sun_path)) >= sizeof(addr.sun_path))
1010     fatal(''ControlPath too long'');
1012   if ((control_fd = socket(PF_UNIX,SOCK_STREAM, 0)) < 0)
1013     fatal(...);
1015   old_umask = umask(0177);
1016   if (bind(control_fd, (struct sockaddr*)&addr,addr_len) == -1) {
       . . .
```

(b) `ssh.c`

```
}
```

FIGURE 9.3: Code fragments of two different call-sites to **bind** in openssh-4.2p1.

illustrative to demonstrate the technique for a procedure such as `bind`, which has a well-documented interface. The `bind` system call takes three parameters, *viz.*, a socket descriptor (type: `int`), the local address to which the socket needs to bind (type: `struct sockaddr *`), and the length of the address (type: `socklen_t`). For a stream socket to start receiving connections, it needs to be assigned to an address, which is achieved by using `bind`. Summarizing the documentation, the necessary conditions that must hold before `bind` can be called are:

(a) A `socket` system call must have occurred.

(b) The return value of `socket` must have been checked for validity.

(c) The address (second parameter to `bind`) corresponds to a specific address family (e.g., AF_UNIX, AF_INET).

The first condition defines a precedence constraint, while the second and third define dataflow properties. Ideally, our goal is to obtain the above information by tracking various calls to `bind` in the source. Figure 9.3 shows code fragments of two procedures (out of eight, total) that invoke the `bind` system call in `openssh-4.2p1`.

Figure 9.3(a) shows a code fragment from the file `sshd.c` where `bind` is invoked from `main`. Before the call to `bind`, as per the documented requirements, observe that there is a call to `socket` on line 1287. The returned value `listen_socket` is checked to ensure that it is a valid descriptor, and the address is set (lines 1075 and 1272). In fact, in a convoluted chain, the procedure `fill_default_server_options` in `main` invokes `add_listen_addr`, which in turn invokes `add_one_listen_addr` where the address that is eventually used in `bind` is set. Apart from these known *requirements*, other operations dependent on the application context are also performed (e.g., the family of the address is checked in line 1273, the `num_listen_socks` is checked in line 1275, etc.). By observing just a single use of `bind` alone, we can generate some properties on the required operations before `bind` is called.

Table 9.1 shows the subset of properties generated for the corresponding `bind` call. For example, we observe a property where a variable `listen_sock` is assigned the return value of `socket`, has a value greater than or equal to 0, and is the first parameter in calls to `setsockopt` and `bind`. As explained earlier, these properties form some of the preconditions for calls to `bind`. However, not all properties generated before this `bind` call need to hold *always* before any other call to `bind`. For example, `ret` is assigned the return value of `getnameinfo` and is equal to 0 before the `bind` call. This property may be relevant in the context of calls to `bind` in `sshd.c`, but may not be relevant in calls made within other files. Unfortunately, simply examining this single call without any a priori knowledge of `bind`'s behavior would not permit us to discard this property from its specification.

TABLE 9.1:   A Subset of Predicates Associated with the **bind** Calls
Shown in Figure 9.3

sshd.c	
Variables	Attributes
(*ai).ai_addrlen	{(arg(3), bind)}
ai	{(:=, options.listen_addrs),($\neq$, 0) }
inetd_flag	{(=, 0)}
listen_sock	{(:=,**res**(socket)),($\geq$, 0),
	(arg(1), bind), (arg(1), setsockopt)}
num_listen_socks	{($<$, 16)}
ret	{(:=, **res**(getnameinfo)),(=, 0)}
ssh.c	
Variables	Attributes
addr.sun_family	{(:=, 1)}
addr_len	{(:=, **res**(strlen), (arg(3), bind)}
old_umask	{(:=, **res**(umask)))}
control_fd	{(:=, **res**(socket)),
	($\geq$, 0),(arg(1), bind)}
options.control_master	{($\neq$, 0)}
options.control_path	{($\neq$, 0)}

   To improve precision, we collect properties from other call sites to **bind**.
Figure 9.3(b) presents one such call site in procedure **ssh_control_listener**
in **ssh.c**. For this call, we obtain properties that include the known *requirements* (see lines 1004, 1005, 1012) and also shown in Table 9.1. We also obtain
other irrelevant operations (e.g., the control path is checked at line 997, size
of path checked in 1008, etc.). Based on the properties here and the properties
previously obtained with respect to the **bind** call in Figure 9.3(a), an *intersection* of the derived properties can be computed. By repeated application of
this process to each call to **bind** at other call-sites, we obtain the necessary
operations that *must* be performed before every call to **bind**.
   To summarize the example, observe that deriving the desired dataflow
conditions using *intersection* must account for the fact that (a) the names
of relevant variables in the two files are not comparable (e.g., **listen_sock**
in **sshd.c** and **control_fd** in **ssh.c**); (b) operations relevant to the bind
call (e.g., **listen_sock** $\geq$ 0 in **sshd.c** and ((**control_fd** = ...) $\geq$ 0) in
ssh.c) are interspersed with irrelevant operations; (c) the types of corresponding parameters to **bind** before casting are different (**struct sockaddr *** in
sshd.c and **struct sockaddr_un *** in **ssh.c**); (d) there is no fixed order
of calls to procedures setting the address family and the call to **socket** in
the two files and (e) there can be different number of attributes associated
with the corresponding variables across call-sites (e.g., **listen_sock** is used

as a parameter in `setsockopt` whereas `control_fd` does not have any such attribute).

9.2.4 Formalization

We formalize our informal discussion above by defining a simple, call-by-value language equipped with first-class procedures and references. Superscripts on expressions denote labels that are used in defining our analysis. The exact semantics for the language is standard and omitted here.

Informally, a `let`-expression binds x in e, $\lambda y.e'$ constructs a lexically scoped first-class procedure, $y(z)$ denotes call-by-value application, $\text{ref}(y)$ constructs a first-class reference cell that holds the value denoted by y, and $\text{deref}(y)$ extracts the value of the cell bound to y. The expression $(\text{set } x := y^{\ell_1} \text{ in } e^{\ell})^{\ell'}$ assigns the value of y to the cell bound to x, and continues with e. Bound and free variables are defined as usual. A program P is a closed expression, and $e^{\ell} \in P$ is true if e^{ℓ} is a subexpression of P.

In addition to the usual assumption that bound variables are distinct from free variables in different expressions, we also assume that all bound variables in a program are distinct. The *last* variable of an expression, which yields the expression's value, is defined as follows:

$$
\begin{aligned}
last(x^{\ell}) &= x^{\ell} \\
last((\text{let } x = t^{\ell_1} \text{ in } e^{\ell})^{\ell'}) &= last(e^{\ell}) \\
last((\text{set } x := y^{\ell_1} \text{ in } e^{\ell})^{\ell'}) &= last(e^{\ell})
\end{aligned}
$$

Our analysis is defined in two steps. First, we compute a flow analysis for the program, F, that associates with every variable and label, a set of *abstract values*. An abstract value is either a constant, a label corresponding to the definition point of a procedure (*abstract procedure*) or reference (*abstract location*), or a primitive operation paired with the abstract values of its arguments. Thus, given variable x, $F(x)$ (or $F(\ell)$, if given label ℓ) defines the set of procedures, constants, references, and primitive operations that x (or the expression with label ℓ) can denote during execution of the program. We do not present details of the analysis here, but any monovariant flow analysis in the spirit of [36, 40] suffices for our purpose.

A judgment is a three-place relation on specification maps, flows, and expressions. Thus, the judgment $\Delta \models_F e^{\ell}$ is read "Assuming a flow analysis F, expression e^{ℓ} has the preconditions defined by $\Delta(\ell)$." Given a flow function F, and program P, we are interested in the least specification map Δ for which the judgment holds.

Specification inference is defined by a collection of inference rules (see Figure 9.4) that leverages the result of the flow analysis. Each rule is of the form:

$$
\frac{c_1, \ldots, c_n}{\Delta \models_F e}
$$

SYNTAX:

$$
\begin{aligned}
e ::=\ & x^\ell\ | \\
& (\texttt{let } x = t^{\ell_1} \texttt{ in } e^\ell)^{\ell'}\ | \\
& (\texttt{set } x := y^{\ell_1} \texttt{ in } e^\ell)^{\ell'} \\
t ::=\ & c\ |\ \lambda x.e\ |\ x(y)\ | \\
& (\texttt{if } x \texttt{ then } e_1^{\ell_t} \texttt{ else } e_2^{\ell_f})\ | \\
& \texttt{ref}(x)\ |\ \texttt{deref}(x)\ | \\
& \texttt{op}(x_1, \ldots, x_n)
\end{aligned}
$$

DOMAINS:

$$
\begin{aligned}
F &\in Flow = Var + Label \to AVal \\
\hat{v} &\in AVal = \mathcal{P}(Label + Constant + \\
& \qquad\qquad Op(AVal \times \ldots \times AVal)) \\
\Delta &\in SpecMap = Label \to \mathcal{P}(Pred) \\
\Lambda &\in ProcMap = Label \to Label \\
\pi &\in Pred = \\
& \mathsf{read}(Label, AVal) + \mathsf{write}(Label, AVal) + \\
& \mathsf{alloc}(Label, AVal) + \mathsf{bind}(Var, AVal) + \\
& \mathsf{cbind}(Var, AVal) + \mathsf{call}(Label \leftarrow Label)
\end{aligned}
$$

(BIND)
$$\frac{\Delta(\ell') \cup \{\mathsf{bind}(x, \{c\})\} \subseteq \Delta(\ell)}{\Delta \models_F (\texttt{let } x = c^{\ell_1} \texttt{ in } e^\ell)^{\ell'}}$$

(REF)
$$\frac{\Delta(\ell') \cup \{\mathsf{alloc}(\ell_1, F(y)), \mathsf{bind}(x, \ell_1)\} \subseteq \Delta(\ell)}{\Delta \models_F (\texttt{let } x = \texttt{ref}(y)^{\ell_1} \texttt{ in } e^\ell)^{\ell'}}$$

(WRITE)
$$\frac{\begin{array}{c} S = \{\mathsf{write}(\ell_i, F(y)) \mid \ell_i \in F(x),\ \texttt{ref}(z)^{\ell_i} \in P\} \\ \Delta(\ell') \cup \{S\} \subseteq \Delta(\ell) \end{array}}{\Delta \models_F (\texttt{set } x := y^{\ell_1} \texttt{ in } e^\ell)^{\ell'}}$$

(PRIM)
$$\frac{\Delta(\ell') \cup \{\mathsf{bind}(x, \texttt{op}(F(x_1), \ldots, F(x_n)))\} \subseteq \Delta(\ell)}{\Delta \models_F (\texttt{let } x = \texttt{op}(x_1, \ldots, x_n)^{\ell_1} \texttt{ in } e^\ell)^{\ell'}}$$

(READ)
$$\frac{\begin{array}{c} S = \{\mathsf{read}(\ell_i, F(\ell_i)), \mathsf{bind}(x, F(\ell_i)) \mid \ell_i \in F(y) \wedge \texttt{ref}(z)^{\ell_i} \in P\} \\ \Delta(\ell') \cup \{S\} \subseteq \Delta(\ell) \end{array}}{\Delta \models_F (\texttt{let } x = \texttt{deref}(y)^{\ell_1} \texttt{ in } e^\ell)^{\ell'}}$$

(IF)
$$\frac{\begin{array}{c} \Delta(\ell') \cup \{\mathsf{cbind}(y, \mathsf{true})\} \subseteq \Delta(\ell_t) \\ \Delta(\ell') \cup \{\mathsf{cbind}(y, \mathsf{false})\} \subseteq \Delta(\ell_f) \\ \Delta\ell' \cup (\Delta(\ell_t) \cap \Delta(\ell_f)) \cup \{\mathsf{bind}(x, F(\ell_1))\} \subseteq \Delta(\ell) \end{array}}{\Delta \models_F (\texttt{let } x = (\texttt{if } y \texttt{ then } e_1^{\ell_t} \texttt{ else } e_2^{\ell_f})^{\ell_1} \texttt{ in } e^\ell)^{\ell'}}$$

(ABS)
$$\frac{\begin{array}{c} \bigcap\{\Delta(\ell_i) \mid (\texttt{let } z_i = x_i(y_i) \texttt{ in } e_i)^{\ell_i}, \ell_1 \in F(x)\} \subseteq \Delta(\ell_1) \\ \{\mathsf{bind}(w, \hat{v}) \mid (\texttt{let } z_i = x_i(y_i) \texttt{ in } e_i)^{\ell_i}, \ell_1 \in F(x), \hat{v} = \cap(F(y_i))\} \subseteq \Delta(\ell_b) \\ \Delta(\ell') \cup \{\mathsf{bind}(x, \ell_1)\} \subseteq \Delta(\ell) \end{array}}{\Delta \models_F (\texttt{let } x = (\lambda w.e_b^{\ell_b})^{\ell_1} \texttt{ in } e^\ell)^{\ell'}}$$

(APP)
$$\frac{\begin{array}{c} S = \{\ell_j \mid \ell_i \in F(y) \wedge (\lambda w_i.e_i)^{\ell_i} \in P \wedge e_j^{\ell_j} = last(e_i)\} \\ \Delta(\ell') \cup \{\mathsf{call}(\Lambda(\ell_1) \leftarrow \ell_i) \mid \\ \ell_i \in F(y) \wedge (\lambda w_i.e_i)^{\ell_i} \in P\} \cup \{\bigcap\{\Delta(\ell_j) \mid \ell_j \in S\} \cup \{\mathsf{bind}(x, S)\} \subseteq \Delta(\ell) \end{array}}{\Delta \models_F (\texttt{let } x = y(z)^{\ell_1} \texttt{ in } e^\ell)^{\ell'}}$$

FIGURE 9.4: Specification inference via flow analysis.

where the consequent defines a judgment whose validity depends upon the satisfiability of the constraints defined by the antecedent. The constraints impose restrictions on the structure of the specification map Δ, a map that identifies a set of preconditions with every program point.

A precondition π of an expression e defines an action or predicate that *must* hold prior to e's execution. Our analysis tracks a number of such actions; these actions are defined with respect to the abstract values computed for each expression in the program by the flow analysis. Thus, an action of the form $\mathsf{read}(\ell, \hat{v})$ asserts that a reference created at label ℓ holding the abstract value $\hat{v}$ is read; $\mathsf{write}(\ell, \hat{v})$ asserts a similar condition for reference assignment; and $\mathsf{alloc}(\ell, \hat{v})$ holds if in an expression $\mathtt{ref}(z)^\ell \in P$ and $F(z) = \hat{v}$. In the same vein, $\mathsf{bind}(x, \hat{v})$ is true whenever variable x is bound to e^ℓ and $F(\ell)$ is $\hat{v}$, and $\mathsf{cbind}(x, \hat{v})$ is used to express predicates that reflect if-splitting of flow values across conditionals; finally, $\mathsf{call}(\ell_1 \leftarrow \ell_2)$ is used to capture control-flow precedence relationships among procedure calls – it holds whenever a procedure with label ℓ_2 is invoked *after* an invocation of a procedure with label ℓ_1, with no intervening invocation of any other procedure.

The rules for expressions that bind constants and primitive operations are straightforward. The preconditions of the expression in the `let`-body within which the binding occurs include the preconditions of the `let` expression, as well as a precondition that reflects the existence of the new binding. If a variable is bound in a `let`-expression to the result of a call to a primitive operation, the preconditions of the expression in the `let`-body must include this action; the values of the arguments to the primitive are approximated by the abstract values of the operation's arguments as determined by the flow analysis.

A reference binding induces a precondition on the `let`-body that includes both the binding as well as a predicate that captures the reference creation. Since references are first-class, a variable occurrence may be bound to many different references during its lifetime. In an expression of the form,

$$(\,\mathtt{let}\ x\ =\ \mathtt{deref}(y)^{\ell_1}\ \mathtt{in}\ e^\ell)^{\ell'}$$

consider the set of references that y may be bound to (defined by $F(y)$). Each element in this set contains a label ℓ corresponding to a reference expression $\mathtt{ref}(z)$ found in the program. The precondition for e^ℓ must therefore include predicates that reflect the potential read of each such location, and predicates that reflect the binding of x to the contents of these locations. Assignment expressions are defined similarly, with write predicates replacing reads as a consequence of the operation. The preconditions following a conditional include the intersection of the specification sets of the two branches; within these branches, an action that reflects the value of the Boolean guard is included as part of the precondition associated with the respective branches.

We now describe the rules dealing with procedure abstraction and call. The precondition associated with the procedure body is defined as the intersection of a collection of sets, each of which represents the specifications extant at a specific (distinct) call point to the procedure. Thus, the specifications defining the entry to a procedure reflect the common preconditions extant at every call point to the procedure. For example, the specification associated with the entry to the procedure body defines a predicate that relates the formal parameter to an abstract value. This value is constructed as the intersection of the abstract values (set of labels, constants, etc.) of the actual parameters to the procedure. Similarly, the intersection of the set of preconditions that exist at each such call defines the smallest set of predicates that is guaranteed to hold whenever the procedure is called.

A procedure call $y(z)$ is defined similarly. Its definition relies on an auxiliary procedure Λ that given the label of an expression $e^\ell \in P$ returns the label of the closest enclosing λ, if one exists, and the distinguished label ℓ_{main}, otherwise. If the set of procedures that y may be associated with is P_y (as determined by our flow analysis), then the intersection of the specifications extant upon *exit* from each procedure $p \in P_y$ defines the conditions present upon exit from the call guaranteed to hold for all procedures p that may be invoked at this call. Observe that these rules are slightly different from typical static analyses that would consider the definition of the procedure independently from its call-sites. This is because preconditions that hold at the entry to a procedure p depend upon the conditions extant at all call-sites to p; similarly, the invariants that hold upon completion of a call depend upon the invariants extant at the return point of all procedures that could be invoked at that call.

As currently defined, the preconditions associated with each program point are constructed by simple unions and intersections of abstract value sets computed by an inter-procedural dataflow analysis. It is straightforward to see that the predicates computed represent a conservative summary of the information present in the flow function.

```
let r = λ z. ref(z)^ℓ1
    ...
    g1 = λ c1. let y1 = λ w. ref(w)^ℓ2    g2 = λ c2. let x1 = ref(c2)^ℓ3
                   y2 = r(c1)                            x2 = λ w'. ...
                   y3 = y1(y2)                              ref(w')^ℓ4 ...
                   y4 = deref(y3)                        x3 = ref(c3)^ℓ5
                   y5 = deref(y2)                        x4 = x2(c4)
               in ... op1(y2, y3)            in ... op2(x1, x4)
                  ... op2(y4, y3)               ... op1(x3, x1)
                  ... set y2 := c1 in f(...)    ... set x3 := c3 in ...
                                                            f(...)
```

FIGURE 9.5: A program fragment illustrating the need for structural matching of predicates. Syntactic sugar is used to simplify the examples.

There are two interesting issues to note about the analysis. First, a predicate is recorded as part of a precondition at a program point *only if* the

$$\text{alloc}(\ell_1, \{\,\mathsf{c}\,\}) \qquad \text{alloc}(\ell_3, \{\,\mathsf{c}\,\})$$
$$\text{read}(\ell_1, \{\,\mathsf{c}_1\,\}) \qquad \text{alloc}(\ell_4, \{\,\mathsf{c}_4\,\})$$
$$\text{write}(\ell_1, \{\,\mathsf{c}\,\}) \qquad \text{alloc}(\ell_5, \{\,\mathsf{c}_3\,\})$$
$$\text{alloc}(\ell_2, \{\ell_1\}) \qquad \text{write}(\ell_5, \{\,\mathsf{c}_3\,\})$$
$$\text{read}(\ell_2, \{\ell_1\})$$
$$\text{op}_2(\{\ell_1\}, \{\ell_2\}) \qquad \text{op}_2(\{\ell_3\}, \{\ell_4\})$$
$$\text{op}_1(\{\ell_1\}, \{\ell_2\}) \qquad \text{op}_1(\{\ell_3\}, \{\ell_5\})$$

$$(a) \qquad\qquad\qquad (b)$$

FIGURE 9.6: A subset of the preconditions that hold prior to the call to procedure f in procedure g_1 (a) and procedure g_2 (b).

predicate occurs on all paths to that point. Consider a module whose designer expects certain preconditions to hold when procedures defined within the module are called. Our analysis would certainly infer these preconditions for correctly written programs, but fail to identify the desired specification in the presence of errors that result in the omission of some of these legitimate predicates. The ability of the analysis to derive meaningful specifications in the presence of errors is consequently poor. There is an obvious conundrum here, given that the inferred specifications are derived from a program source that potentially contains bugs, and can thus potentially compromise the integrity of the specifications themselves.

Second, the intersection of precondition sets fails to consider structural equivalence among predicates. In particular, our specification language does not permit predicates to be abstracted over an arbitrary set of locations, names, or constants. To illustrate this, consider the program fragments shown in Figure 9.5. We are interested in the specification that should be inferred for the entry to procedure f based on the preconditions extant at its two call-sites in g_1 and g_2. Suppose g_1 and g_2 are called from the following expression:

if *pred* then g_1(c) else g_2(c)

At the calls to f in procedures g_1 and g_2, there are a number of preconditions that hold. Ignoring predicates that describe variable bindings, the most interesting are those related to abstract locations ℓ_1 and ℓ_2 (see Figure 9.6(a)) allocated and accessed by procedure g_1 and abstract locations ℓ_3, ℓ_4, and ℓ_5 accessed by procedure g_2 (see Figure 9.6(b)).

Based on the structure of the rules, we would conclude that no interesting preconditions exist that are common to both calls since the sets of locations manipulated by the two procedures are disjoint. This is clearly overly conservative.

For example, it is the case that prior to both calls (i) two locations are allocated and used in operation op_2 (ℓ_1 and ℓ_2 in procedure g_1, and ℓ_3 and ℓ_4 in procedure g_2), and (ii) the contents of one of these locations (ℓ_1 in g_1 and ℓ_3 in g_2) hold the constant c. By "unifying" ℓ_1 and ℓ_3, and ℓ_2 and ℓ_4, we derive the preconditions for f: "there exist a pair of locations (call them a and b) such that a and b are used as arguments in an operation op_2, and hold the constant c."

Surprisingly, by considering an alternative mapping of locations in the two calls, we can deduce another equally valid specification. Prior to both calls it is also the case that (i) two locations are allocated (ℓ_1 and ℓ_2 in g_1, and ℓ_3 and ℓ_5 in g_2) and used in operation op_1; and (ii) one location is written with a constant (ℓ_1 in g_1 and ℓ_5 in g_2).

To extract commonalities such as those among sets of predicates extant at the two calls requires us to match locations, names, and constants across these different sets. As the example illustrates, there are potentially many such matches that can be constructed. Of course, some commonalities could be extracted by examining the body of f, but this would compromise scalability and modularity. Other commonalities can be derived by examining f's signature, the types of values stored in these locations, etc. We exploit some of these heuristics in our implementation.

Our current formulation fails to identify any of them because it does not abstract these components in the sets it constructs. Since the rules that define procedure abstraction and application compute preconditions based on simple intersection of predicates from different call-sites or procedures, respectively, they do not effectively deal with (a) programs that may have bugs (and thus fail to reflect necessary preconditions along some paths) and (b) programs which invoke a procedure at different call-sites whose preconditions at these sites share only structural similarities. To address these limitations, we require a more expressive matching operation than one based on simple set intersection.

As we show in the next section, simply enumerating the set of all possible matches over the predicate sets used to define preconditions is infeasible. We therefore consider an alternate strategy to identify matches among the precondition sets computed at different call-sites (or among procedures called at the same call-site) inspired by data mining techniques. As we shall discuss, these approaches sacrifice optimality for scalability and efficiency; our experimental results reveal that they yield surprisingly valuable specifications even in the presence of complex control- and data-flow, even in the presence of bugs that result in invariants being omitted along certain program paths.

9.2.5   Incorporating Mining

To make our discussion more concrete, consider the program fragment shown in Figure 9.7.

This code fragment is from the procedure add_listen_addr found in file serverconf.c from openssh 4.2p1. This procedure is called from the procedure fill_default_server_options, which in turn precedes a call to bind. In the body of the procedure, there are several calls to add_one_listen_addr, which is responsible for setting an address family, eventually supplied as the

```
399  add_listen_addr(ServerOptions *options,
                      char *addr, u_short port)
400  {
403    if (options->num_ports == 0)
404      options->ports[options->num_ports++]
                                 = SSH_DEFAULT_PORT;
407    if (port == 0)
408      for (i = 0; i < options->num_ports; i++)
409        add_one_listen_addr(options,
                            addr, options->ports[i]);
410    else
411      add_one_listen_addr(options, addr, port);
412  }
```

FIGURE 9.7: A code fragment taken from `openssh-4.2p1`.

second argument to `bind`. There are a number of different ways in which a call to `add_one_listen_addr` can take place. For example, when `port == 0` and `options->num_ports` is less than one, the call does not happen. It so happens that lines 403 and 404 reveal that this situation cannot arise, and thus the loop must be executed at least once whenever `port` is zero. Unfortunately, in the absence of a theorem prover or model checker [17] that can assert `options->num_ports` is always greater than zero at line 407 because of the operations performed at lines 403 and 404, we must conclude that it is not always the case that `add_one_listen_addr` is called from `add_listen_addr`, and thus, the second argument to `bind` need not always be set to a specific address family. Even if there are no bugs in the program, limitations of the analysis in determining a precise set of feasible paths can be overcome using mining techniques. By mining the set of predicates computed along different paths to `bind` calls, we discover that it is only along one path (namely, the infeasible one described above) that the second argument to bind is not set to an address family. By setting confidence thresholds appropriately, the absence of this predicate would not be considered a critical omission, and the predicate asserting that the second argument to bind is always set would be recorded as part of `bind`'s preconditions.

9.2.5.1   Mining Strategies

Recall that our analysis collects control-flow and dataflow predicates. The elements in a set of dataflow predicates have no ordering relationship among one another. Control-flow predicates, on the other hand, do reflect a specific ordering: each element represents a procedure call, and the order of calls defines a precedence relation. We use frequent itemset mining to derive preconditions for dataflow predicate sets, and subsequence mining to derive preconditions for control-flow predicates.

```
void c1() {          void c2() {          void c3() {          void c4() {
  if(packets > 0)      if(packets > 0)      if(packets > 0)      if(packets > 0)
    pack_flag =          size =               i = 0;               i = 0;
true;                MIN_SIZE;              pack_flag =          size =
    size =               buf =            true;                MAX_SIZE;
MAX_SIZE;            allocbuf(size);        size =               buf =
    buf =                if(buf =         MIN_SIZE;            allocbuf(size);
allocbuf(size);      NULL)                  buf =                while(1 =
    readbuf(buf,         while(1 =        allocbuf(size);      lock(buf));
size);               lock(buf));            if(buf =             readbuf(buf,
    ...                               NULL)                size);
    ...              readbuf(buf,           while(1 =            ...
    ...              size);           lock(buf));            ...
    ...                ...                                      ...
}                      ...              readbuf(buf,         }
                       ...              size);
                     }                     ...

                                          }
      (a) c1              (b) c2              (c) c3              (d) c4
```

FIGURE 9.8: Illustrative example.

Frequent Itemset Mining. To obtain a specification on predicates where ordering is not critical, we use maximal frequent itemset mining [11]. In this technique, there is assumed to be a set of *transactions*; each transaction contains a collection of elements. The elements that occur in at least n transactions, where n is a confidence threshold specified by the user, is a frequent itemset. For our application, a transaction is a call-site and the set of predicates that hold at the call-site form the elements of the transaction.

We illustrate the mining process using the code fragments shown in Figure 9.8. We observe that there are four different call-sites to function **readbuf** and each call-site is preceded by a number of operations. For ease of understanding, we use the same names for the associated variables across call-sites. Based on the operations preceding each call to **readbuf**, a number of properties are gleaned and are shown in Table 9.2. Observe that there are four[3] transactions, equal to the number of call-sites of **readbuf** in the example. For example, observe that there are six items for transaction c3. Each item is composed of multiple attributes (e.g., the item associated with variable 1 has two attributes, *viz.*, 1 is assigned the return value of **lock(buf)** and is equal to 0 before the call to **readbuf**). When the frequent items are extracted at confidence 75%, we obtain the following specification:

packets: {>,0}

---

[3]Each transaction encodes properties on all possible paths to the call-site.

TABLE 9.2: Transactions Associated with Calls to **readbuf** Shown in Figure 9.8

Variables	Transactions	
	c1	c2
packets	$\{(>, 0)\}$	$\{(>, 0)\}$
pack_flag	$\{(:=, \textbf{true})\}$	
size	$\{(:=, \text{MAX\_SIZE}),$	$\{(:=, \text{MIN\_SIZE}),$
	$(\textbf{arg}(1), \textbf{allocbuf}),$	$(\textbf{arg}(1), \textbf{allocbuf}),$
	$(\textbf{arg}(2), \textbf{readbuf})\}$	$(\textbf{arg}(2), \textbf{readbuf})\}$
buf	$\{(:=, \textbf{res}(\textbf{allocbuf})),$	$\{(:=,\textbf{res}(\textbf{allocbuf})), (\neq, 0),$
	$(\textbf{arg}(1), \textbf{readbuf})\}$	$(\textbf{arg}(1), \textbf{lock}),$
		$(\textbf{arg}(1), \textbf{readbuf})\}$
l		$\{(=, 0), (:=,\textbf{res}(\textbf{lock}))\}$
i		

Variables	Transactions	
	c3	c4
packets	$\{(>, 0)\}$	$\{(>, 0)\}$
pack_flag		$\{(:=,\textbf{true})\}$
size	$\{(:=, \text{MIN\_SIZE}),$	$\{(:=, \text{MAX\_SIZE}),$
	$(\textbf{arg}(1), \textbf{allocbuf}),$	$(\textbf{arg}(1), \textbf{allocbuf}),$
	$(\textbf{arg}(2), \textbf{readbuf})\}$	$(\textbf{arg}(2), \textbf{readbuf})\}$
buf	$\{(:=,\textbf{res}(\textbf{allocbuf})), (\neq, 0),$	$\{(:=, \textbf{res}(\textbf{allocbuf})), (\neq, 0),$
	$(\textbf{arg}(1), \textbf{lock}),$	$(\textbf{arg}(1), \textbf{lock}),$
	$(\textbf{arg}(1), \textbf{readbuf})\}$	$(\textbf{arg}(1), \textbf{readbuf})\}$
l	$\{(=, 0), (:=, \textbf{res}(\textbf{lock}))\}$	$\{(=, 0), (:=, \textbf{res}(\text{lock}))\}$
i	$\{(:= 0)\}$	$\{(:= 0)\}$

size: $\{(\textbf{arg}(1), \textbf{allocbuf}), (\textbf{arg}(2), \textbf{readbuf})\}$
l: $\{(=,0), (:=,\textbf{res}(\textbf{lock}))\}$
buf: $\{(\textbf{arg}(1), \textbf{lock}), (\textbf{arg}(1), \textbf{readbuf}),$
$(\neq,0), (:=,\textbf{res}(\textbf{allocbuf}))\}$

Depending upon on the level of precision required by the user, the above mining technique can be easily translated into the more restrictive intersection technique by simply fixing n to be the total number of call-sites (confidence = 100%).

Sequence Mining. For control-flow predicates, frequent itemset mining does not suffice since the order of elements in the transaction is not considered. For deriving precedence relations [37], we use sequence mining [2]. A sequence mining algorithm takes as input a set of sequences (I), a user-defined confidence threshold, and outputs a set (S) of sequences that occur as subsequences in a minimum fraction (as specified by the confidence threshold) of input sequences. Observe that if a subsequence s is frequently occurring, all subsequences of s also occur at least as frequently as s. Therefore, we consider only maximal subsequences, i.e., it must be the case that every sequence(s_i) in S is not a subsequence of any other sequence present in S.

For example, if the set of sequences is given by $\{(a \leftarrow b \leftarrow c \leftarrow e)$, $(a \leftarrow d \leftarrow c \leftarrow e)$, $(d \leftarrow a \leftarrow c \leftarrow e)$, $(a \leftarrow c \leftarrow d \leftarrow e \leftarrow f)$, $(e \leftarrow f \leftarrow d \leftarrow c \leftarrow a)\}$, a sequence miner detects $(a \leftarrow c \leftarrow e)$ as a frequently occurring subsequence. Observe that the same set of transactions without ordering in frequent itemset mining would generate the set $\{$a, c, d, e$\}$. For our application, a transaction corresponds to a call-site and the sequence within a transaction corresponds to the sequence of procedure calls that occurred before the call-site. Our implementation uses the Apriori-all algorithm by Agrawal and Srikant [2], which is known to scale to over a million sequences. For the example shown in Figure 9.8, we generate the specification `allocbuf ← lock ← readbuf`.

9.2.5.2   The Structural Similarity Problem

In Figure 9.8, the names of the variables are the same across multiple call-sites whereas this does not hold in real programs (as noted earlier in this section). In other words, as discussed earlier, predicates computed along different paths may share structural, if not syntactic, similarities. In order to capture such similarities, a technique to determine the locations, names, values, etc. that can be abstracted uniformly among different sets is necessary.

Consider every predicate expression as being mapped to a set of locations. Thus, assume a set of location sets,

$$\{L_1 = \{\ell_{11}, \ell_{12}, ...\ell_{1m_1}\}, L_2 = \{\ell_{21}, \ell_{22}, ...\ell_{2m_2}\}, ..., L_k = \{\ell_{k1}, \ell_{k2}, ...\ell_{1m_k}\}\}$$

where L_i corresponds to locations associated with predicates that reach call-site i of procedure P. Now, for every element in L_i, we wish to find a corresponding element in every other L_j such that the cumulative matching of the attribute sets for such a mapping is *maximal*. Given three sets A, B, and C, we say A and B match maximally, if and only if $\mid A \cap B \mid$ is greater than $\mid A \cap C \mid$ or $\mid B \cap C \mid$.

Theorem 1. *The maximal matching problem as stated above is NP-hard.*

Proof By reduction from maximal bipartite $(k, *)$-clique in a bipartite graph [23, 45].

Fortunately, there are a number of heuristics that can be employed to map locations based on semantic information available within programs. We describe below heuristics that match the attribute sets across multiple call-sites that we have used in our implementation.

- **Type:** Attribute sets can be divided based on the type of variable. e.g., two variables, x and y with attributes $[$x: $\{(:=, $ true$)\}]$ and $[$y: $\{(>, 20)\}]$ can never be matched.

- **Parameter:** If variables are supplied as arguments to the same parameter for a given procedure at different call-sites, their attributes can be matched. Note, however, that while using positional parameter information for the purposes of matching may be a useful heuristic, other variables that are not used as parameters, but nevertheless are significant as preconditions, need to be detected as well (e.g., matching attribute sets associated with ℓ in Figure 9.8).

- **Result:** Variables that are assigned the return values of the same function can have their attribute sets matched.

- **Points-to set:** If more attribute sets are present and are unmatched, then pointer analysis is applied to group them.

By using these heuristics, we are able to prune down the number of possible matchings significantly. Available algorithms easily scale to the sizes of the pruned location sets.

9.2.6 Implementation

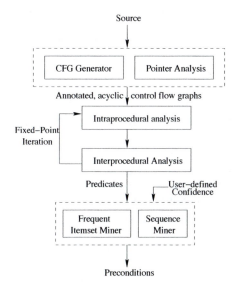

FIGURE 9.9: Software architecture.

Our implementation (see Figure 9.9) takes as input the program source and a user-defined confidence level for determining when a property should form part of a precondition. We first generate the control-flow graph for each procedure using an efficient program analysis tool [6]. The direction of all edges in the control flow graph are reversed, since we are interested in constructing preconditions. Furthermore, all back edges in the control flow graph

```
let a = λ argₐ. let ptr = ref(...) in p(...)
   in ...

let mkptr = λ z. let ptr = ref(...) in ...
   b = λ arg_b. ... mkptr(...) ... p(...)
   in ...

let mkptr = λz. let ptr = ref(...) in ...
   e = λ arg_e. ... mkptr(...)
   c = λ arg_c. ... e (...) ... p (...)
   in ...
```

FIGURE 9.10: Example showing the need for FPA evaluation.

(corresponding to the while loops) are removed. This is because when computing preconditions, the predicates that hold as part of the back edge are uninteresting, since they are not guaranteed to always occur (i.e., the loop may not be processed as the loop guard may evaluate to false). The graphs obtained are fed into the intra-procedural analysis framework, which builds the initial set of predicates. These data are processed by the inter-procedural analysis framework iteratively until a fixed-point is reached.

There are two categories of fixed-point iterations that are essential for generating predicates that cross multiple function boundaries. One iteration (FPA – Fixed Point Iteration A) corresponds to the set of tasks accomplished when a procedure is invoked and which are at a lower level of the invocation tree and the other iteration (FPB – Fixed Point Iteration B) corresponds to the set of operations performed before a call to the procedure. We discuss this issue in detail.

Figure 9.10 presents an example for FPA. From the example, it is clear that calls to procedures a, b, and c always allocate a pointer variable and then call procedure p. Furthermore, procedure mkptr always allocates the pointer variable. To reduce redundant computation of these properties, we maintain a memoization table for each of the procedures in the source, and update the information iteratively until fixed point is reached.

Observe that while the above fixed point iteration accumulates facts in one direction (down the call graph invocation path toward the leaves), there is a necessity for fixed point computation in the reverse direction as well (toward the root in the call graph). Consider the example shown in Figure 9.11. It is clear that before p is invoked, apart from the pointer being allocated, cond is always true. However, to obtain this information, a fixed point iteration (FPB) in the direction toward the root of the call graph needs to be performed.

Figure 9.12 presents pseudo-code describing details on building the control and data flow predicates, apart from computing procedure summaries (memoization tables) used in FPA. The algorithm follows closely from the analysis formalized in Figure 9.4. At the end of FPA, a set of predicates (data_precond

```
let x = λ arg_x. if cond then a(...) else ...
    in ...

let y = λ arg_y. if cond then b(...) else c(...)
    in ...

let call_y = λ arg_k. if cond then y(...)
    in ...
```

FIGURE 9.11: Example showing the need for FPB evaluation.

---

procedure BUILDPREDICATES
　　▷ **Input**: G(V,E), directed, acyclic (reversed) CFG of α;
　　　　　　V is topologically sorted;
　　▷ **Output**: true if dflow or cflow changes from previous
　　　　　　iteration for any node in V; false otherwise;
　　▷ **Auxiliary Information**:
　　　　　LCS: longest common subsequence of multiple strings;
　　　　　data_predicates(i): data predicates generated at i;
　　　　　concat(i,j,k): concatenates strings i, j, k;
　　　　　CALLSITE(i): true if i is a callsite;
　　　　　RETURN(i): true if i is the exit node from procedure α;

```
1    for each node i = 1 to |V|
2        for all neighbors j of i
3            in_data_flow(i) ← ∩dflow(j)
4            in_control_flow(i) ← LCS(cflow(j))
5        dflow(i) ← in_data_flow(i) ∪ data_predicates(i)
6        if CALLSITE(i) is true then
7            dflow(i) ← dflow(i) ∪ data_signature[func(i)]
8            cflow(i) ← concat(cflow(i), func(i),
9                            control_signature[func(i)])
10       if RETURN(i) is true then
11           data_signature[α] ← dflow(i)
12           control_signature[α] ← cflow(i)
```

FIGURE 9.12: Algorithm for building predicates.

and `control_precond`) for all the procedures in the program are obtained. Figure 9.13 presents the pseudo-code that performs the mining process that forms part of FPB iteration. There are two mining implementations that we use in our approach – a frequent item-set miner [11] on dataflow predicates, where ordering is not necessary, and a sequence miner [2] for controlflow predicates. At the end of FPB, the preconditions for the procedures are obtained.

---

procedure CONCATPREDICATES
    ▷ **Input**: α: a procedure in the program;
                $C = \{c_1, c_2, ...c_n\}$ is the set of call sites of α;
                $E = \{e_1, e_2, ...e_n\}$ is the set of enclosing procedures
                for respective call sites;
    ▷ **Output**: `true` if `dflow_precond` or `cflow_precond`
                changes from previous iteration; `false` otherwise;
    ▷ **Auxiliary Information**:
        `in_control_flow`(c_i): see Figure 9.12
        `concat`(i,j,k): concatenates strings i, j, k;

```
1    for each node c_i
2        dflow_t(c_i) ← dflow(c_i) ∪ dflow_precond[e_i]
3        cflow_t(c_i) ← concat( cflow_precond[e_i],
                                 in_control_flow(c_i), -)
4    Input dflow_t for all c_i into the frequent itemset miner
5    dflow_precond[α] ← result of Step 4
6    Input cflow_t for all c_i into the sequence miner
7    cflow_precond[α] ← result of Step 6
```

FIGURE 9.13: Mining preconditions.

9.2.7   Experimental Results

We validate our ideas on selected benchmark sources, with a view to demonstrating its scalability and effectiveness. We extract preconditions for seven sources: `apache`, `linux`, `openssh`, `osip`, `postgreSQL`, `procmail` and `zebra`. Specific details relating to the sources are provided in Table 9.3. The size of selected benchmarks varies from 9K to 1.98MLoc. Since default configurations are used to compile these sources, we believe that the number of control flow nodes represents a more reliable indicator of effective source size than lines of code. The number of control flow nodes ranges from 16K to 958K. We also present the number of procedures examined, the number of precedence and dataflow protocols discovered, and analysis times in Table. 9.4.

We implemented our tool in C++ and perform experiments on a Linux 2.6.11.10 (Gentoo release 3.3.4-r1) system running on an Intel(R) Pentium(R)

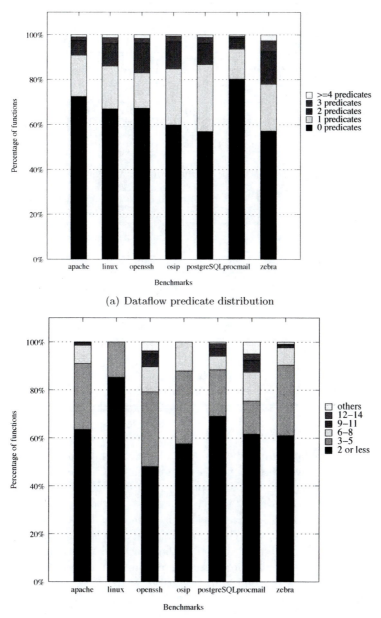

(a) Dataflow predicate distribution

(b) Control-flow predicate distribution

FIGURE 9.14: Predicate distributions.

TABLE 9.3:   Benchmark Information

Source	Version	LoC	CFG nodes	Procedure count
apache	2.2.3	273K	102K	2079
linux	2.2.26	1.98M	958K	7465
openssh	4.2p1	68K	88K	1281
osip	3.0.1	24K	34K	666
postgreSQL	8.1.3	618K	548K	8568
procmail	3.22	9K	16K	298
zebra	0.95a	183K	145K	3342

TABLE 9.4:   Procedure and Specification Counts, and Analysis Times

Source	Total number of specifications		Analysis time(s)
	Data-flow	Control-flow	
apache	556	330	157
linux	5862	101	1258
openssh	625	202	120
osip	213	51	46
postgresSQL	3348	615	1007
procmail	84	105	26
zebra	1397	608	162

4 CPU machine operating at 3.00GHz, with 1GB memory. The time taken for performing the analysis is presented in Table 9.3.

9.2.8   Quantitative Assessment

We derive two kinds of predicates – dataflow and control-flow. For dataflow predicates, we derive assignments to variables and logical relations between variables with other variables and constants. Control-flow predicates specify the procedures that are called before the associate procedure is called. The total number of preconditions generated for procedures mined at 70% confidence is presented in Table 9.3. Our choice of mining at 70% is somewhat arbitrary, chosen to be resilient to latent errors in the benchmark, without comprising accuracy of the results. The predicate size distribution (the number of predicates found within a precondition) for the generated preconditions is given in Figure 9.14. For generated dataflow preconditions, the size of the predicate set is less than three for a majority of the procedures. For example, observe that approximately 95% of the procedures in postgreSQL have fewer than two predicates in their preconditions. In the case of control-flow predicates, we observe the predicate set size to be less than five for a majority of the procedures. Thus, the output of the tool is tractable for further examination and analysis by users.

To further quantify the effect of the confidence threshold on the preconditions derived, we performed experiments on `apache` over different thresholds. Figure 9.15 presents the results on the change in the number of preconditions with change in confidence. As expected, we observe that the number of predicates derived reduces with increase in the confidence threshold, although the change is not dramatic. For example, there are 60 additional procedures for which no preconditions are derived when the confidence level changes from 60% to 100%. This is expected because increase in confidence leads to more aggressive pruning of predicates.

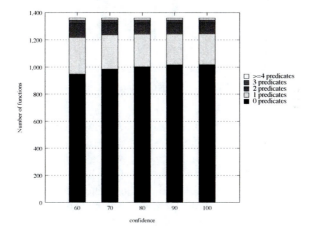

FIGURE 9.15: Reduction in number of predicates in `apache` with increase in confidence threshold.

Although the number of (static) call-sites in these benchmarks may be small (see Figure 9.16), mining may still be profitably applied. Recall that the preconditions derived for a call-site is computed by considering the set of predicates that flow along all paths into that site. Thus, it may be feasible to derive preconditions with high confidence even for a single call-site, provided that the site has a large number of incoming paths. In Section 9.3, we further refine this intuition to also consider the *number* of paths that lead to a specific call-site, using this value as a measure of the significance of that call-site to the establishment of the invoked procedure's preconditions.

9.2.9 Qualitative Assessment

To study the quality of our results, we examine the effectiveness of our technique in discovering protocols associated with library calls made in `openssh`. We mine the predicates at a 100% confidence threshold. We correlate the effectiveness of the analysis by comparing our results manually with the documentation found in the `man` pages of the corresponding library functions.

Out of the 242 library procedures that are invoked in `openssh`, we de-

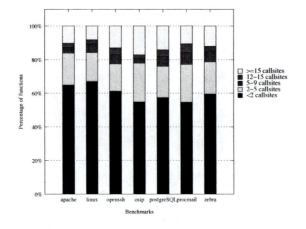

FIGURE 9.16: Distribution of call-sites.

rive preconditions correctly for 199 of them (77.13% accuracy). Moreover, we were able to derive preconditions for an additional nine procedures that were not documented. We observe 12 false-positives (our tool derives preconditions where none exist) and 31 *false negatives* (our tool did not derive the preconditions the documented specification claims should hold). These false negatives are potential sources of bugs. False positives occur primarily because there is an insufficient number of use cases for mining to effectively prune away irrelevant predicates. For example, in a few cases, a predicate is included in the precondition to a procedure call because the procedure was invoked only twice, and in both cases, the calling context contained similar irrelevant invariants.

Besides being potential sources of bugs, false negatives can also manifest because of limitations in the implementation. In addition to the obvious approximations introduced by our heuristics (recall that a precise solution to structural matching, the heart of the precondition inference problem, is NP-hard), there are two other limitations in our approach addressed briefly below:

- **Absence of theorem proving:** A precondition for the procedure BN_mod_word is that the second parameter must not be equal to zero. We do not observe any explicit sanity check on the second parameter in the program source. On further inspection, we notice that there is a chain of assignments leading to the second parameter, where we may be able to prove that the second parameter will be non-zero on any invocation. Automatically formulating this conclusion is possible with the aid of a theorem prover. The integration of theorem proving to the existing infrastructure to handle these predicates is part of our ongoing research.

- **Closed world assumptions:** Sometimes preconditions are formulated with respect to environment variables whose values are directly manifest in the program source. Since our implementation analyzes the program source in a closed-world setting, it is unable to accurately derive pre-conditions for those procedures whose predicates depend upon values of environment variables.

9.2.9.1 Bug Detection

We discuss several bugs detected in `openssh-4.2p1`. In the code fragment shown below, neither variables `p` nor `q` are checked for being non-null. Subsequent use of these values in procedure `prime_test` results in a segmentation fault. The computational complexity of the Miller-Rabin primality testing performed in `prime_test` makes it difficult to generate comprehensive test suites that would detect this bug. We exercised this fault by making the system run out of buffer space, and using the test case (`ssh-keygen -T <outfile> -f <infile>`), the program crashes in the then latest release `openssh-4.4p1`. Based on our report, these bugs are now fixed in `openssh-4.5p1`. We also observe a similar bug associated with invocation of `BN_new` and subsequent absence of sanity check in the procedure `gen_candidates`.

```
473     p = BN_new();
474     q = BN_new();
475     ctx = BN_CTX_new();
```

Observe that return value of `BN_CTX_new` is also not checked as being non-null. Even though this does not result in a crash, this violation potentially leads to a significant degradation in the performance of the library call `BN_is_prime` used in `prime_test`, as documented in the man pages.

There are several other instances of similar errors in the program. The existing documentation for library procedure `initgroups`, for example, claims that the first parameter to this procedure must always be non-null. However, our analysis does not generate predicates to this effect because this check is not performed. Similarly, before invoking procedure `RSA_size`, the field `n` of its parameter must be non-null. Even though the parameter is checked for being non-null, `n` itself is not. A similar bug exists in the invocation of `DH_size`. Any one of these bugs can be exercised with appropriate inputs, and could lead to a server crash.

9.3 Static Path Profiles

As the discussion in the previous section illustrates, the effectiveness of mining critically depends on a sufficient number of use cases that can be examined. For example, if we are interested in inferring the preconditions that must hold prior to a call to a procedure p, we benefit by examining multiple calls to p. The more calls analyzed, the greater the likelihood we can effectively distinguish between predicates present at these calls that are truly part of p's specification from those that, although present, are nonetheless irrelevant. In general, the confidence in a mined precondition is significantly higher if it is observed in 90,000 out of 100,000 occurrences, compared to when it is observed in 9 out of 10 occurrences, even though the underlying percentages of occurrences are the same [27].

With a sufficient number of test cases, dynamic mining techniques can generate execution traces which contain a potentially large number of calls to p. Unfortunately, the cost to generate these traces may be high if we wish to ensure that these traces define a comprehensive enumeration of all possible executions of the program [20, 21, 39]. On the other hand, static techniques can only rely on static properties to identify call points; for example, if a call to p occurs at m different static program points in the source, only the predicates present at those m points can be mined. On the benchmarks used in our study, we observed that on an average, 80-85% of the procedures in these benchmarks are not invoked more than five times statically.

Furthermore, existing static techniques, including the one described earlier, do not take into account the *number* of paths leading to different call-sites of the same procedure. Consider a predicate π that occurs at one call-site c_1, but which is absent at another call-site c_2 of the same procedure p. Static inference techniques would naturally deduce that π is not part of p's precondition. However, the number of paths leading to c_1 may significantly be greater than c_2 (e.g., c_2 may be part of an infrequently occurring error-inducing path). Indeed, it may be precisely the absence of π at c_2 that leads to an error. The approach described in the previous section relaxes this restriction somewhat by allowing a predicate to be included if it occurs at a majority of static known call-sites. But, this majority set may nonetheless represent call-sites that occur infrequently dynamically, while the minority set at which the predicate does not hold may, in fact, correspond to frequently occurring calls at runtime.

The underlying premise of our work is that we can effectively apply the benefits of a dynamic analysis (i.e., generating a desired quantity of data for the purposes of mining) to a static specification mining algorithm. However, exploring all paths and generating the traces associated with each path statically has two significant disadvantages: (1) there are an exponential number of paths that would need to be examined, and (2) if only a subset of all paths are explored, then this approach has the same disadvantage of incompleteness common to any dynamic mining strategy.

In this section, we develop an intelligent, comprehensive path enumeration and summarization scheme that does not lead to exponential time and space costs. This goal is achievable because we are interested in deriving properties that are not path specific, but merely valid over a *majority* of the paths examined.

We define an inter-procedural, path-based static analysis that collects a set of program predicates that define potential preconditions to procedure calls. As before, if procedure p has precondition π, it means that that all the predicates comprising π should hold before any call to p. To compute preconditions, we analyze the predicates present along each control flow edge in the program's control-flow graph. At any join point j, where multiple paths merge, we keep track of the *number* of paths, n_j, leading to the join point and the number of times a predicate π is valid on these n_j paths. This information, which we refer to as a *static path profile*, is transferred to outgoing edges, and the process repeated until all control flow edges are traced. We use procedure summaries to make the approach scalable for inter-procedural analysis. To compute the preconditions of a procedure p, we take the cumulative sets of predicates associated with its different call-sites and their associated path profiles to derive the required specifications.

An essential assumption underlying our approach is that the probability of occurrence of a dynamic path is likely to be equal to that of a static path. Clearly, such an assumption need not hold in general. Static paths may be infeasible, i.e., not be traversable under any dynamic execution. Similarly, a path that occurs frequently statically may occur infrequently dynamically because there may be stringent runtime conditions that dictate when the path can be traversed that are not captured by a static analysis. Conversely, a path that occurs frequently dynamically (e.g. the back edge of a long-lived loop) may occur infrequently statically. Fortunately, for the purposes of specification inference, we demonstrate that static path profiling is robust against inaccuracies introduced by failing to recognize (statically) infeasible, or infrequently occurring static and dynamic paths.

To support this claim, we have also implemented a dynamic specification inference engine that mines comprehensive dynamic executions of the program generated by CUTE [39], an automatic test generation tool. A comparison between the specifications inferred using static path profiles and the dynamic inference engine reveals that infeasibility of program paths (or lack of correlation between probabilities of static *versus* dynamic paths) has little impact on the quality of the specifications generated.

As we have seen earlier, bugs in programs present another challenge to specification inference since they may invalidate correct predicates from a specification or introduce incorrect ones. Test generation tools can help identify commonly occurring bugs since such bugs by definition must occur on many dynamic paths. Because these bugs can be fixed, we assume programs are *mostly* free of errors. Bugs that are found on infrequently occurring dynamic paths are not always captured by unit testing. However, the paths on which these bugs occur must therefore necessarily correspond to profiled static paths with small weights. Consequently, the influence of these bugs on derived specifications is small.

Our experimental results show that the analysis (a) can effectively infer specifications even for procedures with a small number of statically apparent call-sites; (b) exhibits fewer false negatives compared to static specification inference techniques that do not take path profiles into consideration; and (c) displays precision closer to that of an exhaustive dynamic path exploration technique.

9.3.1   Deriving Specifications

A simple technique to derive specifications is to trace each path in the program and then infer the set of valid preconditions from the traced paths. Consider the example shown in Figure 9.17(a). There are seven paths on total to a call-site of some procedure p. If every path is traced statically, it is clear that among five out of the seven paths, the predicate π holds and is a precondition for p with confidence 71.42%. Although this scheme is simple, the cost associated with tracing each path is exponential in the number of edges in the program.

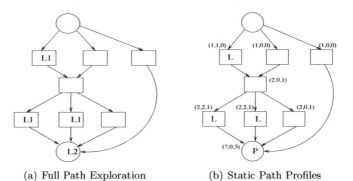

(a) Full Path Exploration   (b) Static Path Profiles

FIGURE 9.17: Illustrative example. Rectangles indicate predicates, circles indicate call-sites. Empty rectangles/circles indicate arbitrary predicates/procedure calls. (With kind permission from Springer Science + Business Media: Protocol Inference Using Static Path Profiles, SAS, 2008, pp. 78–92, M. Ramanthan et al., Figure 3.)

The key insight to our approach is that obtaining aggregate information associated with multiple paths is sufficient for generating interesting preconditions. Knowing the specific paths in which π holds is uninteresting from the perspective of specification inference. A static path profile is the cumulative information of predicates that hold across all possible paths to a specific call-site.

Path information is collected by examining the program's control-flow graph. Each node v in the CFG is annotated as a three tuple (n_v, m_v, q_v) for every predicate π under consideration, where the definition of the tuple components is as follows:

- n_v is the total number of paths leading to v

- $m_v = \begin{cases} n_v, \text{if predicate } \pi \text{ holds at } v \\ 0 \text{ otherwise} \end{cases}$

- $q_v = \Sigma_u \, \texttt{max}(m_u, q_u)$ where $u \in$ predecessor(v) in the CFG

At any given node, we can derive the number of paths any predicate π holds by observing the three-tuple (n_v, m_v, q_v) associated with the predicate π at that node. The number of predicates examined at a node is directly proportional to the number of variables. Intuitively, q_v specifies the number of paths through v in which the predicate is valid. If a predicate π is valid on some number of incoming paths *upto* node v, but in addition also happens to be asserted *at* v, it is clear π holds on all paths *through* v ($m_v = n_v$). The nodes downstream from v decide the number of paths on which π holds using q_v and m_v. If the number of paths for which π holds is i, then $i = \texttt{max}(m_v, q_v)$; the fact that predicate π holds on i paths is denoted as π_i.

For example, consider the annotated graph counterpart of Figure 9.17(a) in Figure 9.17(b) associated with predicate π. Let one of the two nodes annotated (2,0,1) be v. This annotation denotes the fact that there are two possible paths to node v, predicate π is not explicitly valid at v, and the total number of paths on which π is valid is one (written π_1).

Loops pose complications for building path profiles because they represent a potentially infinite set of executions. To make our approach tractable, we perform a simple fixpoint calculation to compute the path profile for back edges in loops. Initially, we assume the back edge does not contribute to the profile weights of any path found within the loop. In subsequent iterations of the analysis, the back edge on the loop contributes exactly once to the profile weights, albeit with the predicates being derived propagated through the back edge multiple times. Since the computation of the tuple is monotonic (since q_v computes the maximum of the profiles of its predecessors which is bounded by the number of paths in the loop body that include the back edge), the analysis is guaranteed to converge.

The annotation marking mechanism must also take into account nodes in the control-flow graph that represent call-sites (e.g., the node labeled p). Path profiles distinguish between incoming and outgoing annotations. The incoming annotation in p's case is (7,0,5). Incoming annotations are used to generate preconditions for p. Thus, to infer the precondition for p requires no inspection of p's body. In this case, π_5 holds true at node p, i.e., five paths of the total set of paths have π to be true. Outgoing annotations (not shown in the figure), on the other hand, capture path profile summary information. The summary information for some procedure p gives the number of paths within p for which the predicate holds upon exit from p, which in turn is given by the annotation at p's *return* node. Summary information is used to define incoming annotations for other call-sites downstream in the graph. We elaborate on this point in the next section.

9.3.2   Implementation

Our algorithm takes as input the program source and a user-defined confidence threshold for determining when a predicate should form part of a pre-condition, and produces as output preconditions (i.e., a set of predicates) for every procedure. These preconditions indicate the conditions that must hold prior to any call of the associated procedure.

We first generate the control-flow graph for each procedure. The resulting graph is processed using the algorithm given in Figure 9.18. The number of

---

procedure BUILDPREDICATES
    ▷ **Input**: $G(V,E)$, directed, acyclic CFG of α; V is topologically sorted;
    ▷ **Output**: Annotated Graph G
    ▷ **Auxiliary Information**:
          predicates(u): predicates generated at u; flow(u): set of
                          predicates valid at u;
          precond(u): set of predicates that are used for generating
                          preconditions associated with procedure at u;
          CALLSITE(u): **true** if u is a callsite; RETURN(u): **true**
                if u is the return node from procedure α;

```
1   iterate ← true
2   while iterate do
3       iterate ← false
4       for each node u = 1 to |V|
5           oldflow ← flow(u)
6           for all predecessors v of u
7               n_u ← n_u + n_v
8               flow(u) ← flow(u) ∪ predicates(v)
9               for each predicate π in flow(v)
10                  q_u(π) ← q_u(π) + max(m_v(π), q_v(π))
11                  m_u(π) ← 0
12          flow(u) ← flow(u) ∪ predicates(u)
13          for each predicate π in data_predicate(u)
14              m_u(π) ← n_u
15          if CALLSITE(u) is true then
16              precond(u) ← flow(u)
17              flow(u) ← flow(u) ∪ proc_summary[func(u)]
18          if RETURN(u) is true then
19              proc_summary[α] ← flow(u)
20          if oldflow ≠ flow(u) then iterate ← true
```

FIGURE 9.18: Algorithm for building predicates. (With kind permission from Springer Science + Business Media: Protocol Inference Using Static Path Profiles, SAS, 2008, pp. 78–92, M. Ramanthan et al., Figure 4.)

paths to each node in the graph is first computed. Subsequently, the q value for the node is computed for each predicate by considering all its parent nodes. If the node is a call-site, then the *procedure summary* associated with that call is also added to the set of predicates that will flow into other adjacent nodes in the graph. The procedure summary is the summary of predicate information along with the total number of paths and the number of paths for which each predicate holds at the *return* node of the procedure. This process is repeated until a convergent path profile for the loop backedge is computed. Yet another fixed point iteration is performed to ensure that dependencies crossing procedure boundaries (as given by the *procedure summary* and *return*) are completely captured.

---

procedure GETPRECONDITIONS
    ▷ **Input**: α: a procedure in the program;
                    $C = \{c_1, c_2, ... c_n\}$ is the set of call sites of α;
                    β = user-defined threshold for generating preconditions
    ▷ **Output**:set of preconditions for α
1   for each node c_i
2   for each predicate π in $\texttt{precond}(c_i)$
3            $q_t(\pi) \leftarrow q_t(\pi) + q_{c_i}(\pi)$
3            $n_t(\pi) \leftarrow n_t(\pi) + n_{c_i}$
4        $\texttt{flow\_t} \leftarrow \texttt{flow\_t} \cup \texttt{precond}(c_i)$
5   for each predicate π in $\texttt{flow\_t}$
6   if $\frac{q_t}{n_t} > \beta$
7   preconditions$[\alpha] \leftarrow$ preconditions$[\alpha] \cup \{\pi\}$

FIGURE 9.19: Generate preconditions. (With kind permission from Springer Science + Business Media: Protocol Inference Using Static Path Profiles, SAS, 2008, pp. 78–92, M. Ramanthan et al., Figure 5.)

At the end of the fixed point calculation, the algorithm shown in Figure 9.19 is executed to obtain the preconditions associated with each procedure in the program. To generate the precondition for a procedure p, each call-site of p is considered. The predicates that can be used in computing the preconditions from each of these call-sites are extracted and the total number of paths in which each predicate holds (q_t) across all call-sites is computed. Similarly, the total number of paths to all call-sites (n_t) is also calculated. If the ratio of the number of paths on which a predicate holds compared to the total number of paths at all call-sites is greater than β, a user-defined threshold, the predicate is added to the precondition for p.

9.3.3 Results

We validate the idea of using static path profiles on selected benchmark sources to demonstrate scalability and effectiveness. We extract preconditions

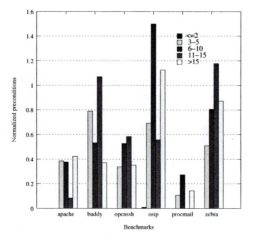

FIGURE 9.20: Comparison with non-profile based inference. (With kind permission from Springer Science + Business Media: Protocol Inference Using Static Path Profiles, SAS, 2008, pp. 78–92, M. Ramanthan et al., Figure 7.)

for six sources: `apache`, `buddy`, `zebra`, `openssh`, `osip2`, and `procmail`; other than `buddy`, the characteristics of these benchmarks were described in Tables 9.3 and 9.4. `Buddy` is a BDD generator, roughly 2.4KLOC, with 173 procedures.

9.3.4   Quantitative Assessment

We derive preconditions containing three different types of predicates – assignment, comparison, and precedence. As their names suggest, assignment predicates reflect the assignment of values (or results of procedure calls) to variables; comparison predicates include six kinds of logical comparison operations ($>, <, \neq, =, \geq$, and $\leq$) between variables and/or constants; a precedence predicate is an ordered sequence of procedures whose calls must precede the call to the procedure being examined. The total number of preconditions generated for procedures, where the predicates are valid on at least 70% of the paths is given in Table 9.3. Our earlier experiments on the predicate distributions (see. Figures 9.14(b) and 9.14(a)) revealed that the size of the predicate set is less than two for a majority of the procedures.

We experimentally compare our approach with a non-profile based inference mechanism that does not leverage path profiles such as the system described in Section 9.2. Briefly, the comparison metric is an analysis that requires a predicate to be satisfied along all paths to a call-site in order to be a valid candidate for inclusion as part of a procedure call's precondition. After accumulating the predicates at each call-site, we declare a predicate as a precondition if the predicate is valid in at least the user-defined threshold percentage of call-sites. We use the same user-defined threshold (70%) in deriving the predicates, i.e., if a predicate is valid in 7 out of 10 call-sites, we declare the predicate as a precondition in the non-profile based inference scheme. In the path-profiling approach, we declare a predicate to be a precondition if it is valid in 70% of the *paths* to call-sites of the procedure.

Figure 9.20 presents the percentage of preconditions derived by non-profile based specification inference as compared to those derived using static path profiling. For example, for procedures with three to five call-sites in `zebra`, the former discovers roughly only half the predicates discovered by the path profile analysis. As expected, for procedures with fewer than three call-sites, the non-profile based inference scheme is not able to derive any preconditions. For example, in the case of `openssh`, no precondition is derived for procedures that have fewer than three statically apparent call-sites.

We also observe that in many cases, the set of preconditions generated with the non-profile based inference is a proper *subset* of the preconditions generated using the static path profiling approach. This is consistent with our expectation that typical static analyzes can lead to over approximation by eliminating valid predicates from preconditions. In some cases, however, such as `osip` or `zebra`, this hypothesis does not hold. Path profiling weights predicates based on the number of paths on which they hold across all call-sites. Consider a predicate π which occurs on k paths at n call-sites to procedure p. Suppose that paths are not evenly distributed among these n call-sites. If on m call-sites, π occurs on all paths, and m is greater than the threshold cutoff, the non-profile based inference will record π as a valid precondition. However, if the number of paths that flow into these m call-sites is much less than k, then the path profile analysis will nonetheless not include π as part of p's preconditions. In other words, a predicate that does not hold on a majority of paths may still hold on the paths to a majority of call-sites. Path profiling thus provides finer control over both the inclusion and exclusion of predicates than non-profile based inference.

9.3.5   Qualitative Assessment

We want to identify the impact of infeasible paths and approximations introduced by static path weights in the program on the quality of the specifications inferred. To do so, we compare our approach with a dynamic inference mechanism. Rather than using an existing test-suite to generate dynamic traces, we use CUTE, an automatic test generation tool, that provides extended coverage of the program, and thus helps reduce the possibility of under-approximation (compared to other dynamic analysis systems) as described in Section 9.1.

The test generation process initially runs with some random input and collects constraints $\{C_1, ..., C_{k-1}, C_k\}$ symbolically along the execution. To explore a previously unexplored path, a new input is generated that satisfies the constraints $\{C_1, ...C_{k-1}, \neg C_k\}$. If this path were explored earlier, then the set of constraints $\{C_1, ...\neg C_{k-1}\}$ would be used to explore a different path. This process repeats until all paths in the program are explored. There are several issues that must be handled by the input generation process. Most

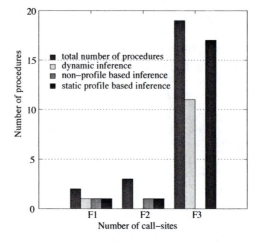

FIGURE 9.21: Correctness of different inference schemes. (With kind permission from Springer Science + Business Media: Protocol Inference Using Static Path Profiles, SAS, 2008, pp. 78–92, M. Ramanthan et al., Figure 8.)

importantly, when it becomes difficult to reason with symbolic constraints, concrete values from the program execution replace symbols to ensure progress of the test input generation process. We refer the reader to [39] for a more detailed description.

We track the predicates along different execution paths of the program and for each call to a procedure, group the set of predicates that precede it from the start of the execution. Thus, across multiple executions, we would generate many such groups of predicates. To generate the precondition for the procedure, we apply frequent item-set mining [11]. The frequently occurring predicates across all the groups form the precondition.

We performed our comparison on buddy, an open source package that implements operations over Binary Decision Diagrams (BDD). We ran CUTE for a bounded number of iterations (1000), which took approximately 30 minutes, and in that process collected specifications for 24 procedures. Of these 24 procedures, only 2 procedures (F1) had more than 10 call-sites, 3 procedures (F2) had call-sites between 5 and 10, and the remaining 19 procedures (F3) had less than 5 call-sites. Using existing documentation, and manual inspection, we computed a reference specification for each of these procedures.

Figure 9.21 presents the results associated with our qualitative analysis. We applied three different schemes: (1) dynamic inference, (2) non-profile based inference, and (3) path-profile based inference on this benchmark. For the set of two procedures in F1, all techniques provide similar precision and were able to detect preconditions correctly for one procedure. Underapproximation confounds the precision of dynamic inference for the set of three procedures in F2. The analysis for the procedures in F3 is more interesting. Because of the lack of frequency of call-sites for the procedures in this set, non-profile based static inference is ineffective in producing specifications with any degree of confidence. In contrast, path-profile based inference correctly identified the correct specification for 17 of the 19 procedures. Surprisingly, under-approximation still poses a problem even for a comprehensive test generation tool like CUTE; it failed to correctly generate specifications for seven of the procedures that were successfully analyzed using static path profiling.

9.4 Related Work

There has been significant research toward automatically validating program properties, and detecting program errors when programs are annotated with partial specifications describing desired invariants [3,9,10,13,17,18,24–26,29,44]. Our approach differs fundamentally from these other efforts insofar we assume *no* input from the programmer on the specifications that need to be validated.

In [4], Ammons et al. perform specification mining by summarizing frequent interaction patterns as state machines that capture temporal and data dependencies when interacting with APIs or abstract data types. Subsequently, Ammons et al. present an approach [5] to debug derived specifications using concept analysis. Ernst et al. [16] present Daikon, a tool for dynamically detecting invariants in a program. Yang et al. [46] present scalable dynamic inference techniques that also work effectively with imperfect traces. While these techniques can indeed be used to derive preconditions, they critically rely on test input providing comprehensive coverage. In this regard, they differ in obvious ways from our approach.

Li and Zhou present PR-Miner [31], a tool that relies on mining [1] to identify frequently occurring program patterns. Our work differs significantly from theirs because we integrate mining within a path-sensitive dataflow framework. Livshits and Zimmermann [34] present a tool which uses mining to analyze revision histories of programs. Li et al. [30] also use data mining techniques to detect copy-paste bugs in large software systems. Mandelin et al. [35] present a technique for synthesizing jungloid code fragments automatically based on the input and output types that describe the code. Their approach is useful for reusing existing code. Because none of these techniques tightly integrate dataflow and control-flow information with the mining engine, it would be difficult to leverage them for deriving useful preconditions. It is precisely this synthesis that is the distinguishing contribution of this work.

There are several other related approaches that address the problem of mining specifications. An automatic specification mining technique that uses information about exceptions and errors to identify temporal safety rules is presented in [42]. Engler et al. [15] use mining to detect relations between pairs of functions, and Kremenek et al. [28] significantly generalize these earlier ideas. However, [28] is domain specific, and requires either machine learning or user specifications to generate initial annotation probabilities, and employs naming conventions for identifying interesting procedures to improve accuracy. As a result, their approach would be ineffective in deriving the specifications for the example programs in Figures 9.2, 9.3, or Section 9.2.9.

Apart from mining based approaches, many other interesting techniques have been devised for bug detection in software systems [21,32,47]. For example, in [21], Godefroid et al. present a technique for automatically generating test cases so that the coverage of the program is increased. Liblit et al. [32] present a technique in which predicate information is collected on actual runs of the software and statistical analysis is employed to find correlation between bugs and causes. Yang et al. [47] use model checking to detect bugs in systems code. Rinard et al. [38] present an approach on failure oblivious computing that enables servers to run even in the presence of memory errors. Castro et al. [12] present an approach where a data flow graph is generated and ensures that the data flow integrity is preserved at run time. Because our work focuses on an entirely new dimension, namely, statically extracting preconditions from program source transparently, it is conceivable that it could be used in conjunction with these other approaches to operate with even greater precision and scale.

Cortes et al. [14] present a domain- specific language HANCOCK for writing mining applications.

Ball and Larus [7] propose an approach for efficient path profiling. In their approach, dynamic runs of a program are profiled to gather information about different path executions. Recently, Vaswani et al. [41], present a scheme to identify a subset of interesting paths and use a compact numbering scheme using arithmetic coding techniques. Our approach is motivated by the algorithm presented by Ball and Larus [7] and is applied statically.

9.5   Conclusions

This chapter discusses the problem of statically deriving specifications using predicate mining. We describe an inference mechanism for detecting the preconditions that must be valid whenever a procedure is invoked. We derive these preconditions using an inter-procedural path-sensitive dataflow analysis that gathers predicates at each program point. We apply mining techniques to these predicates to make specification inference robust to errors. Experimental results on large open-source C programs validate the practicality of our techniques. To gain greater precision, and have static analysis more closely emulate properties that would be revealed under a dynamic evaluation, we also explore the use of static path profiles, a technique that weights the predicates found at a particular call-site based on the number of incoming paths to that site. Taken together, these techniques provide a promising approach toward the realization of automatic, scalable, and efficient specification inference of real-world programs.

Bibliography

[1] R. Agrawal and R. Srikant. Fast algorithms for mining association rules. In *Proc. 20th Int. Conf. Very Large Data Bases, VLDB*, pages 487–499, 1994.

[2] R. Agrawal and R. Srikant. Mining sequential patterns. In *Eleventh International Conference on Data Engineering*, pages 3–14, 1995.

[3] R. Alur, P. Cerny, P. Madhusudan, and W. Nam. Synthesis of interface specifications for java classes. In *POPL '05: Proceedings of the 32nd ACM SIGPLAN-SIGACT Symposium on Principles of Programming Languages*, pages 98–109, 2005.

[4] G. Ammons, R. Bodik, and J. Larus. Mining specifications. In *POPL '02: Proceedings of the 29th ACM SIGPLAN-SIGACT Symposium on Principles of Programming Languages*, pages 4–16, 2002.

[5] G. Ammons, D. Mandelin, R. Bodik, and J. Larus. Debugging temporal specifications with concept analysis. In *PLDI '03: Proceedings of the ACM SIGPLAN 2003 Conference on Programming Language Design and Implementation*, pages 182–195, 2003.

[6] P. Anderson, T. Reps, and T. Teitelbaum. Design and implementation of a fine-grained software inspection tool. *IEEE Trans. on Software Engineering*, 29(8):721–733, August 2003.

[7] T. Ball and J. Larus. Efficient path profiling. In *MICRO-29*, December 1996.

[8] T. Ball, V. Levin, and F. Xie. Automatic creation of environment models via training. In *TACAS '04: Tenth International Conference on Tools and Algorithms for the Construction and Analysis of Systems*, pages 93–107, 2004.

[9] T. Ball and S.K. Rajamani. Automatically validating temporal safety properties of interfaces. In *SPIN 2001, Workshop on Model Checking of Software, LNCS 2057*, pages 103–122, May 2001.

[10] B. Blanchet. A computationally sound mechanized prover for security protocols. In *IEEE Symposium on Security and Privacy*, pages 140–154, 2006.

[11] D. Burdick, M. Calimlim, J. Flannick, J. Gehrke, and T. Yiu. Mafia: a performance study of mining maximal frequent itemsets. In *Workshop on Frequent Itemset Mining Implementations (FIMI'03)*, 2003.

[12] M. Castro, M. Costa, and T. Harris. Securing software by enforcing data-flow integrity. In *OSDI '06: Proceedings of the 7th Usenix Symposium on Operating Systems Design and Implementation*, pages 147–160, 2006.

[13] B. Chin, S. Markstrum, and T. Millstein. Semantic type qualifiers. In *PLDI '05: Proceedings of the ACM SIGPLAN 2005 Conference on Programming Language Design and Implementation*, pages 85–95, 2005.

[14] C. Cortes, K. Fisher, D. Pregibon, and A. Rogers. Hancock: a language for extracting signatures from data streams. In *KDD '00: Proceedings of the Sixth ACM SIGKDD International Conference on Knowledge Discovery and Data Mining*, pages 9–17, 2000.

[15] D. Engler, D. Chen, and A. Chou. Bugs as inconsistent behavior: a general approach to inferring errors in systems code. In *SOSP '01: Proceedings of the 18th ACM Symposium on Operating Systems Principles*, pages 57–72, 2001.

[16] M. Ernst, J. Cockrell, W. Griswold, and D. Notkin. Dynamically discovering likely program invariants to support program evolution. *IEEE TSE*, 27(2):1–25, February 2001.

[17] J. Fischer, R. Jhala, and R. Majumdar. Joining dataflow with predicates. In *ESEC-FSE '05: 10th European Software Engineering Conference and 13th ACM SIGSOFT International Symposium on Foundations of Software Engineering*, pages 227–236, 2005.

[18] J. Foster, T. Terauchi, and A. Aiken. Flow-sensitive type qualifiers. In *PLDI '02: Proceedings of the ACM SIGPLAN 2002 Conference on Programming Language Design and Implementation*, pages 1–12, 2002.

[19] M. Furr and J. Foster. Checking type safety of foreign function calls. In *PLDI '05: Proceedings of the ACM SIGPLAN 2005 Conference on Programming Language Design and Implementation*, pages 62–72, 2005.

[20] P. Godefroid. Compositional dynamic test generation. In *POPL '07*, pages 47–54, 2007.

[21] P. Godefroid, N. Klarslund, and K. Sen. DART: directed automated random testing. In *PLDI '05: Proceedings of the ACM SIGPLAN 2005 Conference on Programming Language Design and Implementation*, pages 213–223, Chicago, Il, 2005.

[22] R. Gopalakrishna. Improving Software Assurance Using Lightweight Static Analysis. Ph.D. thesis, Purdue University, 2006.

[23] D. Gunopulos, R. Khardon, H. Mannila, S. Saluja, H. Toivonen, and R. Sharma. Discovering all most specific sentences. *ACM Transactions on Database Systems*, 28:140–174, 2003.

[24] T. Henzinger, R. Jhala, and R. Majumdar. Permissive interfaces. *SIG-SOFT Softw. Eng. Notes*, 30(5):31–40, 2005.

[25] G.J. Holzmann. *The SPIN Model Checker: Primer and Reference Manual*. Addison-Wesley, 2004.

[26] R. Jhala and R. Majumdar. Path slicing. In *PLDI '05: Proceedings of the ACM SIGPLAN 2005 Conference on Programming Language Design and Implementation*, pages 38–47, 2005.

[27] A.S. Kapadia, W. Chan, and L.A. Moye. *Mathematical Statistics with Applications*. CRC Press, 2005.

[28] T. Kremenek, P. Twohey, G. Back, A. Ng, and D. Engler. From uncertainty to belief: inferring the specification within. In *OSDI '06: Proceedings of the 7th Usenix Symposium on Operating Systems Design and Implementation*, pages 161–176, 2006.

[29] P. Lam, V. Kuncak, and M. Rinard. Generalized typestate checking for data structure consistency. In *VMCAI '05: Proceedings of 6th International Conference on Verification, Model Checking and Abstract Interpretation*, pages 430–447, 2005.

[30] Z. Li, S. Lu, S. Myagmar, and Y. Zhou. Cp-miner: a tool for finding copy-paste and related bugs in operating system code. In *OSDI '04: Proceedings of the 6th Usenix Symposium on Operating Systems Design and Implementation*, pages 289–302, 2004.

[31] Z. Li and Y. Zhou. Pr-miner: automatically extracting implicit programming rules and detecting violations in large software code. In *ESEC-FSE '05: 10th European Software Engineering Conference and 13th ACM SIG-SOFT International Symposium on Foundations of Software Engineering*, pages 306–315, 2005.

[32] B. Liblit, M. Naik, A. Zheng, A. Aiken, and M. Jordan. Scalable statistical bug isolation. In *PLDI '05: Proceedings of the ACM SIGPLAN 2005 Conference on Programming Language Design and Implementation*, pages 15–26, Chicago, IL, 2005.

[33] B. Livshits and T. Zimmermann. Dynamine: a framework for finding common bugs by mining software revision histories. In *Proceedings of the Joint 10th European Software Engineering Conference and 13th ACM SIGSOFT Symposium on the Foundations of Software Engineering*, 2005.

[34] B. Livshits and T. Zimmermann. Dynamine: finding common error patterns by mining software revision histories. In *ESEC-FSE '05: 10th European Software Engineering Conference and 13th ACM SIGSOFT International Symposium on Foundations of Software Engineering*, pages 296–305, 2005.

[35] D. Mandelin, L. Xu, R. Bodik, and D. Kimelman. Jungloid mining: helping to navigate the api jungle. In *PLDI '05: Proceedings of the ACM SIGPLAN 2005 Conference on Programming Language Design and Implementation*, pages 48–61, 2005.

[36] J. Palsberg. Closure analysis in constraint form. *ACM Trans. Program. Lang. Syst.*, 17(1):47–62, 1995.

[37] M.K. Ramanathan, A. Grama, and S. Jagannathan. Path-sensitive inference of function precedence protocols. In *ICSE '07: Proceedings of the 29th International Conference on Software Engineering*, 2007.

[38] M. Rinard, C. Cadar, D. Dumitran, D.M. Roy, T. Leu, and W.S. Beebee. Enhancing server availability and security through failure-oblivious computing. In *OSDI '04: Proceedings of the 6th Usenix Symposium on Operating Systems Design and Implementation*, 2004.

[39] K. Sen, D. Marinov, and G. Agha. Cute: a concolic unit testing engine for C. In *Proceedings of ESEC-FSE*, pages 263–272, 2005.

[40] O. Shivers. Control-Flow Analysis of Higher-Order Languages. Ph.D. thesis, Carnegie Mellon University, May 1991.

[41] K. Vaswani, A.V. Nori, and T.M. Chilimbi. Preferential path profiling: compactly numbering interesting paths. In *Proceedings of POPL '07*, Nice, France, January 2007.

[42] W. Weimer and G. Necula. Mining temporal specifications for error detection. In *TACAS '05: Eleventh International Conference on Tools and Algorithms for the Construction and Analysis of Systems*, pages 461–476, April 2005.

[43] J. Whaley, M. Martin, and M. Lam. Automatic extraction of object-oriented component interfaces. In *Proceedings of the International Symposium of Software Testing and Analysis, ISSTA*, 2002.

[44] Y. Xie and A. Aiken. Scalable error detection using boolean satisfiability. In *POPL '05: Proceedings of the 32nd ACM SIGPLAN-SIGACT Symposium on Principles of Programming Languages*, pages 351–363, 2005.

[45] G. Yang. The complexity of mining maximal frequent itemsets and maximal frequent patterns. In *KDD '04: Proceedings of the Tenth ACM SIGKDD International Conference on Knowledge Discovery and Data Mining*, pages 344–353, 2004.

[46] J. Yang, D. Evans, D. Bhardwaj, T. Bhat, and M. Das. Perracotta: mining temporal api rules from imperfect traces. In *ICSE '06: Proceedings of 28th International Conference on Software Engineering*, May 2006.

[47] J. Yang, P. Twohey, D. Engler, and M. Musuvathi. Using model checking to find serious file system errors. In *OSDI '04: Proceedings of the 6th Usenix Symposium on Operating Systems Design and Implementation*, pages 273–288, San Francisco, CA, 2004.

Chapter 10

Mining API Usage Specifications via Searching Source Code from the Web

Suresh Thummalapenta

Department of Computer Science, North Carolina State University

Tao Xie

Department of Computer Science, North Carolina State University

Madhuri R. Marri

Department of Computer Science, North Carolina State University

10.1 Introduction

The emergence of the web has revolutionized traditional software development. In modern software development, programmers often reuse or adapt existing frameworks or libraries rather than developing similar artifacts from scratch. Furthermore, programmers often learn how to reuse Application Programming Interfaces (APIs) provided by these frameworks or libraries via searching for relevant code examples from open source code, transforming traditional software development to search-driven development. Therefore, open source code available on the web has become a common platform for sharing source code and for developing new projects efficiently. Currently, the amount of open source code available on the web is enormous. For example, source-forge.net, the most popular website for open source software development, hosts about 230,000 projects[1] with two million registered users and a large number of anonymous users.

With such an enormous amount of open source code available on the web, several code search engines (CSE) such as Google code search [11], Krugle [15], Koders [1], and Codase [9] are introduced to effectively search for relevant code examples. These CSEs accept queries such as the names of API classes or methods and return relevant code examples from CVS or SVN repositories of existing open source projects available on the web. The primary reason for the introduction of CSEs is that the normal search engines such as Yahoo (www.yahoo.com) and Google (www.google.com) mainly search based on the textual content of a file. However, a file including source code is more than just a textual file. For example, each word in the source code file has a different meaning, depending on several factors such as the programming language or the location of that word in the source code file. Therefore, to effectively search in available open source code, CSEs index source code based on the semantics of the corresponding programming language. For example, Krugle provides a search criterion that the keyword in the query should appear as a method call among returned code examples. Figure 10.1 shows snapshots of CSEs Google code search and Krugle. For Krugle, the figure also shows the 1564 code examples returned for the RegEx class (of C#), which is used to find specific character patterns. These code examples include information on how to use RegEx such as performing pattern matching using the IsMatch method. In contrast to the MSDN documentation that includes only a single code example,[2] these 1564 code examples gathered from open source code can assist programmers in learning different scenarios of how to use the RegEx class.

Although CSEs can serve as sources for an enormous number of open source codes available on the web, their usage is often limited to simple tasks such as searching for relevant code examples. In this chapter, we show the usage of CSEs in achieving other tasks in software development life cycle such as detecting defects in an application under analysis via software verification. Achieving tasks such as software verification requires API usage specifications that describe programming rules to be followed while writing source code. Without such API usage specifications, existing software verification techniques can detect only robustness-related defects such as division by zero or dereferencing a null pointer. However, these specifications are often not well documented in practice due to various factors such as hard project delivery deadlines and limited resources in the software development process [16].

---

[1]http://sourceforge.net/, 2010

[2]http://msdn.microsoft.com/en-us/library/system.text.regularexpressions.regex.aspx

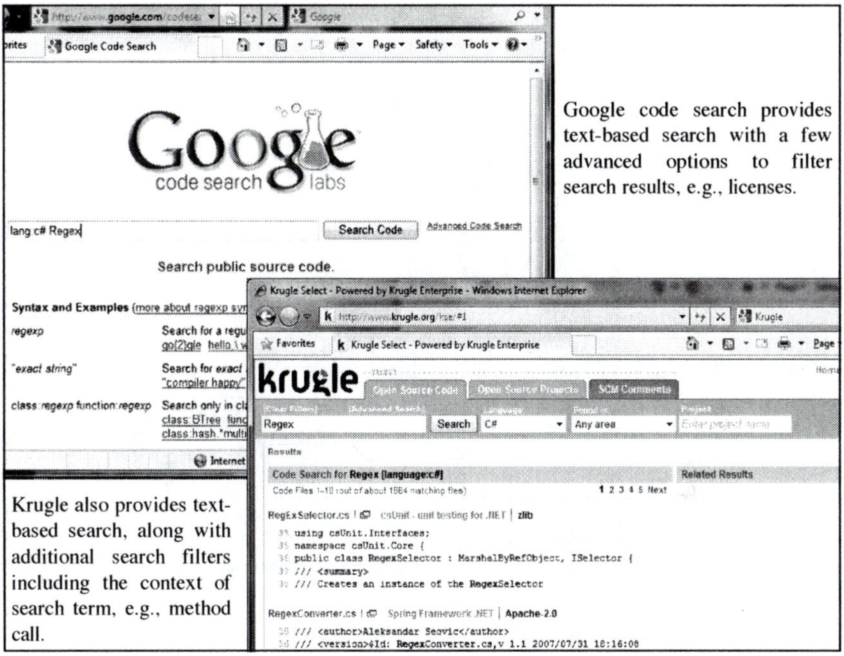

FIGURE 10.1: Snapshots of Google code search and Krugle.

To address this issue of lacking specifications, a new research area, called Mining Software Engineering Data (MSED) [20], has emerged. Recently, MSED has gained focus as shown by its dedicated sessions in major software engineering conferences. MSED primarily targets at applying data mining techniques on software engineering data (such as source code or execution traces) to mine high-level specifications in the form of common patterns (e.g., frequent occurrences of pairs or sequences of API method calls) across a sufficiently large number of data points (e.g., code examples). These mined specifications can be used for improving software productivity via assisting programmers or software quality by using mined specifications as programming rules for verification tools. In this chapter, we show how to use CSEs as sources of information for MSED, rather than a few code bases that are often used by existing approaches [2, 3, 5, 8, 10, 13, 17, 18, 21, 22, 24, 30, 31] in MSED as data points. The major disadvantage of using a few code bases as data points is that many API usage specifications cannot be mined as common patterns, since there are often too few data points in those code bases to support the mining of desirable patterns. In other words, the number of data points to support a pattern related to a particular programming rule is often insufficient.

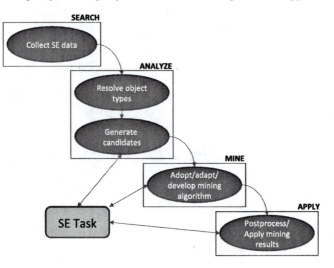

FIGURE 10.2: Phases in the life cycle of approaches developed based on searching and mining.

Since mining entire open source code is not feasible, in this chapter, we introduce a life-cycle model [19] that assists programmers in mining API usage specifications via searching for relevant code examples on demand from the web. In particular, given a software engineering task (SE task) such as detecting defects in an application under analysis that is using a set of APIs, our life-cycle model describes how to search for relevant code examples for the set of APIs and mine API usage specifications for detecting defects.

In the rest of this chapter, we present the major phases of life-cycle model. In particular, we describe how to search for relevant code examples via CSEs and analyze these code examples for mining API usage specifications. We use two example SE tasks for describing the major phases in our life-cycle model. We also show the benefits of mining API specifications via searching for relevant code examples from the web.

10.2   Life-Cycle Model

Figure 10.2 shows the four major phases in the life cycle for achieving an SE task such as detecting defects in API client code via mining API usage specifications. These four phases are *search*, *analyze*, *mine*, and *apply* phases. Given an SE task, the *search* phase collects SE data in the form of code examples by leveraging a code search engine such as Google code search [11].

These collected code examples include necessary information for mining API usage specifications. The search phase also includes additional techniques for addressing the challenges faced while collecting code examples via code search engine. The *analyze* phase analyzes collected code examples to extract relevant SE data such as static method-call sequences.

The *mine* phase transforms extracted SE data into a format suitable for applying a mining algorithm. For example, the mine phase replaces each distinct method call in method-call sequences with a unique symbol. Based on requirements of the SE task, the mine phase either uses an existing off-the-shelf mining algorithm such as frequent itemset mining [7] or produces a new mining algorithm developed based on the requirements unique to the SE task.

The *apply* phase transforms results of mining algorithm into a format required to achieve the SE task. For example, the apply phase replaces each symbol in the results with its corresponding method call. The apply phase next uses mining results for achieving the SE task. For example, the apply phase detects defects in API client code by using a static-verification tool with mined API specifications. Among these four phases, the search phase is independent of target SE task, whereas the remaining phases are specific to the target SE task. In this chapter, we use an SE task, described next, as an example task for describing our life-cycle model. We next explain each phase in detail.

10.3   Example SE Task: Detecting Exception-Handling Defects

Programming languages such as Java and C# provide exception-handling constructs such as `try-catch` to handle exception conditions that arise during program execution. Under these exception conditions, programs follow paths different from normal execution paths; these additional paths are referred to as *exception* paths. Applications developed based on these programming languages are expected to handle these exception conditions and take necessary recovery actions. For example, when an application reuses resources such as files or database connections, the application should release the resources after the usage in all paths including *exception* paths. Failing to release the resources can cause performance degradation, but can also lead to critical issues. For example, consider the code example shown in Figure 10.3. In Statement 9, the method call `executeUpdate` acquires a database lock before updating the contents of the database. This lock can be released either by the `commit` method call (Statement 10) or by the `rollback` method call (Statement 12). Consider that the `rollback` method call is not invoked in Statement 12. In this scenario, if `SQLException` is raised while updating the contents of the database, the database lock is not released and any other process trying to acquire the same lock hangs till the database releases the lock after timeout. We refer to the defects that are caused by such improper handling of exception-handling constructs as *exception-handling defects.*

Software verification for detecting exception-handling defects requires specifications, referred to as *exception-handling rules,* that describe expected behaviors when exceptions occur. Given an application under analysis, this SE task can be achieved by mining exception-handling rules for the APIs used by the application under analysis and using those rules for detecting exception-handling defects. We recommend readers to refer to our CAR-Miner approach [28] for specific details on this SE task and for more technical details.

10.4   Search Phase

Given an SE task, the *search* phase collects SE data in the form of code examples by leveraging a code search engine (CSE) such as Google code search [11]. We next explain how search phase collects code examples via CSE and present additional techniques that help address the challenges faced while collecting those code examples.

To search and collect SE data such as code examples relevant to APIs whose specifications need to be mined, the search phase constructs queries to CSEs. We consider that a code example is relevant to an API, if the code ex-

```
01:    ...
02:    OracleDataSource ods = null; Session session = null;
          Connection conn = null; Statement statement = null;
03:    logger.debug("Starting update");
04:    try {
05:        ods = new OracleDataSource();
06:        ods.setURL("jdbc:oracle:thin:scott/tiger@192.168.1.2:1521:catfish");
07:        conn = ods.getConnection();
08:        statement = conn.createStatement();
09:        statement.executeUpdate("DELETE FROM table1");
10:        conn.commit(); }
11:    catch (SQLException se)  {
12:        if (conn != null)  { conn.rollback(); }
13:        logger.error("Exception occurred");   }
14:    finally {
15:        if(statement != null) statement.close();
16:        if(conn != null) conn.close();
17:        if(ods != null) ods.close();
18:    }
```

FIGURE 10.3: An example scenario where database contents are modified using the `executeUpdate` method call. (From S. Thummalapenta and T. Xie, Mining exception-handling rules as sequence association rules, International Conference on Software Engineering (ICSE) © 2009 IEEE.)

ample includes call sites of methods in API. These constructed queries include key words derived based on the names of APIs. CSEs also provide additional options such as language of API for further filtering out the code examples during the search. For example, the search phase constructs the query "`lang:java org.apache.regexp RE`" to collect relevant code examples of the `RE` class provided by the Apache library [6] via Google code search (GCS). In the preceding query, the option "`lang:java`" describes that the language under consideration is Java. GCS returns around 2000 code examples for this query. These code examples include information that helps in mining API usage specifications for the `RE` class.

Based on our experience with CSEs, we identify that the relevance of code examples returned by CSE is primarily based on the format of the query issued to CSEs. Without a well-formed query, CSEs can result in a high number of irrelevant code examples. For example, a basic search query for collecting code examples of the `fopen` method via GCS is "`lang:c fopen`". GCS returns around 752, 000 code examples for the preceding basic query. When the query is changed to a well-formed query of the form "`lang:c file:.c$ [\s \*]fopen [\s]?\(`" (GCS supports search with regular expressions), GCS returns 689, 000 code examples. Among the top 50 returned code examples, the number of relevant code examples was found to be doubled with the well-formed query compared to the basic query. The relevance (or quality) of collected code examples plays an important role in mining API usage specifications from collected code examples.

These well-formed queries can be formed by using additional features provided by CSEs. We next present the features provided by four popular CSEs for constructing well-formed queries.

- **Google code search** provides features to filter out search results through additional information such as licenses, packages, and filenames. Google code search also supports POSIX regular expressions as part of the search query.

- **Koders** provides features to filter search results based on licenses. Additionally, Koders supports wild-card expressions and context-based search such as class definition or method definition.

- **Krugle** provides features to filter the search results based on projects and also on contexts such as comments and function calls. Additionally, Krugle supports a new kind of search, known as negative terms search, that supports searching for a "<term> - <negativeterm>" and excludes code examples including the "<negativeterm>" among the search results.

- **Codase** provides features to conduct a search based on programming languages and further on contexts such as method calls and method definitions.

Additional techniques. We next present an additional technique that helps address the challenge of duplicate code examples among the code examples returned by CSEs. This technique is based on our observation that the code examples returned by CSEs often include duplicates. We consider a code example ce_i as a duplicate of another code example ce_j, if both ce_i and ce_j belong to the same project and the same source file in that project. For example, among 2000 code examples returned by GCS for the query "`lang:java org.apache.regexp RE`," the source file `JakartaRegexpRegexp.java` is found 13 times. Among these 13 copies, there are 5 different versions of the source file and the remaining 8 copies are duplicates of these 5 versions. There are both desirable and undesirable consequences with duplicates or multiple versions of source files among code examples. For example, code examples that are duplicate of the same source file, such as those belonging to a particular jar file, can be found to be used in various projects. The existence of duplicate or multiple copies for a code example can indicate that the code example is widely used and therefore the code example can be trusted more than those code examples that do not have duplicate or multiple versions. On the other hand, duplicate or multiple copies can bias the results of mining approaches that try to mine common patterns. To mine unbiased patterns used across a large number of code bases, we suggest to identify and filter out duplicate code examples.

10.5   Analyze Phase

We next explain how the analyze phase analyzes SE data collected in the form of code examples. The analyze phase includes two major tasks: resolve object types and generate candidates. Since these code examples are collected from a CSE, traditional program analysis techniques cannot be used for analyzing these code examples. The primary reason is that CSEs often return only individual source files (i.e., code examples) including the search term, and these code examples are often partial and not compilable. In our context, a partial code example indicates that the code example is complete; however, the other source files on which the code example is dependent upon are not available. Therefore, to analyze these code examples, we propose partial-program analysis for resolving object types based on heuristics. These heuristics are contrary to type checking done by a compiler. We first present the heuristics used by our partial-program analysis for resolving object types and next describe how we generate pattern candidates from collected code examples.

10.5.1 Resolve Object Types

We use 16 heuristics for resolving object types such as receiver or argument object type of an API method call in collected code examples. In this chapter, we explain two of our major heuristics used for identifying the return type of an API method call. Our heuristics are not complete as these heuristics cannot resolve entire type information. However, the evaluation results of approaches [25–28] developed based on our life-cycle model show that these heuristics are often effective in resolving required object type information.

Heuristic 1: *The return type of an API method call contained in an initialization expression is the same as the type or a subtype of the declared variable.*

Consider the code example shown below:

```
QueueConnection connect; QueueSession session =
    connect.createQueueSession(false,int)
```

The receiver type of the method `createQueueSession` is the type of `connect` variable. Therefore, the receiver type can be simply inferred by looking at the declaration of the `connect` variable. But as our approach mainly deals with code that is partial and not compilable, it is difficult to get the return type of the method-invocation `createQueueSession`. The reason is the lack of access to method declarations. However, the return type can be inferred from the type of variable `session` on the left-hand side of the assignment statement. As the type of variable `session` is `QueueSession`, we can infer that the return type of the method-invocation `createQueueSession` is `QueueSession`.

Heuristic 2: *The return type of an outermost API method call contained in a return statement is the same (or a subtype) as the return type of the enclosing method declaration.*

Consider code example presented below:

```
public QueueSession test()    { ...
    return connect.createQueueSession(false,int);}
```

In this code example, the method-invocation statement `createQueueSession` is a part of the return statement of the method declaration. In this scenario, we can infer the return type of this method-invocation from the return type of the method `test`. As the method `test` returns `QueueSession`, we can infer that the return type of the method-invocation `createQueueSession` is also `QueueSession`.

10.5.2 Generate Candidates

After type resolution based on preceding heuristics, the analyze phase generates relevant SE data from collected code examples. We refer to these SE data as pattern candidates. In practice, these pattern candidates are based on the requirements of SE tasks. For example, for our example SE task, the

```
01:    Connection conn = null;
02:    Statement stmt = null;
03:    BufferedWriter bw = null; FileWriter fw = null;
04:    try {
05:        fw = new FileWriter("output.txt");
06:        bw = BufferedWriter(fw);
07:        conn = DriverManager.getConnection("jdbc:pl:db", "ps", "ps");
08:        Statement stmt = conn.createStatement();
09:        ResultSet res = stmt.executeQuery("SELECT Path FROM Files");
10:        while (res.next()) {
11:            bw.write(res.getString(1));
12:        }
13:        res.close();
14:    } catch(IOException ex) {  logger.error("IOException occurred");
15:    } finally {
16:        if(stmt != null) stmt.close();
17:        if(conn != null) conn.close();
18:        if (bw != null) bw.close();
19:    }
```

FIGURE 10.4: An example scenario where database contents are retrieved using the `executeQuery` method call.

pattern candidates are in the form of method-call sequences, since we are interested in mining expected behavior as the method calls that need to be invoked when exceptions occur.

In general, control-flow graphs (CFG) can help generate pattern candidates for a majority of the SE tasks, since these graphs represent the flow of program execution. However, for some special tasks such as our example SE Task, CFGs may not be sufficient. For example, the objective of the example SE task is to mine expected behavior during exceptions. Traditionally, CFGs do not include the flow of program execution when exceptions occur. Therefore, we propose a new type of graph, called exception-flow graph (EFG). These EFGs are an extended form of CFGs and includes all paths, including exception paths. In this section, we briefly describe how to construct EFGs and generate pattern candidates from EFGs. The concepts explained based on EFGs are also applicable to CFGs.

We use the example scenario shown in Figure 10.4 for describing how to construct EFGs and generate pattern candidates. Figure 10.5(a) shows the constructed EFG, where each node is denoted with the corresponding statement in Figure 10.4. Initially, we build a CFG that represents flow of control during normal execution and augment the constructed CFG with additional edges that represent flow of control after exceptions occur. We refer to these additional edges as *exception* edges and all other edges as *normal* edges. In the figure, *normal* and *exception* edges are shown in solid and dotted lines, respectively. For example, an exception edge is added from Node 5 to Node 13

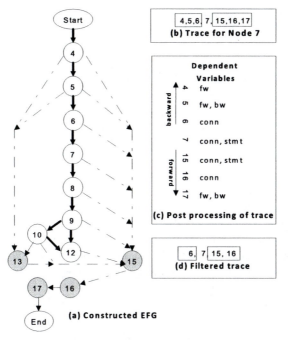

FIGURE 10.5: An example exception-flow graph and a generated pattern candidate. (From S. Thummalapenta and T. Xie, Mining exception-handling rules as sequence association rules, International Conference on Software Engineering (ICSE) ©2009 IEEE.)

as the program can follow this path when `IOException` occurs while creating a `BufferedWriter` object. As code inside a `catch` or a `finally` block gets executed after exceptions occur, we consider edges between the statements within `catch` and `finally` blocks also as exception edges. We show nodes related to method calls in normal paths such as those in a `try` block in white and method calls in exception paths such as those in a `catch` block in gray. Although method calls in a `finally` block belong to both normal and exception paths, we consider these paths as exception paths and show the associated nodes in gray. For simplicity, we ignore the control flow inside exception blocks.

We next describe how we generate pattern candidates from EFGs. We next capture static traces that include actions that should be taken when exceptions occur while executing method calls such as $FC_a \in FCS$. For example, consider the FC_a "`Connection.createStatement`" and its corresponding Node 7 in the EFG. A trace generated for this node is shown in Figure 10.5(b). The trace includes three sections: *normal method-call sequence* $(FC_c^1...FC_c^n)$, FC_a, *exception method-call sequence* $(FC_e^1...FC_e^m)$.

The $FC_c^1...FC_c^n$ sequence starts from the beginning of the body of the enclosing method (i.e., caller) of the FC_a method call to the call site of FC_a. The $FC_e^1...FC_e^m$ sequence includes the longest exception path that starts from the call site of FC_a and terminates either at the end of the enclosing method body or at a node in EFG whose outgoing edges are all normal edges. We generate such traces from code examples and input application for each FC_a $\in FCS$. We next identify method calls in $FC_c^1...FC_c^n$ or $FC_e^1...FC_e^m$ that are not related to FC_a through data-dependency, and remove such method calls from each trace. Failing to remove such unrelated method calls can result in many false positives due to frequent occurrences of unrelated method calls. For example, in the trace shown in Figure 10.5(b), method calls in the normal method-call sequence related to Nodes 4 and 5 are unrelated to the FC_a of Node 7. Similarly, Node 17 in the exception method-call sequence is also unrelated to FC_a.

Figure 10.5(c) shows an example of our data-dependency analysis. Initially, we generate two kinds of relationships: var dependency of a variable and method association of a method call. The var dependency of a variable represents the set of variables on which a given variable is dependent upon. Similarly, a method association of a method call represents the set of variables with which a method call is associated. First, we compute the var-dependency relationship information from assignment statements. For example, in Scenario 2, we identify that the variable `res` is dependent on the variable `stmt` from Line 2.8 and is transitively dependent on `conn` as `stmt` is dependent on `conn` from Line 2.7. We compute the method-association relationship based on the var-dependency relationship. In particular, we identify that a method call is associated with all its variables including the receiver, arguments, and the return variable, and their transitively dependent variables. For example, applying the preceding analysis to the method call of Node 7, we identify that the associated variables are `conn` and `stmt`. We use variables associated with each method call to identify method calls in the normal method-call sequence $FC_c^1...FC_c^n$ or the exception method-call sequence $FC_e^1...FC_e^m$ that are not related to FC_a. Starting from FC_a, we perform a backward traversal of the trace to filter out method calls in $FC_c^1...FC_c^n$ and a forward traversal to filter out method calls in $FC_e^1...FC_e^m$. Assume that variables associated with FC_a are $\{V_a^1, V_a^2,..., V_a^s\}$. Assume that variables associated with a method call, say FC_{ce}^k, in the normal or exception method-call sequence are $\{V_{ce}^1, V_{ce}^2,..., V_{ce}^t\}$.

In each traversal, we compute an intersection of associated variable sets of FC_a and FC_{ce}^k. If the intersection $\{V_a^1, V_a^2,..., V_a^s\} \cap \{V_{ce}^1, V_{ce}^2,..., V_{ce}^t\} \neq \phi$, we keep the FC_{ce}^k method call (either in the normal or exception method-call sequence) in the trace; otherwise, we filter out the FC_{ce}^k method call from the trace. The rationale behind our analysis is that if the intersection is a nonempty set, it indicates that the FC_a is directly or indirectly related to the FC_{ce}^k method call. For example, the intersection of associated variables for Nodes 6 and 7 is non-empty. In contrast, the intersection of associated variables for Nodes 5 and 7 is empty. Therefore, we keep Node 6 in the trace and filter out Node 5 during backward traversal. Similarly, during forward traversal, we ignore Node 17 since the intersection is an empty set. The resulting trace of "4,5,6,7,15,16,17" is "6,7,15,16," where

```
 6 : DriverManager.getConnection
 7 : Connection.createStatement
15 : Statement.close
16 : Connection.close
```

10.6 Mine Phase

The *mine* phase preprocesses analyzed SE data to transform data into a format suitable for applying a mining algorithm. The mine phase next applies a mining algorithm to generate specifications in the form of frequent patterns from the candidates generated by the analyze phase. In general, existing off-the-shelf data mining algorithms [4, 7, 12, 14, 23, 29] can be used for generating frequent patterns from pattern candidates. However, sometimes unique requirements of target SE tasks such as our example SE task require new data mining algorithms. Therefore, the mine phase primarily targets at adopting existing off-the-shelf algorithms or developing new mining algorithms based on the unique requirements of the target SE task. We next describe why existing off-the-shelf algorithms are not sufficient for achieving our example SE task and propose how to develop new mining algorithms based on the requirements of target SE tasks.

For our example SE task, applying existing association-rule mining algorithms can help find rules of the form $FC_a \Rightarrow FC_e$ as specifications, where both FC_a and FC_e are method calls that share the same receiver object in object-oriented programs. These specifications can be used to find exception-handling bugs: if FC_e does not follow FC_a in all exception paths. However, association rules of this form are often insufficient to capture common exception-handling rules. In some situations, FC_a is not necessarily followed by FC_e when FC_a raises exceptions, although both method calls share the same receiver object.

Consider the two code examples shown in Figures 10.3 and 10.4. The code example in Figure 10.3 attempts to modify the contents of a database through the method call `Statement.executeUpdate` (Statement 9), whereas the code example in Figure 10.4 attempts to read the contents of a database through the method call `Statement.executeQuery` (Statement 8). A simple specification in the form of an association rule "`Connection creation` $\Rightarrow$ `Connection rollback`" indicates that a `rollback` method call should occur in exception paths whenever an object of `Connection` is created. However, this form of specification is not a real rule since the `rollback` method call should be invoked only when changes are made to the database. Therefore, we propose sequence association rules of the form $(FC_c^1...FC_c^n) \wedge FC_a \Rightarrow (FC_e^1...FC_e^m)$, which implies that method-call sequence $FC_e^1...FC_e^m$ should follow FC_a in exception paths only when method-call sequence $FC_c^1...FC_c^n$ precedes FC_a. Therefore, the sequence association rule for the code examples shown in Figures 10.3 and 10.4 is expressed as "$(FC_c^1 FC_c^2) \wedge FC_a \Rightarrow (FC_e^1)$," where

FC_c^1 : `OracleDataSource.getConnection`
FC_c^2 : `Connection.createStatement`
FC_a : `Statement.executeUpdate`
FC_e^1 : `Connection.rollback`

We first present a problem definition for mining sequence association rules and then present an algorithm developed for mining these sequence association rules.

Problem definition. Let $F = \{FC_1, FC_2, ..., FC_k\}$ be the set of all possible distinct items. Let $I = \{FC_{i1}, FC_{i2}, ..., FC_{im}\}$ and $J = \{FC_{j1}, FC_{j2}, ..., FC_{jn}\}$ be two sets of items, where $I \subseteq F$ and $J \subseteq F$. Consider a sequence database as a set of tuples (sid, S_i, S_j), where sid is a sequence id, S_i is a sequence of items belonging to I, and S_j is a sequence of items belonging to J. In essence, S_i and S_j belong to two sequence databases, say SDB_1 and SDB_2, denoted as $S_i \in SDB_1$ and $S_j \in SDB_2$, respectively, and there is a **one-to-one** mapping between the two sequence databases. We define an association rule between sets of sequences as $X \Rightarrow Y$, where both X and Y are subsequences of $S_i \in SDB_1$ and $S_j \in SDB_2$, respectively. A sequence $\alpha = \langle a_1 a_2...a_p \rangle$ (where each a_s is an item) is defined as a subsequence of another sequence $beta = \langle b_1 b_2...b_q \rangle$, denoted as $\alpha \sqsubseteq \beta$, if there exist integers $1 \leq j_1 < j_2 < ... < j_p \leq q$ such that $a_1 = b_{j1}$, $a_2 = b_{j2}$,..., $a_p = b_{jq}$.

Mining algorithm. Given two sequence databases such as SDB_1 and SDB_2, the algorithm mines rules of the form $X \Rightarrow Y$, where $X \sqsubseteq S_i \in SDB_1$ and $Y \sqsubseteq S_j \in SDB_2$. We combine both sequence databases in a novel way using annotations to build a single sequence database. These annotations help in deriving association rules in later stages. For example, consider two sequence databases shown in Figure 10.6(a). Figure 10.6(b) shows a single sequence database using annotations combined from the two sequence databases. We next mine frequent subsequences from the combined database, denoted as $SDB_{1,2}$, using the frequent closed subsequence mining technique [29]. The frequent subsequence mining technique accepts a database of sequences such as $SDB_{1,2}$ and a minimum support threshold *min_sup*, and returns subsequences that appear at least *min_sup* times in the sequence database. Given a sequence s, it is considered as frequent if its support $sup(s) \geq min\_sup$. In our context, we are interested in frequent closed subsequences. A sequence s is a frequent closed sequence if s is frequent and no proper super sequence of s is frequent. Figure 10.6(c) shows an example closed frequent subsequence from the combined sequence database. As sequence mining preserves temporal order among items, we scan each closed frequent subsequence and transform the subsequence into an association rule of the form "$X \Rightarrow Y$" based on annotations (as shown in Figure 10.6(d)). We compute confidence values for each association rule using the formula.

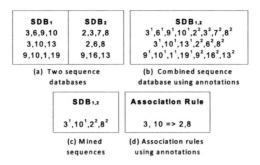

SDB₁	SDB₂	SDB₁,₂
3,6,9,10	2,3,7,8	$3^1,6^1,9^1,10^1,2^2,3^2,7^2,8^2$
3,10,13	2,6,8	$3^1,10^1,13^1,2^2,6^2,8^2$
9,10,1,19	9,16,13	$9^1,10^1,1^1,19^1,9^2,16^2,13^2$

(a) Two sequence databases | (b) Combined sequence database using annotations

SDB₁,₂	Association Rule
$3^1,10^1,2^2,8^2$	3, 10 => 2,8

(c) Mined sequences | (d) Association rules using annotations

FIGURE 10.6: Illustrative examples of general algorithm. (From S. Thummalapenta and T. Xie, Mining exception-handling rules as sequence association rules, International Conference on Software Engineering (ICSE) ©2009 IEEE.)

Confidence $(X \Rightarrow Y)$ = Support $(X\ Y)$ / Support (X)

Although we explain our algorithm using two sequence databases SDB_1 and SDB_2, our algorithm can be applied to multiple sequence databases as well. These multiple sequence databases can also be combined into a single sequence database using the similar mechanism illustrated in Figure 10.6. For mining exception-handling rules for our example SE task, we consider two sequence databases for each method call FC_a: a normal method-call-sequence (NFCS) database and an exception method-call-sequence (EFCS) database. We apply our mining algorithm to generate sequence association rules of the form $FC_c^1...FC_c^n \Rightarrow FC_e^1...FC_e^m$, where $FC_c^1...FC_c^n \sqsubseteq S_i \in$ NFCS and $FC_e^1...FC_e^m \sqsubseteq S_j \in$ EFCS.

10.7   Apply Phase

The apply phase next uses mined API usage specifications for achieving the SE task. These mined specifications can be used for improving software productivity via assisting programmers or software quality by using mined specifications as programming rules for verification tools. We next explain how we achieve the example SE task of detecting exception-handling defects using mined specifications.

Initially, from each call site of FC_a in the application under analysis, we extract the normal method-call sequence, say $C_c^1 C_c^2...C_c^a$, from the beginning of the body of enclosing method of FC_a to the call site of FC_a. If $FC_c^1...FC_c^n \sqsubseteq C_c^1 C_c^2...C_c^a$, then we extract the exception method-call sequence, say $C_e^1 C_e^2...C_e^b$, from the call site of FC_a to the end of the enclosing method body or to a node (in the EFG) whose outgoing edges are all normal edges. We do not report a violation if $FC_e^1...FC_e^m \sqsubseteq C_e^1C_e^2...C_e^b$; otherwise, we report a violation in the application under analysis. We rank all detected violations based on a similar criterion used for ranking exception-handling rules.

We applied the approach [28] developed based on our life-cycle model on static sequences extracted from code examples (found on the web) that use third-party APIs found in five real-world applications (including 285 KLOC), mining 294 real exception-handling rules and detecting 160 exception-handling defects. Among these 294 rules, 88 rules (30%) can be mined by using the source code of the application as a source of information for our approach. However, the remaining 206 rules (70%) can be mined only from the code examples gathered from the web. These results show that approaches developed based on our life-cycle model can mine more API usage specifications, thereby showing the significance of our life-cycle model.

10.8   Summary

In this chapter, we proposed a life-cycle model that describes how to reuse an enormous amount of open source code available on the web for the research in the area of mining software engineering data. Our life-cycle model integrates searching and mining, and addresses a significant issue of lacking sufficient data points to mine desirable patterns from a few code bases provided as input to mining-based approaches. This chapter also presents an example task of detecting exception-handling defects developed based on described life-cycle model. We recommend readers to refer to the papers [25–27] for more approaches developed based on our life-cycle model to address other problems in the software engineering domain such as assisting programmers while writing source code. Our life-cycle model represents a step toward a new direction of leveraging research in the field of search-driven development to assist the research in mining software engineering data, serving as a synergy between these two major research areas.

Bibliography

[1] Koder's Zeitgeist. http://www.koders.com/zeitgeist/.

[2] Mithun Acharya, Tao Xie, Jian Pei, and Jun Xu. Mining API patterns as partial orders from source code: from usage scenarios to specifications. In *Proceedings of the 6th Joint Meeting of the European Software Engineering Conference and the ACM SIGSOFT Symposium on the Foundations of Software Engineering (ESEC/FSE)*, pages 25–34, ACM Press, 2007.

[3] Mithun Acharya, Tao Xie, and Jun Xu. Mining interface specifications for generating checkable robustness properties. In *Proceedings of the 17th International Symposium on Software Reliability Engineering (ISSRE)*, pages 311–320, IEEE Computer Society, 2006.

[4] Rakesh Agrawal and Ramakrishnan Srikant. Fast algorithms for mining association rules in large databases. In *Proceedings of the 20th International Conference on Very Large Data Bases (VLDB)*, pages 487–499, 1994.

[5] Glenn Ammons, Rastislav Bodik, and James R. Larus. Mining specifications. *SIGPLAN Not.*, 37(1):4–16, 2002.

[6] The Apache Jakarta Project, 2007. `http://jakarta.apache.org/regexp/`.

[7] Doug Burdick, Manuel Calimlim, and Johannes Gehrke. MAFIA: a maximal frequent itemset algorithm for transactional databases. In *Proceedings of the 17th International Conference on Data Engineering*, pages 443–452, IEEE Computer Society, 2001.

[8] Ray-Yaung Chang, Andy Podgurski, and Jiong Yang. Finding what's not there: a new approach to revealing neglected conditions in software. In *Proceedings of the 2007 International Symposium on Software Testing and Analysis (ISSTA)*, pages 163–173, ACM Press, 2007.

[9] Codase, 2005. `http://www.codase.com/`.

[10] Dawson Engler, David Yu Chen, Seth Hallem, Andy Chou, and Benjamin Chelf. Bugs as deviant behavior: a general approach to inferring errors in systems code. *SIGOPS Oper. Syst. Rev.*, 35(5):57–72, 2001.

[11] Google code search engine, 2006. `http://www.google.com/codesearch`.

[12] Mark Hall, Eibe Frank, Geoffrey Holmes, Bernhard Pfahringer, Peter Reutemann, and Ian H. Witten. The weka data mining software: an update. *SIGKDD Explor. Newsl.*, 11(1):10–18, 2009.

[13] R. Holmes and G.C. Murphy. Using structural context to recommend source code examples. In *Proceedings of the 27th International Conference on Software Engineering (ICSE)*, pages 117–125, ACM Press, 2005.

[14] Jun Huan, Wei Wang, and Jan Prins. Efficient mining of frequent subgraphs in the presence of isomorphism. In *Proceedings of the 3rd IEEE International Conference on Data Mining (ICDM)*, pages 549–558, IEEE Computer Society, 2003.

[15] Krugle, 2006. `http://www.krugle.com/`.

[16] T.C. Lethbridge, J. Singer, and A. Forward. How software engineers use documentation: the state of the practice. In *IEEE Software*, pages 35–39, 2003.

[17] Zhenmin Li and Yuanyuan Zhou. PR-Miner: automatically extracting implicit programming rules and detecting violations in large software codes. *SIGSOFT Softw. Eng. Notes*, 30(5):306–315, 2005.

[18] V. Benjamin Livshits and Thomas Zimmermann. Dynamine: finding common error patterns by mining software revision histories. *SIGSOFT Softw. Eng. Notes*, 30(5):296–305, 2005.

[19] Madhuri R. Marri, Suresh Thummalapenta, and Tao Xie. Improving software quality via code searching and mining. In *Proceedings of the 2009 ICSE Workshop on Search-Driven Development-Users, Infrastructure, Tools and Evaluation (SUITE)*, pages 33–36, IEEE Computer Society, 2009.

[20] Bibliography on mining software engineering data. `https://sites.google.com/site/asergrp/dmse/`.

[21] Murali Krishna Ramanathan, Ananth Grama, and Suresh Jagannathan. Path-sensitive inference of function precedence protocols. In *Proceedings of the 29th International Conference on Software Engineering (ICSE)*, pages 240–250, IEEE Computer Society, 2007.

[22] N. Sahavechaphan and K. Claypool. XSnippet: mining for sample code. *SIGPLAN Not.*, 41(10):413–430, 2006.

[23] Data Mining Using SAS Enterprise Miner. `http://www.sasenterpriseminer.com/`.

[24] Sharon Shoham, Eran Yahav, Stephen Fink, and Marco Pistoia. Static specification mining using automata-based abstractions. In *Proceedings of the 2007 International Symposium on Software Testing and Analysis (ISSTA)*, pages 174–184, ACM Press, 2007.

[25] Suresh Thummalapenta and Tao Xie. PARSEWeb: a programmer assistant for reusing open source code on the web. In *Proceedings of the 22nd IEEE/ACM International Conference on Automated Software Engineering (ASE)*, pages 204–213, ACM Press, 2007.

[26] Suresh Thummalapenta and Tao Xie. SpotWeb: detecting framework hotspots and coldspots via mining open source code on the web. In *Proceedings of the 23rd IEEE/ACM International Conference on Automated Software Engineering (ASE)*, pages 327–336, IEEE Computer Society, 2008.

[27] Suresh Thummalapenta and Tao Xie. Alattin: mining alternative patterns for detecting neglected conditions. In *Proceedings of the 24th IEEE/ACM International Conference on Automated Software Engineering (ASE)*, pages 283–294, IEEE Computer Society, 2009.

[28] Suresh Thummalapenta and Tao Xie. Mining exception-handling rules as sequence association rules. In *Proceedings of the 31st IEEE International Conference on Software Engineering (ICSE)*, pages 496–506, IEEE Computer Society, 2009.

[29] Jianyong Wang and Jiawei Han. BIDE: efficient mining of frequent closed sequences. In *Proceedings of the 20th International Conference on Data Engineering (ICDE)*, pages 79–80, IEEE Computer Society, 2004.

[30] Andrzej Wasylkowski, Andreas Zeller, and Christian Lindig. Detecting object usage anomalies. In *Proceedings of the 6th Joint Meeting of the European Software Engineering Conference and the ACM SIGSOFT Symposium on The Foundations of Software Engineering (ESEC/FSE)*, pages 35–44, ACM Press, 2007.

[31] J. Yang, D. Evans, D. Bhardwaj, T. Bhat, and M. Das. Perracotta: mining temporal API rules from imperfect traces. In *Proceedings of the 28th International Conference on Software Engineering (ICSE)*, pages 282–291, ACM Press, 2006.

Chapter 11

Merlin: Specification Inference for Explicit Information Flow Problems

Benjamin Livshits
Microsoft Research–Redmond

Aditya V. Nori
Microsoft Research–Redmond

Sriram K. Rajamani
Microsoft Research–Bangalore

Anindya Banerjee
IMDEA Software

The last several years have seen a proliferation of static and runtime analysis tools for finding security violations that are caused by *explicit information flow* in programs. Much of this interest has been caused by the increase in the number of vulnerabilities such as cross-site scripting and SQL injection. In fact, these explicit information flow vulnerabilities commonly found in Web applications now outnumber vulnerabilities such as buffer overruns common in type-unsafe languages such as C and C++. Tools checking for these vulnerabilities require a specification to operate. In most cases the task of providing such a specification is delegated to the user. Moreover, the efficacy of these tools is only as good as the specification. Unfortunately, writing a comprehensive specification presents a major challenge: Parts of the specification are easy to miss, leading to missed vulnerabilities; similarly, incorrect specifications may lead to false positives.

This paper proposes MERLIN, a new approach for automatically inferring explicit information flow specifications from program code. Such specifications greatly reduce manual labor, and enhance the quality of results, while using tools that check for security violations caused by explicit information flow. Beginning with a data propagation graph, which represents interprocedural flow of information in the program, MERLIN aims to automatically infer an information flow specification. MERLIN models information flow paths in the propagation graph using probabilistic constraints. A naïve modeling requires an exponential number of constraints, one per path in the propagation graph. For scalability, we approximate these path constraints using constraints on chosen triples of nodes, resulting in a cubic number of constraints. We characterize this approximation as a probabilistic abstraction, using the theory of probabilistic refinement developed by McIver and Morgan. We solve the resulting system of probabilistic constraints using factor graphs, which are a well-known structure for performing probabilistic inference.

We experimentally validate the MERLIN approach by applying it to 10 large business-critical Web applications that have been analyzed with CAT.NET, a state-of-the-art static analysis tool for .NET. We find a total of 167 new confirmed specifications, which result in a total of 322 *additional* vulnerabilities across the 10 benchmarks. More accurate specifications also reduce the false positive rate: In our experiments, MERLIN-inferred specifications result in 13 false positives being removed; this constitutes a 15% reduction in the CAT.NET false positive rate on these 10 programs. The final false positive rate for CAT.NET *after* applying MERLIN in our experiments drops to under 1%.

11.1 Introduction

Constraining information flow is fundamental to security: We do not want secret information to reach untrusted principals (confidentiality), and we do not want untrusted principals to corrupt trusted information (integrity). If we take confidentiality and integrity to the extreme, then principals from different levels of trust can never interact, and the resulting system becomes unusable. For instance, such a draconian system would never allow a trusted user to view untrusted content from the Internet.

Thus, practical systems compromise on such extremes and allow flow of *sanitized* information across trust boundaries. For instance, it is unacceptable to take a string from untrusted user input and use it as part of an SQL query, since it leads to SQL injection attacks. However, it is acceptable to first pass the untrusted user input through a trusted *sanitization function*, and then use the sanitized input to construct an SQL query. Similarly, confidential data need to be cleansed to avoid information leaks. Practical checking tools that have emerged in recent years [4, 21, 24] typically aim to ensure that all explicit flows of information across trust boundaries are sanitized.

The fundamental program abstraction used in the sequel (as well as by existing tools) is what we term the *propagation graph* — a directed graph that models all interprocedural explicit information flow in a program.[1] The nodes of a propagation graph are methods, and edges represent explicit information flow between methods. There is an edge from node $m_1 \rightarrow m_2$ whenever there is a flow of information from method m_1 to method m_2, through a method parameter, or through a return value, or by way of an indirect update through a pointer.

Following the widely accepted Perl taint terminology conventions [30] — more precisely defined in [14] — nodes of the propagation graph are classified as *sources*, *sinks*, and *sanitizers*; nodes not falling in the above categories are termed *regular* nodes. A source node returns tainted data, whereas it is an error to pass tainted data to a sink node. Sanitizer nodes cleanse or untaint or endorse information to mediate across different levels of trust. Regular nodes do not taint data, and it is not an error to pass tainted data to regular nodes. If tainted data are passed to regular nodes, they merely propagate it to their successors without any mediation.

A classification of nodes in a propagation graph into sources, sinks, and sanitizers is called an *information flow specification*, or just *specification* for brevity. Given a propagation graph and a specification, one can easily run a reachability algorithm to check if all paths from sources to sinks pass through

---

[1]We do not focus on *implicit* information flows [27] in this paper. Discussions with CAT.NET [21] developers reveal that detecting explicit information flow vulnerabilities is a more urgent concern. Existing commercial tools in this space exclusively focus on explicit information flow.

```
1. void ProcessRequest(HttpRequest request,
2.            HttpResponse response)
3. {
4.     string s1 = request.GetParameter("name");
5.     string s2 = request.GetHeader("encoding");
6.
7.     response.WriteLine("Parameter " + s1);
8.     response.WriteLine("Header " + s2);
9. }
```

FIGURE 11.1: Simple cross-site scripting example.

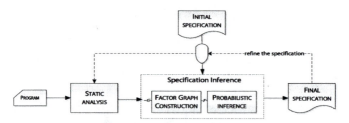

FIGURE 11.2: MERLIN system architecture.

a sanitizer. In fact, this is precisely what many commercial analysis tools in everyday use do [4, 24].

User-provided specifications, however, lead to both false positives and false negatives in practice. False positives arise because a flow from source to sink classified as offending by the tool could have a sanitizer that the tool was unaware of. False negatives arise because of incomplete information about sources and sinks.

This paper presents MERLIN, a tool that *automatically* infers information flow specifications for programs. Our inference algorithm uses the intuition that *most* paths in a propagation graph are secure. That is, most paths in the propagation graph that start from a source and end in a sink pass through some sanitizer.

Example 1 Consider a Web application code snippet written in C# shown in Figure 11.1. While method GetParameter, the method returning arguments of an HTTP request, is highly likely to be part of the default specification that comes with a static analysis tool and classified as a source, the method retrieving an HTTP header GetHeader may easily be missed. Because response.WriteLine sends information to the browser, there are two possibilities of *cross-site scripting vulnerabilities* on line 7 and line 8. The vulnerability in line 7 (namely, passing a tainted value returned by GetParameter into WriteLine without sanizizing it first) will be reported, but the similar vulnerability on line 8 may be missed due to an incomplete specification. In fact, in both .NET and J2EE there exist a number of source methods that return various parts of an HTTP request. When we run MERLIN on larger bodies of code, even within the `HttpRequest` class alone, MERLIN correctly determines that `getQueryString`, `getMethod`, `getEncoding`, and others are sources missing from the default specification that already contains 111 elements. While this example is small, it is meant to convey the challenge involved in identifying appropriate APIs for an arbitrary application. □

Our approach. MERLIN infers information flow specifications using probabilistic inference. By using a random variable for each node in the propagation graph to denote whether the node is a source, sink, or sanitizer, the intuition that most paths in a propagation graph are secure can be modeled using one *probabilistic constraint* for each path in the propagation graph.

A probabilistic constraint is a path constraint parameterized by the probability that the constraint is true. By solving these constraints, we can get assignments to values of these random variables, which yields an information flow specification. In other words, we use probabilistic reasoning and the intuition we have about the outcome of the constraints (i.e., the probability of each constraint being true) to calculate values for the inputs to the constraints. Since there can be an exponential number of paths, using one constraint per path does not scale. In order to scale, we approximate the constraints using a different set of constraints on chosen triples of nodes in the graph. We show that the constraints on triples are a probabilistic abstraction of the constraints on paths (see Section 11.5) according to the theory developed by McIver and Morgan [19, 20].

As a consequence, we can show that approximation using constraints on triples does not introduce false positives when compared with the constraints on paths. After studying large applications, we found that we need additional constraints to reduce false positives, such as constraints to minimize the number of inferred sanitizers, and constraints to avoid inferring wrappers as sources or sinks. Section 11.2 describes these observations and constraints in detail. We show how to model these observations as additional probabilistic constraints. Once we have modeled the problem as a set of probabilistic constraints, specification inference reduces to probabilistic inference. To perform probabilistic inference in a scalable manner, MERLIN uses *factor graphs*, which have been used in a variety of applications [12, 35].

While we can use the above approach to infer specifications *without* any prior specification, we find that the quality of inference is significantly higher if we use the default specification that comes with the static analysis tool as the initial specification, using MERLIN to "complete" this partial specification. Our empirical results in Section 11.6 demonstrate that our tool provides significant value in both situations. In our experiments, we use CAT.NET [21], a state-of-the-art static analysis tool for finding Web application security flaws that works on .NET bytecode. The initial specification provided by CAT.NET is modeled as extra probabilistic constraints on the random variables associated with nodes of the propagation graph. To show the efficacy of MERLIN, we show empirical results for 10 large Web applications.

Contributions. Our chapter makes the following contributions:

- MERLIN is the first practical approach to inferring specifications for explicit information flow analysis tools, a problem made important in recent years by the proliferation of information flow vulnerabilities in Web applications.

- A salient feature of our method is that our approximation (using triples instead of paths) can be characterized formally — we make a connection between probabilistic constraints and probabilistic programs, and use the theory of probabilistic refinement developed by McIver and Morgan [19,20] to show refinement relationships between sets of probabilistic constraints. As a result, our approximation does not introduce false positives.

- MERLIN is able to successfully and efficiently infer information flow specifications in large code bases. We provide a comprehensive evaluation of the efficacy and practicality of MERLIN using 10 Web application benchmarks. We find a total of 167 new confirmed specifications, which result in a total of 322 vulnerabilities across the 10 benchmarks that were previously undetected. MERLIN-inferred specifications also result in 13 false positives being removed.

Outline. The rest of the chapter is organized as follows. Section 11.2 gives motivation for the specification inference techniques MERLIN uses. Section 11.3 provides background on factor graphs. Section 11.4 describes our algorithm in detail. Section 11.5 proves that the system of triple constraints is a probabilistic abstraction over the system of path constraints. Section 11.6 describes our experimental evaluation. Finally, Sections 11.7 and 11.8 describe related work and conclude.

11.2   Overview

Figure 11.2 shows an architectural diagram of MERLIN. MERLIN starts with an initial, potentially incomplete specification of the application to produce a more complete specification. Returning to Example 1, suppose we start MERLIN with an initial specification that classifies `GetParameter` as a source and `WriteLine` as a sink. Then, the specification output by MERLIN would additionally contain `GetHeader` as a source. In addition to the initial specification, MERLIN also consumes a *propagation graph*, a representation of the interprocedural data flow. Nodes of the propagation graph are *methods* in the program, and edges represent explicit flow of data.

Definition 11.2.1 A *propagation graph* is a directed graph $G = \langle N_G, E_G \rangle$, where nodes N_G are methods and an edge $(n_1 \to n_2) \in E_g$ indicates that there is a flow of information from method n_1 to method n_2 through method arguments, or return values, or indirectly through pointers.

The propagation graph is a representation of the interprocedural data flow produced by static analysis of the program. Due to the presence of virtual functions and information flow through references, a pointer analysis is needed to produce a propagation graph. Since pointer analyses are imprecise, edges of a propagation graph approximate information flows. Improving the accuracy of propagation graph involves improving the precision of pointer analysis and is beyond the scope of this chapter. In our implementation, CAT.NET uses an unsound pointer analysis, so there could be flows of data that our propagation graph does not represent. Even though propagation graphs can have cycles, MERLIN performs a breadth-first search and deletes the edges that close cycles, resulting in an acyclic propagation graph. Removing cycles greatly simplifies the subsequent phases of MERLIN. As our empirical results show, even with such approximations in the propagation graph, MERLIN is able to infer useful specifications.

Example 2 We illustrate propagation graphs with an example.

```
public void TestMethod1() {
    string a = ReadData1();
    string b = Prop1(a);
    string c = Cleanse(b);
    WriteData(c);
}

public void TestMethod2() {
    string d = ReadData2();
    string e = Prop2(d);
    string f = Cleanse(e);
    WriteData(f);
}
```

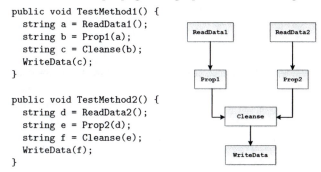

In addition to two top-level "driver" methods, `TestMethod1` and `TestMethod2`, this code uses six methods: `ReadData1`, `ReadData2`, `Prop1`, `Prop2`, `Cleanse`, and `WriteData`. This program gives rise to the propagation graph shown on the right. An edge in the propagation graph represents explicit flow of data, i.e., the value returned by `Prop1` is passed into `Cleanse` as an argument. The edge from `Prop1` to `Cleanse` represents this flow. □

11.2.1 Assumptions and Probabilistic Inference

The crux of our approach is probabilistic inference: We first use the propagation graph to generate a set of probabilistic constraints and then use probabilistic inference to solve them. MERLIN uses factor graphs (see Section 11.3)

to perform probabilistic inference efficiently. As shown in Figure 11.2, MER-
LIN performs the following steps: (1) construct a factor graph based on the
propagation graph; (2) perform probabilistic inference on the factor graph to
derive the likely specification.

MERLIN relies on the assumption that *most* paths in the propagation graph
are secure. That is, most paths that go from a source to a sink pass through
a sanitizer. The assumption that errors are rare has been used before in other
specification inference techniques [3, 10]. Further, we assume that the number
of sanitizers is small, relative to the number of regular nodes. Indeed, developers typically define a small number of sanitization functions or use ones
supplied in libraries, and call them extensively. For instance, the out-of-box
specification that comes with CAT.NET summarized in Figure 11.12 contains
only seven sanitizers.

However, as we show later in this section, applying these assumptions along
various paths individually can lead to inconsistencies, since the constraints
inferred from different paths can be mutually contradictory. Thus, we need
to represent and analyze each path within a constraint system that tolerates
uncertainty and contradictions. Therefore, we parameterize each constraint
with the probability of its satisfaction. These probabilistic constraints model
the relative positions of sources, sinks, and sanitizers in the propagation graph.
Our goal is to classify each node as a source, sink, sanitizer, or a regular node,
so as to optimize satisfaction of these probabilistic constraints.

11.2.2   Potential Sources, Sinks, and Sanitizers

The goal of specification inference is to classify nodes of the propagation
graph into sources, sinks, sanitizers, and regular nodes. Since we are interested
in *string-related* vulnerabilities, we first generate a set of potential sources,
potential sanitizers, and potential sinks based on method signatures, as defined
below:

- Methods that produce strings as output are classified as *potential
  sources.*
- Methods that take a string as input and produce a string as output are
  classified as *potential sanitizers.*
- Methods that take a string as input and do not produce a string as
  output are classified as *potential sinks.*

Next, we perform probabilistic inference to infer a subset of potential sources,
potential sanitizers, and potential sinks that form the inferred specification.

11.2.3   Core Constraints

Figure 11.3 summarizes the constraints that MERLIN uses for probabilistic
inference. We describe each of the constraints below referring to Example 2

A1 For every acyclic path $m_1, m_2, \ldots, m_{k-1}, m_k$, where m_1 is a potential source and m_k is a potential sink, the joint probability of classifying m_1 as a source, m_k as a sink, and all of $m_2, \ldots, m_{k-1}$ as regular nodes is *low*.

B1 For every triple of nodes $\langle m_1, m_2, m_3 \rangle$, where m_1 is a potential source, m_3 is a potential sink, and m_1 and m_3 are connected by a path through m_2 in the propagation graph, the joint probability that m_1 is a source, m_2 is not a sanitizer, and m_3 is a sink is *low*.

B2 For every pair of nodes $\langle m_1, m_2 \rangle$ such that both m_1 and m_2 lie on the same path from a potential source to a potential sink, the probability of both m_1 and m_2 being sanitizers is *low*.

B3 Each node m is classified as a sanitizer with probability $s(m)$ (see Definition 11.2.3 for definition of s).

B4 For every pair of nodes $\langle m_1, m_2 \rangle$ such that both m_1 and m_2 are potential sources and there is a path from m_1 to m_2, the probability that m_1 is a source and m_2 is not a source is *high*.

B5 For every pair of nodes $\langle m_1, m_2 \rangle$ such that both m_1 and m_2 are potential sinks and there is a path from m_1 to m_2, the probability that m_2 is a sink and m_1 is not a sink is *high*.

FIGURE 11.3: Constraint formulation. Probabilities in italics are parameters of the constraints.

where appropriate. We also express the number of constraints of each type as a function of N, the number of nodes in the propagation graph.

A1: Path Safety. We assume that most paths from a source to a sink pass through at least one sanitizer. For example, we believe that if `ReadData1` is a source, and `WriteData` is a sink, at least one of `Prop1` or `Cleanse` is a sanitizer. This is stated using the set of constraints **A1** shown in Figure 11.3. While constraints **A1** model our core beliefs accurately, they are inefficient if used directly: **A1** requires one constraint per path, and the number of acyclic paths could be exponential in the number of propagation graph nodes.

B1: Triple Safety. In order to abstract the constraint set **A1** with a polynomial number of constraints, we add a safety constraint **B1** for each triple of nodes as shown in Figure 11.3. The number of **B1** constraints is $O(N^3)$. In Section 11.5 we prove that the constraints **B1** are a probabilistic abstraction of constraints **A1** under suitable choices of parameters.

11.2.4 Auxiliary Constraints

In practice, the set of constraints **B1** does not limit the solution space enough. We have found empirically that just using this set of constraints allows too many possibilities, several of which are incorrect classifications. By looking at results over several large benchmarks we have come up with four sets of auxiliary constraints—**B2**, **B3**, **B4**, and **B5**—which greatly enhance the precision.

B2: Pairwise Minimization. The set of constraints **B1** allows the solver flexibility to consider multiple sanitizers along a path. In general, we want to minimize the number of sanitizers we infer. Thus, if there are several solutions to the set of constraints **B1**, we want to favor solutions that infer fewer sanitizers, while satisfying **B1**, with higher probability.

For instance, consider the path `ReadData1`, `Prop1`, `Cleanse`, `WriteData` in Example 2. Suppose `ReadData1` is a source and `WriteData` is a sink. **B1** constrains the triple

$$\langle \texttt{ReadData1}, \texttt{Prop1}, \texttt{WriteData} \rangle$$

so that the probability of `Prop1` not being a sanitizer is low; **B1** also constrains the triple

$$\langle \texttt{ReadData1}, \texttt{Cleanse}, \texttt{WriteData} \rangle$$

such that the probability of `Cleanse` not being a sanitizer is low. One solution to these constraints is to infer that both `Prop1` and `Cleanse` are sanitizers. In reality, programmers do not add multiple sanitizers on a path and we believe that only one of `Prop1` or `Cleanse` is a sanitizer. Thus, we add a constraint **B2** that for each pair of potential sanitizers it is unlikely that both are sanitizers, as shown in Figure 11.3. The number of **B2** constraints is $O(N^2)$.

Need for probabilistic constraints. Note that constraints **B1** and **B2** can be mutually contradictory if they are modeled as non-probabilistic boolean constraints. For example, consider the propagation graph of Example 2. With each of the nodes ReadData1, WriteData, Prop1, Cleanse let us associate boolean variables r_1, w, p_1, and c, respectively. The interpretation is that r_1 is true iff ReadData1 is source, w is true iff WriteData is a sink, p_1 is true iff Prop1 is a sanitizer, and c is true iff Cleanse is a sanitizer. Then, constraint **B1** for the triple $\langle$ReadData1, Prop1, WriteData$\rangle$ is given by the boolean formula $r_1 \wedge w \implies p_1$, and the constraint **B1** for the triple $\langle$ReadData1, Cleanse, WriteData$\rangle$ is given by the formula $r_1 \wedge w \implies c$. Constraint **B2** for the pair $\langle$Prop1, Cleanse$\rangle$ states that both Prop1 and Cleanse cannot be sanitizers, and is given by the formula $\neg(p_1 \wedge c)$. In addition, suppose we have additional information (say, from a partial specification given by the user) that ReadData1 is indeed a source, and WriteData is a sink. We can conjoin all the above constraints to get the boolean formula:

$$(r_1 \wedge w \implies p_1) \wedge (r_1 \wedge w \implies c) \wedge \neg(p_1 \wedge c) \wedge r_1 \wedge w$$

This formula is unsatisfiable and these constraints are mutually contradictory. Viewing them as probabilistic constraints gives us the flexibility to add such conflicting constraints; the probabilistic inference resolves such conflicts by favoring satisfaction of those constraints with higher probabilities attached to them.

B3: Sanitizer Prioritization. We wish to bias the selection of sanitizers to favor those nodes that have a lot of source-to-sink paths going through them. We formalize this below.

Definition 11.2.2 For each node m define weight $W(m)$ to be the total number of paths from sources to sinks that pass through m.

Suppose we know that ReadData1 is a source, ReadData2 is *not* a source, and WriteData is a sink. Then $W(\text{Prop1}) = W(\text{Cleanse}) = 1$, since there is only one source-to-sink path that goes through each of them. However, in this case, we believe that Prop1 is more likely to be a sanitizer than Cleanse since *all* paths going through Prop1 are source-to-sink paths and only *some* paths going through Cleanse are source-to-sink paths.

Definition 11.2.3 For each node m define $W_{total}(m)$ to be the total number of paths in the propagation graph that pass through the node m (this includes both source-to-sink paths, as well as other paths). Let us define $s(m)$ for each node m as follows:

$$s(m) = \frac{W(m)}{W_{total}(m)}$$

We add a constraint **B3** that prioritizes each potential sanitizer n based on its $s(n)$ value, as shown in Figure 11.3. The number of **B3** constraints is $O(N)$.

B4: Source Wrapper Avoidance. Similar to avoiding inference of multiple sanitizers on a path, we also wish to avoid inferring multiple sources on a path. A prominent issue with inferring sources is the issue of having wrappers, i.e., functions that return the result produced by the source. For instance, if an application defines its own series of wrappers around system APIs, which is not uncommon, there is no need to flag those as sources because that will actually not affect the set of detected vulnerabilities.

In such cases, we want MERLIN to infer the actual source rather than the wrapper function around it. We add a constraint **B4** for each pair of potential sources as shown in Figure 11.3. The number of **B4** constraints is $O(N^2)$.

B5: Sink Wrapper Avoidance. Wrappers on sinks can be handled similarly, with the variation that in the case of sinks the data actually flow from the wrapper to the sink. We add a constraint **B5** for each pair of potential sinks as shown in Figure 11.3. The number of **B5** constraints is $O(N^2)$.

Given a propagation graph with N nodes, we can generate the constraints **B1** through **B5** in $O(N^3)$ time. Next, we present some background on factor graphs, an approach to efficiently solving probabilistic constraints.

11.3   Factor Graph Primer

In the previous section, we have described a set of probabilistic constraints that are generated from an input propagation graph. The conjunction of these constraints can be looked upon as a joint probability distribution over random variables that measure the odds of propagation graph nodes being sources, sanitizers, or sinks.

Let $p(x_1, \ldots, x_N)$ be a joint probability distribution over boolean variables $x_1, \ldots, x_N$. We are interested in computing the *marginal probabilities* $p_i(x_i)$ defined as:

$$p_i(x_i) = \sum_{x_1} \cdots \sum_{x_{i-1}} \sum_{x_{i+1}} \cdots \sum_{x_N} p(x_1, \ldots, x_N) \qquad (11.1)$$

where $x_i \in \{true, false\}$ for $i \in [1, \ldots, N]$. Since there are an exponential number of terms in Equation 11.1, a naïve algorithm for computing $p_i(x_i)$ will not work in practice. An abbreviated notation for Equation 11.1 is

$$p_i(x_i) = \sum_{\sim \{x_i\}} p(x_1, \ldots, x_N) \qquad (11.2)$$

where the sum is over all variables except x_i. The marginal probability for each variable defines the solution that we are interested in computing. Intuitively, these marginals correspond to the likelihood of each boolean variable being equal to *true* or *false*.

Factor graphs [35] are graphical models that are used for computing marginal probabilities efficiently. These graphs take advantage of their structure in order to speed up the marginal probability computation (known as probabilistic inference). There are a wide variety of techniques for performing probabilistic inference on a factor graph and the *sum-product* algorithm [35] is the most practical algorithm among these.

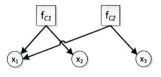

FIGURE 11.4: Factor graph for (11.3).

Let the joint probability distribution $p(x_1, \ldots, x_N)$ be a product of factors as follows:

$$p(x_1, \ldots, x_N) = \prod_s f_s(x_s) \tag{11.3}$$

where x_s is the set of variables involved in the factor f_s. A *factor graph* is a bipartite graph that represents this factorization. A factor graph has two types of nodes:

- *Variable nodes:* one node for every variable x_i.
- *Function nodes:* one node for every function f_s.

Example 3 As an example, consider the following formula:

$$\underbrace{(x_1 \vee x_2)}_{C_1} \wedge \underbrace{(x_1 \vee \neg x_3)}_{C_2} \tag{11.4}$$

Equation 11.4 can be rewritten as:

$$f(x_1, x_2, x_3) = f_{C_1}(x_1, x_2) \wedge f_{C_2}(x_1, x_3) \tag{11.5}$$

where

$$f_{C_1} = \begin{cases} 1 & \text{if } x_1 \vee x_2 = true \\ 0 & \text{otherwise} \end{cases} \tag{11.6}$$

$$f_{C_2} = \begin{cases} 1 & \text{if } x_1 \vee \neg x_3 = true \\ 0 & \text{otherwise} \end{cases} \tag{11.7}$$

The factor graph for this formula is shown in Figure 11.4. There are three variable nodes for each variable x_i, $1 \le i \le 3$ and a function node f_{C_j} for each clause C_j, $j \in \{1, 2\}$.

Equations 11.6 and 11.7 can also be defined probabilistically, thus allowing for solutions that do not satisfy formula 11.4; but such solutions are usually set up such that they occur with low probability as shown below:

$$f_{C_1} = \begin{cases} 0.9 & \text{if } x_1 \vee x_2 = true \\ 0.1 & \text{otherwise} \end{cases} \tag{11.8}$$

$$f_{C_2} = \begin{cases} 0.9 & \text{if } x_1 \vee \neg x_3 = true \\ 0.1 & \text{otherwise} \end{cases} \tag{11.9}$$

If we use this interpretation of f_{C_1} and f_{C_2}, then we can interpret formula 11.5 as a probabilistic constraint.

$$p(x_1, x_2, x_3) = \frac{f_{C_1}(x_1, x_2) \times f_{C_2}(x_1, x_3)}{Z} \tag{11.10}$$

where

$$Z = \sum_{x_1, x_2, x_3} (f_{C_1}(x_1, x_2) \times f_{C_2}(x_1, x_3)) \tag{11.11}$$

is the normalization constant. The marginal probabilities are defined as

$$p_i(x_i) = \sum_{\sim\{x_i\}} p(\vec{x}), \ 1 \leq i \leq 3 \tag{11.12}$$

Here, $p_i(x_i = true)$ denotes the fraction of solutions where the variable x_i has value *true*. These marginal probabilities can be used to compute a solution to the SAT instance in Equation 11.4 as follows: (1) choose a variable x_i with the highest marginal probability $p_i(x_i)$ and set $x_i = true$, if $p_i(x_i)$ is greater than a threshold value, otherwise, set $x_i = false$; (2) recompute the marginal probabilities and repeat Step (1) until all variables have been assigned (this is a satisfying assignment with high probability). Iterative message passing algorithms [12, 35] on factor graphs perform Steps (1) and (2) as well as compute marginal probabilities efficiently. □

11.4   Constructing the Factor Graph

Given a propagation graph G, we describe how to build a factor graph F to represent the constraints **B1** through **B5** associated with G. Figure 11.5 shows the algorithm GenFactorGraph that we use to generate the factor graph from the propagation graph. The construction of the factor graph proceeds as follows. First, in line 1, the procedure MakeAcyclic converts the input propagation graph into a DAG G', by doing a breadth first search, and deleting edges that close cycles. Next, in line 2, the procedure ComputePotentialSrcSanSnk computes the sets of potential sources, potential sanitizers, and potential sinks, and stores the results in X_{src}, X_{san}, and X_{snk}, respectively. On line 3, procedure ComputePairsAndTriples computes four sets defined in Figure 11.7.

These sets can be computed by first doing a topological sort of G' (the acyclic graph), making one pass over the graph in topological order, and recording for each potential sanitizer the set of potential sources and potential sinks that can be reached from that node. Potential sources, sanitizers, and sinks are determined by analyzing type signatures of each method, as described in Section 11.2.2. These sets can be computed in $O(N^3)$ time, where N is the number of nodes in the propagation graph.

GenFactorGraph
Inputs:
$(G = \langle V, E \rangle : PropagationGraph)$,
parameters $low_1, low_2, high_1, high_2, high_3, high_4 \in [0..1]$
Returns:
a factor graph F for the propagation graph G

```
 1: G' = MakeAcyclic(G)
 2: ⟨X_src, X_san, X_snk⟩ = ComputePotentialSrcSanSnk(G)
 3: ⟨Triples, Pairs_src, Pairs_san, Pairs_snk⟩= ComputePairsAndTriples(G', X_src, X_san, X_snk)
 4: s = ComputeWAndSValues(G')
 5: for each triple ⟨a, b, c⟩ ∈ Triples do
 6:     Create a factor f_B1(x_a, x_b, x_c) in the factor graph
 7:     Let f_B1(x_a, x_b, x_c) = x_a ∧ ¬x_b ∧ x_c
 8:     Let probability Pr(f_B1(x_a, x_b, x_c) = true) = low_1
 9: end for
10: for each pair ⟨b_1, b_2⟩ ∈ Pairs_san do
11:     Create a factor f_B2(x_{b_1}, x_{b_2}) in the factor graph
12:     Let f_B2(x_{b_1}, x_{b_2}) = x_{b_1} ∧ x_{b_2}
13:     Let probability Pr(f_B2(x_{b_1}, x_{b_2}) = true) = low_2
14: end for
15: for each n ∈ X_san do
16:     Create a factor f_B3(x_n) in the factor graph
17:     Let f_B3(x_n) = x_n
18:     Let Pr(f_B3(x_n) = true) = s(n)
19: end for
20: for each pair ⟨x_{a_1}, x_{a_2}⟩ ∈ Pairs_src do
21:     Create a factor f_B4(x_{a_1}, x_{a_2}) in the factor graph
22:     Let f_B4(x_{a_1}, x_{a_2}) = x_{a_1} ∧ ¬x_{a_2}
23:     Let probability Pr(f_B4(x_{a_1}, x_{a_2}) = true) = high_3
24: end for
25: for each pair ⟨x_{c_1}, x_{c_2}⟩ ∈ Pairs_snk do
26:     Create a factor f_B5(x_{c_1}, x_{c_2}) in the factor graph
27:     Let f_B5(x_{c_1}, x_{c_2}) = ¬x_{c_1} ∧ x_{c_2}
28:     Let probability Pr(f_B5(x_{c_1}, x_{c_2}) = true) = high_4
29: end for
```

FIGURE 11.5: Generating a factor graph from a propagation graph.

Next in line 4, the function ComputeWAndSValues is invoked to compute $W(n)$ and $s(n)$ for every potential sanitizer n. The function ComputeWAndSValues is described in Figure 11.6. In lines 5–9, the algorithm creates a factor node for the constraints **B1**. In lines 10–14, the algorithm iterates through all pairs $\langle b_1, b_2 \rangle$ of potential sanitizers (that is, actual sanitizers as well as regular nodes) such that there is a path in the propagation graph from b_1 to b_2 and adds factors for constraints **B2**. In lines 15–19, the algorithm iterates through all potential sanitizers and adds factors for constraints **B3**. In lines 20–24, the algorithm iterates through all pairs $\langle a_1, a_2 \rangle$ of potential sources such that there is a path in the propagation graph from a_1 to a_2 and adds factors for constraints **B4**. Similarly, in lines 25–29, the algorithm iterates through all pairs $\langle c_1, c_2 \rangle$ of potential sinks such that there is a path from c_1 to c_2 and adds factors for constraints **B5**.

ComputeWAndSValues(G:Propagation Graph, $X_{src}, X_{san}, X_{snk}$: Set of Nodes)
Precondition:
Inputs:
Acyclic propagation graph G, sets of nodes $X_{src}, X_{san}, X_{snk}$ representing potential sources, potential sanitizers and potential sinks respectively
Returns:
$W(n)$ and $s(n)$ for each potential sanitizer n in G

```
 1: for each potential source n ∈ X_src do
 2:     F(n) := initial probability of n being a source node
 3:     F_total(n) := 1
 4: end for
 5: for each potential sanitizer n ∈ X_san in topological order do
 6:     F(n) := 0
 7:     F_total(n) := 0
 8:     for each m ∈ V such that (m, n) ∈ E do
 9:         F(n) := F(n) + F(m)
10:         F_total(n) := F_total(n) + F_total(m)
11:     end for
12: end for
13: for each potential sink n ∈ X_snk do
14:     B(n) := initial probability of n being a sink node
15:     B_total(n) := 1
16: end for
17: for each potential sanitizer n ∈ X_san in reverse topological order do
18:     B(n) := 0
19:     B_total(n) := 0
20:     for each m ∈ V such that (n, m) ∈ E do
21:         B(n) := B(n) + B(m)
22:         B_total(n) := B_total(n) + B_total(m)
23:     end for
24: end for
25: for each potential sanitizer n ∈ X_san do
26:     W(n) := F(n) * B(n)
27:     s(n) := W(n) / (F_total(n) * B_total(n))
28: end for
29: return s
```

FIGURE 11.6: Computing $W(n)$ and $s(n)$.

11.4.1   Computing $s()$ and $W()$

Recall values $s()$ and $W()$ defined in Section 11.2.4. Figure 11.6 describes ComputeWAndSValues, which computes $s(n)$ for each potential sanitizer node, given input probabilities for each potential source and each potential sink.

The value $s(n)$ for each potential sanitizer n is the ratio of the sum of weighted source-sink paths that go through n and the total number of paths that go through n. The algorithm computes $W(n)$ and $s(n)$ by computing four numbers $F(n)$, $F_{total}(n)$, $B(n)$, and $B_{total}(n)$.

$F(n)$ denotes the total number of sources that can reach n, and $F_{total}(n)$ denotes the total number of paths that can reach n. $B(n)$ denotes the total number of sinks that can be reached from n. Finally, $B_{total}(n)$ denotes the total number of paths that can be reached from n.

For each potential source n, we set $F(n)$ to an initial value in line 2 (in our implementation, we picked an initial value of 0.5), and we set $F_{total}(n)$ to 1 in line 3. For each potential sink, we set $B(n)$ to some initial value in

SET	DEFINITION
$Triples$	$\displaystyle\bigcup_{p\in paths(G')}\{\langle x_{src}, x_{san}, x_{snk}\rangle \mid x_{src} \in X_{src}, x_{san} \in X_{san}, x_{snk} \in X_{snk}, x_{src}$ is connected to x_{snk} via x_{san} in $p\}$
$Pairs_{src}$	$\displaystyle\bigcup_{p\in paths(G')}\{\langle x_{src}, x'_{src}\rangle \mid x_{src} \in X_{src}, x'_{src} \in X_{src}, x_{src}$ is connected to x'_{src} in $p\}$
$Pairs_{san}$	$\displaystyle\bigcup_{p\in paths(G')}\{\langle x_{san}, x'_{san}\rangle \mid x_{san} \in X_{san}, x'_{san} \in X_{san}, x_{san}$ is connected to x'_{san} in $p\}$
$Pairs_{snk}$	$\displaystyle\bigcup_{p\in paths(G')}\{\langle x_{snk}, x'_{snk}\rangle \mid x_{snk} \in X_{snk}, x'_{snk} \in X_{snk}, x_{snk}$ is connected to x'_{snk} in $p\}$

FIGURE 11.7: Set definitions for algorithm in Figure 11.5.

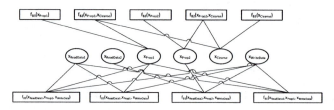

FIGURE 11.8: Factor graph for the propagation graph in Example 2.

line 14 (in our implementation, we picked this initial value to be 0.5), and we set $B_{total}(n)$ to 1 in line 15.

Since the graph G' is a DAG, $F(n)$ and $F_{total}(n)$ can be computed by traversing potential sanitizers in topological sorted order, and $B(n)$ and $B_{total}(n)$ can be computed by traversing potential sanitizers in reverse topological order. The computation of $F(n)$ and $F_{total}(n)$ in forward topological order is done in lines 5–12 and the computation of $B(n)$ and $B_{total}(n)$ in reverse topological order is done in lines 17–24. Once $F(n)$ and $B(n)$ are computed, $W(n)$ is set to $F(n) \times B(n)$ and $s(n)$ is set to

$$\frac{W(n)}{F_{total}(n) \times B_{total}(n)} = \frac{W(n)}{W_{total}(n)}$$

as shown in line 26.

Parameter tuning. The parameters low_1, low_2, $high_1$, $high_2$, $high_3$, and $high_4$ all need to be instantiated with any values between 0.0 and 1.0. In Section 11.5 we show how to compute parameter values for low_1 associated with the constraints **B1** from the parameter values for the constraints **A1**. We have experimented with varying the values of $high_1$, $high_2$, $high_3$ and $high_4$ from 0.8 to 0.95, and the low_1, low_2, values from 0.05 to 0.2 in increments as small as .01. Fortunately, our inference is quite robust: these parameter variations do not significantly affect the quality of results produced by the inference in the applications we have tried.

Example 4   Figure 11.8 shows the factor graph obtained by applying algorithm *FactorGraph* to the propagation graph in Figure 11.2. The marginal probabilities for all variable nodes are computed by probabilistic inference on the factor graph and these are used to classify sources, sanitizers, and sinks in the propagation graph.   □

Path($G = \langle V, E \rangle$)
Returns:
Mapping m from V to the set $\{0, 1\}$

1: **for all** paths $p = s, \ldots, n$ from potential sources to sinks in G **do**
2:     assume($m(p) \notin 10^*1$) $\oplus_{c_p}$ assume($m(p) \in 10^*1$)
3: **end for**
Post expectation: [$\forall$ paths p in G, $m(p) \notin 10^*1$].

FIGURE 11.9: Algorithm Path.

Triple($G = \langle V, E \rangle$)
Returns:
Mapping m from V to the set $\{0, 1\}$

1: **for all** triples $t = \langle s, w, n \rangle$ such that s is a potential source, n is a potential sink and w lies on some path from s to n in G **do**
2:     assume($m(\langle s, w, n \rangle) \neq 101$) $\oplus_{c_t}$ assume($m(\langle s, w, n \rangle) = 101$)
3: **end for**
Post expectation: [$\forall$ paths p in G, $m(p) \notin 10^*1$].

FIGURE 11.10: Algorithm Triple.

11.5 Relationship between Triples and Paths

In this section, we give a formal relationship between the exponential number of constraints **A1** and the cubic number of constraints **B1** in Section 11.2. We use the theory of probabilistic abstraction and refinement developed by McIver and Morgan [19, 20] to derive appropriate bounds on probabilities associated with constraints **A1** and **B1** so that **B1** is a probabilistic abstraction of the specification **A1** (or, equivalently, **A1** is a probabilistic refinement of **B1**). We first introduce some terminology and basic concepts from [20].

Probabilistic refinement primer. Non-probabilistic programs can be reasoned with assertions in the style of Floyd and Hoare [7]. The following formula in Hoare logic:

$$\{Pre\} \ \mathsf{Prog} \ \{Post\}$$

is valid if for every state σ satisfying the assertion *Pre*, if the program Prog is started at σ, then the resulting state σ' satisfies the assertion *Post*. We assume Prog always terminates, and thus we do not distinguish between partial and total correctness.

McIver and Morgan extend such reasoning to probabilistic programs [19, 20]. In order to reason about probabilistic programs, they generalize assertions to expectations. An *expectation* is a function that maps each state to a positive real number. If Prog is a probabilistic program, and Pre_E and $Post_E$ are expectations, then the probabilistic Hoare-triple

$$\{Pre_E\} \ \mathsf{Prog} \ \{Post_E\}$$

is interpreted to mean the following: If the program Prog is started with an initial expectation Pre_E, then it results in the expectation $Post_E$ after execution.

Assertions are ordered by implication ordering. Expectations are ordered by the partial order $\Rightarrow$. Given two expectations A_E and B_E, we say that $A_E \Rightarrow B_E$ holds if for all states σ, we have that $A_E(\sigma) \leq B_E(\sigma)$. Given an assertion A the expectation $[A]$ is defined to map every state σ to 1 if σ satisfies A and to 0 otherwise.

Suppose $A_E \Rightarrow B_E$. Consider a sampler that samples states using the expectations as a probability measure. Then, for any threshold t and state σ, if $A_E(\sigma) > t$, then it is the case that $B_E(\sigma) > t$. In other words, for any sampler with any threshold t, sampling over A_E results in a subset of states than those obtained by sampling over B_E.

Traditional axiomatic proofs are done using weakest preconditions. The weakest precondition operator is denoted by WP. By definition, for any program Prog and assertion A, we have that WP(Prog, A) to be the weakest assertion B (weakest is defined with respect to the implication ordering between assertions) such that the Hoare triple $\{B\}$Prog$\{A\}$ holds.

McIver and Morgan extend the weakest preconditions to expectations, and define for an expectation A_E and a probabilistic program Prog, WP(Prog, A_E) is the weakest expectation B_E (weakest is defined with respect to the ordering $\Rightarrow$ between expectations) such that the probabilistic Hoare triple $\{B_E\}$Prog$\{A_E\}$ holds. Given two probabilistic programs Spec and Impl with respect to a post expectation $Post_E$, we say that Impl *refines* Spec if WP(Spec, $Post_E$) $\Rightarrow$ WP(Impl, $Post_E$).

Refinement between constraint systems. We now model constraints **A1** and **B1** from Section 11.2 as probabilistic programs with an appropriate post expectation, and derive relationships between the parameters of **A1** and **B1** such that **A1** refines **B1**.

Consider any directed acyclic graph $G = \langle V, E \rangle$, where $E \subseteq V \times V$. In this simple setting, nodes with in-degree 0 are potential sources, nodes with out-degree 0 are potential sinks, and other nodes (internal nodes with both in-degree and out-degree greater than 0) are potential sanitizers. We want to classify every node in V with a boolean value 0 or 1. That is, we want a mapping $m : V \to \{0, 1\}$, with the interpretation that for a potential source $s \in V$, $m(s) = 1$ means that s is classified as a source, and that for a potential sink $n \in V$, $m(n) = 1$ means that n is classified as a sink, and that for a potential sanitizer $w \in V$, $m(w) = 1$ means that w is classified as a sanitizer. We extend the mapping m to operate on paths (triples) over G by applying m to every vertex along the path (triple).

We want mappings m that satisfy the constraint that for any path $p = s, w_1, w_2, \ldots, w_m, n$ that starts at a potential source s and ends in a potential sink, the string $m(p) \notin 10^*1$, where 10^*1 is the language of strings that begin and end with 1 and have a sequence of 0's of arbitrary length in-between.

The constraint set **A1** from Section 11.2 is equivalent in this setting to the probabilistic program Path given in Figure 11.9, and the constraint set **B1** from Section 11.2 is equivalent in this setting to the probabilistic program Triple given in Figure 11.10. The statement assume(e) is a no-op if e holds and silently stops execution if e does not hold. The probabilistic statement $S_1 \oplus_q S_2$ executes statement S_1 with probability q and statement S_2 with probability $1-q$. Note that both programs Path and Triple have the same post expectation [∀ paths p in $G, m(p) \notin 10^*1$]. Further, note that both programs are parameterized. The Path program has a parameter c_p associated with each path p in G, and the Triple program has a parameter c_t associated with each triple t in G.

The following theorem states that the probabilistic program Path refines program Triple under appropriate choices of probabilities as parameters. Furthermore, given a program Path with arbitrary values for the parameters c_p for each path p, it is possible to choose parameter values c_t for each triple t in the program Triple such that Path refines Triple.

Theorem. *Consider any directed acyclic graph $G = \langle V, E \rangle$ and probabilistic programs* Path *(Figure 11.9) and* Triple *(Figure 11.10) with stated post expectations. Let the program* Path *have a parameter c_p for each path p. For any such valuations to the c_p's there exist parameter values for the* Triple *program, namely, a parameter c_t for each triple t such that the program* Path *refines the program* Triple *with respect to the post expectation $Post_E = $ [∀ paths p in $G, m(p) \notin 10^*1$].*

Proof: Consider any triple $t = \langle s, w, n \rangle$. Choose the parameter c_t for the triple t to be equal to the product of the parameters c_p of all paths p in G that start at s, end at n, and go through w. That is,

$$c_t = \prod_p c_p \qquad (11.13)$$

such that t is a subsequence of p.

To show that Path refines Triple with respect to the post expectation $Post_E$ stated in the theorem, we need to show that WP(Triple, $Post_E$) $\Rightarrow$ WP(Path, $Post_E$). That is, for each state σ, we need to show that WP(Triple, $Post_E$)(σ) $\leq$ WP(Path, $Post_E$)(σ).

Note that WP(assume(e), [A]) = [$e \wedge A$], and WP($S_1 \oplus_q S_2$, [A]) = $q \times$ WP(S_1, [A])$+(1-q) \times$WP(S_2, [A]) [20]. Using these two rules, we can compute WP(Triple, $Post_E$) and WP(Path, $Post_E$) as an expression tree which is a sum of product of expressions, where each product corresponds to a combination of probabilistic choices made in the program.

First, consider any state σ that does not satisfy $Post_E$. For this state, WP(Triple, $Post_E$)(σ) = WP(Path, $Post_E$)(σ) = 0, and the theorem follows trivially. Next, consider a state ω that satisfies $Post_E$. In this case, WP(Path, $Post_E$)(ω) is the product of probabilities c_p for each path p in G.

Also, in this case $\mathsf{WP}(\mathsf{Triple}, Post_E)(\omega)$ is the product of two quantities $X(\omega)$ and $Y(\omega)$, where $X(\omega)$ is equal to the product of probabilities c_t for each triple $t = \langle s, w, n \rangle$ such that $m(\langle s, w, n \rangle) \neq 101$, and $Y(\omega)$ is equal to the product of probabilities $(1 - c_{t'})$ for each triple $t' = \langle s', w', n' \rangle$ such that $m(\langle s', w', n' \rangle) = 101$. Since c_t's have been carefully chosen according to Equation 11.13 and $Y(\omega) \in [0, 1]$, it follows that $X(\omega)$ is less than or equal to the product of the probabilities c_p for each path p. Therefore, it is indeed the case that for each state ω, $\mathsf{WP}(\mathsf{Triple}, Post_E)(\omega) \leq \mathsf{WP}(\mathsf{Path}, Post_E)(\omega)$. $\blacksquare$

Any solver for a probabilistic constraint system C with post expectation $Post_E$ chooses states σ such that $\mathsf{WP}(C, Post_E)(\sigma)$ is greater than some threshold t. Since we have proved that Path refines Triple, we know that every solution state for the Triple system is also a solution state for the Path system. Thus, the set of states that are chosen by solver for the Triple system is contained in the set of states that are chosen by the solver for the Path system. *This has the desirable property that the* Triple *system will not introduce more false positives than the* Path *system.*

Note that the Path system itself can result in false positives, since it requires at least one sanitizer on each source-sink path, and does not require minimization of sanitizers. In order to remove false positives due to redundant sanitizers, we add the constraints **B2** and **B3** to the Triple system. Further, the path system does not distinguish wrappers of sources or sinks, so we add additional constraints **B4** and **B5** to avoid classifying these wrappers as sources or sinks. Using all these extra constraints, we find that the Triple system performs very well on several large benchmarks and infers specifications with very few false positives. We describe these results in the next section.

11.6   Experimental Evaluation

CAT.NET, a publicly available state-of-the-art static analysis tool for Web application, is the platform for our experiments [21]. MERLIN is implemented as an add-on on top of CAT.NET, using INFER.NET, a library [22] that provides an interface to probabilistic inference algorithms. This section presents the results of evaluating MERLIN on 10 large .NET Web applications. All these benchmarks are security-critical enterprise line-of-business applications currently in production written in C# on top of ASP.NET. They are also subject to periodic security audits.

Benchmark	DLLs	DLL size (kilobytes)	LOC
Alias Management Tool	3	65	10,812
Chat Application	3	543	6,783
Bicycle Club App	3	62	14,529
Software Catalog	15	118	11,941
Sporting Field Management Tool	3	290	15,803
Commitment Management Tool	7	369	25,602
New Hire Tool	11	565	5,595
Expense Report Approval Tool	4	421	78,914
Relationship Management	5	3,345	1,810,585
Customer Support Portal	14	2,447	66,385

FIGURE 11.11: Benchmark application sizes.

Type	Count	Revisions
Sources	27	16
Sinks	77	8
Sanitizers	7	2

FIGURE 11.12: Statistics for the out-of-the box specification that comes with CAT.NET.

11.6.1 Experimental Setup

Figure 11.11 summarizes information about our benchmarks. As we discovered, not all code contained within the application source tree is actually deployed to the Web server. Most of the time, the number and size of deployed DLLs primarily consisting of .NET bytecode are a good measure of the application size, as shown in columns 2–3. Note that in several cases, libraries supplied in the form of DLLs without the source code constitute the biggest part of an application. Finally, to provide another measure of the application size, column 4 shows the traditional line-of-code metric for *all* the code within the application.

To put our results on specification discovery in perspective, Figure 11.12 provides information about the out-of-the box specification for CAT.NET, the static analysis tool that we used for our experiments [21]. The second column shows the number of specifications for each specification type. The last column shows the number of *revisions* each portion of the specification has gone through, as extracted from the code revision repository. We have manually examined the revisions to only count substantial ones (i.e., just adding comments or changing whitespace was disregarded). It is clear from the table that even arriving at the default specification for CAT.NET, as incomplete as it is, took a pretty significant number of source revisions. We found that most commonly revised specifications correspond to most commonly found vulnerabilities. In particular, specifications for SQL injection and cross-site scripting attacks have been revised by far the most. Moreover, after all these revisions,

Benchmark	G		F	
	Nodes	**Edges**	**Vars**	**Nodes**
Alias Management Tool	59	1,209	3	3
Chat Application	156	187	25	33
Bicycle Club App	176	246	70	317
Software Catalog	190	455	73	484
Sporting Field Management Tool	268	320	50	50
Commitment Management Tool	356	563	107	1,781
New Hire Tool	502	1,101	116	1,917
Expense Report Approval Tool	811	1,753	252	2,592
Relationship Management	3,639	22,188	874	391,221
Customer Support Portal	3,881	11,196	942	181,943

FIGURE 11.13: Size statistics for the propagation graph G and factor graph F used by MERLIN.

the ultimate initial specification is also fairly large, consisting of a total of 111 methods.

To provide a metric for the scale of the benchmarks relevant for CAT.NET and MERLIN analyses, Figure 11.13 provides statistics on the sizes of the propagation graph G computed by MERLIN, and the factor graph F constructed in the process of constraint generation. We sort our benchmarks by the number of nodes in G. With propagation graphs containing thousands of nodes, it is not surprising that we had to develop a polynomial approximation in order for MERLIN to scale, as Section 11.5 describes.

11.6.2   Merlin Findings

Figure 11.14 provides information about the specifications discovered by MERLIN. Columns 2–16 provide information about how many correct and false positive items in each specification category have been found. Note that in addition to "good" and "bad" specifications, as indicated by ✓ and ✗, we also have a "maybe" column denoted by ?. This is because often what constitutes a good specification is open to interpretation. Even in consultations with CAT.NET developers we found many cases where the classification of a particular piece of the specification is not clear cut. The column labeled, **Rate**, gives the false positive rate for MERLIN—the percentage of "bad" specifications that were inferred. Overall, MERLIN infers 381 specifications, out of which 167 are confirmed and 127 more are potential specifications. The MERLIN false positive rate, looking at the discovered specifications is 22%, computed as $(7+31+49)/381$. This is decidedly better than the average state-of-the-art false positive rate of over 90% [5]. The area in which MERLIN does the worst is identifying sanitizers (with a 38% false positive rate). This is because despite the extra constraints described in Section 11.2.4, MERLIN still flags

Benchmark	Sources					Sanitizers					Sinks				
	All	✓	?	✗	Rate	All	✓	?	✗	Rate	All	✓	?	✗	Rate
Alias Management Tool	0	0	0	0	N/A	0	0	0	0	N/A	0	0	0	0	N/A
Chat Application	1	1	0	0	0%	0	0	0	0	N/A	2	2	0	0	0%
Bicycle Club App	11	11	0	0	0%	3	2	0	1	33%	7	4	0	3	42%
Software Catalog	1	1	0	0	0%	8	3	0	5	62%	6	3	2	1	16%
Sporting Field Management Tool	0	0	0	0	N/A	0	0	0	0	N/A	1	0	1	0	0%
Commitment Management Tool	20	19	0	1	5%	9	1	2	6	66%	11	8	1	2	18%
New Hire Tool	3	3	0	0	0%	1	1	0	0	0%	17	14	0	3	17%
Expense Report Approval Tool	8	8	0	0	0%	20	2	13	5	25%	20	14	0	6	30%
Relationship Management	44	3	36	5	11%	1	0	0	1	100%	4	0	3	1	25%
Customer Support Portal	26	21	4	1	3%	39	16	10	13	33%	118	30	55	33	27%
Total	114	67	40	7	6%	81	25	25	31	38%	186	75	62	49	26%

FIGURE 11.14: New specifications discovered with MERLIN.

Benchmark	BEFORE				AFTER				-
	All	✓	?	✗	All	✓	?	✗	
Alias Management Tool	2	2	0	0	2	2	0	0	0
Chat Application	0	0	0	0	1	1	0	0	0
Bicycle Club App	0	0	0	0	4	3	1	0	0
Software Catalog	14	8	0	6	8	8	0	0	6
Sporting Field Management	0	0	0	0	0	0	0	0	0
Commitment Management Tool	1	1	0	0	22	16	3	3	0
New Hire Tool	4	4	0	0	3	3	0	0	1
Expense Report Approval Tool	0	0	0	0	2	2	0	0	0
Relationship Management	9	6	3	0	10	10	0	0	3
Customer Support Portal	59	19	3	37	290	277	13	0	3
Total	89	40	6	43	342	322	17	3	13

FIGURE 11.15: Vulnerabilities before and after MERLIN.

some polymorphic functions as sanitizers. An example of this is the method
NameValueCollection.get_Item in the standard class library. Depending on
what is stored in the collection, either the return result will be tainted or not.
However, this function clearly does not *untaint* its argument and so is not a
good sanitizer.

Figure 11.15 summarizes information about the security vulnerabilities we
find based on both the initial and the post-MERLIN specifications. For the purpose of finding vulnerabilities, the post-MERLIN specifications we used are the
"good" specifications denoted by the ✓ columns in Figure 11.14. Columns 2–
10 in Figure 11.15 show the number of vulnerabilities based on the original
specification and the number of newly found vulnerabilities. Just like with
specifications, we break down vulnerabilities into "good," "maybe," and "bad"
categories denoted by ✓, ?, and ✗. The very last column reports 13 former
false positives *eliminated* with the MERLIN specification because of newly discovered sanitizers.

As with many other static analysis tools, false positives are one of the primary complaints about CAT.NET in practice. As can be seen from Figure 11.15
(the column marked with "−"), MERLIN helps reduce the false positive rate
from 48% to 33% (the latter computed as (43-13)/89). Furthermore, if we take
into account all the 322 new (and confirmed) vulnerabilities into account, the
false positive rate drops to 1% (computed as 3/342).

Example 5 Function CreateQueryLink in Figure 11.16 is taken from the
Software Catalog benchmark.[2] The return result of this function is passed into
a known cross-site redirection sink not shown here for brevity.

---

[2]CAT.NET addresses explicit information flow only and does not flag the fact that there is
a control dependency on line 13 because tainted value request.QueryString is used within
a conditional.

```
1   public static string CreateQueryLink(
2       HttpRequest request, string key, string value,
3       List<string> keysToOmit, bool ignoreKey)
4   {
5     StringBuilder builder = new StringBuilder(
6       request.Url.AbsolutePath);
7     if (keysToOmit == null) {
8         keysToOmit = new List<string>();
9     }
10    builder.Append("?");
11    for (int i = 0; i < request.QueryString.Count; i++) {
12        if ((request.QueryString.GetKey(i) != key) &&
13          !keysToOmit.Contains(request.QueryString.GetKey(i)))
14        {
15            builder.Append(request.QueryString.GetKey(i));
16            builder.Append("=");
17            builder.Append(AntiXss.UrlEncode(
18              QueryStringParser.Parse(
19                request.QueryString.GetKey(i))));
20            builder.Append("&");
21        }
22    }
23    if (!ignoreKey) {
24        builder.Append(key);
25        builder.Append("=");
26        builder.Append(AntiXss.UrlEncode(value));
27    }
28    return builder.ToString().TrimEnd(new char[] { '&' });
29  }
```

FIGURE 11.16: Function `CreateQueryLink` for Example 5.

- The paths that go through `request.Url.AbsolutePath` and `request.QueryString` on lines 6 and 15 are correctly identified as new, not previously flagged vulnerabilities.
- CAT.NET flags the path that passes through function `QueryStringParser.Parse` on line 18 as a vulnerability. However, with MERLIN, `AntiXss.UrlEncode` is correctly determined to be a sanitizer, eliminating this false positive. With MERLIN, we eliminate all 6 false positives in this benchmark.

This short function illustrates many tricky issues with explicit information flow analyses as well as the danger of unrestricted manipulation of tainted data as strings. □

Note that while we start with the CAT.NET specification characterized in Figure 11.12, MERLIN can even infer specification entirely *without* an initial specification purely based on the structure of the propagation graph.

Example 6 Consider a short program fragment written in C# consisting of two event handlers shown in Figure 11.17. When run with *no initial specification at all*, MERLIN is able to infer a small, but absolutely correct specification consisting of 13 elements, as shown in Figure 11.18. Starting with even a small specification such as the one above, MERLIN is able to succesfully infer

```
1   protected void TextChanged(object sender, EventArgs e) {
2       string str = Request.QueryString["name"];
3       string str2 = HttpUtility.HtmlEncode(str);
4       Response.Write(str2);
5   }
6
7   protected void ButtonClicked(object sender, EventArgs e) {
8       string str = Request.UrlReferrer.AbsolutePath;
9       string str2 = HttpUtility.UrlEncode(str);
10      Response.Redirect(str2);
11  }
```

FIGURE 11.17: Program for Example 6.

```
Sources     (1):
    string System.Web.HttpUtility+UrlDecoder.Getstring()
Sanitizers  (8):
    string System.Web.HttpUtility.HtmlEncode(string)
    string System.Web.HttpUtility.UrlEncodeSpaces(string)
    string System.Web.HttpServerUtility.UrlDecode(string)
    string System.Web.HttpUtility.UrlEncode(string, Encoding)
    string System.Web.HttpUtility.UrlEncode(string)
    string System.Web.HttpServerUtility.UrlEncode(string)
    string System.Web.HttpUtility.UrlDecodestringFrom...
    string System.Web.HttpUtility.UrlDecode(string, Encoding)
Sinks       (4):
    void System.Web.HttpResponse.WriteFile(string)
    void System.Web.HttpRequest.set_QuerystringText(string)
    void System.IO.TextWriter.Write(string)
    void System.Web.HttpResponse.Redirect(string)
```

FIGURE 11.18: Specification inferred for Example 6.

increasingly larger specifications that fill many gaps in the original CAT.NET specification. □

11.6.3   Running Times

Finally, Figure 11.19 provides information about running time of the various MERLIN components, measured in seconds. Columns 2–4 show the CAT.NET running time, the time to build the propagation graph, and the inference time. The experiments were conducted on a 3 GHz Pentium Dual Core Windows XP SP2 machine equipped with 4 GB of memory. Overall, in part due to the approximation described in Section 11.5, our analysis scales quite well, with none of the benchmarks taking over four minutes to analyze. Given that CAT.NET is generally run once a day or less frequently, these running times are more than acceptable.

Benchmark	CAT.NET P	MERLIN G	MERLIN F	Total time
Alias Management Tool	2.64	4.59	2.63	9.86
Chat Application	4.61	.81	2.67	8.09
Bicycle Club App	2.81	.53	2.72	6.06
Software Catalog	3.94	1.02	2.73	7.69
Sporting Field Management Tool	5.97	2.22	2.69	10.88
Commitment Management Tool	6.41	18.84	2.91	28.16
New Hire Tool	7.84	2.98	3.44	14.27
Expense Report Approval Tool	7.27	3.59	3.05	13.91
Relationship Management	55.38	87.63	66.45	209.45
Customer Support Portal	89.75	29.75	31.55	151.05

FIGURE 11.19: Static analysis and specification inference running time, in seconds.

11.7 Related Work

Related work falls into the broad categories of securing Web applications and specification mining.

11.7.1 Securing Web Applications

There has been much interest in static and runtime protection techniques to improve the security of Web applications. Static analysis allows the developer to avoid issues such as cross-site scripting before the application goes into operation. Runtime analysis allows exploit prevention and recovery during the operation of an application. The WebSSARI project pioneered this line of research [8] by combining static and dynamic analysis for PHP programs. Several projects that came after WebSSARI improve on the quality of static analysis for PHP [9, 33].

The Griffin project proposes scalable and precise static and runtime analysis techniques for finding security vulnerabilities in large Java applications [15, 18]. Several other runtime systems for taint tracking have been proposed as well, including Haldar et al. [6] and Chandra and Franz [1] for Java, Pietraszek and Berghe [25], and Nguyen-Tuong et al. for PHP [23]. Several commercial tools have been built to detect information flow vulnerabilities in programs [4, 24]. All these tools without exception require a specification of information flow. Our work infers such specifications.

11.7.2   Mining Specifications

A number of projects have addressed inferring specifications outside the context of security. For a general overview of specification mining techniques, the reader is referred to Perracotta [34], DynaMine [16], and Weimer and Necula [31]. In particular, Engler et al. [3] infer specifications from code by seeking rules that involve action pairs: `malloc` paired with `free`, `lock` paired with `unlock`, etc. Li and Zhou [13] and Livshits and Zimmermann [16] look at more general patterns involving action pairs by combining data mining techniques as well as sophisticated pointer analyses. Whaley et al. [32] consider inference of interface specifications for Java method calls using static analysis. Jagannathan et al. [26] use data mining techniques for inference of method preconditions in complex software systems. The preconditions might incorporate dataflow as well as control-flow properties.

Kremenek et al. [10] use probabilistic inference to classify functions that allocate and deallocate resources in programs. While similar in spirit to our work, inference of information flow specifications appears to be a more complex problem than inference of allocation and deallocation routines in C code in part because there are more class classifications — sources, sinks, and sanitizers at play. Furthermore, the wrapper avoidance and sanitizer minimization constraints do not have direct analogs in the allocator-deallocator inference. Unlike Kremenek et al. [10] we use the theory of probabilistic refinement to *formally characterize* the triple approximation we have implemented for the purposes of scaling.

11.8   Conclusions

The growing importance of explicit information flow is evidenced by the abundance of analysis tools for information flow tracking and violation detection at the level of the language, runtime, operating system, and hardware [1, 2, 6, 8–11, 15, 17, 18, 23, 28, 29, 33, 36]. Ultimately, all these approaches require specifications.

In this chapter we have presented MERLIN, a novel algorithm that infers explicit information flow specifications from programs. MERLIN derives a system of probabilistic constraints based on interprocedural dataflow in the program, and computes specifications using probabilistic inference.

In order to scale to large programs, we approximate an exponential number of probabilistic constraints by a cubic number of triple constraints, showing that the path-based constraint system is a refinement of the triple-based constraint system. This ensures that, for any given threshold, every solution admitted by the approximated triple system is also admitted by the path system (for the same threshold). Though this connection gives formal grounding to our approximation, it does not say anything about the precision of the results that can be obtained; such an assessment is obtained empirically by evaluating the quality of the specification inferred for large applications, the number of new vulnerabilities discovered, and the number of false positives removed. Based on our observations about large Web applications, we added extra constraints to the triple system (constraints **B2**, **B3**, **B4**, and **B5** in Figure 11.3) to enhance the quality of the results.

With these extra constraints, our empirical results convincingly demonstrate that our model indeed achieves good precision. In our experiments with 10 large Web applications written in .NET, MERLIN finds a total of 167 new confirmed specifications, which result in a total of 322 newly discovered vulnerabilities across the 10 benchmarks. Equally important, MERLIN-inferred specifications also result in 13 false positives being removed. As a result of new findings and eliminating false positives, the *final* false positive rate for CAT.NET *after* MERLIN in our experiments drops to about 1%.

Acknowledgments

We thank Carroll Morgan for explaining his insights about abstraction and refinement between probabilistic systems. We want to thank Ted Kremenek, G. Ramalingam, Kapil Vaswani, and Westley Weimer for their insightful comments on earlier drafts. We are indebted to Mark Curphey, Hassan Khan, Don Willits, and others behind CAT.NET for their unwavering assistance throughout the project. We also thank John Winn for help with using INFER.NET.

Bibliography

[1] Deepak Chandra and Michael Franz. Fine-grained information flow analysis and enforcement in a java virtual machine. In *Annual Computer Security Applications Conference*, pages 463–475, 2007.

[2] Michael Dalton, Hari Kannan, and Christos Kozyrakis. Raksha: a flexible information flow architecture for software security. In *Proceedings of the International Symposium on Computer Architecture*, pages 482–493, 2007.

[3] Dawson R. Engler, David Yu Chen, and Andy Chou. Bugs as inconsistent behavior: a general approach to inferring errors in systems code. In *In*

Proceedings of ACM Symposium on Operating Systems Principles, pages 57–72, 2001.

[4] Fortify. Fortify code analyzer. http://www.ouncelabs.com/, 2008.

[5] Claire Le Goues and Westley Weimer. Specification mining with few false positives. In *Tools and Algorithms for the Construction and Analysis of Systems*, 2009.

[6] Vivek Haldar, Deepak Chandra, and Michael Franz. Dynamic taint propagation for Java. In *Proceedings of the Annual Computer Security Applications Conference*, pages 303–311, December 2005.

[7] C.A.R. Hoare. An axiomatic basis for computer programming. *Communications of the ACM*, 12:576–583, October 1969.

[8] Yao-Wen Huang, Fang Yu, Christian Hang, Chung-Hung Tsai, Der-Tsai Lee, and Sy-Yen Kuo. Securing Web application code by static analysis and runtime protection. In *Proceedings of the Conference on World Wide Web*, pages 40–52, May 2004.

[9] Nenad Jovanovic, Christopher Kruegel, and Engin Kirda. Pixy: a static analysis tool for detecting Web application vulnerabilities (short paper). In *Proceedings of the Symposium on Security and Privacy*, May 2006.

[10] Ted Kremenek, Paul Twohey, Godmar Back, Andrew Y. Ng, and Dawson R. Engler. From uncertainty to belief: inferring the specification within. In *Symposium on Operating Systems Design and Implementation*, pages 161–176, November 2006.

[11] Maxwell Krohn, Alexander Yip, Micah Brodsky, Natan Cliffer, M. Frans Kaashoek, Eddie Kohler, and Robert Morris. Information flow control for standard os abstractions. In *Proceedings of Symposium on Operating Systems Principles*, pages 321–334, 2007.

[12] F.R. Kschischang, B.J. Frey, and H.A. Loeliger. Factor graphs and the sum-product algorithm. *IEEE Transactions on Information Theory*, 47(2):498–519, 2001.

[13] Z. Li and Y. Zhou. Pr-miner: automatically extracting implicit programming rules and detecting violations in large software code. In *Proceedings of the European Software Engineering Conference*, 2005.

[14] Benjamin Livshits. Improving Software Security with Precise Static and Runtime Analysis. Ph.D. thesis, Stanford University, Stanford, CA, 2006.

[15] Benjamin Livshits and Monica S. Lam. Finding security errors in Java programs with static analysis. In *Proceedings of the Usenix Security Symposium*, pages 271–286, August 2005.

[16] Benjamin Livshits and Thomas Zimmermann. DynaMine: finding common error patterns by mining software revision histories. In *Proceedings of the International Symposium on the Foundations of Software Engineering*, pages 296–305, September 2005.

[17] Michael Martin, Benjamin Livshits, and Monica S. Lam. Finding application errors and security vulnerabilities using PQL: a program query language. In *Proceedings of the Conference on Object-Oriented Programming, Systems, Languages, and Applications*, October 2005.

[18] Michael Martin, Benjamin Livshits, and Monica S. Lam. SecuriFly: Runtime Vulnerability Protection for Web Applications. Technical report, Stanford University, October 2006.

[19] A. McIver and C. Morgan. *Abstraction, Refinement and Proof of Probabilistic Systems*. Springer, 2004.

[20] A. McIver and C. Morgan. Abstraction and refinement in probabilistic systems. *SIGMETRICS Performance Evaluation Review*, 32:41–47, March 2005.

[21] Microsoft Corporation. Microsoft Code Analysis Tool .NET (CAT.NET). `http://www.microsoft.com/downloads/details.aspx?FamilyId=0178e2ef-9da8-445e-9348-c93f24cc9f9d&displaylang=en`, 3 2009.

[22] T. Minka, J.M. Winn, J.P. Guiver, and A. Kannan. Infer.NET 2.2, 2009. Microsoft Research Cambridge. http://research.microsoft.com/infernet.

[23] Anh Nguyen-Tuong, Salvatore Guarnieri, Doug Greene, Jeff Shirley, and David Evans. Automatically hardening Web applications using precise tainting. In *Proceedings of the IFIP International Information Security Conference*, June 2005.

[24] OunceLabs, Inc. Ounce. `http://www.ouncelabs.com/`, 2008.

[25] Tadeusz Pietraszek and Chris Vanden Berghe. Defending against injection attacks through context-sensitive string evaluation. In *Proceedings of the Recent Advances in Intrusion Detection*, September 2005.

[26] M. K. Ramanathan, A. Grama, and S. Jagannathan. Static specification inference using predicate mining. In *PLDI*, 2007.

[27] Andrei Sabelfeld and Andrew Myers. Language-based information-flow security. *IEEE Journal on Selected Areas in Communications*, 21(1):5–19, January 2003.

[28] Zhendong Su and Gary Wassermann. The essence of command injection attacks in web applications. In *Proceedings of POPL*, 2006.

[29] Steve Vandebogart, Petros Efstathopoulos, Eddie Kohler, Maxwell Krohn, Cliff Frey, David Ziegler, Frans Kaashoek, Robert Morris, and David Mazières. Labels and event processes in the Asbestos operating system. *ACM Trans. Comput. Syst.*, 25(4):11, 2007.

[30] Larry Wall. Perl security. http://search.cpan.org/dist/perl/pod/perlsec.pod.

[31] Westley Weimer and George C. Necula. Mining temporal specifications for error detection. In *Proceedings of the International Conference on Tools and Algorithms for the Construction and Analysis of Systems*, pages 461–476, 2005.

[32] J. Whaley, M. Martin, and M. Lam. Automatic extraction of object-oriented component interfaces. In *Proceedings of the International Symposium on Software Testing and Analysis*, pages 218–228, 2002.

[33] Yichen Xie and Alex Aiken. Static detection of security vulnerabilities in scripting languages. In *Proceedings of the Usenix Security Symposium*, pages 271–286, August 2006.

[34] Jinlin Yang and David Evans. Perracotta: mining temporal API rules from imperfect traces. In *Proceedings of the International Conference on Software Engineering*, pages 282–291, 2006.

[35] Jonathan S. Yedidia, William T. Freeman, and Yair Weiss. Understanding belief propagation and its generalizations. In *Exploring Artificial Intelligence in the New Millennium*, pages 239–269, 2003.

[36] Nikolai Zeldovich, S. Boyd-Wickizer, Eddie Kohler, and David Mazières. Making information flow explicit in HiStar. In *Proceedings of the Symposium on Operating Systems Design and Implementation*, pages 263–278, 2006.

Chapter 12

Lightweight Mining of Object Usage*

Andrzej Wasylkowski

Computer Science, Saarland University

Andreas Zeller

Computer Science, Saarland University

12.1   Introduction

Whenever we want to use a third-party package, we need to understand the services it provides as well as the services it requires. Such a description typically comes as part of the documentation of the programmer application interface (API), providing a specification for each function provided. Correct usage of these individual functions is also easily checked. Statically typed signatures, for instance, are part of most programming languages; violations can be discovered right within the editor.

What such documentations frequently miss is to describe how the individual functions are supposed to work together. Authors commonly use code examples, showing how the functions dovetail and intertwine with each other to achieve a greater whole. What we miss is formal *specifications* describing

---

*Some text in this chapter from A. Wasylkowski and A. Zeller, Mining temporal specifications from object usage, Proceedings of the 2009 IEEE/ACM International Conference on ASE © 2009 IEEE.

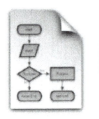 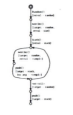 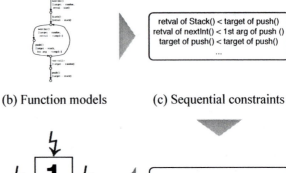

(a) Input program   (b) Function models   (c) Sequential constraints

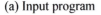

(e) Ranked violations   (d) Patterns

FIGURE 12.1: Mining object usage patterns. A lightweight parser transforms the source code (a) into a set of function models (b), from which sequential constraints are extracted (c). Sets of these sequential constraints are generalized into patterns (d), reflecting "normal" object usage. Pattern violations are reported to the user (e) as potential defects. (From [9]. © 2009 IEEE.)

legal interactions–not so much for instructing the programmer, but again to detect *illegal interaction between functions.*

Unfortunately, such specifications are difficult to write, and hard to get right. In this chapter, we present an approach to *mine* specifications for function interaction from existing code bases. Our approach is based on the notion of *sequential constraints* representing data flow between functions calls.[1] For example, the fact that a call to `fopen()` returns a file object that should later be passed as the first argument to `fclose()` can be represented by the constraint "retval of `fopen()` ≺ 1st arg of `fclose()`," where "≺" represents the dataflow from the left-hand side to the right-hand side. Sets of such sequential constraints can represent quite complicated specifications expressing relationships between multiple different functions and their arguments as well as return values.

Once we have obtained such specifications, we can check for *violations* – that is, detect instances where function usage differs from "normal" usage as mined before. Such places need not be wrong, just unusual – but a usage that is unusual today may become an error or a maintainability issue tomorrow.

---

[1] We will use the term "function" to mean both "method" and "function."

How do we obtain and check these specifications? Essentially, we go through four steps, starting with a program and ending in a set of specifications and their violations, and illustrated in Figure 12.1 as follows:

(a) Apply program analysis to come up with *function models*. These function models are related to control flow graphs, but they are less detailed, while on the other hand containing dataflow information that is necessary to create sequential constraints. (See Section 12.3.)

(b) Obtain sequential constraints from function models. In this step we abstract each function in the program into a set of sequential constraints that represents it. (See Section 12.4.)

(c) Find frequently occurring sets of sequential constraints. These sets are patterns in the program and we expect them to occur frequently for a reason. (See Section 12.5.)

(d) Discover violations of patterns. If a particular pattern occurs frequently and is violated by just a few functions, it is natural to assume that those functions can be buggy. (See Section 12.6.)

12.2 An Example

Before we show details on each step of our approach, let us illustrate them on in example. Consider the `createStack()` function shown in Figure 12.2. The function model created out of it (step a) is shown in Figure 12.3. This model resembles control flow graph, in that it captures control flow through the program, but it also contains useful information about how objects are being used by the function (e.g., `random` is the target of the call to `nextInt()` in the loop, and the return value of that call is assigned to a temporary variable that is used afterward in a call to `push()`). What is important here is that the model is a pretty accurate representation of how objects are being used in the function, but (in contrast to source code) is programming-language-independent. We will later show how to take advantage of this fact.

After the function model has been created, we abstract it into a set of sequential constraints (step b):

$$\text{retval of } \texttt{Random()} \prec \text{target of } \texttt{nextInt()}$$
$$\text{target of } \texttt{nextInt()} \prec \text{target of } \texttt{nextInt()}$$
$$\text{retval of } \texttt{Stack()} \prec \text{target of } \texttt{push()}$$
$$\text{retval of } \texttt{nextInt()} \prec \text{1st arg of } \texttt{push()}$$
$$\text{target of } \texttt{push()} \prec \text{target of } \texttt{push()}$$

These sequential constraints capture temporal information about object usage in a set form. Temporal information that was implicitly present in the function model ("`random` is the target of the call to `nextInt()` in the loop, and the return value of that call is assigned to a temporary variable that is used

```
public Stack createStack () {
    Random random = new Random ();
    int size = random.nextInt ();
    Stack stack = new Stack ();
    for (int i = 0; i < size; i++)
        stack.push (random.nextInt ());
    random = null;
    stack.push (-1);
    return stack;
}
```

FIGURE 12.2: Sample function written in Java. (From [8]. © 2007 Association for Computing Machinery. Reprinted by permission.)

afterwards in a call to push()") becomes explicit in the sequential constraints abstraction, and spurious information (like variables' names) gets abstracted away ("target of nextInt() $\prec$ target of nextInt()," "retval of nextInt() $\prec$ 1st arg of push()").

After we have obtained sequential constraints from each function in the program, we can look for patterns (i.e., frequently occurring sets of sequential constraints; step c). Let us imagine that the createStack() function comes from a program, where stacks are heavily used. It can then happen that the following set of sequential constraints gets identified as a pattern:

retval of Stack() $\prec$ target of push()
target of push() $\prec$ target of push()

This pattern expresses the fact that elements are pushed to stacks, and that typically more than one element gets pushed.

The last step is discovering if any of the patterns found earlier are violated (step d). Let us consider the function fillStack() shown in Figure 12.4. If we create a function model out of it and then abstract it into a set of sequential constraints, the result will be as follows:

target of log() $\prec$ target of log()
retval of Stack() $\prec$ target of push()

Let us now compare this set with the pattern we have shown above. It turns out that the first sequential constraint in the set is not in the pattern, so we can ignore it. The second sequential constraint is part of the pattern, but the pattern contains one additional constraint (target of push() $\prec$ target of push()) that is not in the set. Thus, the set (and thus the fillStack() function) violates the pattern shown earlier: There is only one element pushed, instead of multiple elements. If we take a closer look at fillStack(), we will find the defect: There is a semicolon at the end of the line with the for-loop, and this makes the call to push() being executed just once, as opposed to being executed **num** times.

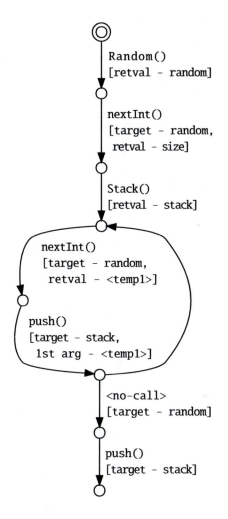

FIGURE 12.3: Function model of the function from Figure 12.2.

```
public Stack fillStack (Object o, int num) {
    log ("Filling the stack");
    Stack stack = new Stack ();
    for (int i = 0; i < num; i++);
        stack.push (o);
    log ("Done");
    return stack;
}
```

FIGURE 12.4: Code violating "normal" stack usage.

To summarize, we have now shown

(a) how to mine function models from function source code;

(b) how to turn these into sequential constraints;

(c) how to generalize instances of these constraints into patterns; and

(d) how to discover violations of these patterns.

In the remainder of this chapter, we will detail these steps.

12.3   Creating Function Models

In the first step, each function is transformed into a function model. Why is this step useful and why are sequential constraints not created directly? Let us assume we want to abstract a function $f()$ into a set of sequential constraints that represents it. To keep things more concrete, let us consider the function shown in Figure 12.2. Some sequential constraints that can be extracted from this function are "target of push() $\prec$ target of push()," "retval (return value) of Random() $\prec$ target of nextInt()" (representing the fact that creating a Random object precedes calling nextInt() on it) and "retval of nextInt() $\prec$ 1st arg(ument) of push()." It can easily be seen that source code is not a representation that is well suited for the purpose of obtaining sequential constraints.

Let us now take a look at the representation shown in Figure 12.3. We can easily obtain sequential constraints based on this representation because it abstracts away a lot of details and contains only the information that is really needed. Additionally, some information that is implicit in the source code is explicit here. Consider for example the line stack.push (random.nextInt ()). There is an object here that is the return value of a call to nextInt() and is passed to push() as the first argument. This piece of information is explicit in the representation shown in Figure 12.2: There is a synthetic variable (<temp1>) introduced in order to achieve this.

How then can we transform a function into a function model We have indicated already in the overview all steps tn which function models are programming-language-independent. If we want to be able to apply the whole approach to an arbitrary programming language, we can in principle create a different analyzer for it and have it create function models out of functions. All the remaining steps build on function models and are not dependent on any specific programming language. However, we can do better.

It turns out that many programming languages share similar syntax. Consider C and Java. Both end statements with semicolons and use curly braces to mark the beginning and end of a code block. Both use the same types of loops with the same syntax: for-, while-, do-loops. Both use parentheses to indicate function calls. The list goes on and on. There are differences, of course,

```
FUNCTION createStack (0) {
    random : Random ();
    size : random.nextInt ();
    stack : Stack ();
    LOOP () {
        stack.push (random.nextInt ());
    }
    random : NO-CALL;
    stack.push (CONST);
}
```

FIGURE 12.5: Generic abstract representation of the function from Figure 12.2.

but these turn out to be essentially inconsequential. Together with Natalie Gruska, we have leveraged these properties to create a *lightweight parser* that is able to analyze code in any C-like language and come up with function models for it [3, 4]. The lightweight parser works in two stages:

(a) Create a *generic abstract representation* of each function.

(b) Transform each abstract representation into a function model.

Generic abstract representation is similar to an abstract syntax tree, but it stores less information and is not bound to a specific programming language. It focuses on representing the code's structure and all the function calls. Describing all the details on how it is created would take too much space, so we will instead give just one example and send the interested reader elsewhere [3, 4]: Consider the source code shown in Figure 12.2. Its generic abstract representation is shown in Figure 12.5. As can be seen, a lot of information has been abstracted away, including the loop-controlling code (because there is no function call in it). This abstract representation is now close enough to a function model to allow a pretty straightforward transformation. The result of this transformation is shown in Figure 12.3.

Using the lightweight parser allows us to apply our pattern- and anomaly-detection technique to programs written in all C-like languages. In our experiments we have shown that despite the loss of accuracy that using the lightweight parser entails (in contrast to programming-language-specific analyzers), we are still able to find real specifications and real defects in real production code written in languages such as C, C++, Java, and PHP [3, 4].

12.4 Obtaining Sequential Constraints

Now let us turn to the second step in our approach: obtaining sequential constraints from function models. Before we give an algorithm for obtaining sequential constraints from a function model (like the one shown in Figure 12.3), let us introduce two definitions.

Definition 12.4.1. An event *is a combination of a function name and a variable used in a call to that function, together with dataflow information that describes the way the variable is used in the call.*

Let us clarify this abstract definition by several examples: "`<temp1>` is a retval of `nextInt()`" is an event, because it is a combination of a function name (`nextInt()`) and a variable (`<temp1>`) together with data flow information ("is a retval of"). So are "`stack` is a target of `push()`" and "`<temp1>` is a 1st arg of `push()`." Based on the definition of an event, we can define what a sequential constraint is.

Definition 12.4.2. A sequential constraint *is an ordered pair of two related events with the variable information abstracted away. Two events are related if they describe the usage of the same variable.*

The definition above tell us that "retval of `nextInt()` $\prec$ 1st arg of `push()`" is a valid sequential constraint, because "`<temp1>` is a retval of `nextInt()`" and "`<temp1>` is a 1st arg of `push()`" are related events (both describe the usage of `<temp1>`).

Not all valid sequential constraints are correct with respect to a function model. For example, "retval of `nextInt()` $\prec$ retval of `nextInt()`" obviously does not make any sense. However, even some sensible sequential constraints are incorrect. Consider the following one: "1st arg of `push()` \$prec 1st arg of `push()`." This is a valid sequential constraint, because there is an event "`<temp1>` is a 1st arg of `push()`" in the function model in Figure 12.3, and yet it is clear that the sequential constraint describes a dataflow that does not happen. For a sequential constraint to be correct with respect to a function model, it must be supported by the dataflow represented by that function model. To put it more formally, there must exist a path through the model, leading from the first event to the second one, with the variable relating the two events not being "killed" by any transition on that path, including the transition that corresponds to the second event. Intuitively, a variable is "killed" if it is assigned to (perhaps by being a return value of a function call).

The algorithm that extracts sequential constraints from a function model looks as follows:

EXTRACT-SEQUENTIAL-CONSTRAINTS(M)
1   $I =$ GET-INCOMING-EVENTS(M)
2   $O =$ GET-OUTGOING-EVENTS(M)
3   $C = \emptyset$
4   **for** each node n in M
5   **for** each event $e_i \in I[n]$
6   **for** each event $e_o \in O[n]$
7   **if** $e_i.var\_name == e_o.var\_name$
8                           $C = C \cup \{e_i.data\_flow \prec e_o.data\_flow\}$
9   **return** C

This algorithm uses two helper functions: GET-INCOMING-EVENTS (shown below) and GET-OUTGOING-EVENTS (which we leave as an exercise for the reader; it is quite similar to GET-INCOMING-EVENTS).

GET-INCOMING-EVENTS(M)

```
1   Killed = INIT-KILLED-VARIABLES(M)
2   // Initialize incoming events for each node
3   I = ∅
4   for each node n in M
5       for each transition t ingoing into n
6           I[n] = I[n] ∪ t. events
7   // Repeatedly update incoming events for each node
8   repeat
9       for each node n in M
10          for each predecessor p of n in M
11              t = transition from p to n in M
12              for each event e ∈ I[p]
13                  if var_name. e ∉ Killed[t]
14                      I[n] = I[n] ∪ {e}
15  until I does not change anymore
16  return I
```

The INIT-KILLED-VARIABLES finds variables "killed" by a transition. We will leave providing an algorithm for this function as an exercise for the reader.

Applying the EXTRACT-SEQUENTIAL-CONSTRAINTS algorithm to the function model shown in Figure 12.3 results in the following sequential constraints being extracted:

$$\text{retval of } \texttt{Random()} \prec \text{target of } \texttt{nextInt()}$$
$$\text{target of } \texttt{nextInt()} \prec \text{target of } \texttt{nextInt()}$$
$$\text{retval of } \texttt{Stack()} \prec \text{target of } \texttt{push()}$$
$$\text{retval of } \texttt{nextInt()} \prec \text{1st arg of } \texttt{push()}$$
$$\text{target of } \texttt{push()} \prec \text{target of } \texttt{push()}$$

We call these sequential constraints a *sequential constraints abstraction* of the function model they were extracted from. We can apply this algorithm to function models of all functions of a program and thus arrive at a sequential constraints abstraction of the program.

12.5 Finding Specifications

In Section 12.1 we said that we can represent specifications as sets of sequential constraints, and in the previous section we showed how to automat-

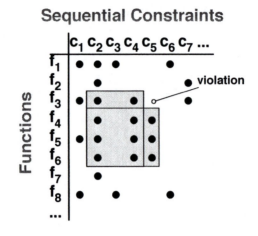

FIGURE 12.6: Sample matrix used as an input to formal concept analysis. Each rectangle corresponds to a pattern; gaps indicate potential violations. (From [4,8,9]. © 2007, 2010 Association for Computing Machinery, Inc. Reprinted by permission; and © 2009 IEEE.)

ically obtain sequential constraints (arriving in the end at a set of sequential constraints particular to each function). However, not every set of sequential constraints is a specification. Consider the following, hypothetical set:

retval of Random() $\prec$ target of nextInt()
target of nextInt() $\prec$ target of nextInt()
retval of Random() $\prec$ 1st arg of println()
target of nextInt() $\prec$ 1st arg of println()

The first two sequential constraints in this set can be thought of as being a specification for one of the possible uses of the Random class, but the same cannot be said about the last two constraints. The fact that the Random object is passed to println() is in reality just *noise*. Such noise can appear in sequential constraints obtained from a particular function, or several functions. To cope with this problem, we will restrict ourselves to sets of sequential constraints that occur frequently (i.e., sets that consist of sequential constraints that occur in sequential constraints abstractions of many functions). In our example above, if there are many functions that use Random and repeatedly call nextInt() on objects of this type, but only a few functions pass these objects to println(), then the last two sequential constraints will be discarded as not being part of the true specification. This learning by eliminating noise is done by *formal concept analysis*.

Concept analysis is, broadly speaking, a technique for finding *patterns* [2]. We use the Colibri/Java tool for formal concept analysis [5]. We feed Colibri/Java with a matrix $A = (a_{ij})$ as an input. In that matrix, rows are functions from the analyzed program (denoted $f_1, \ldots, f_k$, where k is the number of the functions), and columns are sequential constraints (denoted $c_1, \ldots, c_n$, where

n is the number of different sequential constraints). The matrix is binary[2]; if a particular sequential constraint c_j occurs in the sequential constraint abstraction of a particular function f_i, the entry a_{ij} in A is 1; otherwise it is 0. Thus, the input matrix contains information saying which sequential constraints can be found in which functions. Figure 12.6 shows a sample matrix, with filled circles denoting 1's in the matrix, and empty cells denoting 0's.

Before proceeding further, let us define a useful metric called *support* of a set of sequential constraints.

Definition 12.5.1. *Let* $A = (a_{ij})$ *be a binary matrix (assumed to be an input matrix to formal concept analysis) and* $C = \{c_{j_1}, \ldots, c_{j_m}\}$ *be a non-empty set of sequential constraints. Support of* C *is defined as* $|F|$, *where* $F = \{f_i : \forall c_j \in C . a_{ij} = 1\}$.

Intuitively, support of a set of sequential constraints C is the number of functions that "support" it (i.e., whose sequential constraints abstractions contain all of the elements in C). For example, in Figure 12.6 support of $\{c_1, c_2\}$ is 3, and support of $\{c_2\}$ is 7.

Colibri/Java finds sequential constraints that are common to many functions; intuitively, these are rectangles (not necessarily contiguous) in the matrix. Figure 12.6 shows two such rectangles, each representing a frequent set of sequential constraints: $\{c_2, c_4\}$ and $\{c_2, c_4, c_5\}$. To determine what is frequent and what is not, Colibri/Java needs a parameter called *minimum support*. This parameter states the minimum support (as defined above) that a particular set of sequential constraints must have for this set to be treated as frequent (for example, if we use 4 as the minimum support value, the second of the sets above would not be reported as frequent, because its support is 3). We treat each such frequent set of sequential constraints as a specification.[3] Here is a sample specification mined from AspectJ 1.5.3, with minimum support set to 20:

retval of `CompilerAdapter()` $\prec$ target of `compile()`
retval of `getAbsolutePath()` $\prec$ 1st arg of `compile()`
retval of `openFile()` $\prec$ target of `getAbsolutePath()`

This specification corresponds to the following code snippet[4]:

```
CompilerAdapter ca = new CompilerAdapter ();
ca.compile (getAbsolutePath (openFile (...)), ..., ...)
```

Code similar to the one above must thus occur in AspectJ in at least 20 different functions, and it does in fact occur in exactly 20 functions.

---

[2]That is, each element of the matrix is either 0 or 1.

[3]These are not necessarily specifications; it can always happen that there are sets of sequential constraints that just occur frequently, but do not form a specification. This is a problem that is common to all automatic specification mining techniques and is in general undecidable [1].

[4]We know the number of arguments of each function, because it is in practice part of an event, and thus a sequential constraint; we omit it from events for clarity.

12.6   Discovering Violations

Specifications found by the process described in the previous section can be useful as they are, but it turns out that we can try to find functions that violate them – hoping that these violations will be real defects. To check if a particular function violates a particular specification, we can compare sequential constraints obtained from the function with the sequential constraints that constitute the specification. Consider the following specification:

1st arg of `initialiseProject()` $\prec$ 1st arg of `build()`

1st arg of `build()` $\prec$ 1st arg of `build()`

If a particular function first calls `initialiseProject()` on some project and then repeatedly calls `build()` on this project, it is clear that this function satisfies the specification above, and the set of sequential constraints obtained from the function will contain the two constraints that constitute the specification. But if, say, the call to `initialiseProject()` is missing, we we would say that such a usage violated the specification, and this time the set of sequential constraints obtained from the function contains the second constraint from the specification, but not the first one. Most probably such a usage would indicate a defect. Generally, we can say that *if there are sequential constraints that are present in a specification, but do not occur in the sequential constraints abstraction of a function, the function violates the specification.*

Unfortunately, the condition above is a bit too strict. Imagine that the same specification is violated in the same way by many functions; in the example above this could be the case if the call to `initialiseProject()` were entirely optional, and, for example, half the functions that call `build()` used it, and the other half did not. In this case it is more likely that the specification is too restrictive and that all the violating functions are defective. To deal with such cases, let us introduce a new metric called *confidence* of a violation.

Definition 12.6.1. *Let $A = (a_{ij})$ be a binary matrix (assumed to be an input matrix to formal concept analysis), $S = \{c_{j_1}, \ldots, c_{j_m}\}$ be a specification, and $V \subset S$ be a violation of the specification (i.e., in the sequential constraint abstraction(s) of the violating function(s) only sequential constraints in V are present; those in $S - V$ are missing). Confidence of V is defined as $support(S)/support(V)$.*

From the definition above we can see that confidence ranges from 0 (for specifications that are never true) to 1 (for specifications that are never violated). In practice, of course, these two extreme values do not occur, because in the first case there is no specification to be violated, and in the second there is no violation, so there is no such thing as "confidence of a violation." Intuitively, confidence measures the relative frequency with which a specification

TABLE 12.1: Two Sample Projects Used for Evaluation

Project	Language	SLOC	Functions	Analysis time
AspectJ 1.5.3	Java	320,906	33,559	2.09
GMyth 0.7.1	C	10,198	444	0.07

Note: Analysis time encompasses the time needed for all the steps, from parsing to detecting violations of specifications.

is violated in a given way. We can use a parameter called *minimum confidence* to cope with the problem of too frequently occurring violations: We simply filter out all violations whose confidence is below the given minimum confidence value.

Violations can be detected using Colibri/Java [5]. Detecting violations is equivalent to detecting "gaps" in the concept analysis matrix [6]. In Figure 12.6 we see that the specification $S_1 = \{c_2, c_4, c_5\}$ is violated by f_3 with the violation being $V_1 = \{c_2, c_4\}$ (i.e., c_5 is missing in the sequential constraints abstraction of f_3; this "gap" is shown in the figure). Confidence of this violation is $support(S_1)/support(V_1) = 3/4 = 0.75$. Another specification, $S_2 = \{c_1, c_2\}$, is violated by f_2, f_4, f_6, and f_7 with the violation being $V_2 = \{c_2\}$. Confidence of this violation is $support(S_2)/support(V_2) = 3/7 \approx 0.43$.

12.7 The Real World

Now that we have shown how we can automatically find specifications and their violations, let us show some examples of violations, detected in two different projects written in two different programming languages (see Table 12.1). These will serve to illustrate the type of specifications that can be found, as well as potential severity of their violations.

Our first sample project is AspectJ 1.5.3.[5] AspectJ is a compiler for the AspectJ language, which is an aspect-oriented extension to the Java language. AspectJ is written in Java, and is a sufficiently large project to put scalability of the whole approach to test: It encompasses 320,906 SLOC in .java files.[6] One sample specification found was the following:

target of `next()` $\prec$ target of `next()`
retval of `iterator()` $\prec$ target of `next()`

In a nutshell, this specification (with support of 687) says that iterators

---

[5] http://eclipse.org/aspectj/
[6] All SLOC counts were generated using David A. Wheeler's "SLOCCount."

are used to iterate through a collection using multiple calls to `next()`. This does not seem like a terribly useful specification, and yet it is violated by the following function (the confidence of the violation being ≈ 0.99):

```
public String getRetentionPolicy() {
    ...
    List values = ax.getBcelAnnotation().getValues();
    for (Iterator it = values.iterator(); it.hasNext();) {
        ...
        retentionPolicy = ...;
        return retentionPolicy;
}
    ...
}
```

This function does use an iterator, but only the first element of the collection being iterated through is ever investigated – there cannot be more that one call to `next()`. It turns out this code is correct, as this particular collection cannot have more than one element, but using a for-loop to get just the first element is simply confusing and an example of a *code smell* – a programming antipattern, so to speak.

Here is another specification found in AspectJ:

retval of `FileReader()` $\prec$ 1st arg of `BufferedReader()`
retval of `BufferedReader()` $\prec$ target of `readLine()`

This one (with support of 34) says that buffered readers are typically used to read data from files line by line. This is true to a certain extent. However, it is also possible to use `BufferedReader` just for its buffering capabilities and still read data byte by byte if need be. In fact, this specification is violated in exactly this way by one of the functions in AspectJ (the confidence of the violation being ≈ 0.97), which is a false alarm in this particular case.

One more specification found in AspectJ:

retval of `stack()` $\prec$ target of `peek()`
target of `stack()` $\prec$ target of `stack()`
target of `stack()` $\prec$ target of `constraintViolated()`

This specification (with support of 72) is difficult to understand without knowing the details of the code it comes from. It came to be roughly as follows: One part of AspectJ is BCEL (ByteCode Engineering Library), and it contains verifiers that check Java bytecode's correctness. This includes (among others) checking that all the instructions get parameters of appropriate type. Now, Java virtual machine is a stack machine, so all the calculations are done on a stack. So the verifier checks for each instruction if the stack will be in a proper state when this instruction is executed, and this is the meaning of the first two sequential constraints: Stack must be accessed (typically more than once), and values on the stack must be inspected. The last sequential constraint says that there must be a call to `constraintViolated()` somewhere – and this call happens in BCEL if the verifier encounters a problem. To summarize, the specification above says that if there is a function that verifies correctness of a specific bytecode instruction, it should actually look at what is on the stack and then, if need be, report a problem. This specification is violated by the following function:

```
public void visitCALOAD(CALOAD o){
    Type arrayref = stack().peek(1);
    Type index = stack().peek(0);

    indexOfInt(o, index);
    arrayrefOfArrayType(o, arrayref);
}
```

This function is supposed to check the correctness of a `CALOAD` instruction. This instruction loads an element from an array of `char`'s. So, there are the following conditions that must be satisfied: There must be an `int` index on the stack, and an array reference, and the array reference must hold elements of type `char`. Only the first two of these three conditions are checked (albeit indirectly) by this function; the third one is ignored. Adding the check for the third condition would have to involve calling `constraintViolated()` if it is not satisfied, and this is how the violation points to a real defect: This function is indeed buggy and it leads to BCEL accepting wrong bytecode as correct.

Our second sample project is GMyth 0.7.1.[7] GMyth is a library to access MythTV[8] backend services. In contrast to AspectJ, GMyth is written in C (that is, a procedural, not an object-oriented language) and is quite small: It encompasses 10,198 SLOC in .c files. This obviously means less data to mine specifications from. One sample specification found was the following (we replaced the actual function name prefix `gmyth_string_list` with `gsl` to help readability):

retval of `g_string_new()` ≺ 1st arg of `g_string_free()`
retval of `g_string_new()` ≺ 2nd arg of `gsl_append_string()`
2nd arg of `gsl_append_string()` ≺ 1st arg of `g_string_free()`
retval of `gsl_new()` ≺ 1st arg of `g_object_unref()`
retval of `gsl_new()` ≺ 1st arg of `gsl_append_string()`
1st arg of `gsl_append_string()` ≺ 1st arg of `g_object_unref()`

This specification (with support of 25) corresponds roughly to the following code snippet:

[7]http://gmyth.sourceforge.net/index.html
[8]http://www.mythtv.org/

TABLE 12.2: Results Obtained on the Sample Projects Used for Evaluation

Project	Total	# Violations Investigated	Defects	Code smells	Accuracy
AspectJ 1.5.3	216	54	2	13	**27%**
GMyth 0.7.1	11	3	1	1	**66%**

Note: For both projects we ranked the violations found and investigated top 25% of them.

```
list = gmyth_string_list_new ();
str = g_string_new (...);
gmyth_string_list_append_string (list, str);
g_string_free (str);
g_object_unref (list);
```

One of the functions in GMyth violates this specification by not calling g_string_free(), which causes both sequential constraints with this call inside to be missing from this function's sequential constraints abstraction. The result of this is that the violating function contains a memory leak.

Table 12.2 summarizes the results we obtained by analyzing AspectJ 1.5.3 and GMyth 0.7.1. We ranked the violations and then investigated the top 25% of them for each project. As we can see, there were a lot more violations detected for large AspectJ than for small GMyth. Accuracy (i.e., the percentage of true positives amongst the investigated violations) differs very much between the two projects, but it is decent for both of them. Investigating 54 violations to find 15 code issues (including 2 defects) seems quite productive, not speaking about 2 code issues (including 1 defect) found by investigating just 3 violations for GMyth 0.7.1. Overall, we can see that despite very lightweight and programming-language-independent parsing, the approach is still accurate enough to find real defects, and – as the paragraphs above have shown – some quite subtle defects, too.

12.8   Scaling to Multiple Projects

The results shown above are based on single-project analysis: Specifications are mined from one single project, which is then investigated for violations. One drawback of such an approach is that some APIs are used very rarely and analyzing one project is not enough to mine any specifications for them. However, the approach described in this chapter is not inherently limited to one project at a time. As described in Section 12.5, specifications are found by applying formal concept analysis, and its input is just a matrix showing which sequential constraints occur in which functions. Therefore, we can put into the matrix the data for functions that stem from different projects. Our idea is to have a set of *reference projects* to mine specifications from, and one *tested project* to check for violations of those specifications.

Unfortunately, there is one fundamental *scalability problem* that we need to solve to put the idea above into use: If we put data from all the reference projects and the tested project into the matrix, it can become huge. There are two reasons for this: First, there can be a lot of reference projects – and therefore a lot of rows in the matrix. Second, the reference projects will differ one from another in the functions that are called in them. This will result in a huge variety of possible sequential constraints – meaning a lot of columns in the matrix. Formal concept analysis will most likely choke on such a huge matrix and this would make the whole idea impractical. How can we scale up our approach?

Recall that our goal is finding violations of mined specifications in the tested project, in the hope that these are defects. In other words, if a specification cannot possibly be violated in the tested project, it might just as well not have been mined at all. This leads to an important observation: If not all specifications stemming from reference projects are useful, then also not all sequential constraints stemming from the reference projects are useful. If reference projects use a certain library that is not used in the tested project, all sequential constraints related to this library can be safely ignored. This will reduce the number of columns in the matrix, and might even reduce the number of rows, too, if it so happens that some reference projects are completely unrelated to the tested project (i.e., use completely different APIs). It turns out that this (coupled with increasing minimum support; see Section 12.5) is enough to make the idea above scale and work very well in practice.

How do we decide which sequential constraints to keep and which to remove? We limit ourselves to sequential constraints that *pertain* to the tested project.

Definition 12.8.1. *A sequential constraint $e_1 \prec e_2$ pertains to the tested project iff there exists in the tested project a function, whose sequential constraints abstraction contains $e_1 \prec e$ or $e \prec e_2$, where e is an arbitrary event.*

This definition can be straightforwardly translated into an algorithm that chooses sequential constraints to be included in the matrix. We will leave this task as an exercise to the reader.

Limiting the matrix size by removing sequential constraints that do not pertain to the tested project is quite effective, but is not enough if the tested project is very large. Therefore, we exploit the minimum support parameter: If a sequential constraint occurs less than minimum support times in the matrix, it cannot be part of any specification (and thus neither of any violation). So we can count the number of times each sequential constraint occurs in the matrix and remove those that are too rare to be of use. We can do this step as

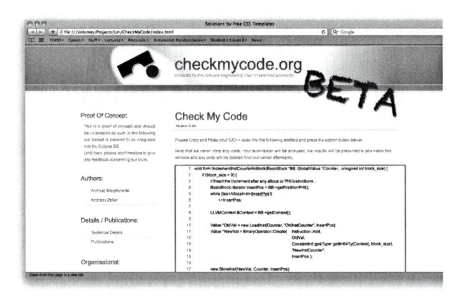

FIGURE 12.7: At `www.checkmycode.org`, programmers can have their code checked against 6000 reference projects from the Gentoo Linux distribution.

many times as we want until we find the minimum support value that results in a matrix of a size we can handle. To limit the number of rows, we simply remove all empty rows. There are bound to be such rows after the number of columns in the matrix has been reduced, and we can now take advantage of them.

We have used the technique above to test projects against specifications mined from the whole of the Gentoo Linux distribution. That is more than 6000 reference projects with over 200,000,000 lines of code. In our experiments, we were able to find defects and code issues in tested projects such as GIMP 2.6.6, Glade 3.6.4, MPICH 1.2.7p1, etc. Some problems found were impossible to find using single-project analysis, with even high-level design issues cropping up. Our analysis ran in less than 20 minutes on GIMP (which was the largest of the tested projects we used), which is an excellent running time for a project of almost 600,000 SLOC tested against the Gentoo Linux distribution.

The result of our work is publicly available in a web site. At *checkmycode.org* (Figure 12.7), interested programmers can have their code checked against the reference projects from the Gentoo Linux distribution. Such a check can reveal API usage errors that would otherwise require an extensive API specification to be checked against; our approach learns these specifications from code, and at a massive scale. Details on the approach and our experiments can be found in a separate paper [4].

12.9 Conclusion and Future Work

In this chapter, we have shown how to mine patterns of object usage using lightweight, language-independent analysis. The resulting specifications can be used to detect violations – deviations from "normal" usage that frequently turn out to be errors. The approach easily generalizes to arbitrary bodies of source code, and could also be easily adapted to additional languages.

At the present time, the approach is effective enough to detect real problems in existing software. Despite these successes, there are several possible ways how this work could be further extended:

Improve accuracy. When it comes to improving accuracy, the first direction to go would be using better analysis techniques, in particular language-dependent techniques. Better flow analyses, points-to analyses, and liveness analyses would all contribute to accuracy, in particular as they become interprocedural. At the same time, though, the approach would also become much more heavyweight; and it would be harder to analyze large bodies of code in reasonable time.

Better abstractions. Our most successful abstraction so far is to use Computation Tree Logic formulas to represent so-called *operational preconditions* of functions [7]. We do not want to go into detail here; suffice it to say that Computation Tree Logic allows representing much more sophisticated dataflow facts than in the case of sequential constraints, and the concept of operational preconditions further improves accuracy by adding more focus than is possible when working on a function level.

Detecting anomalies across projects. When starting a new project from scratch, there would not be many object usages to learn from. But would it be possible to learn from *other* projects? In our experiments, we have applied lightweight object usage mining to learn specifications from over 6000 Gentoo Linux distribution projects. These specifications allowed us to find defects that would have been impossible to detect when focusing on a single project at a time. Also, some of the violated specifications turned out to be in reality high level design properties. Finding such specifications is nearly impossible when using a single-project approach.

All in all, the field of mining specifications is still in its infancy – there is still much to do in terms of analysis, models, and applications. With the abundance of automated software verification methods, specifications are more required than ever – and this is where we can and where we should leverage all the information there is.

For more information on mining models of object usage, go to

http://www.st.cs.uni-saarland.de/models/

Bibliography

[1] Glenn Ammons, Rastislav Bodík, and James R. Larus. Mining specifications. In *POPL 2002: Proceedings of the 29th ACM SIGPLAN-SIGACT Symposium on Principles of Programming Languages*, pages 4–16, ACM Press, New York, 2002.

[2] Bernhard Ganter and Rudolf Wille. *Formal Concept Analysis: Mathematical Foundations.* Springer-Verlag, Berlin, 1999.

[3] Natalie Gruska. Language-Independent Sequential Constraint Mining. Bachelor thesis, Saarland University, 2009.

[4] Natalie Gruska, Andrzej Wasylkowski, and Andreas Zeller. Learning from 6,000 projects: lightweight cross-project anomaly detection. In *ISSTA 2010: Proceedings of the Nineteenth International Symposium on Software Testing and Analysis*, pages 119–130, AC, New York, 2010. DOI=10.1145/1831708.1831723. http://doi.acm.org/10.1145/1831708.1831723.

[5] Daniel Norbert Götzmann. Formale Begriffsanalyse in Java: Entwurf und Implementierung effizienter Algorithmen. Bachelor thesis, Saarland University, 2007. Available from http://code.google.com/p/colibri-java/ (accessed 6 April 2010).

[6] Christian Lindig. Mining Patterns and Violations Using Concept Analysis. Technical report, Saarland University, Software Engineering Chair, 2007. Available from http://www.st.cs.uni-sb.de/publications/; the software is available from http://code.google.com/p/colibri-ml/ (accessed 6 April 2010).

[7] Andrzej Wasylkowski and Andreas Zeller. Mining temporal specifications from object usage. In *ASE 2009: Proceedings of the 24th IEEE/ACM International Conference on Automated Software Engineering*, pages 295–306, IEEE Computer Society, Los Alamitos, CA, 2009.

[8] Andrzej Wasylkowski, Andreas Zeller, and Christian Lindig. Detecting object usage anomalies. In *Proceedings of the 6th Joint Meeting of the European Software Engineering Conference and the ACM SIGSOFT Symposium on the Foundations of Software Engineering (ESEC-FSE '07)*, pages 35–44, ACM, New York, 2007. DOI=10.1145/1287624.1287632. http://doi.acm.org/10.1145/1287624.1287632.

[9] Andrzej Wasylkowski and Andreas Zeller. Mining temporal specifications from object usage. In *Proceedings of the 2009 IEEE/ACM International*

Conference on Automated Software Engineering (ASE'09), pages 295–306, IEEE Computer Society, Washington, DC, 2009. DOI=10.1109/ASE.2009.30 http://dx.doi.org/10.1109/ASE.2009.30.

Index

A

Abstract history, 164, 166, 168, 171, 173, 175, 177
  pointer information and, 165
Abstract interpretation, 10, 165
  flow sensitive and context-sensitive, 162
  with future abstraction, 176
  output of, 179
  with past abstraction, 175
Abstract object, 164, 170–171
  abstract state with single, 170
  alias information and histories, 167
  partitioning, 170
  tracking, 178
Abstract program state, 165, 171
  collapse of, 176
Abstract semantics, 169–179
Abstract trace collection, 161, 164, 165, 167–179, 187, 192
Access rewriting strategy, 47–48
Active inference, 71
Active learning, 9, 10, 71–73
Alias analysis, 162, 164, 189
  type-based, 195
Alias contexts, 171
Anomaly detection, 2
  run-time, 295
API. *See* Application Programming Interface (API)
Application Programming Interface (API), 8
  clean-up, 138
  collaboration patterns, 95–96
  coverage, 101–102

  critical, 134, 136, 141
    identification of, 143
  details, 134
  enclosed procedure, 135
  error and normal trace generation, 139
  error-check specifications, 136, 141, 144, 148
  error-check violations, 138, 148
  error-handling specifications, 138–139, 141, 142
  exceptional-handling support, 134
  invariants, 202
  multiple specifications, 139, 144–145
  multiple violations, 139, 150
  postconditions, 114
  preconditions, 114
  send procedure, 134
  socket, 137
  uncommon usage patterns, 95
  usage patterns, 89, 92
    encoding commonly observed, 96
    recurring, 95
  usage protocols, 88–97, 101
    performance and scalability of, 102–104
    quality of, 102
  usage specifications, mining of, 357–372
  user-defined procedures, 135
  violations, 150
Apriori algorithm, 208, 210, 212, 213
Automatic repair, 244